Japanese Law

Japanese Law

Hiroshi Oda LL.D(Tokyo)
Sir Ernest Satow Professor of Japanese Law
University College
University of London
Attorney at Law

Butterworths
London, Dublin, Edinburgh
1992

United Kingdom	Butterworth & Co (Publishers) Ltd, 88 Kingsway, LONDON WC2B 6AB and 4 Hill Street, EDINBURGH EH2 3JZ
Australia	Butterworths, SYDNEY, MELBOURNE, BRISBANE, ADELAIDE, PERTH, CANBERRA and HOBART
Belgium	Butterworth & Co (Publishers) Ltd, BRUSSELS
Canada	Butterworths Canada Ltd, TORONTO and VANCOUVER
Ireland	Butterworth (Ireland) Ltd, DUBLIN
Malaysia	Malayan Law Journal Sdn Bhd, KUALA LUMPUR
New Zealand	Butterworths of New Zealand Ltd, WELLINGTON and AUCKLAND
Puerto Rico	Equity de Puerto Rico, Inc, HATO REY
Singapore	Butterworths Asia, SINGAPORE
USA	Butterworth Legal Publishers, AUSTIN, Texas; BOSTON, Massachusetts; CLEARWATER, Florida (D & S Publishers); ORFORD, New Hampshire (Equity Publishing); ST PAUL, Minnesota; and SEATTLE, Washington

Reprinted 1993

Cover illustration by Hideko Matsubara

A CIP Catalogue record for this book is available from the British Library.

ISBN 0 406 66921 X

Printed and bound in Great Britain by
Biddles Ltd, Guildford and King's Lynn

Preface

Several decades ago, people who were interested in Japanese law outside Japan were limited to a small number of comparativists. Since then, with the internationalisation of the Japanese economy, interest in Japanese law has increased rapidly.

It is now fairly well known abroad that the Japanese legal system is based upon the Civil Law system with some influence from American law. However, when it comes to more specific issues, information on Japanese law available in foreign languages still seems to be limited. There are various areas of Japanese law where such information is almost non-existent. This book is intended to fill this void and provide an accurate knowledge of all relevant areas of Japanese law.

In this book, instead of emphasising peculiar aspects of Japanese law, I have endeavoured to illustrate the Japanese legal system as a fair and rational system based upon values shared by industrially developed countries. This is because it is my impression that, in the past, the uniqueness of Japanese law has been overstressed. This has led to a perception of Japanese law as a peculiar system in which, behind its modern facade, traditional values and rules still remain. The inclination of the Japanese to depict themselves as different and unique may have helped in developing this perception. However, in this day and age, when countries are making efforts to harmonise their laws in the face of intertwining economies, I have thought it might be better to place the emphasis elsewhere.

In every legal system, there is always a gap between statutes and their implementation. In order to study foreign law, one has to go beyond the statutes. This also applies to Japanese law, although there is no evidence that the gap is wider than in other jurisdictions. I have focused on how the courts interpret the law and solve specific problems, rather than summarising the statutes and reiterating the official or majority view. My intention here is to shed more light on case law, which is one of the primary sources of law, and illustrate how the Japanese legal system actually works.

I have three kinds of reader in mind. First, there are the people who are interested in comparative law or foreign law in general. In addition, the way the Japanese tackle problems in specific areas of law attracts the attention of specialists in other jurisdictions. For example, an expert in competition law in Europe might want to see how Japanese competition law operates. It is these people who are the primary target of this book.

Secondly, with the internationalisation of the Japanese economy in the past decades, more and more businessmen have come to be involved in business with Japanese companies. Naturally, this has contributed to the expansion of Japanese-related business by foreign law firms. Government officials and international organisations quite often come across issues related to Japanese law. This is particularly relevant when multilateral and bilateral trade talks are taking place. A good operating knowledge of Japanese law is crucial.

Thirdly, courses on Japanese law are given in the United States, Europe, U.K., Australia and some other places. This book will be useful as a textbook for these courses.

I am indebted to many people who have kindly supported me while writing this book. My special thanks are due to Professor Bernard Rudden of Brasenose College, Oxford, who, despite his heavy workload, scrupulously read the entire draft and made valuable comments. Without his encouragement and support, this book could never have been completed. I am also grateful to my colleagues at University College London, namely Professors Bob Hepple and Jeffrey Jowell, for their understanding and warm support.

I would like to add that my experience as a visiting professor at Cornell Law School in the United States in the past several years has contributed to adding some new dimensions to the book. In this respect, I am grateful to Dean Russell Osgood and his colleagues at the Law school. I am also indebted to my former colleagues at the Faculty of Law of the University of Tokyo, namely Professor Ichiro Kato, former president of the University of Tokyo, and my mentors, Professors Koya Matsuo and Junichi Murakami. I would like to thank Mr. Denzil Millichap, former assistant at University College London, for assisting me with an earlier version some years ago; and Mr. Shunichi Himeno, Managing Director of the International Business Law Institute, for providing me constantly with valuable information and material. I am much indebted to IBM Japan and the Matsushita Foundation for their generous assitance. I would also like to express my gratitude to the editors of Butterworths for their patience.

My very special thanks go to my wife Midori, who has supported me warmly all through the preparation of this book, and assisted me in sorting information and typing the manuscript.

This book is dedicated to my late grandfather, Professor Shozaburo Sugimura.

Hiroshi Oda
August 1992

Contents

Table of statutes

Table of cases

Case reports referred to in the book are as follows:

Minshū The Supreme Court Reporter (Civil Cases)
Keishū The Supreme Court Reporter (Criminal Cases)
(*Minshū* and *Keishū* also cover the judgments and decisions of the
Supreme Tribunal between 1922 and 1947)
Saikō-saibanshō Saibanshū Collection of the judgments of the Supreme
Court
Kō-minshū The Appellate Court Reporter (Civil Cases)
Kō-keishū The Appellate Court Reporter (Criminal Cases)
Kaminshū Collection of the Judgments and Decisions of Lower Courts
(Civil Cases)
Gyōsai-reishū Collection of Judgments and Decisions on Administrative
Cases
Rōmin Collection of Judgments and Decisions on Labour Cases
Kagetsū Collection of Judgments and Decisions of the Family Court
Shinketsu-shū Decisions and Awards of the Fair Trade Commission
Minroku The Supreme Tribunal Reporter (Civil Cases; 1895–1921)
Keiroku The Supreme Tribunal Reporter (Criminal Cases; 1895–1921)
Hanji Hanrei-jiho (commercial publication)
Hanta Hanrei Times (commercial publication)
Kinyū-shōji-hōmu Financial and Commercial Law (commercial publica-
tion)

In Japan, cases are not cited by the name of the parties as is the case
with some major jurisdictions. Instead, cases are referred to by the date
and the volume and number of the case report. In some areas, e.g.
Constitutional, Labour and Anti-Monopoly Law, cases are often
referred to by the name of one of the parties or the place where the
dispute took place. Some celebrated cases in other areas are also cited in
this way. Therefore, as a rule, cases are referred to in this book without
specifying the name of the parties. Only when the case is known by the
name of the parties or a place are these names indicated.

Supreme Tribunal

Supreme Court

Appellate courts

1 Introduction

1. Japanese law as an object of study in comparative law

The study of comparative law has attracted academics in Europe and the United States since the end of the last century. Although the primary focus is usually on the comparison of laws within Europe, or the comparison between the Anglo-American system and the Civil Law system, legal systems outside the Common Law and Civil Law system were not entirely ignored. There have been attempts by some pioneer comparativists to include laws outside Europe and North America in their field of research.[1] Systematic research on Soviet law started in the 1920s in Breslau, which at that time was part of Germany. Also there has been a long tradition of the study of Chinese law in France and Holland. However, Japanese law failed to attract much attention from European and American specialists of law in the pre-Second World War era.

This did not mean that the Japanese legal circle had no links with either Europe or the United States in this period. In the course of modernisation which started in the mid–19th century, Japan relied heavily on advisers invited from Europe in enacting laws and developing legal education. A number of Japanese students were sent to Europe to study law and they returned with extensive knowledge, mainly of the Civil Law system. However, the relationship remained basically unilateral; the Japanese kept learning from European countries and there was a constant flow of knowledge of European Law into Japan, but there were only a few persons in Europe or the United States who were interested in disseminating knowledge of Japanese law in the West. O. Rudolff, a German legal adviser to Japan, was an exception. He translated the Codes of the Tokugawa Shogunate in 1889. Works by J. H. Wigmore on the law of the same period

---

1 T. Gorai, 'Influence du Code Civil français sur le Japon', in *Le Code Civil: Livre du Centenaine*, Paris 1904, pp. 783–784.

and by de Becker on the Civil Code of Japan can be considered major contributions in the dissemination of knowledge about Japanese Law.[2] Also some Japanese lawyers, namely Naojiro Sugiyama and Kotaro Tanaka, have taken part in various international activities in the field of Comparative Law, but they remain a minority.

After the end of the Second World War, the scope of the study of Comparative Law expanded significantly in three directions. Firstly, Eastern European countries came under the control of the Soviet Union and China shifted to socialism. Thus, the socialist legal system came to carry more weight than it did in the pre-War period. The Cold War made the study of socialist law indispensable to the formulation of policy towards the Eastern bloc. Secondly, the abolition of colonial rule in third world countries led to the emergence of various legal systems which are copies of neither the Civil Law system nor the Common Law system. These legal systems needed serious research. Thirdly, the Allied Occupation of Japan necessitated a comprehensive study of Japanese political and legal institutions. This was later enhanced by the emergence of Japan as an economic superpower in the 1980s. The increasingly powerful Japanese economy resulted in a growing interest not only in commercial law, but also in the cultural and historical background of the Japanese legal system.

The United States was probably the first country where systematic studies in Japanese law developed. Already during the War, the United States, in anticipation of victory, had been promoting Japanese studies in order to formulate its occupation policy. The study of legal institutions was one of the primary topics of Japanese studies. Under the Allied occupation, American legal advisers worked together with Japanese lawyers to reshape the Japanese legal system. The knowledge which they accumulated during this period has further developed the study of Japanese law in the United States.

With this background and the close economic links with Japan, it is not surprising that the study of Japanese law first developed in the United States and not in Europe. One of the earliest accomplishments was *Law in Japan: The Legal Order in a Changing Society*, edited by Arthur von Mehren, which resulted from a joint project of Japanese and American lawyers in 1963.

Interest in Japanese Law also developed in Australia and Germany in the 1970s. In Australia, developing commercial ties with Japan have led to the introduction of Japanese law courses

---

2 A. F. Schnitzer, *Vergleichende Rechtslehre*, Basel 1945, S. 271–272.

in several universities. In Germany, reflecting the strong ties between Japan from the pre-War period, Japanese law studies began in Hamburg and Freiburg. A series of Japanese law books written mainly by Japanese lawyers and translated into German (*Japanisches Recht*) is published on an annual basis in Freiburg.

In Japan, lawyers became aware of the need to enhance the understanding of Japanese Law in foreign countries. In 1967, Japanese lawyers and American specialists in Japanese law began to jointly publish an annual, *Law in Japan*. Furthermore, books written in foreign languages by Japanese professors in their respective fields of specialty started to appear.[3] Today, it is not uncommon for Japanese law professors to give a course on Japanese law at foreign universities.

2. The *Rechtskreis* of Japanese law

Despite the developments of the study of Japanese law, comparativists are yet to agree on the position of Japanese law within the world legal system. At the beginning of this century, a French legal historian named A. Esmein classified the legal systems of the world into five major groups: Roman, German, Anglo-Saxon, Slavonic and Muslim.[4] In discussing the problem of families of law (*Rechtskreis*), some comparativists have thought that Japanese law is part of the Far Eastern legal system, mainly because of geography or the role of Confucianism. In 1945, A. Schnitzer published *Vergleichende Rechtslehre*, which was among the first books on comparative law after the Second World War. This book covered not only Anglo-American and Continental European legal systems, but also 'the law of the people with ancient culture', 'religious law' and 'law of Asian countries'. Schnitzer classified Japanese law as a member of the Asian legal system together with Turkish, Persian, Hindu, Mongolian and Afghan law and devoted four pages to Japanese law. Religion seems to have played a major role in his classification, which is understandable in light of the role Shintoism played in Japan at that time.[5]

---

3 For instance, Z. Kitagawa, *Rezeption und Fortbildung des europäischen Zivilrechts in Japan*, Frankfurt/M 1970.
4 Cited in K. Zweigert, 'Zur Lehre von den Rechtskreisen', K. N. Nadelmann et al eds., *XXth Century Comparative and Conflicts Law*, Leyden 1961, p. 44.
5 Schnitzer, *supra* note 2, S. 88–89, 268–272.

In 1950, two books on comparative law were published in France. There was still very little information on Japanese law available in any foreign language. In *Traité de droit comparé*, P. Arminjon, B. Nolde and M. Wolf emphasised the influence of German law on Japan and described Japanese law as German law in the Far East.[6] This is probably because the German Bürgerliches Gesetzbuch served as a basis for the Japanese Civil Code. In contrast, *Traité élémentaire de droit civil comparé*, written by René David, stressed the affinity of Japanese Law with Chinese law. In his view, rites played a dominant role in China and Japan, and law was secondary.[7]

David later elaborated on this topic in his book with J. E. C. Brierley, *Major Legal Systems in the World Today* (1968). Here, the connection of Japanese law with the Romano-Germanic family of legal systems is acknowledged, but the book still deals with Japanese Law as one of the 'Laws of the Far East,' together with Chinese law under the heading of 'Religious and Traditional Law'.[8]

The common feature of the 'Laws of the Far East', according to David and Brierley, is that laws in this part of the world are formally connected to either the Romano-Germanic family or to the family of Socialist laws. But they proceed to point out that:

> The reception of Western ideas and institutions, decreed by their rulers, has not wholly eliminated those traditional ideas which were considered as morality and the social order. For a long time yet modern law may very well remain a mere 'veneer', behind which the traditional ways of acting, thinking and living will be perpetuated.[9]

This pattern was followed in more recent works by K. Zweigert and H. Koetz, as well as K. H. Ebert. Ebert categorised Japanese and Chinese Law as Far Eastern Law, but he failed to produce any persuasive argument to support this.[10] Zweigert and Koetz also classifed Japanese Law as part of the 'Far Eastern Legal Family,' together with Chinese Law, and found the reliance on extra-judicial methods of settling disputes as a salient feature of this group. In their view, positive law imported from foreign countries has not fully taken root in Japan and China.

---

6 P. Alminjon, B. Nolde and M. Wolff, *Traité de droit comparé*, Paris 1950, Tome II, pp. 427–428.

7 R.David, *Traité élémentaire de droit civil comparé*, Paris 1950, pp. 388–389.

8 R. David and J. E. C. Brierley, *Major Legal Systems in the World Today*, London 1968, pp. 20, 450–460.

9 *Ibid.*

10 K. H. Ebert, *Rechtsvergleichung:Einführung in die Grundlagen*, Bern 1978, S. 112–118.

Instead of recourse to the courts, people resort to informal procedures of dispute settlement, characteristic of Confucianism, which discourages the settlement of conflicts in public.[11] Presumably these authors based their views on the work of Professors T. Kawashima and Y. Noda. In an article published in 1963, Professor Kawashima pointed out as follows:

> Traditionally, the Japanese people prefer extrajudicial, informal means of settling a controversy. Litigation presupposes and admits the existence of disputes and leads to a decision which makes clear who is right or wrong in accordance with standards that are independent of the will of the disputants. . . . There is a strong expectation that a dispute should not and will not arise; even when one does occur, it is to be solved by mutual understanding. . . .Because of the resulting disorganisation of traditional social groups, resort to litigation has been condemned as morally wrong, subversive and rebellious.[12]

Professor Noda went even further in his book, *Introduction to Japanese Law* (1976):

> Japanese generally conceive of law as an instrument of constraint that the State uses when it wishes to impose its will. Law is thus synonomous with pain or penalty. To an honorable Japanese the law is something that is undesirable, even detestable, something to keep as far away as possible. To never use the law, or be involved with the law, is the normal hope of honorable people. To take someone to court to guarantee the protection of one's own interests, or to be mentioned in court, even in a civil matter, is a shameful thing; and the idea of shame. . .will be the keystone to the system of Japanese civilisation.[13]

Whether this notion of the 'non-litigiousness of the Japanese' is a myth or not has been a focus of contention for some years. Thus, in the latest edition of Zweigert and Koetz's book, the tone has slightly changed:

> . . .it is clear that until well into the twentieth century these imported statutes had very little practical effect on Japanese legal life. . . .But

11 K. Zweigert and H. Koetz, *Einführung in die Rechtsvergleichung auf dem Gebiet des Privatrechts*, erste Auflage, Bd. 1, Tübingen 1971, S. 431–434. Translated into English by T. Weir, *An Introduction to Comparative Law*, vol. 1, Oxford 1977, pp. 362–365.
12 T. Kawashima, 'Dispute resolution in Contemporary Japan', in A. von Mehren, ed., *Law in Japan*, Ann Arbor 1963, pp. 43–45.
13 Y. Noda, *Introduction to Japanese Law*, Tokyo 1976, pp. 159–160.

it would be wrong to overemphasise the Japanese preference for resolving disputes uncontentiously. Many people familiar with Japan believe it to be a myth that the Japanese are reluctant to litigate.[14]

In fact the usefulness of the *Rechtskreis* concept is rather questionable, especially when applied to peripheral area such as the law of the Far East. It should also be noted that those who promoted this notion of families of law have focused on private law rather than public law, and therefore the classification may not be applicable to the legal system as a whole. For the purposes of this book, it is sufficient here to point out that Japanese law is part of the Romano-Germanic family of law, with some elements of American law.

Contrary to the views of the leading comparativists, it is meaningless to put Japanese and Chinese law in the same category on any basis except geographical. After all, China turned to socialism in 1949 and despite some residual elements from the time of Imperial China, its legal system can be regarded as part of the Socialist legal family. Japan did introduce some legal institutions from China in the past, but the influence of Chinese law on contemporary Japanese law is minimal. There may be some common features such as the preference for informal methods of dispute settlement, but in contemporary China, it is doubtful whether this is due to the ideas of Confucius or is a result of an underdeveloped court system, or even the reluctance of the rulers to adjudicate in civil cases. In any case, it seems that these ostensibly common features are not sufficient to surmount the large gap which exists between various legal systems in the Far East.

Moreover, the idea of the Japanese legal system as part of the Far Eastern 'family' is contrary to the perception of the majority of Japanese lawyers, who believe that they are working within what is basically a Western legal system. This view had already been expressed in the early 20th century by Nobushige Hozumi, who was a Professor of Civil Law at the University of Tokyo. He divided major legal systems into seven groups: Chinese, Hindu, Mohammedan, Roman, Germanic, Slavonic and English law. Referring to the Civil Code, he pointed out that Japanese law had shifted from the family of Chinese law to the family of Roman law:

> . . .the new Japanese Civil Code stands in a filial relation to the European systems, and with the introduction of Western Civilization,

---

14 Zweigert and Koetz, *Einführung in die Rechtsvergleichung auf dem Gebiet des Privatrechts*, zweite Auflage, Tübingen 1984, S. 416–419. Translated into English by T. Weir, *An Introduction to Comparative Law*, second edition, Oxford 1988, pp. 370–372.

the Japanese civil law passed from the Chinese Family to the European Family of law.[15]

However, David's view on Japanese law, regardless of its appropriateness, has significance since it seems to represent a notion common to foreign observers. His view is essentially that firstly, Japanese law has been influenced by various foreign legal systems, mainly Romano-Germanic and American. Secondly, due to the persistence of traditional morals and values, these 'imported' modern legal systems did not fully succeed in taking root in Japanese society. Therefore, thirdly, 'the question is still very much open whether behind this facade of westernisation Japan really has undergone any kind of significant transformation and whether it has accepted the idea of justice and law as understood in the West'.[16] Zweigert and Koetz more or less follow this line.

It is natural in a way to imagine frictions arising between imported foreign laws on the one hand and traditional morals and values on the other. However, in Japan, during the modern period, foreign law was imported and accepted fairly smoothly without any significant resistance. The gap between modern codes based upon foreign law and social reality in Japan has not been as wide as believed by foreign observers.

In every legal system, there is a gap between the law in books and the law in action. This applies to Japanese law as well, but the assumption that this gap is wider in Japan than in other countries simply because foreign law was introduced to a 'traditional' society cannot be substantiated. In order to clarify this matter, it is necessary to examine the way in which Japan has imported and digested foreign law in the modern period.

Foreign law was received into Japan in three different stages. The first stage was in the 7th – 8th century when Japan imported the Chinese political and legal system. However, the legacy of Chinese law is minimal in contemporary Japanese law. The second and third stages are of particular significance, since these two stages have direct bearing on contemporary Japanese law.

The second stage was between the overthrow of the Tokugawa Shogunate in the mid–19th century and the early 20th century when the industrialisation of the country was accomplished. In this period of modernisation, European law, namely French and German codes, was imported into Japan and served as a model for the major Japanese codes. The third stage began after the

---

15 N. Hozumi, *Lectures on the New Japanese Civil Code as Materials for the Study of Comparative Jurisprudence*, Tokyo 1904, p. 19.
16 David and Brierley, *supra* note 9, p. 456.

Second World War and continued during the period of the Allied occupation. During this stage, some laws were amended or replaced on the basis of American law. Nevertheless, the strong influence of the Civil Law system remains until today.

Despite two-and-a-half centuries of isolationist policy under the Tokugawa shogunate, when major reforms took place after the fall of the Shogunate, the existing social and economic system in Japan was fairly well-developed and certainly ready for further steps of development. For instance, a money economy had developed to such an extent that large mercantile and money-lending capital enjoyed dominant power in the economy. This enabled the introduction of the modern banking system under the new government. Another example is ownership of land. Despite lacking the modern concept of land ownership, some rights of land-holding had developed before the modernisation and land was traded extensively under the Tokugawa shoguns' rule. This made it possible to introduce a modern system of land ownership smoothly.

Furthermore, unlike some countries under colonial rule, the reception of foreign law in Japan occurred without any substantial resistance. Although modernisation began in response to both pressure from foreign countries to open up and the desire of Japan to renegotiate unequal treaties, the need for modernisation itself was never doubted. The government's slogan of emulating and surpassing Western powers was shared by most political leaders and largely supported by ordinary people. Therefore, psychological barriers to the reception of foreign law were minimised, making the implementation of laws modelled on foreign laws easier than in countries where foreign law was imposed from above by colonial rulers. Admittedly, there was conflict in the 1890s involving the draft Civil Code, but this mostly concerned family law and was primarily a conflict between specialists trained in different foreign legal systems.

Furthermore, due to the absence of commitment to a specific country, the Japanese legislature usually did not carbon-copy foreign legislation in its entirety without considering its adaptability to Japanese society. At the very beginning of the modernisation, there were attempts to translate French Codes and implement them directly, but these attempts were quickly abandoned and a more prudent approach prevailed. The reception of foreign law in Japan was selective, i.e. it was introduced only in so far as it met specific social demands at the time. It is often pointed out, for instance, that the present Civil Code is primarily influenced by German law, yet it is neither a replica of the draft German BGB nor even primarily influenced by the German Code. In fact, in the process of preparation, French law, German law and English law were studied and the Code incorporated those parts considered to be most preferable, regardless of the source. One of the authors of the Code later stated that legislative materials were collected from all over the civilised world and that the Code was 'a fruit of comparative jurisprudence'.[17]

This was not possible without understanding and considering the then existing social reality. The legislature in the period of modernisation did not fail to take into account the existing customs and conventions in Japan, especially commercial practice. Naturally, some traditional customs and conventions needed to be abandoned for the sake of modernisation, but justifiable practices were preserved under the new regime. In order to meet specific conditions in Japan, foreign law was often modified, sometimes to the extent that its origin became difficult to identify. This careful consideration of social reality existing in Japan minimised the friction between the new laws and established social practice.

This applies more or less to the reception of American law during the Allied Occupation after the Second World War, but in a slightly different way. American advisers sometimes strongly urged the Japanese to amend some laws, which they considered to be undemocratic, on the model of American law. The Code of Criminal Procedure serves as an example. However, even in such instances, the views of Japanese experts who took part in the drafting process carried some weight. Social and cultural conditions unique to Japan were cited by Japanese participants and often were accepted by the Americans. It should be noted that these uniquely Japanese conditions were occasionally equivalent to the values which had been developed and promoted in the pre-War era and sometimes served as pretexts for resisting the liberal reforms. However, despite the initiatives taken by the Allied Forces, all in all, legislation enacted during this period, including the present Constitution, was mostly welcomed and accepted by the general public.

Therefore, although modern Japanese law has been heavily influenced by foreign law, namely German and French law, Japan has not taken over foreign legal institutions without considering their adaptability and suitability to Japan. Foreign law was carefully examined in light of the existing social reality of Japan, and only that which met the specific requirements of the day was accepted, but often with substantial modification. This

---

17 N. Hozumi, *supra* note 12, pp. 21–22.

cautious approach still did not eliminate the possibility of some discrepancy between law and reality. In such cases, it was not uncommon that a different practice which was not always compatible with the law emerged. This can be seen, for instance, in the field of real securities. However, once established, these practices were endorsed by the court, if not by the legislature, and became fully compatible with the law.

Thus, Japan has been fairly successful in assimilating foreign laws and transplanting them in different soil. The gap which initially existed between the 'imported' laws and social reality has been filled in one way or another and statutory laws are duly implemented and generally enforced. Therefore, an overemphasis on the disparity between law and practice is often misleading and results in the 'mystification' of Japanese Law.

3.   Purposes of Japanese law studies

Apart from the general objectives of studying comparative law which are often discussed in the work of comparativists,[18] Japanese law deserves serious study for the following purposes.

Firstly, Japanese law is probably one of the most interesting topics of study in comparative law, and law in general. In the past, Japan has been influenced by all the major legal systems of the world. However, none of these systems enjoys an 'absolute share' in the present system. It remains a unique hybrid of different legal systems. Therefore, by studying Japanese law, one inevitably encounters some fundamental problems of comparative law, including the problem of the relationship between law and culture as affected by the reception of foreign law and how and to what extent law can be successfully transplanted from one country to another.

Another example is the problem of the role of law in modernising a country i.e. how far law can affect social change. In the process of modernisation, Japan has relied heavily on law as a tool of social engineering. Modernisation was inconceivable without an advanced legal system. The experience of Japan, especially in the modern period, serves as an experimental ground for theories of law in general as well as comparative law.

Secondly, some institutions of Japanese law may be of practical significance to foreign legislators. For example, several sophisticated institutions of alternative dispute resolution in the field of traffic accidents, pollution control, consumer credit, construction

---

18 Zweigert and Koetz, *supra* note 14, S. 14–26. In English, pp. 14–22.

and the protection of consumers have developed in Japan in recent years. In the case of traffic accidents, attorneys work part-time in the Centre for the Settlement of Traffic Accident Disputes, advising clients and trying to arrange a settlement. If this attempt fails, an arbitration board within the Centre takes over. The advantage of this system lies in the flexibility of its solution as well as in saving the time and money needed. The services of the Centre are free for victims and are less time consuming than litigation. Whether this kind of development represents a peculiar preference of the Japanese for informal procedures has been discussed for years. Regardless of the outcome of this dispute, these institutions for extra-judicial settlement may serve as models for the development of alternative conflict-resolution systems in other countries.

Another field in which foreign legislatures may learn from Japanese Law is pollution control. As a by-product of high economic growth in the 1960s, pollution became particularly serious in Japan. In 1970, the Diet passed a group of laws aimed at controlling pollution and providing measures for the relief of victims. At the same time, new theories have been worked out by courts and lawyers in Tort law in order to cope with pollution cases. After some years, the situation has improved, although a number of people still suffer from pollution and its after effect. Legislative measures, case law and the development of legal theories concerning remedies serve as a model, either negatively or positively, for countries facing similar problems.

Thirdly, in this age of close economic interdependence, some problems cannot be solved without international cooperation. For example, in the law of securities, Tokyo, as one of the largest financial centres, is closely linked with foreign securities markets. If the control of insider trading is ineffective in Japan, this is not only a concern of Japan but of London, New York and Hong Kong as well. Therefore, international cooperation and, in some areas, the harmonisation of regulations are needed. In fact, agencies supervising the securities markets of various countries, including the Securities and Exchange Commission of the United States, Ministry of Finance of Japan and the Department of Trade and Industry of the United Kingdom are now cooperating in the harmonisation and standardisation of controls over insider trading. This kind of work naturally presupposes knowledge about not only the law or statute concerned, but also of the entire legal system in each country. The same applies in competition law where approximation of controls over cartels is essential.

Fourthly, since Japan has become an economically, if not politically, powerful country, the opportunity for foreign businessmen to deal with Japanese companies and invest in the Japanese market had considerably increased. This is particularly true in light of gradual trade and financial liberalisation in the last ten years. According to the statistics of the Ministry of Finance, direct investment into Japan by foreign companies amounted to 2.86 billion dollars in 1989.[19] Japanese direct investment abroad also has sharply increased in recent years.[20] The number of contracts concluded with Japanese companies where Japanese law is chosen as the governing law is steadily growing.

When a foreign company intends to invest in Japan, it encounters various legal problems such as foreign exchange controls, Competition law, Company law, Trade Mark law and taxation, not to mention 'invisible barriers' such as the *keiretsu* system and the practice of bid-rigging, which are often pointed out as inhibiting entry into Japanese markets. Also it is likely that a foreign company may come across 'administrative guidance' from the ministries and go through a maze of administrative bureaucracy. Basic knowledge of Japanese law will certainly help to sort out these problems.

It should also be noted that although the common belief in foreign countries is that law plays only a minor role in Japanese society, law does play a significant role in Japanese business. Contracts used for international transactions are detailed and sophisticated and are usually strictly implemented in a way equivalent to that found in Europe or the United States. Major companies are equipped with a legal department staffed with experts in business law who review significant transactions from a legal point of view. This alone necessitates some knowledge of Japanese law on the part of foreign businessmen who want to negotiate with these legal experts.

In addition, the possibility of litigation with Japanese companies is not as small as believed. Those foreign businessmen who expect that Japanese companies prefer to settle differences amicably and informally will be surprised to find that Japanese companies do not hesitate to bring the case to court when it is really necessary. It is even expected by members of legal departments in major companies that disputes with foreign companies might increase in the future. This naturally requires foreign companies to know about the Japanese system of settling disputes.

Finally, since law, as a set of rules observed by people, is a significant part of the culture of a country, understanding the law

19 JETRO, *NIPPON: Business Facts & Figures*, Tokyo 1991, p. 108.
20 *Ibid.*, p. 78.

of a country enhances the understanding of the country itself. There are some views which stress the uniqueness of Japanese law or the attitude of the Japanese towards law. It is largely believed that despite the reception of Western Civilisation, traditional values and virtues still prevail in Japan. By studying the way modern Japanese law operates, one may reach a different conclusion not only about the nature of contemporary Japanese law, but also the nature of Japanese society as a whole. One might also question whether it is really fruitful to discuss the distinctiveness or uniqueness of Japanese law when approximation and harmonisation of rules in various fields are being pursued.

2   The history of Japanese law

1.   The emergence of a unified state and the *Ritsuryō* codes

The first unified state, or at least a close approximation, in Japan was the *Yamatai* state of the late 2nd or early 3rd century. The existence of this state was referred to in Chinese historical sources, namely the *Wei-chih Wojen-ch'uan*, but the exact location of this state – whether it was located in Kyushu (near Fukuoka) or Yamato (close to Nara) is still in dispute. According to the Chinese sources, this state was ruled by Queen Himiko, whose authority emanated from her position as a religious leader. She was assisted by her brother in governing the state. After the death of Himiko in the mid–3rd century, the *Yamatai* state was taken over by Emperor Sujin who was succeeded by generations of emperors.[1] An official history of Japan, compiled in the 8th century, claimed that Sujin was the tenth of the emperors starting from Emperor Jinmu who founded the country in 660 B.C., but there is little historical evidence to support the existence of nine emperors preceding Sujin.

In the archaic period which lasted until the 7th century, the Emperor, who was a religious leader as well as a ruler, governed the country through a system of clans (*uji*) which were led by a patriarchal chieftain. Law in this period was basically customary law of Japanese origin. Law and religion (Shintoism) were inseparable. For instance, punishment of offenders was justified on the ground that the commission of a crime had displeased the gods and an act of purification was needed. Trial was by ordeal, which usually required the witness to retrieve a stone from boiling water.

In the 7th century, the powerful Soga clan consolidated their power over the successive emperors and empresses. The Sogas used Buddhism, which was imported from China in the previous century, to countervail traditional Shintoism.[2] Buddhism was

---

1 R. Ishii, *A History of Political Institutions in Japan*, Tokyo 1908, pp. 4–16.
2 *Japanese Religion; A Survey by the Agency of Cultural Affairs*, Tokyo 1972, pp. 47–69.

also supported by the Prince Regent, Prince Shōtoku. Inspired by Buddhism and Confucianism, the Prince promulgated the seventeen-article constitution in 604. Despite the nomenclature, this was more of a moral code for officials and the general public.

At that time, the T'ang dynasty ruled China. The Sogas sent envoys regularly to China to learn from the most advanced civilisation of the day. Together with Buddhism, various institutions of Chinese origin, including Chinese characters and the system of court ranks came to Japan.

The rule of the Soga clan did not last long. In 645, the clan was eliminated in a coup d'état by Prince Naka no Ōe. The Prince started large-scale political and social reforms, declaring that only the government of the Emperor (*ōkimi*) was legitimate. The country was to be directly ruled by the Emperor, instead of through the clans and their chieftains. In order to realise this goal, the land which had belonged to the clans were confiscated and re-allotted to the people. These fundamental changes in the governmental system followed the model of the T'ang system. The secularisation of the traditionally semi-religious political system was completed around this period.

In the latter half of the 7th century, the power of the Emperor was further strengthened and a highly centralised state emerged under the direct rule of the Emperor. The Emperor's government was composed of two major offices: the *daijōkan* which administered the country and *jingikan* which was in charge of Shintoist rites. Legal codes known as *ritsuryō*, which were gradually transplanted in the 7th century from China, served as the basis of the political system. In general terms, *ritsu* is a penal code whereas *ryō* is an administrative code. The earliest *ritsuryō*, the *Ōmi-ryō*, was promulgated in 668 followed by *Tenmu ryō* (689), *Taihō ritsuryō* (701), and *Yōrō ritsuryō* (718). Although these codes were of Chinese origin, they were modified in order to suit the existing conditions in Japan. *Ritsu* was close to its Chinese model, but penalties were more lenient. The Japanese *ryō* were substantially revised from their Chinese models, and included some new rules.[3]

It should be noted that specialists skilled in interpreting *ritsuryō* of foreign origin emerged in this period. With the exception of these specialists, the legal profession was not very developed in Japan until the late 19th century.

A new era began in 794 when the emperor moved the capital from Nara to Kyoto. Kyoto remained the capital until 1182 when

---

3 R. Ishii, *ibid.*, p. 23. J. Aomi ed., *Nihon no Shakai to Hō* (*Society and the Law in Japan*), Tokyo 1987, pp. 36–37.

the Kamakura Shogunate took over power from the Taira family. The *ritsuryō* system, based upon direct rule by the emperor, gradually eroded with the rise of the nobles (*kuge*). In the first half of this period, nobles and major Buddhist temples and Shintoist shrines accumulated large estates (*shōen*) and eventually established the privilege of immunity from taxes and the right to bar court officials from entering the estate. In place of the centralised system of the monarchy, a feudal system of divided estates emerged. Through inter-marriage with the Emperor's family, one of these *kuge* families, the Fujiwara family, consolidated its power and virtually ruled the country as regents (*sesshō*) or chief imperial advisers (*kampaku*). From 967 onwards, the position of the regent and chief imperial adviser became permanent positions reserved solely for the Fujiwara family while the role of the Emperor was greatly reduced.

The *ritsuryō* codes of the earlier period were nominally in effect until the mid–19th century. However, these codes had already fallen behind the developments in the mid-10th century when the nobles came to power. The nobles attempted to fill the gap between the codes and reality by 1) enacting new laws; 2) approving prevailing customs which were against the codes; and 3) interpreting the codes through commentators in a more flexible way. The laws which thus developed in the later period of the *ritsuryō* codes under the rule of the nobles are called *kuge* laws.[4] These *kuge* laws were largely superseded by *buke* (feudal warriors) law from the 12th century onwards.

2.   The law of the early Shogunates

Under the rule of the nobles, the country was divided into a number of feudal estates. The nobles found it necessary to employ warriors to defend their estates. Warriors were also employed to preserve public order in the capital, Kyoto, where factional war often took place. These warriors intermarried with nobles and came to form a class of warriors called *bushi* or *samurai*. Thus, powerful military clans such as the Taira and Minamoto emerged. The Taira family first took over power from the nobles, specifically the Fujiwara family. Kiyomori Taira became the chief imperial adviser, backed by his military strength and his marriage to the daughter of the Emperor. However, after his death, the Taira family was defeated in battle by the Minamoto family, another military clan.

4 *Ibid.*, p. 39. See also F. G. Bock ed., *Engi-shiki*, three volumes, Tokyo 1970.

In 1192, Yoritomo Minamoto was appointed 'great general who conquered barbarians' (*seii-taishōgun*) by the Emperor and moved the seat of government to Kamakura. He also obtained the title of 'general defender of feudal estates' (*zenkoku sō-shugo jitō*). His government, which was primarily staffed with warriors and resembled a military command, was designated as a Shogunate (*bakufu*). This particular shogunate is called Kamakura Shogunate after the name of its capital. Yoritomo Minamoto's successors also obtained the title of *Shōgun* from the emperor. Therefore, the title came to be associated with the position of the chief of the warriors. The Kamakura Shogunate lasted for 140 years, although in the later period, the *Shōgun*'s power was in fact exercised by regents, which were from the Hōjō family and not the Minamoto family.

With the accession to power of the warrior class, a vertical relationship developed between the warlords (leaders of the warriors) on one hand and the retainers on the other. The Shogun held the position of the supreme leader in the hierarchy of the leader-retainer relationship. Retainers swore loyalty to the leader and offered services, namely military service. In return, they were allotted land or rights to the proceeds from land. Unlike the Medieval European feudal system, it was a unilateral relationship. The leaders were not formally obliged to compensate their retainers and protection and benefits granted by the leader were regarded as favours, not legal rights of the retainers. Another difference from the European system was that the emperor was not involved with feudal relations, leaving the Shōgun as the highest feudal leader in Japan.[5]

Under the Kamakura Shogunate, the system of feudal estates which had developed under the rule of the nobles formally remained intact, although the power of the court and nobles had been reduced to a minimum. There were three kinds of estates: estates controlled by the nobles, estates controlled by *shōen* owners and estates controlled by warriors. However, the Kamakura Shogunate began to undermine the system of feudal estates held by the nobles. Formally, privileges of exemption from taxes and non-entry of officials were unscathed even after the Kamakura Shogunate was established. However, the Shogunate appointed stewards (*jitō*) and posted them in the existing *shōen*s. The *jitō*s abused their power by appropriating tax income and services from the estate for themselves and by interfering with parts of estates over which they had no jurisdiction.[6] The

---

5 Ishii, *supra* note 1, pp. 37–39, 42.
6 *Ibid.*, pp. 43–44.

abortive coup by the retired Emperor Go-Toba against the Shogunate in 1221 led to the confiscation of his supporter's estates, contributing further to the decline of feudal estates.

In 1333, the Kamakura Shogunate was defeated by the Emperor and his supporters, and a spell of direct imperial rule followed until Takauji Ashikaga, another leader of warriors, took over in 1338. Under the Ashikaga Shogunate, the system of feudal estates further declined. Military governors (*shugō*) in rural areas gradually gained power in the provinces and appropriated feudal estates. Although the Ashikaga Shogunate lasted until the mid–16th century, its authority eroded with the emergence of powerful military governors and territorial lords (*daimyō*) after the mid–15th century, some of whom ignored the orders of the Shogunate, enacted their own laws and conducted adjudication within their territory.

The legal system under the Kamakura and Ashikaga Shogunates was composed of three sub-systems: *kuge* law, *shōen* or *honjo* law, and *buke* law (the law of military households). Naturally, under both Shogunates, the law of military households was the most powerful of these three. These medieval laws were primarily unwritten customary laws which had developed after the demise of the *ritsuryō* codes. Written laws played only a secondary role, amending or supplementing the existing customary laws.

An important example of the law of military households is the *Jōei-shikimoku*, which was enacted by the Kamakura Shougunate in 1232. This Code, comprised of 51 articles, mainly dealt with criminal law and procedure. It was primarily a codification of customary laws, but some new provisions were added. This Code embodied the basic moral principles of warriors and remained in force under the Ashikaga Shogunate, although with subsequent amendments and supplements.

The judicial system of the Kamakura Shogunate was initially divided into civil and criminal law. Later, cases involving real property (the estates of warriors) and cases concerning chattels and credits were distinguished. Claims on estates increased in number and formed a significant proportion of legal disputes. This reflected the warriors' growing consciousness of their rights over their estates. The Shogunate found it crucial to develop legal protection for the property of warriors in order to ensure their loyalty.

Civil procedure was conducted by written evidence, but hearings were not uncommon. Deeds were considered to be the most reliable evidence, followed by testimony of witnesses and affidavits. The case was heard by a council of hearing officers, which drafted decisions subject to approval by a majority vote of the Shogunate advisers. When the hearing officers or advisers to the Shogunate failed to reach a conclusion, they resorted to divine guidance.[7] Procedures under the Ashikaga Shogunate were similar to those of the Kamakura Shogunate.

Whereas the criminal law under the *ritsuryō* system had a strong religious meaning, the criminal law under the Kamakura and Ashikaga Shogunates had more practical aims, namely the maintenance of the regime and the moral code of warriors. Confiscation of estates played a significant role in the punishment system.[8]

The Ashikaga Shogunate became almost completely powerless after the Civil War (*Ōnin-no-ran*), which was fought between two major families of military governors between 1467 and 1477. The country was deeply divided and a new type of rulers, territorial lords, emerged in the rural areas. These territorial lords fought against each other for a century after the Civil War. Therefore, the later period of the Ashikaga Shogunate is called 'a period of warring countries'. Both the Shogun and the Emperor were merely nominal figures in this period. In such chaotic times, it was inevitable that the law of the shogunate lost its significance. Territorial lords started to enact their own laws, which were often based on the *Jyōei shikimoku*, with some modifications.

Hideyoshi Toyotomi eventually emerged from among the warring territorial lords and unified the divided country by subjugating the *daimyōs* in 1587. He was appointed chief minister (*daijyō daijin*) and chief imperial adviser (*kampaku*) by the Emperor. His rule was short, but some important developments took place during his reign. First, a rigid status system was introduced. A firm line was drawn between the warrior class and other social classes. Hideyoshi Toyotomi ordered those other than warriors to surrender their weapons throughout the country. He also banned warriors from becoming merchants or peasants and prohibited peasants from leaving their land. Secondly, he conducted a nationwide cadastral survey (*kenchi*) and rearranged the system of land ownership. All land was publicly declared to be under direct control of the central government and was registered and allotted to *daimyōs*, who were granted the right of administration and taxation. This marked the formal end of the feudal *shōen* system, replacing it with a system of villages under the control of territorial lords.

Despite the continuous war between the warlords, trade and

---

7 Ishii, *ibid.*, p. 47.
8 Ishii, *Hōsei-shi* (*History of Law*), Tokyo 1964, p. 138.

commerce made significant progress in the 15th and 16th centuries. Warlords needed a strong financial and commercial base and therefore encouraged commerce and trade in their territory. Local cities developed into commercial centres and some of them even obtained an autonomous status. Some territorial lords increased relations with China and even some European countries, and in the 16th century Christianity first reached Japan via Jesuit missionaries, and was accepted by several territorial lords.[9]

3.   The law of the Tokugawa Shogunate

After the death of Hideyoshi Toyotomi, Ieyasu Tokugawa, a territorial lord who ruled the eastern part of Japan, came to power by defeating Hideyoshi's son and his supporters in 1600. Ieyasu Tokugawa founded a shogunate in Edo (present Tokyo) which lasted through fifteen generations of shōguns until 1867. He was granted the title of *seii-taishōgun* which Yoritomo Minamoto had received by the Emperor and became the supreme leader of warriors.

The political system under the Tokugawa Shogunate was a unique combination of centralised control exercised by the Shogunate and autonomous domains ruled by territorial lords. The Tokugawa family directly controlled a quarter of the country, while the remaining three quarters were ruled by 260–270 territorial lords who were subordinated to the Shōgun. Territorial lords swore obedience to each Shōgun, and in return, the territorial lord was made the supreme leader of the vassals and subjects within his domain (*han*).

Unlike the feudal lords in Europe, territorial lords under the Tokugawa Shogunate did not enjoy total autonomy; they were strictly controlled by the Shogunate. It was not rare that the Shogunate interfered with the internal affairs of the domain, especially when there was a dispute concerning succession or a wide scale peasant uprising. In some cases, the Shogunate held a territorial lord liable for mismanagement and confiscated his domain or transferred him to another domain. In this sense, the Shogunate was much more powerful vis à vis its subordinates than the European feudal kings.

Within their domain, territorial lords were entitled to enact laws, conduct adjudications and levy taxes. Parallel to the laws

9 Agency for Cultural Affairs, *supra* note 2, p. 76.

enacted by the territorial lords, the Shogunate enacted laws concerning matters which required nationwide regulation, including religious matters such as the ban on Christianity. Direct contacts between the territorial lords and the imperial court were also prohibited under the law of the Shogunate.

Territorial lords were classified into three categories. First came the family of Tokugawa. Next came hereditary vassal lords (*fudai*), whose families had already been serving Tokugawa before the defeat of the Toyotomis. Finally came outside lords (*tozama*) who pledged obedience after the establishment of the Shogunate. The Shōgun also had direct retainers (*hatamotos* and *gokenins*). It was the *fudais* that occupied senior positions as councilors, chief censors and commissioners within the Shogunate.

The Shogunate was composed of senior councillors (*rōjyū*), junior councillors (*wakadoshiyori*), chief censors (*ometsuke*) and commissioners (*bugyo*). Chief censor monitored the activities of territorial lords, while three commissioners dealt with finance, supervision over the temples and shrines, and the administration of the city of Edo, respectively.

As with the Kamakura and Ashikaga Shogunates, the legal system under the Tokugawa Shogunate was primarily based upon customary law, rather than a comprehensive code. However, the number of written acts increased significantly during this period. The shogunate promulgated two significant laws at the beginning of its reign, which were the Law on Military Households and the Law on the Imperial Court and Nobles of 1615. The former was intended to curb the power of the territorial lords and prohibited them from forming political alliances, moving troops outside their territory, maintaining more than one castle within their domain, and marrying without the approval of the Shōgun. It also obligated them to spend alternate years living in Edo.

By the latter act, the Shogunate imposed various restrictions on the imperial court. The Emperor was deprived of any kind of political power, while the Shōgun was empowered to interfere with significant matters concerning the imperial court. Appointments to senior positions within the court were strictly controlled by the Shogunate. The Emperor and the nobles were prohibited from leaving Kyoto without permission. The only power left to the Emperor was the power to decide the change of calendars and the power to award honours.[10]

One of the most important acts by the Tokugawa Shogunate, which had a long-lasting effect on the development of Japan, was

10 Mason and Caiger, *A History of Japan*, North Melbourn 1972, pp. 160–161.

the adoption of the isolationist policy in 1638. Trade with foreign countries had developed since the 16th century. Portuguese, Spaniards, Dutch and British came to Japan, as well as the Chinese. Christianity reached Japan at the same time and gained some support among the territorial lords, peasants and merchants. Although Christianity was tolerated at the beginning of the reign of the Tokugawa Shogunate, the tide changed soon afterwards. Firstly, Christians were found among the supporters of the son of Hideyoshi Toyotomi during their war against the Tokugawa Shogun. Secondly, because of factional rivalry, the Dutch and British denounced the Spaniards and Portuguese for subversion. Finally, a large scale rebellion, led by Christians against a territorial lord, occurred in Kyushu, where Christianity was the strongest. In 1637, Japanese nationals were banned from leaving the country. It was declared that no Catholic nationals were to be allowed to enter Japan, and further trade and diplomacy were to be conducted only in Nagasaki, a port in Kyushu. Thus, the only foreign contacts Japan had for the next two centuries were with the Dutch and Chinese. It was mainly through the Dutch that knowledge of European civilisation was imported into Japan during the period of isolationist policy.[11]

Until 1742, cases were decided on the basis of precedent and individual decrees. That year, a systematic code, *kujikata osadamegaki*, was enacted, which was compilation of acts and precedents comprising two volumes. The first volume was a collection of various acts while the second volume mainly covered civil and criminal law. It is interesting to note that the second part of the *osadamegaki* was a secret code which was accessible only to three commissioners and other senior officials of the Shogunate. It was considered unnecessary to let ordinary people know the contents of the code.

Territorial lords were empowered to adjudicate in cases within their domain. In the same way, the Shogunate adjudicated in cases in the territory under its direct control. If the case involved more than one domain, the Shogunate had jurisdiction.

There were two different procedures, *deiri-suji* and *ginmi-suji*, were administered by the Shogunate. The former was criminal procedure and the latter was civil procedure, but in some instances the distinction was blurred because some kinds of penalties could be imposed in the latter procedure. In civil procedure, the commissioner's office (*bugyō-sho*) accepted the petition of the plaintiff and summoned the defendant. The commissioner examined the case with both parties present and

11 *Ibid.*, pp. 166–171.

rendered the judgment. In criminal procedure, the defendant was examined in the open court of the commissioner's office. Since confession was considered to be crucial, torture was allowed, although limited in scope.

Punishments imposed in the early period of the Tokugawa Shogunate reflected the style of the period of 'warring countries' and were rather harsh. Since vertical relationship was the basis of the society, crimes against one's master or parents were severely punished. For instance, the punishment for homicide of a master was beheading by a saw. Punishments varied according to the status of the offender. The military character of the Shōgun's rule gradually faded in the later period, reflecting the changing societal values, and the punishments became milder.

Ginmi-suji, which involved disputes between private individuals was regarded as secondary to *deiri-suji*. Such disputes were expected to be settled without the involvement of the authority if possible, and it was thought to be a favour on the part of the authority to trouble themselves with such trivial matters. Therefore, informal settlement of disputes (*naisai*) by conciliation arranged by local officials or elders was encouraged. In fact, the Shogunate, as a rule, dispensed of cases without hearing and sometimes even forced the parties to reach a compromise under pain of punishment.[12]

Under the reign of the Tokugawa Shogunate, the Shōgun and the territorial lords had the right to levy taxes on the land in their respective domains. At the same time, the actual holder of the land (landlords) were regarded as private holders of the title. The rights they exercised were not so remote from modern ownership, although they were subject to various restrictions. For example, in 1643, the permanent sale of arable land held by landlords was prohibited and in 1673, division of land was restricted. However, in the 18th century, these restrictions came to be circumvented by wealthy merchants who accumulated newly developed land and became absentee landlords.[13] It was not uncommon to use land as collateral; the practice of using land as security for loans was also seen in this period.

The period of Tokugawa Shōguns' rule was a period of peace after the final fall of the Toyotomi family in 1615. A market economy developed on a national scale with growing monetisation all over Japan. Although industrial capital was yet to accumulate, commercial capital fully developed in this period. The merchant class flourished in the later period, and territorial

---

12 Aomi, *supra* note 3, pp. 53–54.
13 Ishii, *supra* note 1, pp. 87–88.

lords and warriors became heavily indebted to wealthy merchants. The ancestors of later business conglomerates (*zaibatsu*) such as Sumitomo and Mitsui, which controlled the Japanese economy in pre-Second World War Japan, emerged in this period. The development of the merchant class led to the emergence of commercial practices such as trading in futures and the use of limited companies. Bills of exchange also came to be extensively used in this period.

In light of these developments, it is no wonder that the radical modernisation which took place in the latter half of the 19th century, with strong influence of the West European countries, was largely successful. A sufficient basis to absorb a modern commercial and economic system had gradually developed in the period preceding the modernisation.

4. The period of modernisation

The arrival of Commodore Perry of the United States Navy in 1853 marked the beginning of the political turmoil which led to the fall of Tokugawa Shogunate. The Shogunate initially compromised steps and signed treaties to open up the country to foreign nations. Outside territorial lords who had traditionally kept their distance from the Shogunate gathered around the Emperor in opposition to the Shōgun and supported a firm approach to foreigners. Ideologically, they found support in the Emperor-centered nationalism, which was based on Shintoism as opposed to Confucianism and had been revived in the early 19th century to serve as the official ideology of the Shogunate.[14] The position of the Shogunate became too weak to counter the Emperor's stand on isolationism. The 15th Shōgun, Keiki Tokugawa, surrendered his power to the Emperor and resigned from his position as Shōgun in 1867. Domains of the territorial lords and the Shōgun remained intact for a year, but then the territorial lords surrendered their lands and were appointed governors in their domain. In the same year, the Emperor declared that imperial rule should be restored.

Finally in 1871, the feudal system of domains was replaced by a new system of prefectures directly under control of the Emperor's government and run by officials appointed by the Emperor. A new government was formed on the model of the

14 R. Storry, *A History of Modern Japan*, revised edition, Harmondsworth 1982, p. 82.

dajōkan system, which dates back to the 8th century. Under the new regime, the Emperor directly ruled the country with the assistance of the prime minister (*dajō-daijin*), ministers and councillors.

Three significant measures were taken at the beginning of the new regime. First, a modern tax system replaced the obsolete land tax system, which had been the major source of revenue. In 1873, a new system of taxation was introduced, under which all land was surveyed, assigned a definite monetary value, and a uniform rate of taxation was imposed. It was the landlord, not the village as under the previous system, who was to pay taxes. Land certificates, which were transferrable, were issued to landlords. This reform was a step towards the modern concept of land ownership.[15]

The second measure was the introduction of mandatory military service. This proved to be successful in light of rebellions which occurred during the early period of the Emperor's rule, where conscripts defeated rebels comprised of former *samurai* warriors.

Third, the Confucian civil status system (the distinctions between *samurai*, peasants, artisans and merchants) was abolished. This did not mean an overall abolition of the status system. A new nobility, which was comprised of former nobles as well as former territorial lords and those who were instrumental in the overthrow of the Shogunate, was established. Next to these nobles were former upper echelons of the *samurai* class, which were also called nobles (*kazoku*). Others were classified as commoners (*heimin*). However, the distance between the different ranks was greatly reduced. For instance, commoners were now permitted to have surnames.

At this initial stage, major positions were filled by nobles and former territorial lords. After several years, junior ranking men, who had served under these territorial lords and were instrumental in overthrowing the Tokugawa Shogunate, rose to power. Despite their initial chauvinism, these men quickly realised that the knowledge of foreign civilisation and the use of advanced technology developed in the West were indispensable to the modernisation of Japan. Modernisation was considered to be an urgent task if Japan was to avoid being colonised like many other Asian countries. Therefore, after a spell of return to the ancient *dajōkan* system, the new government turned to Western countries as a model. The system of *dajōkan* underwent several changes in the first decade of the Emperor's rule. The senate

15 Ishii, *supra* note 1, pp. 108–110.

(*genrōin*) was founded in 1875 followed by the Supreme Tribunal (*taishinin*). Then the *dajōkan* system was abolished altogether and replaced by a modern cabinet system based upon the European model.

Since the introduction of direct imperial rule, the government was in urgent need of a systematised legal system to replace obsolete feudal law. Laws of the previous period were unsystematic and varied from domain to domain. In order to consolidate the rule of the Emperor, a powerful and highly-centralised political system was required. Codified law was to play a significant role in supporting such a system.

There was another reason to develop a modern system of law. The Shogunate had no choice but to sign treaties with foreign countries at the end of its reign, which had imposed unequal terms on Japan. For example, foreigners were granted immunity, primarily because they thought the Japanese legal system was insufficiently developed to be applied to them. Japanese rulers considered it necessary to modernise the legal system in order to convince foreign countries that there was no problem in acknowledging Japanese jurisdiction over foreigners in Japan.

The Emperor's government initially resorted to Chinese Law. The first criminal code – *shinritsu-kōryō* – of 1870 was primarily based upon the *ritsuryō* codes as well as the laws of Ming and Ching China. However, the *ritsuryō* codes and the Chinese codes proved to be obsolete and unsuitable for a nation with aspirations to achieve a status equal to that of European countries in economic and military strength. It is only natural, then, that political leaders turned to Europe for a better model.

It should be stressed that the legislature broke away from traditional Japanese Law at this stage and sought new models in Europe. Unlike countries which introduced foreign law within their system of indigenous law, Japan almost entirely abandoned traditional law and turned to foreign law.

In fact, despite its long isolationist policy, the Dutch had already introduced some European political and legal ideas to the Japanese under the Tokugawa Shogunate. For instance, the idea of natural law was imported into Japan from Holland in the early 19th century. However, it was French law and not Dutch law which first had some influence on Japanese law. France was considered to have the most developed codified legal system when the Emperor's government began looking for a model in the 1870s. The first minister of justice, Shinpei Etoh, was particularly in favour of French Law and had French codes translated into Japanese. Two advisers from France, George

Boussquet and Gustave Boissonade, helped the Japanese understand the French system.

The first Criminal Code, enacted in 1880, was based upon the French Code, though with some influence from the Belgian and Italian codes. The earlier judicial system, including the system of practicing attorneys, already closely reflected the French system. The first Code of Criminal Instruction, also a replica of the French Code, was enacted in the same year.

This period of French influence did not last long. There was a gradual shift to Prussian Law in the 1880s. The fall of Etoh was not the only cause of this shift. Rather, it was the different political system of these countries which really mattered. In the light of the Popular Rights Movement which demanded the introduction of a parliamentary system, the government presumably developed some reservations about the French system. The Prussian constitutional monarchy suited Japanese requirements, since the Kaiser was seemingly free from parliamentary control. Moreover, Prussia was in the process of enacting codes of its own and therefore was the country with the latest codified laws.

The first influence of the Prussian system was seen in the Code of Civil Procedure of 1890. The Commercial Code was drafted with the assistance of a German adviser and was promulgated in the same year. However, these codes were caught in a fierce controversy concerning the Civil Code and it took another decade for the Commercial Code to take effect. Additionally, some earlier laws of French origin were replaced by new laws under Prussian influence. Thus, the Law on Court Organisation of 1890 partly replaced the Code of Criminal Instruction and the Criminal Code was replaced by a new Code in 1907.

The history of the Civil Code is more complicated and will be dealt with in a separate chapter. It is sufficient to mention here that the original Code was prepared by a French adviser, Gustave Boissonade, and was promulgated in 1890, but was abandoned in the face of strong opposition. A new Code, primarily based upon the *Pandekten* system, was finally enacted in 1896–1898.

The enactment of the Constitution, together with the introduction of the cabinet system and the opening of the Imperial Diet in 1890, marked the consolidation of the Emperor's power and signalled a final turn from French Law to Prussian Law.

While the Charter of Oath by the Emperor in 1868 proclaimed that public opinion should be consulted, this merely meant that territorial lords should be consulted in the decision-making. However, inspired by the parliamentary systems of Western Europe, and strengthened by disillusionment and discontent with the autocratic system of the new government, a movement to establish a publicly-elected parliament gained wide support in the 1870s. Different trends were discernable within this movement, which was called the Popular Rights Movement (*jiyū minken undō*). Some extremist factions waged outright rebellion, which was quickly suppressed by the government.[16] However, the government finally yielded to the demands of the movement. In 1875, the Emperor proclaimed that a national Diet would be established and a constitutional monarchy founded by 1890. At the same time, the government enacted the Libel Law and the Regulations on Newspapers in order to limit freedom of speech and gain control over the movement. Further restrictions on public meetings were introduced in 1880.

The enactment of the Constitution was a development closely related to the establishment of the national Diet. Already in the 1840s, the Dutch Constitution had been translated into Japanese followed by a translation of the French Constitution in 1873, and some Japanese had vague ideas about the role of a Constitution. The Senate had drafted a Constitution commissioned by the Emperor in 1876, but it was considered to be unsuitable for Japan and was abandoned. The government intended to proclaim the divine origin of the imperial family and the sovereignty of the Emperor, and the draft had been unsatisfactory from this point of view.

As the Popular Rights Movement gained momentum, various private drafts of the Constitution appeared, primarily of a British parliamentary type. In contrast to these private drafts, there were also drafts which supported an Emperor-centered, semi-religious political system. Thus, Eifu Motoda's draft Constitution provided for the divine character of the imperial family as well as its perpetuity as the sovereign of Japan. It was a clear proclamation of Emperor-centered absolutism.

Tomomi Iwakura, who was a councillor at that time, considered it most appropriate to enact the Constitution on the initiative of the Emperor. In 1882, Hirobumi Itoh, later to become the first prime minister under the cabinet system, was sent to Europe to study the constitutions of European countries. Prussia was chosen as the primary place of research. Itoh consulted Lorenz von Stein and Rudolf von Gneist, both of whom represented the conservatives among German and Austrian scholars.

The Prussian Constitution of 1850 was intentionally selected as a model, presumably for three reasons. Firstly, at that time, Prussia was a fairly backward country which had embarked on a

---

16 K. Nakamura, *The Formation of Modern Japan: As Viewed from Legal History*, Tokyo 1962, pp. 48–56.

modernisation process, and its situation was considered to resemble that of Japan. Secondly, the Japanese delegation which visited Prussia earlier was impressed by Bismarck and von Morthke's political thinking. Thirdly, in Prussia, the Kaiser seemingly had strong power and authority over the parliament. In contrast, the British and French constitutions were regarded as too liberal and democratic.

Itoh prepared a draft Constitution with the assistance of a German adviser, Hermann Roesler, after his return from Europe. Roesler defended a constitutional system which was more conservative than that found in the Prussian Constitution. He wanted to eliminate democratic and liberal institutions which had been imported from England via France and Belgium. The Japanese drafters went even further. Roesler refused to give the Emperor a religious status in the constitution; 'for him it was a contradiction to build a modern constitutional state on a mystic foundation'.[17] The Japanese intended to provide for the eternity of the Emperor's rule. Another point of disagreement arose because Roesler defended universal suffrage for the lower house.[18]

There was a firm belief on the part of the Japanese drafters that the power of the Emperor should be left as free as possible from any control exercisable by the Diet (parliament). The imperial family was to be left outside the realm of the Constitution. Towards this end, rules concerning the succession of the Emperor and other matters regarding the imperial household were left outside the Constitution and a separate act was adopted. This Act, the Act on the Imperial Household (*kōshitsu-tenpan*), was not promulgated, ostensibly because it was a private act of the imperial household.

The draft Constitution was discussed in the Privy Council and not the Senate. People were not informed of its contents until the day of promulgation. This led to protests from various quarters, but the government's enactment of the Public Security Regulations (*hoan jōrei*) suppressed such opposition. This first Constitution of Japan was 'granted' to the subjects by the Emperor in 1889, the day the first Imperial Diet was convened.

17 J. Siemes, *Hermann Roesler and the making of the Meiji State*, Tokyo 1968, pp. 43–44.
18 The history of this constitution is given in Tadakazu Fukase, 'Meiji Kenpō Seitei o meguru Hō-shisō (Legal Thoughts concerning the enactment of the Meiji Constitution)', in Y.Noda and J.Aomi eds., *Gendai Nihon Hō Shisōshi* (*History of Modern Japanese Legal Thoughts*), Tokyo 1979, pp. 164–214. See also R.H.Minear, *Japanese Tradition and Western Law*, Cambridge (Mass.), 1970, pp. 105–147.

The Constitution began with a proclamation of the sanctity and inviolability of the Emperor and the perpetuity of his rule. Accordingly, the legend that the ancestor of the Emperor had founded the nation around 660 B.C., which has never been substantiated historically, gained official endorsement. The Emperor was the sovereign who ruled the country in accordance with the provisions of the Constitution. However, there was a wide range of issues which were left to the prerogative of the Emperor. The Imperial Diet existed merely to assist and support the Emperor. Laws were enacted by the Diet but needed imperial approval. The Emperor also had broad power to issue imperial edicts. It should be added that only 1.1% of the populace could vote for the lower house of this Diet.

Cabinet ministers were appointed by the Emperor while the Diet had no say in the selection. Ministers were responsible to the Emperor, not to the Diet. Later it became constitutional practice that the power of the Emperor as the supreme commander of the armed forces was outside the control of the Diet and the cabinet.

Supporters of Emperor-centered nationalism were not fully satisfied with the seemingly secular nature of the Constitution. They favoured a more religious and ethical constitution. In order to appease this opposition, the Imperial Rescript of Education was promulgated by the Emperor. The Rescript was a mixture of revived Confucianism and Shintoism and was targeted against Westernisation. It proclaimed that loyalty to the Emperor, Confucian obligation of filial piety, and obedience were the essence and virtue of the nation. Subjects were to offer themselves courageously to the State, which was identified with the Emperor, should any emergency arise.[19] This was intended to be the fundamental ethical code of the nation and indeed served as such until the end of the Second World War.

It should be noted that the combination of Shintoism and the Emperor's rule, with some elements of Confucianism, had not always been the rule before the restoration of the Emperor's rule in 1867. Some former emperors retired in a Buddhist temple or were enthroned in a Buddhist fashion. In fact, Shintoism and Buddhism were not necessarily strictly demarcated. One school of thought maintained that the supreme goddess in Shintoism was Buddha reborn, and another school of thought reversed this order, i.e. Buddha was the goddess reborn. The new government, formed after the fall of the Tokugawa Shogunate, adopted a policy to favor Shintoism in order to strengthen the authority of

19 Storry, *supra*, note 15, p. 119.

the Emperor. Shintoism, which had largely been a spontaneous religion of the people emanating from ancestor worship, was thus transformed into a state religion.

The enactment of the major codes was completed in the 1890s. In the meantime, legal education had developed rapidly. The Ministry of Justice founded a school of law in 1871, which primarily taught French Law. In the *Kaisei* School, which dated back to the Tokugawa period, lectures on English law were given. The schools were merged and became the law faculty of the University of Tokyo. Some private schools of law were founded in the same period. Initially, most lectures were given by legal advisers and professors invited from abroad. It was only in the 1890s that most courses came to be taught by Japanese professors.[20]

In the late 19th century, Japan embarked on a rapid industrialisation process under the slogan 'Enrich the country and strengthen the army'. The development of the economy created a considerable gap between the wealthy industrialists on one hand and the deprived peasants and urban workers on the other. Instances of social unrest among poor peasants and the urbanised poor began to increase in the late 19th century. The government took legislative measures in order to control such unrest and to control the movement of the workers and peasants. Firstly, in order to protect the rights of those in a weaker social position, laws such as the Law on the Lease of Land and the Law on the Lease of Houses were enacted in 1922. Secondly, a conciliation procedure was introduced for settling disputes concerning labour and the tenancy of arable land. It was hoped that the introduction of conciliation would mitigate social conflict. At the same time, laws aimed at controlling political and labour movements were enacted. The Public Security and Policing Act of 1900 proved to be effective in controlling labour movements. This was replaced by a harsher law, the Law on the Maintenance of Public Security in 1925.

In terms of internal politics, there were developments in the 1910s which moved in the direction of strengthening democracy. Some political parties developed and there were for a time cabinets supported by a political party within the Diet. Universal suffrage for men was introduced, but women had to wait until the end of the Second World War. However, party cabinets proved to be powerless in the face of growing interference from the military. The Diet gradually turned itself into a ceremonial body

---

20 University of Tokyo, *Tokyo-daigaku Hyakunen-shi* (*Centennial History of the University of Tokyo*), Tokyo 1984, pp. 25, 29, 33, 82.

supporting the invasion of China and eventually the Second World War.

After the start of the war between China and Japan in 1932, whatever was left of embryonic democracy in Japan was removed. Japan withdrew from the League of Nations in 1933. Two successive rebellions by a group of army officials, the second of which involved battalions of the army, finally led to the demise of civilian rule in 1936. An official creed of the Emperor as a sacred entity, a descendant of the sun goddess demanding selfless devotion of people, was promoted even further. Deviance from the official ideology was not tolerated. Freedom of thought and expression was severely restricted by the Law on the Maintenance of Public Security which was amended to make the punishment more severe. The maximum punishment for forming an organisation aimed at altering the fundamental structure of the nation or becoming a leader of it was increased to death in 1933. This totalitarian regime under the Emperor lasted until the eventual defeat of the country in 1945.

5.   Post-war reforms

The Second World War ended with the acceptance of the Potsdam Declaration in 1945. Japan was placed under the control of the Supreme Commander of the Allied Powers (SCAP). The Occupation took the form of indirect military rule, i.e. the Japanese government was allowed to function under the strict supervision of the SCAP. The Occupational Forces were overwhelmingly American and therefore, the reforms were carried out under a strong American influence. Demilitarisation and democratisation were the first steps taken by the Allied Forces. The armed forces were dismantled and suspected war criminals were prosecuted. Those who were responsible for promoting the War were expelled from their positions. The Law on the Maintenance of Public Security was abolished and political prisoners were released. It was proclaimed that Shintoism was to be separated from the State.

The Allied Forces recommended five major reforms in 1945: introduction of equality of the sexes, encouragement of trade unions, liberalisation and democratisation of education, liberation from autocratic rule, and democratisation of the economy. This was followed by a directive on agrarian reform. As for the equality of sexes, part of the Civil Code which dealt with family law and succession underwent a total revision. Women were given the vote for the first time in the election of 1946. As for labour law, three major labour laws which enhanced the rights of the workers were promulgated. The educational system also underwent a significant change and education in Shintoism and Confucian ethics was abolished. The Fundamental Law on Education, enacted in 1947, emphasised peace, justice and respect of individuals. Democratisation of the economy was realised by the dissolution of business conglomerates (*zaibatsu*) which had controlled the economy by monopoly power. The Anti-Monopoly Law was enacted in 1947 in order to prevent monopolisation and maintain fair competition.

These measures signified a radical change of the then existing political, economic and social system, almost amounting to a revolution. Civilian experts and advisers who accompanied the military from the United States played a significant role in shaping these reform policies.

The reform measures were embodied in the Constitution of 1947. This Constitution, which remains in effect to date, introduced significant changes in the political and social system of Japan. Firstly, it proclaimed that sovereignty rested with the people and not the Emperor. The Diet elected by universal election became the supreme body of State power instead of an advisory body as it had been previously. The Emperor was made a 'symbol of the State and the unity of the people' and was deprived of any political power. Secondly, the Constitution provided for the renunciation of war as a sovereign right of a nation and the use of force or threat as a means of settling international disputes. After the dissolution of armed forces in 1945, Japan did not maintain any military force for some years. Thirdly, the new Constitution incorporated a bill of rights, which was far more extensive than that in the previous constitution and safeguarded by the introduction of judicial review.

The Constitution and most of the other laws which were enacted during the Occupation were strongly influenced by American Law. For instance, the three major labour laws, the Code of Criminal Procedure and the Anti-Monopoly Law were all strongly inspired by American Law. This was only natural, since the legal advisers to the SCAP were primarily Americans, some of whom were keen 'New Dealers'. On the other hand, most major codes dating back to the pre-War period remained intact. The Criminal Code, Code of Civil Procedure and the Commercial Code were left without any significant amendment. The Civil Code remained in force, except parts four and five which dealt with family law and succession respectively.

As early as 1948, there was a shift in the occupation policy, which was caused by the increasing tension between the United States and the Eastern Bloc. Policies such as disarmament, encouraging the trade union movement and dissolution of business conglomerates were thought to have gone too far. With the outbreak of the Korean War and the development of the Cold War, the governmental policy shifted from disarmament to rearmament. The Police Auxiliary Force was founded and later developed into the Self Defense Force. The compatibility of the Self Defense Force has been contested in the court on some occasions, but the Supreme Court has declined to rule on this matter.[21] Today, the Japanese Self Defense Force is one of the most powerful armed forces in Asia.

In 1951, Japan signed the Peace Treaty with the Allied Nations which took effect the next year. At the same time, the U.S.-Japan Security Treaty was signed, which provides for a bilateral duty of defence. It has been renewed up to the present.

The policy of 'rectifying the excess' of the initial reforms continued to a certain extent after the Occupation. For instance, the Anti-Monopoly Law of 1947 was substantially amended in 1953 'in order to adapt it to the situation in Japan'. This is not to say that the 'pre-War system' was restored after the Occupation. After all, the Japanese were never reluctant to accept measures adopted on the initiative of the Allied Forces. On the contrary, most people had suffered under the military regime before 1945 and actually welcomed these measures. This is substantiated by the fact that the radical changes introduced by the Allied Forces had been successfully put into practice without overt resistance from the general public. Political and social values such as democracy and human rights promoted during the post-War reform were embedded firmly in the minds of most Japanese. This has probably worked against various attempts to bring substantial changes to the achievements of the post-War reforms. Attempts to amend the Constitution, ostensibly imposed by the Americans, have never gained popular support and there has not been a single amendment to the Constitution so far.

---

21 Judgment of the Supreme Court, 16 December, 1959 (*Keishū* 13–13–3225; Sunagawa case).

3 The sources of law

1. The Rule of Law

The Rule of Law is a fundamental principle underlying the present Constitution. The previous Constitution, which was enacted in 1890 (hereinafter referred to as the 1890 Constitution), did incorporate the principle of *Rechtsstaat* in the pre-War German sense. Thus, State power was to be exercised within the framework of statutory laws enacted by the Emperor with the 'participation' of the Imperial Diet. The emperor was to rule the nation in accordance with the provisions of the Constitution (Art. 4). However, this principle was undermined by the power of the Emperor to issue imperial edicts in order to maintain public security or to cope with natural disasters (Art. 8, para. 1). It was also provided that the provisions of the Constitution did not prevent the Emperor from exercising his power during a war or an state of emergency (Art. 31). Fundamental rights of citizens were guaranteed by the Constitution only within the limits established by statutory law. Constitutional review did not exist, and judicial control over the administration was allowed only on occasions specified by law.

In contrast, the present Constitution, which was enacted in 1946, is regarded as the Supreme Law of the nation. It provides that no law, ordinance, imperial edict or other act of the government against the Constitution is to have legal effect (Art. 97). Fundamental rights guaranteed by the Constitution are regarded as inviolable even by way of legislation. In order to safeguard the supremacy of the Constitution, the courts are now empowered to review the constitutionality and legality of laws and ordinances as well as administrative decisions.

The present Constitution explicitly guarantees due process of law. It provides that no person shall be deprived of life or liberty, nor shall any other criminal penalty be imposed, except in accordance with the procedure established by law (Art. 31). This provision was modeled on the 14th Amendment of the U.S. Constitution which primarily deals with procedural due process.

However, unlike its U.S. counterpart, the Japanese provision is interpreted by the courts to cover both substantive and procedural due process (see Chapter 6).[1]

Japanese law is primarily based on codified laws. Unlike the Anglo-American system, statute law plays the primary role. This, however, does not mean that judicial precedent and other sources of law are not significant. On the contrary, case law represents a significant part of Japanese law. Some foreign observers even point out that, although codified laws are said to constitute the Japanese legal system, in fact, they merely provide the outline; details are left to judicial precedent and often to administrative practice.

Major statutes which set out the basic legal framework in a certain area are denoted as codes. There are six major Codes in addition to the Constitution: the Civil Code, the Criminal Code, the Commercial Code, the Code of Criminal Procedure, and the Code of Civil Procedure. Apart from the Constitution and the Code of Criminal Procedure, other codes were enacted in the late 19th or early 20th century. Parts of the Civil Code concerning family and inheritance were totally amended after the Second World War. Also the Commercial Code underwent a number of amendments. Furthermore, the Law on Civil Enforcement and the Law on Civil Interlocutory Measures replaced part of the Code of Civil Procedure. Apart from these changes, the Codes have remained basically the same since their enactment.

In addition to the Codes, there are individual laws which deal with more specific matters. For instance, while there is no administrative code, various individual laws such as the Cabinet Law, Law on Administrative Litigation, Law on Government Tort Liability, City Planning Law etc exist in the field of administrative law.[2] Labour law consists of the Labour Standards Law, the Trade Union Law, the Law on Adjustment of Labour Relations etc. These individual laws are of the same rank as the Codes, but the fields they cover are more limited than those of the Codes.

Written laws form a hierarchy in accordance with their effect. The Constitution is the Supreme Law of the nation, next come statute laws enacted by the Diet, then cabinet orders and ministerial ordinances. As a rule, provisions of specialised laws take precedence over the provisions of a more general law if

---

1 See the judgment of the Supreme Court, 10 September, 1975 (*Minshū* 29-8-489: Tokushima kōan jyōrei case).
2 As for an outline of Japanese administrative law, see K. Tsuji ed., *Public Administration in Japan*, Tokyo 1984.

there is a conflict. For instance, when provisions of the Civil Code and the Commercial Code are applicable, the latter takes priority. In addition to the laws and ordinances enacted by the central government, local authorities are empowered to enact local regulations within the limit of the law.

A card index of laws and ordinances in force is compiled by the Ministry of Justice. As of September 1983, there were 1,519 laws, 1,706 cabinet orders, and 2,375 ministerial ordinances. Furthermore, there are 130 imperial decrees and 18 pre-War cabinet orders which are still in force. The oldest law in force is the law which prohibits duels, enacted in 1889. In 1982 alone, 94 statutes, 324 cabinet orders and 629 ministerial orders were enacted or amended.[3]

2. The Constitution

1) Historical Backgrounds

The present Constitution was adopted in 1946 and took effect the following year. In 1945, shortly before the end of the Second World War, the United States and the United Kingdom issued the Potsdam Declaration calling for Japan's surrender and its subsequent demilitarisation and democratisation. The acceptance by the Japanese government of this declaration made the radical amendment of the Constitution of 1890 inevitable. After its unconditional surrender, the Japanese government formed a committee to conduct research on possible amendments to the Constitution. The primary concern of this committee was to preserve the basic features of the Constitution of 1890, namely the status of the Emperor. Safeguarding of individual rights was given little attention. The committee eventually worked out a draft, which was essentially conservative, preserving the system under the Constitution of 1890 as much as possible. At this time, Japan was under occupation by the Allied Forces. Therefore, the draft had to be submitted to the Supreme Commander of the Allied Powers (SCAP) for approval.

The SCAP and the U.S. legal advisors found this draft to be unsatisfactory in light of the declared aims of demilitarisation and democratisation. Therefore, the SCAP sent guidelines of a new Constitution to the Japanese government, which then developed another draft in accordance with the suggested line. This draft

---

3 N. Kikuchi, '*Seibun hōten no seibi jyōkyō* (The Current Status of Laws and Ordinances)', *Jurist* No. 805, 1984, pp. 176–180.

was sent to the Imperial Diet pursuant to the procedure as provided by the Constitution of 1890 and was adopted in 1946. This Constitution remains in force to the present day.[4]

Since the new Constitution was drafted on the initiative of the Allied Forces during the occupation, and was against the intention of the ruling elite at that time, some people believe that the Constitution was 'imposed' on Japan under the threat of the Allied Forces. They propose to amend the present Constitution and restore some features of the Meiji Constitution, including the removal of the renunciation of the war clause, formal recognition of the Self Defense Force, and the recognition of the Emperor's status as the sovereign head of the state. It is also argued that the present Constitution overemphasises the rights of the individuals, while neglecting their duties towards the nation.[5]

Proposals like this surface from time to time, mostly from conservative quarters. The ruling Liberal Democratic Party and its predecessors have always maintained that an 'original Japanese Constitution' is necessary, but so far they have not been successful. Despite the strong influence of the Allied Forces on the drafting process of the Constitution under unusual circumstances, its basic principles such as the renunciation of war, the inviolability of fundamental rights, and above all, democracy, have been accepted by a great majority of the Japanese. It should also be remembered that the lower house of the Imperial Diet, which discussed the draft Constitution, approved it by an overwhelming majority.[6]

2)   Fundamental principles underlying the constitution

There are three fundamental principles which are set out in the Constitution. First, sovereignty rests with the people and not the Emperor, as it did under the previous Constitution. The Diet, the 'Supreme Body of Legislation,' is composed of members who are elected representatives of the people. The Emperor, who was the sovereign before the end of the Second World War, now assumes the function of a 'symbol' of the nation and the unity of the people. The Emperor performs a limited range of acts upon the advice and approval of the Cabinet. These acts include the promulgation of amendments to the Constitution, laws,

---

4 H. Tanaka, "The Conflict Between Two Legal Traditions in Making the Constitution of Japan", in R. E. Ward and Y. Sakamoto eds., *Democratizing Japan: The Allied Occupation*, Honolulu 1987, pp. 107–126.

5 J. M. Maki, *Japan's Commission on the Constitution*, Seattle 1980, pp. 244–289.

6 M. Itoh, *Kenpō (Constitutional Law)*, Tokyo 1984, p. 172.

ordinances and treaties, the convocation of the Diet, the dissolution of the Lower House, the attestation of the appointment of ministers and other officials, and the reception of foreign ambassadors. The Emperor also appoints the Prime Minister and the Chief Justice. The appointment is actually a formality. The Prime Minister and the Chief Justice are nominated by the Diet and the Cabinet respectively. Thus, the power of the Emperor is limited to ceremonial matters and the real decision-making power resides elsewhere.

The second fundamental principle of the Constitution is pacifism and peaceful cooperation with foreign countries. The Constitution has a clause which renounces 'war as a sovereign right of a nation' and the 'threat or use of force as a means of settling international disputes'. It is declared that 'land, sea and air forces as well as other war potentials are not to be maintained' (Art. 9). It is understood that the right of defense is not waived by this clause, and opinion is divided as to whether the maintenance of the Self Defense Force is compatible with this clause or not. The government contends that the maintenance of a 'minimum necessary force' for defense is compatible with the Constitution and thus has developed a powerful Self Defense Force. Whether the present Self Defence Force is within the limit of 'minimum necessary' force is rather questionable.

As regards nuclear weapons, it is the official policy of the government not to develop them, not to allow them to be brought into the country, and not to keep them.

The third fundamental principle of the present Constitution is the respect for fundamental human rights. There is an extensive bill of rights which will be discussed in Chapter 6. Fundamental rights guaranteed by the Constitution are 'conferred upon the people as eternal and inviolable rights' (Art. 11). In order to safeguard these rights and freedoms, the courts are given a general power of constitutional review. Furthermore, actions of the executive branch are generally subject to judicial review in so far as they affect rights or freedoms of the people. The Law on the Courts provides that the courts are empowered to decide 'all legal disputes' (Art. 3, para. 1).

Accordingly, the Special Law on Administrative Litigation, enacted in 1948, provided for exceptions to the Civil Procedure Code. This Law was replaced in 1962 by a new comprehensive Law on Administrative Litigation.[7] Administrative litigation is supplemented by the administrative complaints system.[8] As for

---

7 Law No. 139, 1962.
8 Law No. 160, 1962.

controls over the decision-making process of administrative agencies, the enactment of a Code of Administrative Procedure is being proposed and a private draft has been published, but the legislature has been slow to react. On the other hand, a body of case law has developed in this respect. For instance, requirement of a hearing and notice in administrative procedure has been acknowledged by the courts (see Chapter 6).

3)   Procedure of Constitutional amendment

The present Constitution has strict requirements for effecting constitutional amendments. Any amendment must be proposed by the Diet with the support of two-thirds majority of each house. Furthermore, a majority vote in a popular referendum is needed (Art. 96). It is in practice very difficult to meet these requirements, and since the enactment in 1946, not a single amendment has been made.

Whether the Constitution can be amended by a *fait accompli* instead of by the formal procedures laid down in the Constitution has been an issue of controversy for some time. This is usually discussed in relation to the status of the Self Defense Force. The military forces of Japan were dismantled after the Second World War. The Constitution explicitly renounced both war as a sovereign right of the nation and the threat of force as a means for the settlement of international disputes. It also declared that Japan would never maintain military forces (Art. 9).

The outbreak of the Korean War resulted in a change in U.S. policy. The rearmament of Japan was considered to be indispensable as a barrier against Communism. Therefore, the existing Police Auxiliary Forces were transformed into the Self Defense Force, which has developed into a powerful military force in the three following decades. This development was not foreseen by the Constitution.

The constitutionality of the Self Defense Force has been contested in the courts several times. Some lower court decisions have found it unconstitutional, but the Supreme Court has refrained from ruling on this issue, allowing the question to remain open.

Some people argue that the shift in governmental practice and the accumulation of facts like this may alter the Constitution without recourse to a formal amendment procedure. However, without the judgment of the Supreme Court on this matter and with the absence of the popular acceptance of the change, it is difficult to acknowledge such 'transformation of the Constitution'

(*Verfassungswandel*). A majority of specialists of constitutional law reject this theory which was originally imported from Germany.[9]

It is generally agreed that there is a limit to the amendment of the Constitution. The Constitution itself declares in its preface that democracy is the 'universal principle of mankind' and forms the basis of the Constitution. Also one provision proclaims that the fundamental rights guaranteed by the Constitution are held 'for all time inviolable' (Art. 97). Whereas the German, Italian, and French Constitutions have a provision which explicitly prohibits amendments which contradict the principles underlying the Constitution, the Japanese Constitution does not have such a provision. However, despite the absence of an explicit provision, basic principles, such as the sovereignty of the people, pacifism and respect for human rights are understood to be unchangeable even with a constitutional amendment.[10]

4) Judicial review

The Separation of Powers is a basic principle underlying the political system embodied in the Constitution. The Diet is the supreme legislative body, while executive power lies with the Cabinet and judicial power belongs to the courts. These three powers are interrelated by checks and balances.

The Constitution has adopted a system in which the cabinet is jointly responsible to the Diet. The Diet nominates the Prime Minister from among the members of the Diet. If the nomination of both houses differ and the difference cannot be solved via a meeting of representatives of both houses, or if the House of Councilors fails to make a decision within ten days after the House of Representatives, the decision of the latter prevails. Thus, in practice, the leader of the majority party of the Lower House is nominated as a Prime Minister.

Under the previous Constitution, the Prime Minister was *primus inter pares*. In contrast, the present Constitution provides that the Prime Minister is the 'head' of the Cabinet. He selects and dismisses his Cabinet ministers, a majority of whom must be members of the Diet. Ministers, including the Head of the Defense Agency, must be civilians.

The House of Representatives may pass a vote of no confidence in the Prime Minister by a simple majority. The

---

9 Y. Higuchi and T. Fukase, *Le constitutionalisme et ses problèmes au Japon: une approche comparative*, Paris 1984, pp. 108–122.
10 Itoh, *supra* note 6, pp. 632–633.

Cabinet must resign or alternatively, the Prime Minister may dissolve the House of Representatives. After a general election, the Cabinet must resign.

The Cabinet is empowered to and responsible for, *inter alia*, administering the law and conducting the affairs of the State, concluding treaties and administering foreign affairs, and preparing and presenting the budget. It also has the power to enact Cabinet orders.

The supremacy of the Constitution is safeguarded by judicial review. The system of judicial review was introduced to Japan from the United States after the Second World War. In general, it has worked fairly well in post-War Japan.

The scope of judicial review has been an issue of debate. Some emphasise that there are issues the constitutionality of which can not be reviewed by the courts because of their political nature. The doctrines of 'political questions' in the United States or '*actes de gouvernement*' in France are often cited as examples. It is argued that since the courts cannot bear political responsibility, unlike the Cabinet or the Diet, they should forego reviewing sensitive political issues.[11] It is generally agreed that there is a certain limit to judicial review, but opinion varies as to where to set this limit. One school asserts that highly political issues such as the constitutionality of the Self Defense Force, or the U.S. – Japan Security Treaty cannot be reviewed by the courts, since these political issues should be decided by a representative body, the Diet. Others argue that there can be cases where the intervention of the courts is necessary even on such issues, especially when fundamental rights are concerned.

The Supreme Court has once refrained from ruling on the constitutionality of the U.S. – Japan Security Treaty. In that case, defendants were prosecuted for trespassing on a U.S. Air Force base. The defendants argued that the posting of the U.S. forces in Japan on the basis of the Security Treaty was against the Constitution. The Supreme Court ruled that such a political issue was beyond the scope of judicial review and should be left to the decision of the Cabinet which has the power to conclude treaties, and the Diet, which has the power to ratify them. On the other hand, the Court pointed out in passing that there may be instances where the treaty in question was apparently unconstitutional. In such cases, judicial review is possible.[12]

---

11 Cited in N. Ashibe, '*Shihō sekkyoku shugi to shōkyoku shugi* (Judicial Activism and Passivism)', in *Kenpō to Gikaisei* (*The Constitution and Parliamentalism*), Tokyo 1976.

12 Judgment of the Supreme Court, 12 December, 1959 (*Keishū* 13–13–3225: Sunagawa case).

There have been four situations in which the Supreme Court has found a provision of a law to be unconstitutional. Firstly, a provision of the Customs Law, which allowed confiscation of property not belonging to the offender without notice or hearing was found to be against due process.[13] Secondly, a provision of the Criminal Code had made homicide of an ascendant different from ordinary homicide, punishable either by death or life imprisonment. This was found to be against the equality clause of the Constitution.[14] Thirdly, a provision of Pharmaceutical Law which controlled the location of pharmacies was ruled to be unconstitutional, since it imposed unreasonable restrictions of the right to choose one's occupation.[15]

Finally, the Public Election Law was found unconstitutional because the demarcation of the boundaries of constituencies under it resulted in a wide difference in the number of votes needed to win a seat. In the 1972 general election, in a constituency where the population was not dense, only 35,000 votes were needed, while in major cities, almost five times as many votes were needed. The Supreme Court found the demarcation to be unconstitutional, unless measures to rectify the situation were not taken in due time.[16] This was followed by a judgment concerning the 1983 general election where the largest discrepancy was 4.4:1. The Supreme Court acknowledged the demarcation as provided by the Public Election Law to be unconstitutional.[17] It should be noted that in cases concerning the boundaries of the constituencies, the Supreme Court did not refrain from reviewing constitutionality, although the issue might be categorised as political.

A judgment of the Supreme Court which finds a certain provision of a law to be unconstitutional does not automatically make that provision void. The provision is regarded as null and void only in relation to the specific case before the Court. When the Supreme Court finds a provision of a law to be unconstitutional, it publishes the judgment in an official gazette (*kanpō*) and sends the original to the Cabinet and the Diet for consideration. The Cabinet and the Diet are then expected to take appropriate action.

However, such actions do not always follow. In the above-mentioned four cases, in the first and the third cases, i.e. the

13 Judgment of the Supreme Court, 28 November, 1962 (*Keishū* 16–11–1593).
14 Judgment of the Supreme Court, 4 April, 1973 (*Keishū* 27–3–265 : *Sonzoku-satsu* case).
15 Judgment of the Supreme Court, 30 April, 1975 (*Minshū* 29–4–572).
16 Judgment of the Supreme Court, 14 April, 1976 (*Minshū* 30–3–223).
17 Judgment of the Supreme Court, 17 July, 1985 (*Minshū* 39–5–1100).

Custom Law case and the Pharmaceutical Law case, the government acted promptly, either passing a provisional law or deleting the provision at issue. In the second case involving the homicide of an ascendant, the Cabinet and the Diet were slow to react although the Public Prosecutors' Office decided not to enforce this provision. Some members of the ruling party claimed that the provision was needed to maintain respect for parents, supposedly one of the highest virtues in Japan. As yet, years after the judgment, no legislative measure has been taken. On the other hand, the Supreme Court itself seems to have changed its stance. In a judgment in 1974, the Supreme Court found a provision constitutional even though it punishes assault resulting in the death of an ascendant more severely than the same act on others.[18]

As for the electoral boundaries issue, the Supreme Court did not invalidate the election in the first of its successive judgments on this issue, although it found the demarcation to be unconstitutional. The Court considered that the invalidation of the election as a whole would result in the disqualification of the members of Diet and thus bring the Diet to a standstill. The Law on Administrative Litigation provides for the option of declaring an administrative decision unlawful, while maintaining its effect in the interest of the public (Art. 31).[19] Although this provision was not directly applicable, the Supreme Court based its judgment on this provision. It should be noted that this judgment was influenced by a judgment of the U.S. Supreme Court.[20]

The Supreme Court had expected that the Diet would take the necessary action to rectify the inequality among different constituencies within a reasonable period. However, no action had been taken when a second case reached the Supreme Court. Noting the failure on the part of the government to take action, the court nevertheless maintained that a reasonable period to rectify the inequalities had not expired.[1] However, in a third case involving the election of 1983, the Supreme Court acknowledged that the legislature had failed to rectify the inequality within a reasonable time and found the demarcation of the boundaries to be unconstitutional.[2]

In 1986, the Diet passed an amendment to the Public Election Law as a provisional measure. However, the difference is still

---

18 Judgment of the Supreme Court, 26 September, 1974 (*Keishū* 28–6–329).
19 Law No. 139, 1962.
20 H. Tanaka, '*Teisu-haibun Fubyōdō ni taisuru Shihōteki-kyūsai* (Judicial Remedy for Unequal Constituency system)', *Jurist* No. 823 (1985), pp. 45–48.
 1 Judgment of the Supreme Court, 27 April, 1983 (*Minshū* 37–3–345).
 2 Judgment of the Supreme Court, 17 July, 1985 (*Minshū* 39–5–1100).

higher than three to one and some specialists of Constitutional law argue that in light of the inactivity on such a crucial issue, the court may invalidate the election and go even further to work out a provisional constituency system in lieu of the Diet.[3]

3. Statute law

The present Constitution provides that the Diet is the supreme and the only law-making body of the State (Art. 41). This is in contrast to the Constitution of 1890 in which the legislative power belonged to the Emperor and the Imperial Diet merely assisted him in law-making. The Emperor was empowered to issue imperial decrees between the sessions of the Imperial Diet, which replaced the laws for the maintenance of public security.

The scope of issues required to be regulated by statute under the present Constitution has been discussed for some time. A theory which developed under the previous Constitution maintained that norms imposing duties or limiting the rights of the citizens should take the form of statute enacted by the Diet. The current Cabinet Law, which provides that Cabinet orders may not impose duties or restrict rights unless such a power is delegated by law, is based upon this theory (Art. 11).[4] The underlying idea of this theory is that the Executive Power is basically free from restrictions but should be exceptionally limited in cases involving the rights and freedoms of citizens. For instance, various government subsidies do not necessarily need statutory sanction, but the levying of taxes does.

Whether this theory is still valid under the present Constitution or not is an issue of controversy. It is now pointed out that, since the Constitution is based upon the sovereignty of the people proclaimed in the supremacy of the Diet, instead of the Emperor, the scope of issues which should be regulated by law must be much broader than before. For example, financial subsidies to local government are not an imposition of duties nor a restriction of rights, but it may affect the rights and interests of citizens in various ways. The pension system and the unemployment benefit system are not intended to limit the rights of the citizens, but nevertheless, it is desirable to regulate them by law. In addition,

3 K. Takahashi, '*Giin-teisū Iken-hanketsu no mondai to kongo no Kadai* (Problems and Perspectives of the Judgment of the unconstitutionality of the constituency system)', *Jurist* No. 844, pp. 28–30.
4 Law No. 5, 1947.

issues previously considered to be internal matters of administration should be controlled by law, in so far as they affect the rights of citizens. Therefore, new theories are gaining support which assert that legal norms which in one way or another concern the relationship between the citizens and the state should take statutory form.[5]

The Constitution provides that the Diet is the 'highest body of State power' and that it shall be the 'sole lawmaking body of the State' (Art. 41). The Diet is composed of the House of Representatives and the House of Councilors. The Constitutional position of the former is much stronger than the latter. Every person over 20 years of age may vote. The House of Representatives is composed of 471 members elected from 129 constituencies. In the constituency system for the House of Representatives, each constituency elects two to five representatives roughly in accordance with the number of inhabitants. The House of Councillors has 252 members out of which 100 are elected proportionally from a list prepared by political parties. Each political party prepares a list of candidates and arranges them in order and seats are allotted in proportion to the number of votes the party obtains.[6]

The Constitution does not have an explicit provision empowering the Cabinet to submit a bill to the Diet, although there is a provision in the Law on the Cabinet. In practice, a majority of bills are submitted to the Diet by the Cabinet. From 1947 to 1983, out of 6,225 bills submitted to the Diet, 67% were submitted by the Cabinet while the rest were submitted by members of the Diet. Of the bills actually passed by the Diet, 85% were submitted by the Cabinet. The high proportion of Cabinet-initiated bills is not unique to Japan. In the United Kingdom, 90% of bills passed by Parliament are submitted by the executive branch.[7]

Bills submitted to the Diet are usually drafted by the relevant ministry. For instance, when the new Foreign Exchange and Foreign Trade Control Law was enacted in 1980, the Ministry of Finance and the Ministry of International Trade and Industry prepared the draft, although not without some departmental conflict.[8] In complicated issues where the advice of specialists is

---

5 N. Harada, *Gyōsei-hō-yōkō* (Administrative Law), 2nd ed., Tokyo 1989, pp. 72–76.

6 For details, see A. Stockwin, *Japan: Divided Politics in a Growth Economy*, second edition, London 1982, pp. 88–114.

7 T. Fukase, '*Nihon no Rippō-katei no Tokushoku* (Characteristics of the Legislative Process in Japan)', *Jurist*, No. 805, 1984, p. 23.

8 An example of a drafting process can be found in J. Horne, *Japan's Financial Markets*, Sydney 1985, pp. 153–162.

necessary, or when the reform involves major codes, advisory committees are consulted.

Advisory committees are usually attached to the ministries. Their task is to investigate issues in the ministry's portfolio and make recommendations and proposals. The advisory committee on taxation, for example, is composed of 58 members selected by the Ministry of Finance. They include university professors, trade union representatives, industry representatives and local governors and mayors. One of the peculiarities of the Japanese system is that interested parties are also made members of the committee, unlike the American system, where such interested parties are normally summoned as witnesses. Another peculiarity is that these committees invariably have ex-ministerial officials as members. After retiring from the ministries, they 'parachute' to the boards of quasi-governmental bodies or private companies and also become members of the committees.

Although members of the advisory committees are selected from various walks of life, three or four members who have close links with the ministry in charge tend to steer discussions in the direction favoured by the ministry. Actually, the draft report is often prepared by the ministry with the assistance of a working group composed of several experts and adopted by the plenary session with only minor revisions. Thus, the ministry's influence in the decision-making process of the advisory committee can be overwhelming.

Hence, these advisory committees are at times criticised for their lack of independence which results in a mere rubberstamping of decisions already finalised inside the ministries. However, they often play a crucial role in law-making. For instance, the Advisory Committee on Securities and Exchange has been instrumental in working out the latest amendments to the Securities and Exchange Law.[9]

When an enactment or amendment of a major code, such as the Commercial Code or Criminal Code, is contemplated, the Legislative Advisory Committee is consulted. This committee, which is attached to the Ministry of Justice, is composed of prominent law professors, appellate court judges, practicing lawyers, the Prosecutor General, the Head of the Secretariat of the Supreme Court, and the Director of the Cabinet Legislative Bureau. It has subcommittees on criminal law, civil law, commercial law, conflict of laws etc. Currently, the Committee is

---

9 H. Oda, 'Regulation of Insider Trading in Japan', in Oda and G.Grice ed., *Japanese Banking, Securities and Anti-Monopoly Law*, London 1988, pp. 86–93.

working on amendments to the Commercial Code and the reform of the Code of Civil Procedure.

A bill which has been prepared by a ministry is reviewed by the Cabinet Legislative Bureau. The Bureau and other interested ministries are usually consulted at an earlier stage as to the outline of the bill. The Bureau is staffed with 'counsellors' who were seconded from the court, the public prosecutor's office or a ministry.[10]

After review by the Cabinet Legislative Bureau, the ministry requests the Cabinet to consider the bill at a Cabinet meeting. What is peculiar is that the bill is simultaneously sent to the ruling party where it is normally examined by the Political Affairs Commission of the ruling Liberal Democratic Party. Key members of the ruling party as well as major opposition parties are informed of the contents of the bill and their prior consensus is sought. A bill which was approved by the Political Affairs Commission is then sent to the General Affairs Commission. For the most part, the approval of this latter commission is a prerequisite of any cabinet discussion on the bill. Thus, in a majority of cases, the bill has already been discussed and a compromise been reached before it is submitted to the Diet.

A bill can be submitted to either house but it is usually submitted to the House of Representatives, and then referred to one of the standing committees. Only when the bill is of major significance is it first explained to the general assembly of the House. Since the sessions of the general assembly are not held very often, and because the time allocated for discussion is limited, standing committees play a major role in the Diet. At present, there are 18 standing committees in the House of Representatives and 16 of them in the House of Councilors. Both Houses have the constitutional power to investigate legislation (Art. 62), and this power is primarily exercised by the standing committees.

The committee system was introduced from the United States after the Second World War, but present practice is somewhat different from the U.S. system. While discussions in general assembly are open to the public, standing committee sessions are usually closed. Only reporters and other persons who have the special permission of the chairman are allowed to observe. After debate and voting, the bill is sent to the general assembly, where it is discussed and voted upon. Discussion before the assembly is limited not only in time, but in effect. The consent of a minimum

---

10 Cabinet Legislation Bureau, 'Legislative Review', in Tsuji ed., *supra* note 2, pp. 139–152.

of 20 members is required in the House of Representatives in order to place a motion of amendment.

When one of the Houses passes a bill, the bill is then sent to the other House and discussed in the same manner. If the House of Representatives passes the bill but the House of Councillors does not agree, the former may overrule the latter by two-thirds majority. If the House of Councillors does not approve a bill which has been referred by the House of Representatives within 60 days, the latter may regard the bill as having been vetoed by the former.

A bill which the Diet has passed is signed by the minister in charge, together with the Prime Minister. The Emperor, upon advice and approval of the Cabinet, promulgates the law in the official gazette.[11] The law usually designates the date on which it is to take effect, but if not, it comes into force 20 days after promulgation.

Laws which are applicable only to a specific and limited area require a special legislative procedure. After the Diet has passed such a bill, it must be approved by a majority vote at a referendum in the locality in which it is expected to be applied.[12] This system was inspired by the laws of several states in the United States. These kinds of laws occasionally were enacted in the first decade after the promulgation of the Constitution, but since then this provision of the Constitution has been interpreted narrowly and there has been no recent case of such a referendum.

4.   Delegated legislation

Legislative power is often delegated to Cabinet orders, ministerial ordinances, and administrative rules, although this delegation is not provided for in the Constitution explicitly. It provides for the power of the Cabinet to issue orders, but only to 'implement the provisions of the Constitution and the laws' (Art. 73, para. 6). However, since the same provision states that Cabinet orders may not include criminal sanctions unless so delegated by the law, it is generally understood that the Constitution presupposes delegated legislation.

In practice, it is impossible to regulate everything by primary legislation in a modern society. It is even preferable, for

11 The Constitution, Arts. 7, para. 1, 76.
12 *Ibid.*, Art. 95.

example, to leave matters which require technical expertise, matters which need to be adapted promptly to changing circumstances, or matters which presuppose political neutrality for delegated legislation.

On the other hand, the delegation of legislative power is not unlimited. It is allowed only insofar as it does not undermine the supremacy of the Diet in law-making. Delegation of legislative power must be specific and concrete; giving *carte blanche* to the executive branch is not permitted. The Supreme Court has acknowledged this in principle, but in practice, it tends to allow a fairly broad delegation of power.[13]

There are various kinds of delegated legislation, classified in accordance with the body which enacts them. Cabinet orders (*seirei*) are issued by the Cabinet, while ministerial and prime ministerial ordinances (*shōrei* and *sōrifurei*) are issued by ministries and the Prime Minister's Office respectively. Administrative commissions, such as the Fair Trade Commission, also enact such legislation in the form of rules. In addition, legislative power may also be delegated to local authorities.

Matters left to delegated legislation are fairly broad in Japan. For example, in the field of water pollution controls, the emission standards are set by an order of the Prime Minister's Office.[14] The Foreign Exchange and Foreign Trade Control Law provides that a person who intends to export goods may be required to obtain the license of the Ministry of International Trade and Industry as provided by cabinet order.[15] Goods and technology subject to export license are listed in ministerial ordinances. Also the Anti-Monopoly Law provides for the delegation of power to the Fair Trade Commission, which issues guideline and notices.[16]

One of the most controversial issues in this respect is the constitutionality of Art. 102 of the Law on Government Employees.[17] This provision prohibits government employees from being involved in political activity under threat of a maximum three years' imprisonment. The definition of 'political activities' is not given in the Law, but is left to rules enacted by the Government Personnel Authority, one of the administrative commissions. The constitutionality of this provision is questionable because this provision involves fundamental rights of govern-

13 Judgment of the Supreme Court, 13 May, 1952.
14 The Law on Water Pollution Controls, Law No. 138, 1970, Art. 3, para. 1.
15 Law No. 228, 1949, Art. 48, para. 1.
16 Law No. 54, 1947, Art. 2, para. 9.
17 Law No. 120, 1947.

ment employees, but nevertheless, gives broad discretion to administrative rules.

The issue was contested in court when a post office employee was prosecuted for taking part in an industrial action under this provision. The district court and the appellate court acquitted the defendant on the ground that imposing of criminal sanctions for political activity was an unreasonable and excessive restriction on the actions of government employees. The appellate court explicitly referred to the 'less restrictive alternative' test adopted by the United States Supreme Court to reach this conclusion. However, the Supreme Court quashed the judgment of the appellate court and found the provision constitutional.[18]

The majority opinion ruled that the delegation of legislative power was sufficiently specific. Since it was possible to derive the purpose of the delegation and the scope and standards for its implementation from the given provision of the Law, the delegation of power was constitutional. There were four dissenting opinions which maintained that the Diet should first discuss the necessity of restricting political activities in detail, and only then decide the scope of restrictions. Most specialists in constitutional law view the broad and unlimited delegation of legislative power effected by this Law as unconstitutional.[19]

Not in all cases, however, has the Supreme Court found a delegation of legislative power to the Cabinet constitutional. In one case, a provision of the Law on Agricultural Land was acknowledged to have unduly restricted the possibility of the owner selling the land.[20]

5. International treaties

The Constitution provides that international treaties as well as the established laws of nations should be faithfully observed (Art. 98, para. 2). It is the Cabinet which is empowered to conclude international treaties. A plenipotentiary signs a treaty and the Cabinet ratifies it with the attestation of the Emperor. The attestation is merely a formality. The approval of the Diet is required, normally in advance, but an *ex post facto* approval is justified in cases of urgency or other extraordinary situations.

---

18 Judgment of the Supreme Court, 6 November, 1974 (*Keishū* 28–9–393: Sarufutsu case).
19 N. Asibe, *Kenpō-soshō no gendaiteki Tenkai* (*Contemporary Developments of Judicial Review*), Tokyo 1983, p. 261.
20 Judgment of the Supreme Court, 20 January, 1971 (*Minshū* 25–1–1).

When the opinions of the Houses differ, and the difference cannot be solved via a coordinating meeting, or when the House of Councilors does not take any action within 30 days after receiving the draft treaty, the decision of the House of Representatives is regarded as final (Arts. 61, 60, para. 2).

In an official opinion in 1974, the government listed the following categories as within the scope of treaties required to be approved by the Diet: first, treaties concerning matters which fall within the competence of the Diet, such as treaties involving territorial issues or tax treaties (commerce and navigation treaties also are included in this category); second, treaties which require special financial arrangements or undertaking of obligations, such as a treaty to establish an international organisation in which the contribution of funds is needed, or a treaty of compensation for losses caused by war; and third, treaties of political significance which establish fundamental links with other countries.[1]

The majority of scholarly opinion maintains that the Diet may not alter a treaty when approving it. The conclusion of treaties is an exclusive power of the Cabinet and the Diet may only approve or reject the treaty *in toto*.

In order to implement an international treaty in a sovereign state, it is necessary to incorporate it into the national legal system. In some countries, treaties must be transformed into national law by an enabling act of the legislature. In other countries, treaties are accepted without being so transformed. Japan has taken the second approach. Treaties are promulgated as such in the same way as statutory laws and are not always converted to national laws.

Since treaties can be incorporated into the national legal system without transformation, the relationship between domestic law and international treaties must be determined. The Constitution provides that international treaties to which Japan is a party should be observed faithfully and since the approval of the Diet is needed, it is generally agreed that international treaties are superior to statute laws.

There are, however, diverse opinions on the relationship between the Constitution and international treaties. The prevailing view is that the Constitution has priority over international treaties. The Cabinet's power to conclude treaties and the Diet's power to approve them are derived from the Constitution. Therefore, it is logically impossible to justify the superiority of a treaty which is against the Constitution. This view is also

1 Opinion of the Government, 20 February, 1974.

supported by the fact that the procedure for amending the Constitution is much more difficult than that for concluding treaties.

A problem may arise when the government concludes a treaty which is later found to be unconstitutional by the Supreme Court. Even those who assert the supremacy of the Constitution over international treaties do not claim that the treaty is null and void in relation to other parties to the treaty. From the viewpoint of international law, it is still valid. The government, however, must negotiate with the other parties to withdraw from or revoke the treaty. It should be added that Japan is a signatory to the Vienna Convention on the Law of Treaties. The Convention provides that a nation may not justify the non-fulfillment of obligations arising from treaties on the ground of its national law.

In the background of this debate is the issue of the Japan – U.S. Security Treaty. Some people claim that this treaty, which provides for defensive actions against attacks to either party within the territory of Japan and for the stationing of U.S. armed forces in Japan, is against the Japanese Constitution. When the constitutionality of this treaty was brought to the courts, the Supreme Court stated that an international treaty can be reviewed by the Court only when it is apparently unconstitutional and null and void.[2]

The Constitution provides that the 'established law of nations' is to be faithfully observed (Art. 98, para. 2), which includes international custom. This provision was interpreted in a case where the extradition of a person to his home country was contested. The Supreme Court ruled that the non-extradition of political offenders was yet to become an established international custom.[3]

6. Judge-made law

The Japanese legal system is primarily based on codified law. This, however, does not mean that judicial precedents are insignificant. On the contrary, court judgments, especially those of the Supreme Court, are respected and followed as one of the primary sources of law. New rules often emerge from case law and therefore, the study of court judgments is an essential part

2 Judgment of the Supreme Court, 16 December, 1959 (*Keishū* 13–13–3225: Sunagawa case).
3 Judgment of the Supreme Court, 26 January, 1976 (*Shōmu-geppō* 22–2–578).

of discussing legal problems. Judgments and decisions of the Supreme Court as well as the lower courts are studied and commented on by scholars and practicing lawyers. These comments are regularly published in legal periodicals, and often influence the courts in their decision-making.

The courts have played a crucial role in the development of modern Japanese law. In some areas, for instance, the law relating to real security rights, the law on land and housing lease and tort law, the law has been supplemented by precedent in a significant way.

Since the early codes were somewhat general in character, the gaps had to be closed by court judgments. This is illustrated in tort law, for example. The Civil Code has a provision on tortious liability (Art. 709) which was intentionally made general so that it could cover various kinds of situations emerging in the future. The concepts of negligence, causality, unlawfulness, etc. were not defined by the Code, but have developed out of court judgments, and today a substantial body of case law has emerged in this field.

Similar developments have taken place in the field of administrative law. The Law on Administrative Litigation which was enacted in 1962 provided for an 'objecting action', i.e. an action aimed at having an administrative decision revoked or altered. The Law provided for four such types of litigation, but left room for other types of litigation to be developed through academic research and court judgments. For instance, the availability of litigation mandating the administration to take a certain measure (*Verpflichtungsklage*) is discussed in this respect.

The courts have also been instrumental in mitigating the effect of provisions of a law which, when literally and strictly applied, may result in unfairness. Thus, in labour law, the courts have developed a rule that the exercise of the employer's right to dismiss an employee may be null and void, if the dismissal lacks reasonable grounds and is socially unacceptable. Similar developments have taken place to protect a lessee's rights.

Sometimes, the courts do not hesitate to deviate from the provisions of law in order to attain equitable results. The development of atypical real security rights serves as an example. Despite the provisions of the Civil Code which prohibit the creation of real rights by way other than law and require the transfer of possession in order to effect security over movables, various kinds of atypical real securities have developed and been upheld by the courts. Also, in the field of consumer loans where 'loan sharks' have charged extremely high interest, the Supreme Court has made efforts to control such high rates and reimburse excess interest to the debtor.

There are different views among specialists as to the status of court judgments as a source of law. There is no explicit provision in the law which directly provides for the status of judicial precedent in Japan. The Constitution provides that judges should fulfill their duties independently, and are bound only by law (Art. 76, para. 3). Some people feel that since this provision does not refer to court judgments, they should not be a source of law. However, the prevailing view is that court judgments are sources of law, but in a supplementary way. This is because precedents are not binding on the courts in the same way as statutory laws are binding on them. The doctrine of *stare decisis* has no explicit basis in Japanese Law. Therefore, the courts are, theoretically, free to render judgments against established precedent.

It should be stressed that the lower courts occasionally defy the precedents of the Supreme Court. For example, the Supreme Court in 1967 ruled that the right to compensation for non-pecuniary loss could be inherited without an express intention on the part of the inheritee to claim compensation.[4] However, some lower courts, in accordance with the prevailing view of scholars, still maintain that such a right cannot be inherited; instead, those heirs who had been dependent on the deceased should be allowed to claim damages in their own right.

Sometimes, the accumulation of lower court judgments which are contrary to Supreme Court precedent has eventually led to a change of view by the latter. Generally, lower courts are closer to everyday life and more sensitive to changes in society than higher courts. They are thus likely to have good reason to deviate from inappropriate precedents of the Supreme Court.

On the other hand, the Code of Criminal Procedure provides that deviation from precedents of the Supreme Court is a ground for appeal (Art. 405, para. 2). The Rules of Civil Procedure also have a similar provision (Art. 48). Thus, the lower courts must take the risk that their judgments will be quashed or reversed by the Supreme Court. Because of this possibility, the lower courts usually follow the precedents of the Supreme Court. This is often denoted as the *de facto* binding force of precedent.[5] Furthermore, Japanese judges are career judges almost without exception. The Supreme Court wields great power in promoting and transferring lower court judges. Judges have a fixed term of ten years, and the renewal of the term is not necessarily guaranteed. Therefore, lower court judges may find it psychologically difficult

---

4 Judgment of the Supreme Court, 1 November, 1967 (*Minshū* 21–9–2249).
5 T.Nakano ed., *Hanrei no Yomikata (How to read Cases)*, Tokyo 1986, pp. 14–16.

to rule against precedents of the Supreme Court. Some argue that despite the absence of the doctrine of *stare decisis*, lower courts are bound by precedents even more than in the countries where this doctrine exists, because of this career judge system.

Another reason that precedent is followed may be that the scope of the binding force is much broader in Japan. While the binding effect of precedent in Anglo-American jurisdiction is limited to the *ratio decidendi*, in Japan, the demarcation between the *ratio decidendi* and *obiter dicta* is not necessarily strict. General explanations or guidelines given in the judgments of the Supreme Court are often treated as precedents and are cited in lower court judgments.[6]

The binding force of judicial precedent, although it is not *de lege*, is explained mainly by the hierarchical system of the courts (i.e. judgments of the higher courts are superior to those of the lower courts), rather than by the need to treat similar cases in an equal fashion. A possible corollary of this view is that the Supreme Court itself is not necessarily bound by its precedents. The issue was raised when the Supreme Court refused to follow its previous judgment concerning the constitutionality of restrictions of political activities imposed on government employees. The Supreme Court had ruled that the imposition of criminal sanctions on government employees for political activities was an excessive restriction on their basic rights, and therefore, unconstitutional. However, eight years later, the Supreme Court explicitly changed its position and found the imposition of criminal penalties in such cases to be constitutional.[7]

This was not the first case where the Supreme Court has declined to follow its own precedents, but this case was peculiar in that the decision is contrary to the prevailing view of lawyers. Additionally, the judgment was also controversial because there had been a change of justices since the previous judgment. Furthermore, in this case, a change of precedent was not needed to reach the same substantive conclusion. Nevertheless, the majority opinion, supported by eight justices, elaborated on this issue and rejected the approach taken by the previous judgment. Five dissenting justices stressed that in order to alter the interpretation of the Constitution and to change a precedent, the

---

6 *Ibid.*, pp. 142–147. See also Y.Higuchi, '*Hanrei no Kōsoku-ryoku Kō* (On the Binding Force of Precedent)', in Higuchi and M.Shimizu eds., *Nihon-koku Kenpō no Riron* (*Theories of the Constitution of Japan*), Tokyo 1987, p. 684.

7 Judgment of the Supreme Court, 25 April, 1973 (*Keishū* 27–4–547: Zennōrin keishokuhō case). See also Judgment of the Supreme Court, 26 October, 1966 (*Keishū* 23–5–305: Zentei-chūyū case).

court should cautiously examine the necessity and reasonableness of the change and argued that there was no need to change the precedent in this case.

Court judgments are published in court reports. Supreme Court judgments are selected by its precedents commission and published by the Supreme Court. There are also collections of selected appellate court judgments and lower court judgments.

7. Circulars

Circulars of ministries and other administrative bodies are categorised as administrative rules and are contrasted with administrative orders. Circulars are issued by ministers, directors of bureaus and departments and other officials. They are addressed to lower echelons of the administration and local governments in order to give guidelines for the interpretation of the law and the exercise of discretion on their part. Administrative rules are *not* regarded as a source of law because they do not address the public directly and are basically internal rules.

In the field of public administration, for instance, taxation, finance and urban development and planning, circulars play a crucial role. Although the law is fairly general, the discretion of lower echelons of the administration and local government is narrowly limited by circulars. It often happens that a certain system or procedure, which does not have explicit legal basis, develops through circulars and becomes an established practice.

Since circulars are regarded as internal rules or guidelines, breaches of a circular cannot be contested in court and generally do not serve as a ground for citizens to claim damages. Even so, there are cases where circulars affect the rights and duties of citizens in a direct way. A lower court judgment has allowed the validity of a circular to be contested in court, provided that there is no alternative way of redress.[8]

8.   Local regulations

Under the Constitution of 1890, political power was highly centralised and there was little room for the autonomy of local government. Governors, mayors and other key officials of local authorities were all appointed by the central government. The

---

8 Judgment of the Tokyo District Court, 8 November, 1971 (*Gyōsaireishū* 22–11/12–1785).

Ministry of Internal Affairs exercised enormous power over local authorities whose task was to implement the policy set by the central government.

After the Second World War, the democratisation of the local government system was part of the reforms. The Ministry of Internal Affairs was abolished and replaced by the Agency of Local Administration. The police was separated from this agency, unlike its predecessor. The current Constitution has a chapter on local self-administration and guaranteed the autonomy of local government. Shortly afterwards, the Law on Local Self-Administration was enacted, which provides for the organization and powers of local governments.[9]

This reform was aimed at democratisation and decentralisation, following the models of the United States, but went only half way, partly due to the strong opposition from the Japanese government. While significant reforms such as the introduction of public election for governors and mayors were made, some features of the pre-War system of local administration remain intact, or have been restored. The power of the central government vis à vis local government is still dominant. Sometimes, local administration is denoted as 30% autonomy because local authorities are allocated only 30% of public funds.

As part of the post-War reform, local government was given the right to enact local regulations. The Constitution provides that local authorities, including prefectures, cities, towns and villages, may enact regulations within the scope of law (Art. 94). The Law on Local Self-Administration provides that local authorities may enact regulations on matters listed in the Law within the framework of laws and ordinances (Arts. 14, 2, para. 2). These issues range from the maintenance of public order and public health, protection of the environment, consumer protection, as well as the promotion of industry and commerce. It is also possible to provide for criminal sanctions in local regulations, with a maximum two years' imprisonment or a fine of 100,000 yen (Art. 14, para. 5).

The enactment of local regulations falls within the competence of the assembly of the local government, composed of members elected by the inhabitants. Local regulations are published by the local authorities.

The relationship between the general law and local regulations is a much debated topic. The issue was first raised when a person was charged with a breach of local regulation which punished prostitution. Prostitution *per se* is not a criminal offence in

9 Law No. 67, 1947.

Japan. The defendant argued that the regulation was contrary to due process of law. However, the Supreme Court ruled that the wordings of the Law on Local Self-Administration enabling local regulations to provide for criminal sanctions were sufficiently clear and specific to justify such a delegation of power. The judgment also took into account that local regulations are enacted by representative bodies.[10]

A similar issue came before the Supreme Court when a person was prosecuted for violation of a local regulation punishing indecent behaviour towards minors. Among other issues, the constitutionality of providing for such 'offenses' in local regulation was at issue. The Supreme Court cited the judgment discussed above and found punishment to be constitutional.[11]

The relationship between the general law and local regulations came into focus when pollution became a serious problem in the 1960s. Since the national government was slow in reacting to the increasingly serious problem of pollution, some local authorities, especially those in highly industrialised areas, enacted local regulations to cope with the problem, introducing stricter standards than those in the national anti-pollution law by their local regulations. Sometimes, local regulations controlled a scope of activity wider than that of national laws. Whether regulations with higher standards and broader applicability were legal or not was a matter of debate.

Previously, the prevailing view had been that local regulations could not cover issues which had already been regulated by national legislation. A corollary of this was that local regulations could not strengthen or broaden national control. However, the development of local regulations on pollution control led to a reconsideration of this theory. It is now asserted that when the law has established norms which are meant to be enforced throughout the country in a uniform fashion, i.e. when the law has established a maximum standard, local regulations may not regulate the same activity in a stricter or broader way. On the other hand, when the law is intended to establish a minimum standard, local authorities may enact stricter regulations by taking into account local peculiarities.[12] In this sense, the above-mentioned judgments of the Supreme Court concerning prostitution and indecent behaviour are questionable, since in these

10 Judgment of the Supreme Court, 15 October, 1958 (*Keishū* 12–14–3305).
11 Judgment of the Supreme Court, 23 October, 1985 (*Keishū* 39–6–413).
12 H. Shiono,'*Jyōrei-sono Igi to Genkai* (The significance and Limits of Local Regulations), in *Jurist: 100 Selected Local Regulations*, 1983, pp. 10–13.

cases, the silence of the law seems to indicate the Diet's intention to leave these acts outside the scope of criminal law.

The Supreme Court has acknowledged this view in its *obiter dictum* in a strange way. A case arose where the issue was the constitutionality of a public security regulation, which required participants in public demonstrations to observe traffic rules and provided for criminal sanctions for violations. Because this regulation in fact conflicted with the Law on Road Traffic, the district court acquitted the defendant, who had been prosecuted for a violation, on the ground that the regulation overlapped with national law. The appellate court upheld this judgment. However, the Supreme Court reversed the judgment of the appellate court, ruling that this was a case where the Diet had intended to set minimum standards and thus allowed further restrictions by local authorities.[13]

It should be added that some laws explicitly provide for local authorities to establish higher standards or broaden the scope of control. For example, the Law on Prevention of Air Pollution provides that when the prefectures find that the standards set by the Law are insufficient due to the natural and social environments of the locality, they may establish standards stricter and broader than those set by the law (Art. 4).[14]

9.   Custom

As a general principle, the Law on the Application of Laws (*hōrei*) provides that where custom is not contrary to public order nor morals it has an effect equivalent to law, on the condition that the law expressly provides for the custom to be applied, or when there is no law on the issue (Art. 2).[15] The Civil Code has a provision which allows the application of custom when the parties had such intention (Art. 92).

Since the codes adopted at an earlier stage were modelled after foreign codes, there was inevitably a gap between the law and social reality. Custom, together with court judgments, played an important role in filling this gap and adapting the codes to changing social conditions. Sometimes, custom which was contrary to the mandatory provisions of law has developed and eventually been upheld by the courts. Atypical real security rights

13 Judgment of the Supreme Court, 10 September, 1975 (*Keishū* 29–8–489: Tokushima City kōan jyōrei case).
14 Law No. 97, 1968 as amended in 1970.
15 Law No. 10, 1898.

are such an example. Furthermore, in commercial law, a practice of issuing blank bills of exchange has developed. This is contrary to law, but has been accepted by the courts.

10. Administrative guidance

Administrative guidance by government agencies and local authorities plays a significant role in Japan, although it is usually *not* regarded as a source of law. Administrative guidance is an informal instrument of an administration usually addressed to private corporations, designed to influence and steer their behaviour in order to achieve a specific policy goal.[16] It takes various forms, such as recommendation, encouragement, suggestions, or advice.[17] For instance, the Ministry of Finance, which has general supervisory powers over financial institutions, often resorts to administrative guidance instead of formal regulatory instruments. Thus, after a sharp rise in the price of land which was partly due to speculative investments financed by banks, the banks were recently 'discouraged' from lending money to 'non-bank' financial institutions and companies for investment in property. This policy was implemented by administrative guidance. Banks have also been 'discouraged' from lending over a certain amount of money to a single company by way of administrative guidance. In the securities market, various restrictions are imposed on trading and soliciting by administrative guidance instead of statutes.[18] In addition to such 'regulatory' administrative guidance, 'reconciliatory' administrative guidance is used as an instrument to reconciliate conflicting interests, for instance in city planning.

Although administrative guidance is not binding in nature, it is often accompanied by the power of administrative agencies to give licenses, grant permissions or provide some other benefits. For example, in 1964, the Ministry of International Trade and

16 H. Shiono, 'Administrative Guidance', in K. Tsuji ed., *Public Administration in Japan*, Tokyo 1984, p. 204.
17 H. Shiono, 'Administrative Guidance', in K. Tuji ed., *supra* note pp. 203–204. See also B. W. Semkow, 'Japanese Banking Law: Current Deregulation and Liberalization of Domestic and External Financial Transactions', *Law and Policy in International Business*, vol. 17, 1985, pp. 90–91. R. A Yeomans, 'Administrative Guidance:A Peregrine View', *Law in Japan* vol.19, 1986, p. 125 ff.
18 For an example of administrative guidance by the Ministry of International Trade and Industry, see F.K.Upham, *Law and Social Change in Postwar Japan*, Cambridge 1987, pp. 176–184.

Industry encouraged steel companies to decrease production of crude steel by way of administrative guidance. One steel company refused to follow this, since the plan prepared by the ministry seemed unfairly disadvantageous to them. In response, the ministry decreased the allocation of oil to the company, although the ministry and the company later reached a compromise.

Administrative guidance may also contribute to mitigate conflicting interests, for example, in planning law. While statutes provide for various restrictions on development in urban areas, these are not always sufficient, and therefore local government often establishes its own stricter guidelines. These guidelines are not formally binding, but those who want to apply for building permission are expected to comply with them.

The Supreme Court has rendered judgments on administrative guidance on several occasions. One such case concerned the Anti-Monopoly Law and will be discussed in the relevant chapter. In a recent case the Supreme Court ruled on adminstrative guidance involved planning permission. In this case, the Tokyo Metropolitan Government withheld building permission for a block of flats until a dispute between the developer and the neighbouring inhabitants had been resolved. Although the Metropolitan Government attempted to arbitrate in the dispute by way of administrative guidance, the developer filed an official complaint. When permission was still withheld, the developer brought the case to court seeking damages for loss caused by the delay from the Metropolitan Government.

The District Court found the withholding of permission to be legal. However, the Appellate Court overruled this judgment and was upheld by the Supreme Court. The Supreme Court acknowledged that it is possible to delay the granting of building permission while an administrative agency is trying to control development by way of administrative guidance. However, once the addressee of the guidance refuses to accept it voluntarily, it is no longer legal to withhold permission.[19]

As the Ministry of International Trade and Industry has proclaimed, an aim of administrative guidance is to implement effective measures in a flexible way on the basis of consent and cooperation of the addressees. It has played an important role in the development of Japanese economy, and may continue to do so in the future.[20] Resort to administrative guidance is justified because it is well-suited to react promptly to changing circumstances, while legislative measures require time. Moreover,

19 Judgment of the Supreme Court, 16 July, 1980 (*Minshū* 39–5–989).
20 Cited in Shiono, *supra* note 17, p. 212.

circumstances which necessitate action on the part of an administration are not always lasting enough to justify legislative measures. Also, by utilising administrative guidance before taking formal action, it is possible to avoid unnecessary conflict and reach a flexible and agreeable solution.

On the other hand, administrative guidance has its drawbacks. Administrative guidance often lacks procedural fairness and transparency. Moreover, unofficial 'sanctions' imposed for non-compliance with administrative guidance sometimes result in violations of the rights of individuals and the companies. However, since administrative guidance is not formally binding in nature, it is difficult for citizens and companies to seek redress against wrongful administrative guidance.

The shortcomings of administrative guidance are recognised in Japan and recommendations have been made to improve the situation.[1] There is also mounting criticisms from foreign countries on the extensive use of administrative guidance, since such informal means often work against foreign companies who are unfamiliar with the *modus operandi* of the Japanese market. However, reforms are yet to be made.

11. Scholarly opinion

Scholarly opinions are not regarded as a source of law and are rarely cited explicitly in the judgments of the courts. However, this does not mean that scholarly opinions do not have influence on the court. Since the major codes were of foreign origin, the courts in the early years had no experience in interpreting the codes. Therefore, the assistance of scholars who were familiar with foreign law was indispensable. This process was repeated after the Second World War, when American law served as a model for various laws, such as the Labour Standard Law, the Code of Criminal Procedure, the Anti-Monopoly Law and most importantly, the Constitution.

The courts often accept the views of law professors and form their judgments accordingly. Cases where academic criticism of a precedent eventually led to a change are not rare. For instance, it had been an established precedent in tort law that when determining contributory negligence on the part of minors, only the act of the victim should be taken into account, even when

---

1 H. Shiono, ' On the Occasion of the Publication of the Administrative Procedure Law Study Commission Report', *Law in Japan*, vol.19, 1986, pp. 90–92. A draft administrative procedure law is available in pp. 121–122.

parents are at fault by poorly supervising minors. The precedents of the Supreme Court were subject to criticisms by scholars for years, and finally the Supreme Court ruled that negligence of other persons should also be taken into account.[2]

Judges study scholarly opinions extensively when making a decision. At the Supreme Court, law clerks qualified as judges or assistant judges, consult scholarly opinions when they assist justices writing their opinions. Commentaries written by law clerks often refer to the opinions of law professors. There are informal study groups of judges, prosecutors, attorneys and law professors, who exchange views and study specific problems.

2 Judgment of the Supreme Court, 26 November, 1959 (*Minshū* 13–12–1573).

4 The administration of justice

1. An outline of the system

Japan's modern system of courts can be traced back to the reforms of the mid–19th century. The Statute on Judicial Matters (*shihō-shokumu-teisei*) of 1872, which was the first legislative act concerning the judicial system, was strongly influenced by French Law. This decree was replaced by the Code of Criminal Instruction of 1880, which was modelled on the French Code *d'Instruction Criminelle*. This Code provided for the organisation of courts dealing with criminal cases as well as the rules of criminal procedure. By the early 1880s, a network of courts was established. Civil and criminal cases started at the courts of first instance, followed by appellate courts, and finally, the Supreme Tribunal (*taishinin*) Great Court of Judicature which was founded in 1875.

However, the French system was found to be excessively complicated, and already in 1886, the drafting of a new law started as part of the legal reforms necessitated by the planned adoption of the Constitution. Since the Constitution itself was to be primarily based on the Prussian model, German advisers played a major part in redesigning the court system. The Law on Court Organisation, which replaced the Statute on Judicial Matters, was enacted in 1890.[1] According to this Law, district courts were to be the courts of first instance in ordinary cases, while ward courts were given jurisdiction for minor cases. Appeals could be brought to the courts of appeal, and finally to the Supreme Tribunal.

Under the Constitution of 1890, the independence of the court was guaranteed to a certain extent. Judges could not be removed unless they had been sentenced for committing a crime, or were dismissed by way of disciplinary proceedings. However, the Ministry of Justice was in charge of the overall administration of

---

1 Law No. 6, 1890. K. Takayanagi, 'A Century of Innovation,' in H. Tanaka ed., *The Japanese Legal System*, Tokyo 1976, pp. 167–171.

the courts and even had the power to appoint judges. The Courts had to render judgement in the name of the emperor. Furthermore, the public prosecutor's office was attached to the court at each level. Due to their close relationship with the Ministry of Justice, the status of public prosecutors was regarded as being higher than that of the judges.

The jurisdiction of the courts was limited to civil and criminal cases under this Constitution. Administrative cases were to be handled by administrative courts, which were part of the administration. These courts were empowered to review only a limited category of cases.[2]

After the Second World War, large scale law reform aimed at democratisation of the judicial system took place on the initiative of the Allied Forces. The independence of the judiciary was explicitly guaranteed by the new Constitution adopted in 1946. Whereas the judicial power belonged to the Emperor and was exercised in his name under the previous Constitution, the new Constitution granted judicial power to the courts. The courts were also given jurisdiction over administrative cases, similar to the American system.[3]

In 1947, the Law on Courts and the Law on the Public Prosecutor's Office were adopted. The public prosecutor's office was separated from the courts and formed an independent office at the level corresponding to the courts. They were followed by the Law on Attorneys enacted in 1949. These laws, which replaced the former Law on Court Organisation, are the basic legislation concerning the present judicial system.[4]

The Constitution provides that the entire judicial power is vested in the Supreme Court and the lower courts established under the Constitution. There are five kinds of courts: the Supreme Court, appellate courts, district courts, summary courts, and family courts. The Constitution prohibits the establishment of extraordinary tribunals (Art. 76, para. 2). It follows from this provision that neither a military tribunal nor a special tribunal for the Imperial Family outside the system of ordinary courts can be established. Furthermore, it provides that any organ or agency which is a part of the executive branch should not be given 'final judicial power.' On the other hand, this provision is understood not to prohibit the establishment of courts specialised in certain

2 H. Kaneko and M. Takeshita, *Saibanhō (Judicial Process)*, Tokyo. Second edition, 1983, pp. 49–50.
3 R. Ishii, *A History of Political Institutions in Japan*, Tokyo 1980, pp. 127–131.
4 Laws No. 59, 60, 61, 1947, No. 205, 1949.

fields, such as tax tribunals or administrative courts within the ordinary court system.

It is one of the characteristics of the Japanese court system that although Japan originally modelled its judicial system after the Continental legal system, it did not introduce specialised courts of the German or French type except for the pre-War administrative courts. For example, Germany has labour courts, finance courts, social courts, and administrative courts.[5] In contrast, in Japan the only court specialised in specific matters at present is the family court. Administrative cases are handled by ordinary courts.

Along with the courts, there are administrative commissions which are vested with quasi-judicial power as well as quasi-legislative power. They are attached to the ministries or local authorities, but enjoy independence in their operation. The Government Personnel Authority, the National Public Security Commission, the Fair Trade Commission, the Labour Commission, and the Coordination Commission on Matters concerning Pollution are examples of these administrative commissions.[6] They were founded in areas where political neutrality is particularly needed, some specialised expertise is required, or mitigation of conflicting interests is the main issue. Introduced to Japan as part of the post-War reforms, the commissions are modelled after 'self-regulating bodies' in the United States.

Decisions of these commissions are subject to the court's review. For instance, the decisions of the Fair Trade Commission can be appealed to the Tokyo Appellate Court. In such cases, the substantial evidence rule applies, i.e. the court is bound by the facts found by the commission, in so far as the facts are based upon substantial evidence.

The scope of judicial power under the new Constitution is much broader than in the pre-War period due to the addition of the power of constitutional review. The Constitution provides that the Supreme Court may determine the constitutionality of any law, ordinance or administrative decision (Art. 81). Until 1985, there were three cases in which the Supreme Court found a law unconstitutional. On several occasions since 1985, the Supreme Court has found the constituency system unconstitutional because of discrepancies in the value of votes.[7]

5 J. Baumann, *Einführung in die Rechtswissenschaft*, 8 Auflage, München 1989, S. 481–488; R. David, *French Law* (Translated by M. Kindred), Baton Rouge 1972, pp. 39–40.
6 K. Tsuji ed., *Public Administration in Japan*, Tokyo 1978.
7 Judgment of the Supreme Court, 17 July, 1985 (*Minshū* 39–5–1100).

Despite the silence of the Constitution on the power of constitutional review of the lower courts, it is acknowledged that the lower courts also have such power.[8] In fact, there are a number of cases where the lower courts found certain laws or acts to be unconstitutional.

Judicial review, including constitutional review, is possible only when it is necessary to render judgment on a specific case. Abstract normative control (*abstrakte Normenkontrolle*) without reference to a specific case, as exercised by the German Constitutional Court, does not exist in Japan. The limit of Judicial power is discussed in relation to judicial review (see Chapter 3).

The Law on Courts provides that the court, except in cases specifically provided by the Constitution, shall have jurisdiction over all kinds of legal disputes (Art. 3, para. 1). Thus, administrative cases previously not within the jurisdiction of the court are now handled by the court. The courts accept around one thousand administrative cases a year.[9]

2.   The court system

Japan has a three-tiered court system. Two appeals are allowed against the original judgment. In ordinary civil and criminal cases, the case is first handled by the district court. The party may appeal judgments of the district court to the appellate court. If the party is not satisfied with the judgment of the appellate court, he may appeal to the Supreme Court.

District Courts

District courts are the primary court of first instance. At present, there are 50 district courts, located in the center of each prefecture. There are around 900 judges and 460 assistant judges working at this level.[10] District courts have original jurisdiction over ordinary civil and criminal cases. The district court also hears appeals against the decisions and judgments of the summary courts in civil cases.

---

8 Judgment of the Supreme Court, 8 October 1952 (*Minshū* 6–9–783).
9 Supreme Court of Japan, *Shihō-tōkei-nenpō* (*Annual Report of Judicial Statistics*) 1990, Civil Cases, p. 6.
10 Supreme Court of Japan, *Outline of Japanese Judicial System*, Tokyo 1987, p. 7.

As a rule, one judge presides over cases brought before the district court, but in the following instances, the case must be heard by a bench composed of three judges, which may include assistant judges: 1) criminal cases where capital punishment, life imprisonment, and/or imprisonment exceeding one year is provided; and 2) cases of appeal against the judgment of the summary court (Law on Courts, Art. 26). In addition, in complicated cases, the court may exercise discretion and hear the case with a full bench. Assistant judges, who have finished legal training and have been appointed to the court, may not handle cases on their own, except where provided by the law. However, in order to cope with the shortage of judges, assistant judges who have more than five years' experience and who are specifically designated by the Supreme Court, are entitled to exercise a judge's full powers.[11]

Large district courts such as Tokyo and Osaka have divisions within the court. For instance, the District Court of Tokyo has divisions specialising in administrative cases, traffic cases, intellectual property cases, bankruptcy cases etc.

Appellate courts

Appellate courts primarily handle appeals against judgments of the district court and family courts. Appellate courts are located in eight major cities. They are staffed with a total of 280 appellate court judges.[12] In criminal cases initiated at the summary court, appeal is made to the appellate court, bypassing the district court. The appellate court is a court of final instance for civil cases initiated at the summary court and reviewed (appellate review) by the district court.

In some cases, such as treason or on the validity of an election provided by the Public Election Law, the appellate court has original jurisdiction. In addition, the appellate court is empowered to review the decisions of quasi-judicial bodies such as the Fair Trade Commission, the Patent Office, the High Maritime Board, etc. In such cases, and also in treason cases, five judges instead of the normal three consider the case. The Tokyo Appellate Court has a special division which deals with cases involving anti-monopoly litigation.

---

11 The Law on Special Rules concerning the Power of Assistant Judges, Law No. 146, 1948.
12 *Supra* note 9, p. 6.

The Supreme Court

The Supreme Court is the highest court of Japan. It is located in Tokyo and is composed of fifteen justices, including the Chief Justice. The Supreme Court sits either in full bench or petit bench with five justices. Each case is first assigned to the petit bench. The case must be transferred to the full bench in cases where 1) the appellant claims that the law, ordinance, order or administrative decision was unconstitutional; 2) the Supreme Court considers the law, regulation, order or administrative decision to be against the Constitution, regardless of any assertion by the appellant, and 3) the Supreme Court's opinion differs from its own precedent. In the first case, if the Supreme Court had already found the act constitutional before, the case can be handled by the petit bench. Most cases are handled by the petit bench and the full bench handles less than ten cases annually.

The Supreme Court is responsible for the standardisation of the interpretation and application of law. As a court of appeal, it reviews mainly appellate court judgments. In exceptional cases, the judgment of the district court can be appealed directly to the Supreme Court. For example, in civil cases both parties may agree to bypass the appellate court and appeal to the Supreme Court directly from the district court. In criminal cases, when the district court finds the law, ordinance, or administrative decision to be unconstitutional, the public prosecutor may appeal directly to the Supreme Court. In such cases, if the defendant appeals to the appellate court, the case must first be tried by the appellate court. In addition, in cases involving the *habeus corpus* procedure, the Supreme Court, when it feels it is especially needed, may itself may decide the case even while it is before the lower court. Normally, the petition is handled by the district court or the appellate court.[13] Incidentally, *habeus corpus* is seldom used in criminal procedure; instead, it is used in cases concerning disputes on parental rights over a child or cases involving those who were compulsorily hospitalised in a psychiatric institution.

The possibility of appeal to the Supreme Court is limited so that the Supreme Court will not be overburdened with minor issues. In criminal cases, the only grounds for appeal to the Supreme Court are the unconstitutionality of the appellate court's judgement or a deviation from precedent. In addition, the Supreme Court accepts appeals on its own discretion. In civil

13 *Habeus Corpus* Law, Law No. 199, 1948.

cases, the grounds for appeal are errors in the interpretation of the Constitution and other breaches of the Constitution, as well as breaches of law which substantially affect the decision of the lower court.

The caseload of the Japanese Supreme Court is not light. In 1990, the Supreme Court accepted 3,109 civil and administrative cases and 1,913 criminal cases. Most appeals to the Supreme Court are dismissed. Thus, in criminal cases, out of 1,446 cases disposed of in 1987, 1,193 cases were dismissed and 245 cases were withdrawn by the appellants. The Supreme Court quashed the judgment of lower courts only in two cases. In civil cases, 26 judgments out of 2,004 cases were quashed in 1990.[14]

The Supreme Court is responsible for the administration of courts. It is empowered by the Constitution to make rules regarding procedure and practice of the courts as well as matters relating to attorneys, internal discipline of the lower courts and court administration (Art. 77). Before the end of the Second World War, the Ministry of Justice was responsible for court administration. This system proved to be a serious threat to the independence of the courts. Therefore, the American advisers who took part in preparing the present Constitution strengthened the independence of the judiciary by vesting the Supreme Court with the same rule-making power as courts in common law countries exercise.

The Supreme Court makes rules at the general meeting of the justices. The Supreme Court's general secretariat, which is staffed with judges and assistant judges, handles routine matters and implements the decisions of the justices' meeting.

The Supreme Court has been fairly active in exercising its rule-making power. As of October 1983, there were approximately 150 rules, 55 of which relate to procedural matters, two are related to attorneys, and the rest concern internal matters of the court. Some are minor in nature, but more important ones include the Rules on Criminal Procedure and Rules on Civil Procedure.[15]

The rule-making power of the Supreme Court is not as wide as that of American Courts. For example, its procedural rules coexist with the procedural codes enacted by the Diet. Furthermore, since the Constitution has a provision which guarantees due process of law in criminal procedure, matters concerning the right of defendants must be regulated by statute law, and not by

14 *Supra* note 9, Civil Cases, p. 188; Criminal Cases, pp. 2, 7.
15 T. Hattori, 'The Role of the Supreme Court of Japan in the Field of Judicial Administration,' 60 Wash. L. Rev 69, pp. 83–85 (1984).

rules emanating from the court itself. The Bar is given broad autonomy over internal matters, so issues which can be regulated by the rules established by the Supreme Court are limited.

The relationship between the rules made by the Supreme Court and the statute law was once an issue of debate. Some people stressed the superiority of rules which derive from the inherent power of the court. The prevailing view is that the statute law is superior to the rules promulgated by the court, since the statute law is made by the Diet, which is the supreme body of state power by the Constitution. This view is supported by the practice of the Supreme Court.

The Constitution provides that Supreme Court Justices are appointed by the cabinet and 'attested' by the Emperor (Art. 79, para. 1). The Chief Justice is appointed by the Emperor on the advice of the Prime Minister. The Law on Courts provides that the justices should be selected from learned individuals who have received legal education, and they should be not less than 40 years of age. At least ten out of fifteen justices are required to have over 20 years' experience as either president of an appellate court, judge, summary court judge, public prosecutor, or law professor (Arts. 9 and 10).

When the Supreme Court was founded in 1947, it was composed of five professional judges, five practicing attorneys, and five individuals from other professions, including law professors. The composition of the Court has changed significantly since then. As of December 1990, six justices were 'career judges' promoted from the lower courts, two were former public prosecutors, four were former attorneys, one was a law professor, one a former Head of the Cabinet Legislative Advisory Bureau, and one a former senior diplomat. Of the six career judges, two had been Secretary General of the Supreme Court, and one had spent most of his career in the Ministry of Justice, seconded from the court. Taking into account two former public prosecutors who worked in the Ministry of Justice, five justices had long experience in the administration. Judges who have been Secretary General of the Supreme Court have, without exception, later become Supreme Court justices.

The Constitution introduced a system of referendum by which justices of the Supreme Court are reviewed after their appointment and every ten years afterwards (Art. 79, Paras. 2 and 3). The appointment itself takes effect immediately, but judges may be recalled by a national referendum which takes place at the same time as the first general election after their appointment. This system of general referendum was introduced after the

Second World War, influenced by the practices of some states in the United States of America. In fact, there has never been a case where a Supreme Court Justice was recalled. Some people criticise the referendum system on the ground that it has become mere routine. However, despite this fact, the symbolic significance of this system as a form of democratic control over the Supreme Court cannot be denied.

Family courts

The family court is a court specialising in family affairs and juvenile delinquency. Family courts and their branches are located in the same places as district courts. There are about 200 judges and 150 assistant judges, plus 1,500 probation officers working in the family courts.[16]

The family court is an innovation of post-War reforms. In the pre-War period, family affairs were handled by the family division of the district court, while juvenile tribunals under the control of the Ministry of Justice handled juvenile affairs. Family Law at that time was based upon the traditional concept of the family which denied the equality of the sexes and emphasised the authority of the head of the family. In contrast, the Constitution of 1946 provided for the equality of the sexes and strengthened the rights of females. The family under the new Constitution is more democratic and liberal than under traditional Japanese Law. This required a total reform of both the Civil Code and the organisation and procedure for handling family cases. At the same time, it was considered preferable to transfer juvenile cases to courts from the Ministry of Justice, since these juvenile cases entailed sanctions equivalent to those of the Criminal Law.

The idea of establishing a court which specialises both in juvenile cases and family affairs came from the United States, where it was believed that stable family relations were prerequisites to the healthy upbringing of juveniles and the prevention of delinquency. This was originally the idea of Judge Lindsay and his followers. Thus, in 1947, family courts were established in Japan primarily on the initiative of the SCAP.[17] However, although family affairs and juvenile cases are both handled by the family courts now, it is questionable whether the initial idea of linking both matters has really worked as intended. It is often pointed out that the family division and the juvenile division of the family court lack effective coordination.

16 *Supra* note 9, p. 7.
17 Supreme Court, *Guide to the Family Court of Japan*, Tokyo 1991, pp. 5–7.

In 1990, the family court handled 340,232 family cases out of which 244,948 cases were adjudicated. It also accepted 483,442 juvenile cases, a majority of which were traffic offenses.[18] The procedure in juvenile cases, as well as family affairs adjudication, is conducted *in camera* and is fairly informal.

The family court proceedings represent one of the rare opportunities in which laymen are able to take part in court proceedings (another example is the civil conciliation proceedings at the district court and summary court levels). The staff of the family court is comprised of not only judges and assistant judges but also other specialists. First, family court probation officers carry out pre-hearing investigations and probationary functions in juvenile cases. They are also involved in some family cases. Three to four probation officers are assigned to each judge in the family court. These officers are appointed by the Supreme Court from among university graduates with degrees in sociology, psychology, medicine or education, after they have passed an examination which the Supreme Court administers. Secondly, there are family affairs conciliation commissioners and family court councillors, who are part time government officials selected from laymen with broad knowledge and experience, but not necessarily a legal education.

The jurisdiction and procedure of the court on family affairs is based on the Law on Family Affairs Adjudication of 1947.[19] It covers both adjudication proceedings and conciliation proceedings. Matters such as the declaration of incompetence in civil transactions, declaration of disappearance, and correction of civil registers, which by their nature can only be determined by the decision of the court, are handled by adjudication at the family court. Matters which should be settled in accordance with the intention of the parties, such as divorce or dissolution of adoptive relations, are dealt with primarily by conciliation proceedings. Some cases, such as distribution of matrimonial property resulting from divorce or matters concerning probate, are required to go through conciliation proceedings first; these cases are adjudicated only when conciliation has failed. The family court generally handles adjudication of family affairs, except for divorce cases. In divorce cases, when the parties do not reach agreement at the conciliation proceedings, the case is decided by the district court. It should be added that if the parties agree, no court proceedings are necessary.

Family affairs adjudication is handled by a single judge with

18 *Supra* note 9, Family Cases, pp. 2–3, Juvenile Cases, pp. 2–3.
19 Law No. 152, 1947.

the participation of family court councillors. In contrast, family affairs conciliation proceedings are handled by a conciliation committee which is composed of a judge and two family affairs conciliation commissioners.

Other cases handles by the family court include cases of delinquency by minors under 20 and cases involving adults who have committed crimes against the welfare of juveniles. In addition, the family court is empowered to place juveniles who have not actually committed a crime but are likely to do so in the future under supervision. The law which provides for the jurisdiction and procedure of juvenile cases is the Law on Juveniles of 1948.[20] All cases of juvenile delinquency are first brought to the family court. The court may transfer a case to the district court or the summary court provided that the juvenile is not younger than sixteen.

Summary courts

Summary courts have jurisdiction over minor criminal and civil cases. There are currently 453 summary courts and a total of 790 summary court judges.[1]

In civil cases, summary courts handle cases involving claims not exceeding 900,000 yen (approximately 3,800 pounds sterling). This amount was increased from 300,000 yen in 1983. In criminal cases, offenses which may result in a fine and/or short term detention of up to fifteen days fall within the jurisdiction of the summary courts. Summary courts are not empowered to impose deprivation of freedom. If the judge finds it necessary to impose a custodial sentence, he must transfer the case to the district court.

In summary courts, a single judge handles the case. Summary court judges are not always career judges, i.e. judges who have been appointed assistant judge and then promoted to a full judge. In addition to those who have passed the uniform state examination, those who have worked for a certain period in the court or the public prosecutor's office as a clerk, can be appointed summary court judge (Law on Courts, Art. 45, para. 1).

Summary courts were established in 1947 with the intention of attracting laymen with broad knowledge and a good reputation as judges. Those who drafted the law evidently had in mind the

20 Law No. 168, 1948.
1 *Supra* note 10, p. 8.

magistrates' courts or small claims courts in Anglo-American law. However, this idea has not been fully implemented. Currently, those who qualify as judges, public prosecutors, or attorneys comprise only a quarter of summary court judges. Others are mostly former court clerks.[2]

Unlike ward courts of a German origin which existed before the Second World War, summary courts were intended to be courts easily accessible to the public and able to handle small claims without undue delay. This idea was inspired by the small claims court in the United States, where citizens can bring minor claims for speedy settlement. So far, summary courts have contributed to alleviating the burden of the district court, but it is arguable whether they have made justice more accessible to the public.

In 1987, summary courts newly accepted 1,579,705 civil cases. The number is almost double the figure for 1980.[3] This is primarily due to the increase in the maximum amount of claims which may be brought to the summary court from 300,000 to 900,000 yen. However, small claims brought by citizens occupy a very small portion of cases handled by the summary court. The majority of civil cases disposed by the summary courts are cases where a credit company or loan company is suing a debtor for default. Civil disputes between citizens involving small amounts and small claims by citizens against private firms, such as cases involving consumer protection, are the exception.[4] The expansion of the summary court's jurisdiction has been criticised on the ground that it merely increased the burden of the summary court while doing nothing to make the court more accessible to the citizens. The maximum amount of 900,000 yen is also said to be rather high for a 'small claims court.'[5]

There are several reasons why the summary court does not function as a forum for small claims. Firstly, the procedure adopted by the summary court is identical to that of the district court. The code of civil procedure provides for a simplified procedure applicable in summary courts, but these provisions are rarely used. This makes access to the summary court difficult for citizens, especially without the assistance of an attorney.

---

2 K. Konno, '*Kansai no Minji Jibutsu-kankatsu Kakuchō* (The Expansion of Jurisdiction of Summary Courts)),' in Tokyo Bar Association ed., *Arubeki Shihō o Motomete* (*In Quest of Justice*), Tokyo 1983, pp. 113–14.

3 *Supra* note 9, Civil Cases p. 3.

4 K. Miyakawa, '*Shōgaku Saibansho* (Small Claims Court), *Jiyū to Seigi*, 1984 No. 7, pp. 34–35.

5 Konno, *supra* note 22, pp. 11–112.

Secondly, the cost involved is not necessarily low and legal aid is limited. Thirdly, proceedings are time-consuming, although not as much as in higher courts. In 1987, only half of the ordinary civil cases disposed of by summary courts were settled within two months. The average length of time until judgment was around three months.[6] Fourthly, summary courts are not necessarily located properly. There are about 150 summary courts where a judge does not work regularly. In small summary courts, the annual caseload is less than ten, while summary courts in large cities are overburdened by credit cases.

In 1986, the Ministry of Justice announced a plan to re-organise the network of summary courts. Since then, some summary courts in rural areas have been abolished, while summary courts in major cities have been merged.

3. Lay participation in justice

One of the unique features of the Japanese court system is that lay participation is extremely limited. Despite its foreign origin, the Japanese court system does not accomodate a jury system nor a system of lay assessors. There are some lay elements in the system, such as civil conciliation commissioners and family court councillors. However, these people are required to have certain knowledge and experience, and a majority of conciliation commissioners are attorneys.[7]

A jury system in criminal cases was introduced in Japan in 1923 and had existed until 1943.[8] Early in the period of modernisation, there were proposals to introduce trial by jury. The first draft of the Code of Criminal Instruction which was prepared in the early period included provisions for jury trials, as did the original French Code. However, opponents of the jury trial argued that it was inappropriate to leave fact-finding to laymen. They also asserted that the jury would be too lenient and sometimes acquit those who were apparently guilty. The opponents prevailed and provisions concerning jury trial were deleted from the draft. In the early 1890s, discussions regarding

6 "*Minji-saiban no gaikyō* (Current State of Civil Litigation)", *Hōsō-jihō*, Vol. 43 (1991), No. 9, pp. 83/93.
7 Y. Kawabata, '*shokugyō to shite mita Bengoshigyō* (Lawyers as a Profession),' *Hōritsu Jihō*, vol. 53, No. 2, pp. 13–22.
8 For the history of jury trial in Japan, especially its political background, see T. Mitani, *Kindai Nihon no Shikōken to Seitō* (*Judicial Power and Political Parties in Modern Japan*), Tokyo 1980.

the introduction of the jury trial resumed and after a prolonged debate, the Law on Jury Trial was enacted in 1923.

This Law provided that in cases where imprisonment of over three years can be imposed, the case could be tried by jury and in cases where capital punishment was possible, jury trial was obligatory. However, there was a wide exception to this rule. Treason, military crimes and other serious crimes against the State were exempted from mandatory jury trial. In addition, the defendant was entitled to waive his right to be tried by a jury. Jury decision was by simple majority, like the French jury. This was intended to avoid hung juries, which were said to be common in England.

Although it was inspired by French and German law, the Japanese jury system had certain peculiarities. The verdict of the jury was not binding on the court and the judge was able to remand the case for retrial as many times as he wished, until the verdict conformed with his opinion. Although the defendant was not entitled to an appeal against the verdict on factual grounds, the prosecution was able to do so.

The Law was actually a compromise between the views of a government anxious to prevent too many unjustified acquittals and the proponents of the jury system. The democratic contents of the jury system have been thus substantially watered down. As can be expected, jury trial as provided by this Law did not gain popularity. In the first year, more than 100 cases were tried by jury. However, the waiver of jury trial by defendants increased, later reaching more than 90% of the eligible cases. Finally, in 1943, the law was suspended due to its cost and inefficiency.

The failure of the Japanese jury is explained in various ways. First, it is often pointed out that the Japanese have a tendency to trust a trial by professional judges rather than by their peers. Modernisation in Japan was led by the government rather than by the *bourgeoisie*. Therefore, the government and officialdom were regarded as positive and progressive forces rather than necessary evils which require constant control by the people. Common people had an inclination to defer to officialdom while distrusting their peers. Therefore, trial by peers was not as attractive as trial by a professional judge. Secondly, the fact that the verdict was not binding on the court and that appeal was not allowed on factual grounds discouraged defendants from jury trial. The Japanese jury system was never given a real chance of success because of its status as a mere consultative body.[9]

9 M. Urabe, 'A Study of Jury Trial in Japan,' in H. Tanaka ed., *supra* note 1, pp. 483–491.

After the Second World War, the Code of Criminal Procedure was replaced by a new code, heavily influenced by American law. The first draft of the Code on Criminal Procedure did include provisions for jury trial. However, there was strong opposition from Japanese members of the drafting committee, who cited the failure of the jury system before the Second World War. The Americans did not press hard because, as one of the Americans stated later, they did not feel it necessary to introduce the jury system, which was an institution historically rooted in very different soil.[10]

The introduction of trial by jury in criminal cases is still proposed from time to time.[11] There are various reasons for this. Some proponents want to enhance the 'democratisation' of the courts and bring them closer to everyday reality. Others support trial by jury, since it may 'vitalise' the criminal trial, which relies heavily on written evidence. Recently the Supreme Court decided to start examining the possibility of introducing jury trial.

4. Delays in court proceedings

The Japanese Court system is notorious for its lengthy delays. In civil cases in 1990, the average length of a trial was 11.9 months in the district court and 13.2 months in the appellate court, and 3.1 months even for summary courts. Of 1,376 cases pending at the Supreme Court, there were 211 cases where it had taken more then 10 years after the case was brought to the court.[12] In contested cases at the district court level, it takes in average 27.5 months until the judgment is rendered.

In criminal cases, the average length of trial at the district court and the summary court was 2.6 months and 3.5 months respectively, in 1990. It took an average of 13.2 months until a judgment of the appellate court was rendered, and 23.3 months from prosecution until judgment of the Supreme Court was given.[13]

Civil and criminal cases pending for more than a year are not uncommon. In civil cases in 1990, of 112,140 cases disposed by

---

10 Opler, *Legal Reform in Occupied Japan*, Princeton 1980, pp. 145–47.
11 K. Ueji, '*Kokumin no Shihō Sanka* (Participation of Citizens in the Judicial Process),' in Tokyo Bar Association ed., *Shihō Kaikaku no Tenbō* (*Perspectives of Judicial Reform*), Tokyo 1982, pp. 145–47.
12 "*Minji-jiken no Gaikyō* (Current State of Civil Cases)", *Hōso-jihō*, 1992 vol. 9, pp. 82, 88, 93. *Supra* note 9, Civil Cases, pp. 186–187.
13 *Supra* note 9, Criminal Cases, p. 21.

the district court level, 2,761 cases had been pending for more than five years. In criminal cases disposed by the district courts, there were 1,147 defendants whose trial took more than a year. A majority of these cases involved tax offenses, offenses arising from labour disputes and offenses involving public demonstration.[14]

One of the causes of the delay is the shortage of judges. There are approximately 2,000 judges, excluding summary court judges. At one time before the Second World War, the number of judges was almost 1,600, while the population was 72 million. 2,000 judges for a 121 million inhabitants is claimed to be too small, taking into account the increased caseload. For instance, in 1975, district courts accepted 95,861 new civil and administrative cases. This number increased to 132,430 in 1985 while the number of judges increased by only 100.[15] An increase in the number of judges is proposed from time to time, but the Supreme Court has been reluctant to do so since it may affect the quality of the judges and also because the capacity of the Legal Training and Research Institute is limited. With the recent reform of the state examination system, an increase in the number of judges is expected, but not on a major scale.

A second related reason is that hearings are not held consecutively in Japan. The average interval between hearings in criminal cases is one month. The average number of hearings needed for each case was 2.9 in 1988. In civil cases, the average interval between hearings is about the same.[16]

In criminal cases, the Constitution guarantees a speedy trial (Art. 37, para. 1). This provision of the Constitution was modelled after the sixth amendment of the United States Constitution. If the delay in a criminal case is serious, it is considered to be in breach of the Constitution.

In one extreme case, a trial was suspended for 15 years. The defendants were prosecuted for allegedly taking part in a riot. A majority of the defendants were simultaneously prosecuted in a related case. The court decided to hear one case at the end of the trial of the other. When the trial of the related case came to an end, the defendants made it clear to the court that they had no objections to the reopening of the first case. However, the public prosecutor did not take any measures to speed up the trial. The

14 *Ibid.*, Civil Cases, p. 122, Criminal Cases, p. 122.
15 Special Issue of *Jurist* on the reform of the State judicial examination, 1987, pp. 85, 92.
16 *Supra* note 7.

district court, 17 years after the incident, accepted the argument of the defendants and dismissed the case on the ground of infringement of constitutional rights to a speedy trial. The case was eventually brought to the Supreme Court. The Supreme Court found that nothing could justify the failure on the part of the district court in leaving the case unheard for such a long time. Therefore, the Supreme Court ruled that the defendants' right to a speedy trial had been infringed in this case. Although there was no explicit provision in the Code of Criminal Procedure allowing the dismissal of a case on this ground, the Supreme Court decided that the case should be dismissed by way of 'extraordinary remedy.'[17]

In passing, the Supreme Court ruled that whether the right to a speedy trial had been infringed or not should not be judged solely by the length of trial, but also by taking into account other factors, such as the cause and the reason for the delay, and to what extent the interests of the defendant had been infringed. Since this judgment, similar delayed cases have been brought before the Supreme Court. However, the Supreme Court has been reluctant to acknowledge any alleged violation of constitutional rights to a speedy trial. None of these cases, including a case where it took 25 years until the appellate court rendered a judgment, were found unconstitutional.[18]

In criminal procedure, various measures have been taken to speed up criminal trials by alleviating the courts' workloads. In 1953, summary proceedings were introduced in order to cope with minor offenses. This procedure can be used in cases except those where capital punishment, life imprisonment or imprisonment for not less than a year is provided. It is utilised when the defendant admits his guilt at the beginning of the trial. The evidentiary rules are relaxed and hearsay evidence can also be used with the consent of the defendant.[19] This proceeding was influenced by the arraignment procedure in the United States. However, unlike arraignment in the United States, examination of evidence is required even though the defendant has pleaded guilty.

In addition to this summary procedure, in 1953 a special procedure for traffic offenses at the summary court was introduced. Finally, in 1968, some minor traffic offenses were

---

17 Judgment of the Supreme Court, 20 December 1972 (*Keishū* 26–10–631: Takada case).
18 Judgment of the Supreme Court, 7 February 1980 (*Keishū* 34–2–15).
19 The Code of Criminal Procedure, Article 291–2 and 307–2.

excluded from the jurisdiction of the court. In cases of minor traffic offenses, the offender will not be prosecuted if he pays a fine to the police commissioner.[20]

5.   Legal aid

Litigation in Japan is just as expensive as in other industrialised countries. Attorney's fees are generally not included in an award of costs, and therefore, they are not recoverable from the other party. On the other hand, legal aid leaves much to be desired.

In criminal cases, when the defendant is not able to retain counsel, the State assigns him an attorney. This right to have the assistance of an attorney assigned by the State is guaranteed by the Constitution. However, it is limited to post-prosecution stages; at the pre-trial stage, the suspect may only retain an attorney at his own expense. In 1990, attornies were assigned by the state in 61% of defendants at the district court level.[1]

In civil cases, the Code of Civil Procedure merely provides for stay of payment of costs. This does not cover attorney's fees. Since this system has proved to be insufficient, private foundations have been established in order to assist those who are not financially capable of having the assistance of an attorney. The largest is the Japan Legal Aid Association, which was founded on the initiative of the Japan Federation of Bar Associations. It is subsidised by the Ministry of Justice, local government and receives donations from other institutions and individuals.

The aid covers court costs as well as attorney's fees. Apart from being short of money, applicants are required to have a reasonably good case. Generally, the amount received by the applicant must be repaid after the dispute is settled. Only in exceptional cases is the applicant exempted from repayment. There are around 6,000 to 8,000 applications for legal aid every year. In 1990, legal aid was provided in 4,072 cases. The average amount paid was 170,000 yen.[2] It recently has been reported that the Association is suffering from a shortage of funds since the number of applicants has increased. This is attributed to the increase in litigation in consumer credit cases, especially in the

---

20 Law No. 113, 1954.
1 *Supra* note 9, Criminal Cases, p. 146.
2 H. Kumagai, "*Hōritsu-fujyo-kyōkai no Genjyō to Kadai* (Present State of the Legal Aid Association and the Perspective of its Activities)", *Jiyū to Seigi*, vol. 42 (1991), No. 12, p. 6.

summary courts. There is some difficulty in recovering the money borrowed by parties in such disputes.[3]

In 1987, less than 40% of the applicants received monetary aid from the Association. The annual budget was 340 million yen that year. As compared with the United States and European Countries, legal aid in Japan is far from sufficient.

6. Alternative means of dispute-settlement

There are various alternatives to adjudication in Japan. The most formal of those is the conciliation proceedings which are widely utilised in the district courts, summary courts and family courts. In civil disputes, parties may agree to initiate civil conciliation proceedings at the summary court or district court instead of filing a suit. Even after the suit has been filed, the court may transfer the case to conciliation proceedings if it is considered suitable. In 1990, 97,355 law suits were brought to the summary courts while 59,120 new cases were accepted for civil conciliation proceedings at the same level.[4]

Conciliation at the court is primarily regulated by the Law on Civil Conciliation and the Family Affairs Adjudication Law, as well as relevant rules enacted by the Supreme Court.[5] In the pre-War period, a series of laws on conciliation in different areas, such as tenant farming, housing, commerce, family affairs, etc. were enacted. These laws were superseded by the laws mentioned above, which were enacted in 1951 and 1947 respectively.

The Law on Civil Conciliation provides as the aim of conciliation the resolution of disputes through mutual concession of the parties by way of taking into account 'actual state of affairs and in conformity with reason' (Art. 1).

Conciliation proceedings are handled by a conciliation committee composed of a judge and two civil conciliation commissioners. Civil conciliation commissioners are part-time governmental employees appointed by the Supreme Court for a two year term. They are selected from among people aged between 40 and 69 with profound general knowledge. They should either be qualified as attorneys, have knowledge useful in the resolution of civil disputes, or have sufficient skills and experience in social life. In family cases, conciliation is handled by a judge and two

---

3 *Mainichi Daily*, February, 1987.
4 *Supra* note 9, Civil Cases, p. 3.
5 Law No. 222, 1951.

family court councillors, who are also part-time government employees.

When the parties reach agreement in the conciliation proceedings, the documented agreement has the same effect as a court judgment. If the parties do not reach agreement, the judge may, after consulting the conciliation commissioners and considering relevant circumstances, make a recommendation as to the solution of the dispute. If neither party files an objection to this recommendation it has the same effect as a successful conciliation.

The *raison d'etre* of conciliation is usually explained in two ways. Firstly, it enables the parties to avoid litigation, which is expensive and time-consuming. Secondly, in certain kinds of cases, it is preferable for the parties to reach agreement through concession and without confrontation. This is particularly so in disputes which presuppose a long-term relationship between the parties, such as family disputes or landlord-tenant relations.

On the other hand, it should be borne in mind that conciliation cannot be a full substitute for litigation. After all, not all disputes are suitable for amicable settlement. There are various cases which should be settled in a more legalistic way. In conciliation, there is always a possibility that the rights and interests of people are sacrificed in pursuit of a mutually acceptable agreement. A recent survey shows that people are not always satisfied with the present system of conciliation. While a majority of people who have not experienced the conciliation process thought that conciliation was impartial and in line with common sense, only 18% of those who have experienced it thought that it was impartial.[6]

Apart from conciliation proceedings before the courts, there are some informal means of dispute settlement outside the courts. These range from commercial arbitration to conciliation and mediation, as well as agreements reached by the parties in the dispute by compromise (*jidan*). Disputes covered by these devices include pollution, consumer credits, traffic accidents, construction and building problems, intellectual property disputes, securities transactions, medical malpractice cases, and consumers protection. However, not all of these devices are extensively utilised. For instance, commercial arbitration is not widely used in Japan, although the Code of Civil Procedure provides for arbitration.

International commercial arbitration is handled by the Japan

---

6 Japan Federation of Bar Associations ed., *Shimin to Hōritsu-mondai* (*Citizens and Legal Problems*), Tokyo 1986, pp. 175–77.

Commercial Arbitration Commission and the Japan Shipping Exchange.[7] Rules for arbitration are set out in the Code of Civil Procedure. These rules, which came from the German Civil Procedure Code of the last century, are considered to be rather obsolete, and currently the enactment of a new law on arbitration is being proposed.

The Japan Commercial Arbitration Association, which was founded in 1950 under the auspices of the Chamber of Commerce, handles arbitration, conciliation and mediation of commercial disputes. The number of cases which it handles is rather small; from 1980 to 1990, 65 cases were filed with the Commission.[8] Foreign parties may be represented by practicing attorneys. The 1986 Special Measures Law on Foreign Law Solicitors does not exclude representing a party in arbitration from their scope of business.

Arbitrators are chosen from a list prepared by the Association. All members of the panel must be residents of Japan. Therefore, Japanese nationals are overrepresented in the list (164 out of 186). The limited scope for parties to select arbitrators is said to be one of the primary reasons for such unpopularity.[9]

In contrast, in some areas, conciliation and mediation have come to be widely utilised. In pollution control, a Coordinating Commission for Pollution was established in 1970 as an administrative commission attached to the Prime Minister's Office with quasi-judicial power. It is empowered to conciliate and arbitrate disputes concerning pollution. Since 1971, the committee has handled 592 cases of conciliation plus one case of arbitration. The former includes 555 cases concerning the amount of damages in Minamata disease which resulted from serious mercury pollution caused by a major chemical company. Other conciliation cases include a dispute between the inhabitants near an international airport and the government.[10]

There are various private non profit-making bodies which handle disputes. One such example is the Center for Settlement of Traffic Accidents Disputes which was established in 1978. Although the Center is funded by the Association of Marine and

---

7 T. Sawada, 'International Commercial Arbitration: practice of Arbitral Institutions in Japan', *The Japanese Annual of International Law*, No. 30, 1987, p. 69ff.

8 Information provided by Mr.Hiroshi Hattori, Japan Commercial Arbitration Association.

9 Y. Aoyama, '*Saiban-gai Funsō-shori-kikō no Genjyō to Tenbō* (Current State and the Future of Organizations for Informal Dispute Settlement),' *Jiyū to Seigi*, 1981 Nos. 9 and 11.

10 Coordinating Committee for Pollution ed., *White Paper on the Settlement of Disputes Arising from Pollution*, Tokyo 1987, pp. 21–66.

Fire Insurance Companies, it operates independently of them. The Center retains more than 100 attorneys on a part-time basis and it is these attorneys who give advice and act as conciliators in disputes. The Center gives advice and conducts conciliation from the viewpoint of how the court would have decided had the case been brought to the court.

When a person comes to the Center for advice and decides to proceed to possible amicable settlement, the Center contacts the opposite party and invites him along for mediation. Usually, it is not the tortfeasor, but a representative of the insurance company, who is the opposite party to the proceedings. If both parties agree to proceed to conciliation, the attorney at the Center presides over the conciliation process. If the parties reach an agreement, a written agreement is signed. This is regarded as a contract of compromise as provided by the Civil Code. If they fail to reach agreement, either party may ask the conciliation board of the Center to consider the case. This board is composed of attorneys and law professors, and it hears the view of both parties and makes a recommendation as to the settlement of the dispute. The recommendation is binding on the insurance company, but not on the victim. If the victim does not agree with the recommendation, the proceedings are terminated, but in the majority of the cases, the parties follow its conclusion.

In the 1988 fiscal year, the Center advised on 12,445 cases; in 1,934 cases, the parties reached compromise. 189 cases were forwarded to the conciliation board. In some complicated cases, the Center recommends the clients to go to court.

Compared with the full judicial process, the use of such proceedings at the Center is advantageous for both parties, since delays and expense are less. In most cases, the dispute is settled after four to five visits to the Center, and the time needed is about 100 days.[11]

Sometimes the preference of conciliation and other alternative means of dispute settlement is attributed to the peculiar attitude of the Japanese towards litigation. There is a pervasive opinion among Japanese academics as well as foreign lawyers that the Japanese are particularly non-litigious. A learned professor of the sociology of law, Professor Kawashima, pointed out that the Japanese have traditionally preferred to avoid litigation in favor of informal settlement of disputes. This is supported by the relatively small number of civil litigations. In his view, bringing a lawsuit constitutes a provocative and public challenge to either

11 *Japan Center for Settlement of Traffic Accident Disputes*, in *Hanrei Times*, No. 728 (1990), pp. 173–177.

party. Litigation presupposes and admits the existence of a dispute and leads to a decision which makes clear who is right or wrong in accordance with standards that are independent of the wishes of the parties. There is a strong expectation that a dispute should not and will not arise. Even when one occurs, it is to be solved by mutual understanding.[12]

This previously influential view of 'non-litigiousness' of the Japanese is now being questioned. Firstly, it has been pointed out that the extensive system of conciliation did not emerge as a result of popular demand for alternative means of dispute settlement. It has long been an intentional policy of government to divert civil cases to informal proceedings, and thus alleviate the burden of cases on the court. In the Tokugawa period, compromise was regarded as the preferable way of settling disputes, and people were encouraged or even forced to reach a compromise.

The present system of conciliation in various fields of social relations goes back to the 1920s and 1930s. The introduction of conciliation in each field has had its specific reason. For instance, conciliation in landlord-tenant farmer relations had nothing to do with the non-litigiousness of the latter. Rather, it was the intention of the government to appease the increasing unrest of tenant-farmers without resort to the court.[13]

Secondly, the comparison of the number of lawsuits between countries does not necessarily reflect the difference in attitude of people. If the amount of civil litigation per 100,000 inhabitants in Japan is compared with that of the United States, it is obvious that the amount of litigation is smaller by far in Japan. But the contrast is not as sharp when we compare the amount of litigation in Japan with that in Germany or the United Kingdom. In Scandinavian countries, the amount of civil litigation is less than half that of Japan.[14] It should be noted that the scope of jurisdiction of the courts differs from country to country and this kind of comparison can be misleading.

Thirdly, it is questionable whether the relatively small amount of civil litigation and the broad utilisation of conciliation is caused by the traditional attitude of the Japanese or is the result of some

12 T. Kawashima, 'Dispute Resolution in Contemporary Japan,' in A. von Mehren ed., *Law in Japan*, Ann Arbour 1963, pp. 43–45; Y. Noda, 'The Far Eastern Conception of the Law,' in R. David, et al, eds., *International Encyclopedia of Comparative Law*, Vol. II, Paris 1974, pp. 129–37.
13 J. O. Haley, 'The Myth of the Reluctant Litigant,' *Journal of Japanese Studies*, vol. 4, 1978, pp. 371–378.
14 *Ibid.*, p. 364.

institutional problems. In other words, do the Japanese avoid civil litigation although they can resort to it, or is there an institutional barrier which makes the Japanese reluctant to go to court? In fact, this question had already been raised by Professor Kawashima decades ago; along with cultural factors, he pointed out some institutional problems which inhibit the Japanese from going to court.

The possibility cannot be denied that delays in court proceedings, the fact that the successful party does not recover all his costs from the other party, the poorly funded legal aid service and other factors make litigation unattractive. A survey of the popular image of litigation shows that almost 85% of citizens responded that litigation takes too much time. 67% of the respondents held the popular view that lengthy litigation will result in the loss of one's property.[15] There may be a peculiar attitude prevalent among the Japanese in preferring the extra-judicial settlement of disputes, but the above-mentioned institutional factors also seem to contribute to the phenomenon in some way.[16]

7.   The public prosecutor's office

The post of public prosecutor was first introduced to Japan in 1872, when the influence of French law was predominant. Therefore, the primary task of the public prosecutor was to supervise judicial proceedings on behalf of the government as is the case with French *ministère public*. However, the role of the public prosecutor soon shifted from that of a supervisory agency into that of a prosecuting agency. The Law of Court Organization of 1890 created the Public Prosecutor's Office as an agency of state prosecution.[17]

The Public Prosecutor's Office was a highly centralised and hierarchical body. It was made part of the judiciary, together with the court. The public prosecutor's office at each level was attached to the court of the same level. Public prosecutors regarded themselves as equal to judges, and were in fact treated

15 Japan Federation of Bar Associations, ed., *supra* note 46.
16 See further, S. Miyazawa, 'Taking Kawashima Seriously: A Review of Japanese Research on Japanese Legal Consciousness and Disputing Behaviour', *Law and Society Review*, vol.21, p. 219ff. M. Ramseyer, 'Reluctant Litigant Revisited: Rationality and Disputes in Japan', *Journal of Japanese Studies*, 1988, pp. 111ff.
17 Y. Noda, *Introduction to Japanese Law* (Translated by A. Angelo), Tokyo 1976, pp. 135–36.

as such. They were often transferred to the Ministry of Justice and occupied important positions there. Since the Ministry of Justice was in charge of the administration of justice, this made public prosecutors closer to the ministry, and thus more prestigious than judges. Furthermore, some of them had links with major political parties, which made them even more powerful.

Public prosecutors had, and still have, broad powers in prosecuting offenders and investigating crimes. Since private prosecution was not allowed in Japan, public prosecutors monopolised the power to prosecute. They wielded a broad discretionary power to decide whether or not to prosecute the offender. This included a power not to prosecute the offender even if his guilt had been established by the prosecutor, by considering the nature of the crime, character of the offender, and various other factors. This discretionary power was not provided by law in the pre-War period, but developed from the practice of the prosecutors. Together with their broad power to issue warrants, the Public Prosecutor's Office became a powerful body, not only in relation to the court, but also within the political system as a whole. This led to political bias and excess of power on the part of public prosecutors in the 1920s, and in some cases they exercised their discretionary powers in favor of a political party.[18]

One of the major purposes of the post-war judicial reform was to curtail the power of the Public Prosecutor's Office and to democratise its structure. However, this attempt at reform was only partly successful. The Public Prosecutor's Office was separated from the court, but its highly centralised and hierarchical system remained intact. The proposal of the American advisors to divide the office into four regional offices was turned down by the Japanese. While the power to issue warrants was given exclusively to the court, the discretionary power of the prosecutors remained intact. An attempt to control this discretionary power by introducing a grand jury system met with strong resistance from the Japanese member at the drafting stage. The Prosecution Review Board, which was eventually established, has only limited powers compared to those of a U.S. grand jury.[19]

At present, the Law on the Public Prosecutor's office of 1947 is the basic law regulating the organisation and the powers of the

18 As for the history of the Public Prosecutor's Office, see K. Matsuo, *Keiji-shihō no Genri* (*Principles of Criminal Justice*), Tokyo 1978, pp. 124–26.
19 Opler, *supra* note 31, pp. 104-06.

public prosecutors.[20] The Code of Criminal Procedure also has relevant provisions. The public prosecutor's main functions are the investigation of crimes and the prosecution of the offender. At the trial, the public prosecutor proceeds with the prosecution and requests the court to apply the appropriate law. Supervision of the execution of judgments also falls within the competence of the public prosecutor. In addition, a public prosecutor acts as a plaintiff or a defendant representing the public interest in civil cases.

The Public Prosecutor's Office retains a hierarchical organisation and is headed by the Prosecutor-General. Public prosecutors are subordinate to their superior prosecutors and ultimately to the Prosecutor-General. The four levels of the public prosecutor's office are the Supreme Prosecutor's Office, High Prosecutor's Offices, District Prosecutor's Offices, and Ward Prosecutor's Offices. Each level corresponds to the Supreme Court, appellate courts, district courts and summary courts, respectively.

Each prosecutor is empowered to perform his duties individually. However, unlike judges, public prosecutors do not exercise their powers entirely independently. They are subject to the instructions and orders of their superiors in general issues as well as in specific cases. The superior prosecutor may transfer a case from one prosecutor to another, or take charge of the case personally.

The Minister of Justice is vested with a supervisory power over the public prosecutors. He may give general instructions as well as instructions on a specific case. In the latter case, he may only address the Prosecutor-General and may not directly instruct the prosecutor who is in charge of the case.

There was a celebrated case where the Minister of Justice, when consulted by the Prosecutor-General as to whether a member of the Diet should be arrested for corruption, instructed the Prosecutor-General to wait for a while. The investigation was not successful, allegedly because of this delay, which was criticised as a 'covering up' of a political scandal. The Minister of Justice was forced to resign and eventually, the cabinet resigned after a non-confidence vote by the Diet.

There is an established practice by which the Prosecutor-General seeks the opinion of the Minister of Justice when initiating his investigation and prosecution of 'especially significant cases.' In addition, when the arrest of a member of the Diet endowed with a privilege of freedom from arrest during the session is at issue, or when the case is likely to have political

20 Law No. 61, 1947.

ramifications, the Prosecutor-General also consults the Minister of Justice.[1]

Japanese law does not allow private prosecution. The public prosecutor is the sole agency for prosecution, except in cases of compulsory prosecution proceedings. Prosecutors have broad discretionary power to decide whether to prosecute or not. The Code of Criminal Procedure provides that the prosecutor may refrain from prosecution by taking into account the character of the offender, his age and life history, the seriousness of the crime and mitigating factors, as well as circumstances after the crime, i.e. whether the offender has repented or whether he has paid compensation, etc. (Art. 248).

Japanese prosecutors fully utilize this discretionary power. Approximately 36% of those cases which could have been technically brought to trial are dropped by the prosecutor.[2] Public prosecutors claim that from a criminological point of view, this discretionary power given to the prosecutors contributes to the rehabilitation of the offender and facilitates his correction by liberating him from the procedure at an early stage. However, it also has a negative aspect. Since the prosecutors have to collect information to make a decision whether to prosecute or not, the investigation tends to be excessively thorough. Furthermore, since the prosecutor may refrain from prosecution, if he is to prosecute, he has to be fully convinced that the offender is actually guilty. Thus there is a strong implication of guilt once a person is prosecuted. In fact, the conviction rate is 99.9%.[3] Therefore, the pretrial stage rather than the trial becomes the crucial step in the criminal process.

The need to control the broad discretionary power of the public prosecutor was acknowledged during the judicial reforms after the War. As a result, two devices to control the discretionary power of the prosecutor were introduced. The first is the Prosecution Review Board. The board is designed to review the decisions of the prosecutor not to prosecute. It is composed of eleven citizens who are selected at random, who serve on the board for one year. There are around 200 such boards throughout Japan. The board may initiate review proceedings either upon the request of the citizens or on its own initiative. The board is empowered to demand the prosecutor to

---

1 E. Ito, *Kensatsu-chō-hō Chikujyō-kōgi* (*Commentaries on the Law on the Public Prosecutor's Office*), revised edition, Tokyo 1986, pp. 100–101.
2 Ministry of Justice, *Kensatsu-tōkei-nenpō* (*Annual Report of Statistics on Prosecution*), Tokyo 1987, p. 154.
3 *Supra* note 8, Criminal Cases, p. 204.

submit materials and give explanations. It may also summon persons who initiated the proceedings and other people involved. When members of the board agree, the board may render a decision that the prosecutor should prosecute the offender.[4]

The competence of the board is narrower than that of the grand jury. The board itself does not have the power to prosecute and its decision is not binding on the prosecutor. Moreover, the board is entitled to review the decision of prosecutors not to prosecute, but has no power to review their decision to prosecute. But despite its limited power, the board has been functioning effectively. They disposed of 1,189 cases in 1989 and in 58 cases, they found the decision of the public prosecutor inappropriate. In 8 cases, the public prosecutors accepted the decision of the board and initiated criminal prosecution.[5]

The second device to check the discretionary power of the public prosecutor, though limited in scope, is the proceeding to remand the case to trial in cases involving abuse of power by government officials. When a person who brought complaints or accusations of abuse of power by government officials is not satisfied with the decision of the prosecutor not to prosecute, he may request the court to initiate the proceedings to remand the case for trial. If the court finds the request well-founded, the prosecution shall be deemed to have been initiated without the involvement of the public prosecutor. At the trial, an attorney specially designated by the court performs the function of the public prosecutor.[6]

Another peculiarity of the Japanese prosecutorial system is the active role of public prosecutors in the investigation process. Under the Criminal Procedural Code of 1922, the public prosecutors investigated the case while police officers assisted them. In contrast, the present Code of Criminal Procedure provides that the primary responsibility for investigation lies with the police and that investigation by the public prosecutor is supplementary (Arts. 189 and 191, para. 1). In practice, public prosecutors actively participate in investigation. In some cases, such as corporate offenses which are likely to have significant social impacts, public prosecutors themselves initiate the investigation. In routine cases, public prosecutors investigate cases which have been sent to them by police officials. When conducting an investigation, public prosecutors and police

---

4 Law on the Prosecution Review Board, Law No. 147, 1948.
5 Ministry of Justice, '*Keiji-jiken no Gaiyō* (An Overview of Criminal Justice),' *Hōsō Jihō*, vol. 43 (1991), No. 1, pp. 179–183.
6 The Code of Criminal Procedure, Arts. 262–70.

officials are expected to cooperate. The former may issue general instructions and commands to the latter. When the public prosecutor conducts an investigation himself, he is entitled to issue orders and have police officers' assistance.[7]

7 *Ibid.*, Arts. 192 and 193.

5 The legal profession

1. The *'hōsō'*

Judges, public prosecutors and attorneys form a distinct social group which is called the *'hōsō.'* The term originally came from China where it denoted people administering the law. Although it is often translated as 'legal profession' in English, this may be misleading because the term 'legal profession' usually presupposes a system where judges and public prosecutors come from the rank of attorneys and therefore have a common basis. In contrast, Japanese judges are 'career judges,' who join the court immediately after completing legal training. Public prosecutors are also recruited directly from the Legal Training and Research Institute. Thus, the mobility between different professions is very much limited.

What members of the *'hōsō'* have in common is that they are required to pass the same State examination and have been trained in the Legal Research and Training Institute for two years. Regardless of their future profession, they go through the same training at the Institute.

The Japanese judicial system originally came from Continental Europe where there is a distinct line between judges and public prosecutors on the one hand and attorneys on the other. In Germany, public prosecutors are regarded as part of the judiciary together with the judges, although there is a state examination and common training with the *Rechtsanwalts*. In France, judges and *procureurs* are both categorised as *magistrats*; there is neither a common examination nor training with the *avocats*. Japan initially adopted the French system but later introduced a common examination for all three professions and then, after the Second World War, a common training as well. Therefore, the current system is similar to the German system, except that public prosecutors are no longer considered to be part of the judiciary as they were before the War. However, the tradition continues and judges and public prosecutors are seen as representing 'authority,' while attorneys often take pride in acting for citizens.

In addition to the '*hōsō*,' whose number is limited (less than 20,000), there are various kinds of professions involved in the legal business. Apart from people in corporate legal departments, all of them must pass a special state examination and go through some training. These people perform functions which are often performed by attorneys in other countries.

2. Judges

Judges of the appellate courts, district courts, family courts and summary courts are appointed by the Cabinet from a list prepared by the Supreme Court. The Supreme Court assigns a judge to a specific court. As of 1991, the fixed number of judges is 2,022 (excluding summary court judges).

With the exception of summary court judges, lower court judges are 'career judges.' They begin their careers as assistant judges at a district court or a family court after finishing their training at the Legal Training and Research Institute. They must accumulate ten years' experience as an assistant judge in order to become a full judge. Almost all judges of appellate courts, district courts, and family courts start their careers in this way. Appellate court judges are promoted from among district court and family court judges. The Law on Courts provides that public prosecutors and attorneys can be appointed to the Bench. Law professors may also be appointed to judicial posts under certain conditions. The legislature had apparently intended to allow some exchange of personnel between the three legal professions: judges, public prosecutors, and attorneys. However, the appointment of judges from professions other than public prosecutor is rare. Taking into account that lay participation is very limited in Japan, this may make the court an institution remote from ordinary people and social reality. The Japanese Bar Association has been proposing the appointment of judges from among attorneys for some time and since 1988, the Supreme Court has started to invite attorneys to apply for the Bench. So far, there have been around ten such appointments.[1]

The term for judges is ten years. This term is renewable and judges are almost automatically reappointed. Most judges work in the court until their retirement age of 65. For Supreme Court

---

1 *Mainichi Daily*, 16 June, 1988.

justices and summary court judges, the retirement age is 70. Although the renewal of the term has been almost automatic, the Supreme Court is of the opinion that it has the power to refuse renewal without giving reasons. In one case, a judge who refused to accept a transfer was not reappointed after the expiration of his term.

Similar problems occur when an assistant judge is appointed judge after the expiration of a ten year term. This had been almost automatic until the late 1960s when the Supreme Court started to block the promotion of some of the assistant judges. In one celebrated case, the Supreme Court rejected the application of an assistant judge to be appointed a full judge. The Supreme Court did not give any reasons for the refusal. Because this assistant judge was a member of the Young Lawyers Association, an organisation denounced by the Supreme Court as being leftist, the Supreme Court was criticised for discrimination on political grounds. Although the Supreme Court has a certain degree of discretion in making appointments and reappointments, it is questionable whether it exercised its power properly in this case.[2]

The personnel administration department of the Supreme Court's general secretariat has the power to transfer and promote judges. Judges are usually moved among large, medium, and small courts within their ten year terms. On the other hand, some select individuals are seconded to the Supreme Court secretariat and then return to the lower courts where they occupy key positions. At present, three out of fifteen Supreme Court justices have worked in the secretariat at one stage of their career.

Although most judges work in the courts throughout their careers, the exchange of personnel between the courts on the one hand, and the Ministry of Justice and the Public Prosecutors Office on the other, is not exceptional. This kind of exchange was known in the pre-War period when the Ministry of Justice supervised the administration of the courts. Able judges were induced to work in the Ministry of Justice instead of the courts and were promoted to key positions within the Ministry. After the Second World War, this practice was considered to be incompatible with the impartiality of the judiciary and was abandoned in the course of the democratisation of the judiciary.

However, a similar practice has re-emerged in the past two decades, with the number of exchanges increasing dramatically in the 1970s. In 1982, fourteen judges and assistant judges were

2 H. Tanaka ed., *The Japanese Legal System*, Tokyo 1976, pp. 558–62.

transferred to the Ministry of Justice, while fourteen people were transferred from the Ministry of Justice to the courts. The latter fourteen were all career judges who returned to the courts after working in the Ministry or the Public Prosecutor's office for several years. In 1981, the total number of transfers was 47. In some years, not only those who had begun their careers as judges but also those who had worked in the Public Prosecutor's Office from the beginning of their careers were transferred to the courts. Of those transferred to the courts from 1975 to 1982, three quarters were former judges seconded to the Ministry and then returning to the courts, while the remaining quarter were public prosecutors.[3]

Judges who are transferred to the Ministry of Justice mostly work in the litigation department acting as representatives of the state in administrative cases and government tort cases. Those who return from the Ministry eventually hold key positions within the court, such as president of the district courts and appellate courts as well as the director of the Supreme Court secretariat. One Supreme Court justice who was promoted from the lower court, actually had worked in the Ministry of Justice for more than 29 years.[4]

The main reason for the increase of this kind of exchange is the necessity to fill the departments of the Ministry of Justice with specialists of sufficient legal knowledge and experience. In particular, the increase in administrative cases and government tort cases has forced the Ministry to strengthen its litigation department. Furthermore, the personnel department of the Supreme Court claims that the exchange will broaden the knowledge and experience of judges.

This practice of personnel exchange is not without its drawbacks. Judging from Japan's pre-War experience, close links among the courts, the Ministry of Justice, and the Public Prosecutor's Office may affect the impartiality of the court. Also the emergence of an elitist career structure within the courts may influence judges in a perverse way. This is particularly so in the Japanese career judge system, where the appointment, transfer and promotion of judges is in the hands of the Supreme Court secretariat. Furthermore, citizens may doubt the impartiality of the court if they find a former prosecutor or a representative of

---

3 K. Mizuno, '*Saibansho to Hōmushō no Jinji-kōryū* (Exchange of Personnel between the Courts and the Ministry of Justice),' in *supra* note 2, pp. 75–79, 81–82.
4 *Supra.*

the State sitting on the Bench. Despite criticisms, however, this practice seems to be continuing.

The Constitution of 1890 did not explicitly provide for the independence of the court, but the present Constitution has a provision which provides that all judges shall exercise their power independently in accordance with their conscience and bound only by the Constitution and laws. As a corollary, the Constitution guarantees that judges are not to be dismissed unless they have been either impeached, or found by a court decision to be mentally or physically unfit (Art. 78). The Law on Courts further guarantees that judges are not to be transferred, suspended, or have their salaries reduced (Art. 48).

The procedure for impeachment is provided by the Law on Impeachment of Judges.[5] The Impeachment Tribunal is attached to the Diet and is composed of fourteen members who are members of the Diet, seven from each House. The Tribunal exercises its power independently from the Diet, and is not bound by the decisions of the Diet. There is a Diet Prosecuting Committee which decides whether to bring a case to the Tribunal or not. The grounds for impeachment are serious breach or gross neglect of duties, and misconduct which affects the authority and credibility of the judge, independent of whether it took place in the course of his duty or not. Any person may file a complaint with the Prosecution Committee requesting the impeachment of a judge. The Code of Criminal Procedure is applied in the impeachment procedure, the accused may have the assistance of attorneys, and the hearing is held in public. The tribunal may only dismiss or acquit the judge, and other disciplinary measures fall solely within the jurisdiction of the Supreme Court and the appellate courts. In order to dismiss a judge, the consent of two-thirds of the members of the Tribunal who actually took part in the proceedings is required.

In addition to the impeachment procedure, judges may lose their position if they have been sentenced to imprisonment or declared incompetent or quasi-incompetent with respect to civil transactions by the court.

The Constitution provides that disciplinary actions against judges cannot be taken by an administrative agency. Therefore, disciplinary proceedings are handled by the court. The basic law in this regard is the Law on Disciplinary Actions against Judges, which is supplemented by the rules enacted by the Supreme Court.[6] Disciplinary action against the judges of the district or

---

5 Law No. 137, 1947.
6 Law on Disciplinary Measures on Judges, Law No. 127, 1947.

summary courts is handled by the appellate court, while action against Supreme Court justices and appellate court judges is handled by the Supreme Court.

Grounds for disciplinary action are breaches of professional duties, neglect of duty, and misconduct which undermines the dignity of judges. Reprimand or a fine not exceeding 10,000 yen can be imposed in such proceedings.

3. Public prosecutors

There are approximately 1,200 public prosecutors in Japan. Anyone who has passed the uniform state examination and finished their training at the Legal Training and Research Institute can be appointed public prosecutor. Judges and assistant judges as well as law professors and associate professors are qualified to become public prosecutors under certain conditions.[7] Most public prosecutors, however, are recruited directly from among graduates of the Legal Training and Research Institute. The Prosecutor General and his deputy and the President of the high public prosecutor's office are appointed by the cabinet with the attestation of the Emperor. Other public prosecutors are appointed by the Minister of Justice.

The Law on Public Prosecutor's Office guarantees that public prosecutors shall not be dismissed, suspended or have their salaries reduced against their will, unless so provided by law (Art. 25).

Disciplinary action against public prosecutors falls within the jurisdiction of the Public Prosecutor's Attestation Board. This board is composed of six members of the Diet, the Prosecutor-General, Deputy Minister of Justice, a Supreme Court justice, a member of the Japanese Academy, and the Chairman of the Japan Federation of Bar Associations. It was established as a result of a compromise between American advisors who attempted to introduce public election for public prosecutors and Japanese officials who vigorously opposed it.[8]

The Board also reviews the suitability of each public prosecutor every three years. However, the periodic review by this Board is more or less routine. So far, there has not been even a single case of dismissal by the Board.

---

7 Law on the Public Prosecutor's Office, Arts. 15, 18 and 19.
8 H. Kaneko and M. Takeshita, *Saiban-hō (Judicial Process)*, Tokyo 1983, p. 298.

4.   Attorneys

Until the mid–19th century, professional attorneys were not known in Japan. The law of 1872 allowed the participation of representatives of parties in civil disputes for the first time. It was only in 1890, with the enactment of the Code of Criminal Instruction, that attorneys were allowed to participate in criminal trials as a defense counsel.

The first Law on Attorneys was enacted in 1893. Under this Law, attorneys had to register at the district court. Attorneys formed a local bar, which was supervised by the chief prosecutor of the district court. Disciplinary action against attorneys was not taken by the bar, but by the appellate courts.

At this stage, attorneys were treated differently from judges and public prosecutors, who were government officials. The Law on Attorneys of 1893 required prospective attorneys to pass an examination which was different from that for judges and public prosecutors. Judges and public prosecutors, as well as graduates of the law faculties of the imperial universities, were entitled to become attorneys without taking the examination. Training for attorneys was separated from that for judges and public prosecutors and was poorly organised. These circumstances, combined with the traditional respect for officialdom, created a negative image of attorneys as somewhat less prestigious than judges and public prosecutors.[9]

In 1914, the special examination for attorneys was abolished, requiring prospective attorneys to take the same examination as judges and public prosecutors. However, the practical training for attorneys was kept separate from that of judges and public prosecutors until after the Second World War.

As part of the post-War reforms, a new Law on Attorneys was enacted in 1949.[10] The Law abolished the supervision of attorneys by the Ministry of Justice in favor of supervision by the courts and the public prosecutor's office. The autonomy of the Bar was considerably broadened. The Bar was given the power to admit its own members and bring disciplinary actions against them. People who are qualified as attorneys are those who have passed the uniform State examination for judges, public

9 Tanaka, *supra* note 2, pp. 549–53. *See also* R. Brown, *Legal Aspects of Doing Business in Japan*, Chicago 1983; R. M. Spaulding, Jr., *Imperial Japan's Higher Civil Service Examinations*, Princeton 1967, p. 77.
10 Law No. 205, 1949.

prosecutors and attorneys and have finished two years' practical training. Former judges and public prosecutors, as well as law professors and associate professors are exempted from examination under certain conditions (Art. 4 and 5). It is not uncommon for judges and public prosecutors to become attorneys after retirement.

Attorneys are registered with local bars which form the Japan Federation of Bar Associations (*Nichibenren*). Local Bars may refuse registration in certain cases where the applicant is likely to discredit the bar or disturb the order of the bar. Unsuccessful applicants may appeal to the Japan Federation of Bar Associations, and eventually to the Tokyo Appellate Court.

Attorneys are required to open their offices within the territory of the local bar with which they are affiliated. The size of practice is small compared to that of American law firms. Approximately 80% of attorneys work in one-man offices. Although some law offices have more than 30 attorneys, law offices with more than four attorneys are the exception.[11] Unlike in the United States, it is rather unusual for attorneys to work as staff members of a corporation, government agency or local government. Only in the last decade have major corporations begun to retain in-house counsel.

The Japan Federation of Bar Associations has an ethical code which was modelled after the American Bar Association Canons of Professional Ethics. Disciplinary action can be taken against members who have violated the rules of the local Bar or the Japan Federation of Bar Associations, discredited or disturbed the order of the bar or committed an act which undermined the dignity of the bar.

Any person may request the initiation of a disciplinary proceeding against an attorney. The ethical commission of each bar, composed of attorneys, investigates the case and decides whether disciplinary proceedings should be initiated. When the committee comes to a conclusion to proceed with the case, the case is sent to the disciplinary commission of the bar. The disciplinary committee is composed of attorneys, judges, public prosecutors and academics. The disciplinary measures which can be applied are reprimand, suspension of business for up to two years, an order to leave the local Bar, and dismissal. The decision of the disciplinary committee can be appealed to the Japan Federation of Bar Associations, whose decision can be appealed to the Tokyo Appellate Court (Arts. 56–71).

---

11 Japan Federation of Bar Associations, *Nihon no Hōritsu-jimusho* (*Law Offices in Japan*), Tokyo 1988, pp. 29–31.

As of 1990, there are 14,433 attorneys in Japan. This number seems small when compared with the United States, which has more than 700,000 attorneys. However, the contrast is not so marked when compared with European countries. Although the United Kingdom has around 60,000 barristers and solicitors, France has only 22,000 *avocats*. The number of inhabitants per attorney is 358 in the United States and 879 in the United Kingdom, while it is 9,199 in Japan.[12] This contrast may be striking, but it should be kept in mind that in Japan, there are a number of para-legals who perform functions which are performed by attorneys in other countries. The number of these para-legals has substantially increased in recent years. For instance, the number of tax specialists has increased by 50% in the last decade.[13] A recent survey on the number of attorneys and the number of civil cases in Germany and Japan revealed that while the number of attorneys in Germany was three times as much as that in Japan, the number of civil cases was also three times larger as compared with that in Japan. The author pointed out that the difficulty in having access to attorneys may be a cause of the relatively small number of civil cases in Japan.[14]

Usually, it is not an easy task for ordinary people to find a reliable attorney. A majority of attorneys are concentrated in major cities. Tokyo and Osaka, the two largest cities in Japan have 17.9% of the total population, but 61.9% of the attorneys.[15] This makes it difficult for people in rural areas to find an attorney.

Some people hesitate to consult attorneys, since their fees are not necessarily foreseeable or recoverable. Attorneys' fees are not regulated by law. The Japan Federation of Bar Associations does have a standard scale for attorneys' fees, but it is merely a guideline and is not binding. The fees set by this guideline are vague and offer little information for prospective clients. In a survey by the Japan Federation of Bar Associations published in 1986, approximately three quarters of the respondents replied that it is desirable to inform the client of at least an estimate of the expected fees and costs in advance.[16] What is more,

12 Special issue of *Jurist* on the reform of the State legal examination, 1987 pp. 86–87.
13 Brown, *supra* note 9.
14 R. Hayashiya, '*Minji-soshō no Genkyō no Nichidoku Hikaku* (Comparison of the Current State of Civil Procedure between Germany and Japan),' *Hōsō-jihō*, 1988 No. 10, pp. 36–39.
15 *Ibid.* at p. 12.
16 Tokyo Bar Association ed., *Shimin to Hōritsu-mondai* (*Citizens and the Law*), Tokyo 1986, pp. 150–51.

attorneys' fees are generally not recoverable even if the party wins the case.

Partly because of these difficulties, some people choose to represent themselves in court. In 1990, in 82.3% of civil cases before the summary courts neither parties retained an attorney. At the district court level, the percentage was much lower, 13.4%.[17]

Japanese attorneys concentrate on litigation and matters directly related to it. Their work primarily consists of preparing for litigation and acting as representatives of clients in court, but non-contentious work is sometimes performed by attorneys. However, according to a survey conducted in 1977, Japanese attorneys spend only 12% of their working time on legal advice, 4.2% in drafting contracts and other documents and 6.6% in negotiating business deals. The shares that these kinds of work represent in the attorneys' total income is 7.4%, 3.3%, and 6.7%, respectively. Since then, there has been a steady increase in the share of non-contentious work, especially in major cities. In Tokyo, it reached 31.9% in 1990.[18]

The Japanese seldom consult an attorney unless a dispute actually arises. According to a survey by the Tokyo Bar Association, citizens turn to attorneys either when they have exhausted every other possible remedy, or when they find the issues too difficult for laymen to handle.[19] As for companies, the drafting of contracts and other documents is usually handled by members of in-house legal departments. Japanese companies consult an attorney when a dispute actually arises, although they seek legal advice from time to time.[20]

5. Para-legals

Together with attorneys, there are various professions which perform functions related to legal issues. Tax attorneys, patent attorneys, judicial scriveners as well as in-house legal counsel perform functions which in some other countries are performed by attorneys.[1]

17 Supreme Court of Japan, *Shihō-tōkei-nenpō* (*Annual Report of Judicial Statistics*), Civil Cases 1987, pp. 104, 134.
18 *Supra* note 16 at p. 100. "Nihon no Hōritsu Jimusho (Law Firms in Japan)", *Jiyū to Seigi*, 1991 No. 13, p. 39.
19 *Ibid.* at pp. 60–64.
20 *Kaisha Hōmu-bu* (Corporate Legal Departments), special issue, *New Business Law*, 1986, p. 134.
 1 R. Brown, 'A Lawyer by any Other Name,' *supra* note 9, pp. 366–71.

Tax attorneys

A system of tax attorneys (*zeirishi*) was introduced in Japan as part of the post-War tax reform. The American tax system was thereby introduced and tax assessment by taxpayers replaced the previous system of tax assessment by government. Thus, the necessity for tax advisors increased, and in 1950, the Law on Tax Attorneys was enacted.[2] As of 1986, there were 47,342 tax attorneys.[3]

There is a special State examination for tax attorneys. Attorneys and accountants as well as certain categories of tax officials are exempted. The tax attorney's main functions are the calculation of taxes and drafting of documents to be filed with the tax office on behalf of individuals and private firms. Tax attorneys also submit claims on behalf of their clients for refunds and represent tax payers before tax tribunals.

Patent attorneys

Patent attorneys (*benrishi*) offer advice and draft documents on patent issues. They also appear in court and assist the client in patent and trademark cases. There is a State examination for patent attorneys, but those who have worked in patent offices as patent examiners for more than seven years are exempted from examination. Attorneys are *ipso facto* qualified as patent attorneys. As of 1986, there are 2,947 patent attorneys.[4]

Judicial scriveners

The profession of judicial scrivener is as old as that of attorneys. In fact, attorneys and judicial scriveners were not treated as separate professions in the 19th century. It was only in 1919 that a special law on judicial scriveners was enacted.[5] The primary function of judicial scriveners is drafting legal documents and filing them with courts, the public prosecutor's office, and legal bureaus on behalf of the client. They also represent the clients in the registration of immovable property or companies, and in placing deposits in various proceedings.[6]

As of 1986, there are 15,260 judicial scriveners. As a rule,

---

2 *Supra* note 12, p. 98.
3 M. Young, 'Foreign Lawyers in Japan', *Law in Japan*, vol.21, 1988, p. 116.
4 *Supra* note 12, p. 98.
5 Brown, *supra* note 21.
6 Law on Judicial Scriveners, Law No. 197, 1950.

those who wish to become judicial scriveners are required to pass a special examination for scriveners. Until recently, the examination was prepared and administered by the Association of Judicial Scriveners, but in 1978, a State examination was introduced. Although this examination is substantially easier than the examination for judges, public prosecutors and attorneys, the introduction of a State examination has increased the prestige of the profession. Apart from those who passed the examination, court and public prosecutor's office clerks with more than ten years' experience and sufficient knowledge can become judicial scriveners with the permission of the Minister of Justice.

Judicial scriveners form legal associations, which in turn form the National Association of Judicial Scriveners. The autonomy of the judicial scrivener's association is more limited than that of the attorney's bar. For example, disciplinary action can be taken against judicial scriveners by the head of the local legal affairs bureau, which is part of the Ministry of Justice. The National Association of Judicial Scriveners must have its rules sanctioned by the Ministry of Justice.

Judicial scriveners are not allowed to represent clients in court proceedings, nor to give legal advice to clients. The latter is within the exclusive competence of attorneys. In practice, however, judicial scriveners do give legal advice to their clients in the course of drafting documents. A report published by the Association of Judicial Scriveners stated that judicial scriveners give advice to clients on various issues such as property transactions and inheritance. Especially in localities where there are not many attorneys, citizens rely on judicial scriveners for legal advice. In a way, judicial scriveners are regarded by the public as attorneys of inferior rank, but easily accessible.[7] In fact, there is a proposal pending to allow judicial scriveners to represent clients at summary courts and thus make it easier for citizens to bring small claims to such courts.

There are advangtages and disadvantages in broadening the role of judicial scriveners. Considering the shortage of attorneys and the relatively high cost of retaining them, it would be convenient to allow the judicial scrivener to give legal advice and even to represent clients in court. On the other hand, there are people who are cautious about broadening the activity of judicial scriveners. They are sceptical as to whether it is really in the interest of citizens to allow legal advice and representation to be

---

7 T. Tashiro, '*Shihō-shoshi kara mita Bengoshi-gyōmu tono Kōsaku* (The Boundary of Business between Judicial Scriveners and Attorneys),' *Jurist* No. 842, 1985, pp. 76–77.

offered by judicial scriveners, who are not as highly qualified as attorneys.

There is some friction between attorneys and judicial scriveners over the boundary of their work. The Law on Attorneys gives attorneys a monopoly over legal services. It provides that no person other than an attorney shall perform legal services with the aim of obtaining remuneration (Art. 72). Violation of this provision may result in a fine or deprivation of freedom not exceeding two years. In one case, a judicial scrivener systematically and repeatedly handled civil disputes. He gave legal advice and represented his clients in negotiations for an amicable settlement. This person was prosecuted for violation of the Law on Attorneys. The district court interpreted the competence of judicial scriveners rather broadly and acquitted the defendant on most of the counts. The appellate court, however, quashed the decision of the district court and found the defendant guilty. The appellate court denied the right of judicial scriveners to provide legal advice in general, but acknowledged that the judicial scriveners may advise the client on certain legal issues and give guidance to the clients concerning the handling of a case before the courts.[8]

Corporate in-house counsels

Major corporations in Japan usually have a department or section which handles legal matters. It is often part of the general affairs department, but the number of companies with a specialised legal department is increasing. This is partly attributable to the increased number of international transactions, and disputes related to intellectual property, anti-monopoly law, and product liability.

According to a survey of corporate legal departments, 60% of such employees are graduates of law faculties. They are mostly highly qualified specialists, who often have studied either in the United States or in Europe. On the other hand, only 4% of companies had an attorney on their legal department staff. This is in contrast to legal departments in American companies, which are staffed primarily by attorneys. In Japan, attorneys are consulted usually when the issue is too complicated and is likely to result in litigation.

The primary functions of law departments are to review contracts, coordinate with attorneys retained as legal advisors with respect to litigation, give advice on civil, commercial, anti-

8 Judgment of Takamatsu Appellate Court, 11 June, 1979 (*Hanta* 388–57).

monopoly and industrial property law, and to handle the administration of affairs concerning shares, including the preparation for the general meetings of shareholders.[9]

6. Foreign attorneys

The Law on Attorneys was enacted in 1949 and initially allowed lawyers who were qualified in foreign countries to practice in Japan. Japanese nationality was not a prerequisite to practicing law. This open-door policy, however, was short-lived. In 1955, the Law was amended to make Japanese nationality a prerequisite. Only those foreign attorneys who had qualified before the amendment were allowed to practice.

In recent years, a significant number of foreign attorneys have come to Japan to work as foreign 'trainees.' The Japan Federation of Bar Associations imposed restrictions on these trainees in 1972.[10] In the mid–1970s, there were instances where some American attorneys who intended to open an office and practice in Japan were refused a visa. This eventually became a trade issue between the United States and Japan. Demands to lift restrictions also came from the European Community.

In response, the Japanese government proposed the gradual liberalisation of restrictions on foreign attorneys in the 'Trade Action Program,' which was aimed at easing trade friction with the United States. Because of the autonomy of the Bar, the matter was largely left to the Japan Federation of Bar Associations. After negotiations with the American Bar Association and an exchange of views with its members as well as the Ministry of Justice and the Supreme Court, it finally decided to allow foreign attorneys to practice in Japan. The Diet passed the Law on Special Measures for Handling of Legal Business by Foreign Attorneys in 1986.[11]

Foreign attorneys who are allowed to practice in Japan are called 'foreign law solicitors (*gaikoku-hō jimu-benngoshi*).' In order to qualify as a foreign law solicitor, foreign attorneys have to apply to the Ministry of Justice for a license (Art. 9). There are various requirements, including a sound financial basis on which they can conduct business properly and reliably, an

9 *Supra* note 20.
10 C. Sheehy, 'Japan's New Foreign Lawyer Law,' *Law and Policy in International Business*, 1987 No. 2, pp. 362–69.
11 K. Tadaki, 'The Gaikokuhō Jimu Bengoshi System: Circumstances of Acceptance and Scope of Practice', *Law in Japan*, vol. 21, 1988, pp. 122–128.

adequate coverage for professional risks, and a good legal or professional standing in the jurisdiction of primary qualification (Art. 10). The two most troublesome requirements for foreign attorneys are the requirement of reciprocity and the requirement of five-year experience. Thus, it is required that the home country of the applicant offers Japanese attorneys essentially the same treatment as that provided to foreign attorneys in Japan. The latter requirement affects young 'trainees' who have been working in Japan. Some of them may have to return to their home country to accumulate the necessary experience and in the meantime, will lose the contacts made while working in Japan.

After obtaining approval from the Ministry of Justice, foreign attorneys must register with the Japan Federation of Bar Associations (Art. 24). Once they are registered, they will be admitted as members of the Federation as well as the local Bar. These bodies are responsible for the oversight of foreign law attorneys. The attorneys are subject to the rules and ethical codes of the Federation and the bar and can be disciplined by a special committee of the Federation (Art. 51).

The scope of practice of foreign law solicitors is generally limited to the law of their own country (jurisdiction of their primary qualification) and does not extend to Japanese law (Art. 3). This is because there is no guarantee that foreign law solicitors have sufficient knowledge and expertise in Japanese law. In the case of attorneys from the United States, each state is treated as a separate country. Therefore, a Wisconsin attorney may advise on Federal Law and Wisconsin law, but he is not allowed to handle matters relating to New York law. Foreign law solicitors may also practice law of designated jurisdictions other than the law of their primary qualification, but they either must be qualified as an attorney in that jurisdiction or have the same level of learning as a person qualified to practice in that jurisdiction and have five years' practicing experience (Art. 5).

Foreign law solicitors may not represent the client in court, the public prosecutor's office, or other public agencies in Japan, nor prepare documents for submission to these bodies. It should be noted that a similar system exists in most countries which allow foreign lawyers to practice. Foreign law solicitors are also not entitled to act as defense counsel in a criminal procedure (Art. 3). Foreign law solicitors are not allowed to employ a Japanese attorney (Art. 49). This is intended to prevent circumvention of the ban on practicing Japanese law by employing Japanese attorneys. Another restriction concerns the formation of partnerships with Japanese attorneys (Art. 49).

Not surprisingly, foreign attorneys intending to practice, or already practicing in Japan, have voiced some discontent with the new Law. Indeed, the new Law is seen by some people as a starting point for further negotiations between foreign countries and Japan and not the ultimate solution to the dispute.[12]

As of April 1991, 78 foreign law solicitors were registered in Japan and there are currently 38 foreign law firms with offices in Japan. These firms advise Japanese companies and individuals on international mergers and acquisitions, joint ventures, and financial transactions including floating of bonds. It is interesting to note that in the previously cited survey of corporate legal departments, 33% of the respondents (companies) had consulted foreign attorneys. North American attorneys were most frequently consulted, but European and Asian attorneys were also often consulted. 57.4% of respondents were in favor of allowing foreign attorneys to practice in Japan, while 23.6% replied that it was not necessary.[13]

7. The uniform State examination and legal training

Graduating from a law faculty does not qualify a person to become a judge, a public prosecutor or an attorney in Japan. Those who intend to join one of these professions are required to pass a uniform State examination for judges, public prosecutors and attorneys, which is known for its low pass-rate. As compared with the total number of law faculty graduates, which is annually around 36,000, only a small portion of them become lawyers. Many years of preparation are required for this annual examination and the applicants take the examination more than six times on average before passing it. The average age of those who pass the examination is over 28.[14]

Proposals for the reform of the examination include the increase in the number of successful applicants and the introduction of some restrictions on the number of times an applicant may take the examination. In Germany, for instance, applicants are not allowed to take the State examination more than twice.[15] The Supreme Court, the Ministry of Justice and the Japan Federation of Bar Associations finally agreed on reform measures in 1991. Beginning in 1992, the number of those

---

12 S. Cone, 'The Future of Foreign Law Offices in Japan', *Law in Japan*, vol. 21, 1988, pp. 77–78.
13 *Supra* note 20, p. 129.
14 Special issue of *Jurist* on the reform of the State judicial examination, 1987, pp. 35, 41.
15 *Jurist*, No. 907, 1988, pp. 41–42.

who pass the examination will be increased by 200. Restrictions on the number of times the applicant may take the examination were not introduced, but 200 out of the 700 successful applicants will be selected from among those who first took the examination not more than three years ago.

Those who pass the State examination are entitled to enter the Legal Training and Research Institute, which is run by the Supreme Court. During their two years at the Institute, prospective judges, public prosecutors and attorneys undergo the same training. The trainees select their future profession at the end of the training. The first and last four months of training are spent in training at the institute. The intermediate sixteen months are allocated to practical training at the courts, public prosecutor's offices and attorney's offices. Four months are spent in a public prosecutor's office and an attorney's office respectively, while eight months are spent in the court.

Since most trainees have graduated from the law faculty of universities where law is taught at the undergraduate level, it is assumed that they have a basic knowledge of law. Therefore, the training is highly practice-oriented. At the end of the two year training period there is a final examination. Those who pass this final examination are then qualified as lawyers. In 1991, out of those who passed the final examination, 19% became assistant judges, 9% became public prosecutors, and the remaining 72% became attorneys.[16]

While the Legal Training and Research Institute gives practical training to prospective judges and others, legal education at the university level is more academic than practical. As can be assumed from the number of the students who pass the examination for judges, public prosecutors and attorneys, only a limited number of law graduates become lawyers. Only ten out of 90 law faculties annually produce more than ten graduates who pass the state examination for judges, public prosecutors, and attorneys. Remaining graduates enter either civil service or work in a company as businessmen.

Thus, Japanese law faculties are not necessarily designed to educate and train professional lawyers. Rather, their primary purpose is to produce people with a sound legal mind, but not necessarily lawyers. Law faculties may be better characterised as institutions which offer advanced social science education in the form of legal studies.

---

16 *Hōsō-yōsei-seido-kaikaku* (The Reform of the Legal Training System), *Jurist*, Special Issue, 1991, p. 97.

6   The protection of human rights

1.   Developments in Human Rights Law

The concept of individual rights was unknown to Japan until the mid 19th century. Under the rule of the Tokugawa Shogunate, a status system had developed, in which ordinary people had few rights against the ruling territorial lords (*daimyōs*) and warriors (*samurais*). But by the end of the Tokugawa Shogun's rule, Western ideas gradually had begun to penetrate Japan, and this flow of ideas continued after the overthrow of the Tokugawa Shogunate. Works of British and French philosophers such as J. S. Mill, J. Bentham, and J. J. Rousseau were translated into Japanese and influenced many intellectuals. Initially, ideas of the school of Natural Law were widely accepted and inspired a movement called the 'Civil Rights and Freedom Movement (*jiyū minken undō*),' which gained momentum in the 1870s. Although radical movements were quickly suppressed by the government, this movement led to the establishment of the Imperial Diet under the Emperor.[1]

In 1889, the first Constitution of Japan was 'granted' to the subjects by the Emperor. This Constitution was modelled on the Prussian Constitution of 1850, since the Emperor's advisers considered that the monarchy of Prussia should be the model which Japan should follow. It should be noted that what was left of the liberal and democratic elements included in the Prussian Constitution, which had in turn been influenced by the Constitution of Belgium, were effectively omitted from the Japanese Constitution. Instead, the existence of harmonious relations between the ruler and the ruled under the religious and ethical authority of the 'sacred and inviolable' Emperor was stressed.

The guarantee of individual rights under this Constitution was far from sufficient. There was a short list of individual rights

1 See R. H. P. Mason and J. G. Caiger, *A History of Japan*, North Melbourne 1972, pp. 234–243.

which were guaranteed in a chapter entitled 'The Rights and Duties of the Subjects'. These rights were considered to be granted by the Emperor and not inherent natural rights. Moreover, most of the rights listed in the Constitution were guaranteed only 'in accordance with the provisions of the law,' theoretically giving the legislature freedom to limit individual rights by way of legislation. In fact, the adoption of the Constitution was preceded by the suppression of the opposition by the Public Security Regulation.

Institutions designed to guarantee individual rights were also limited. There was no possibility of constitutional review. An administrative court did exist, but its jurisdiction was very much limited, and it was made part of the administration, not the judiciary.[2]

In the latter half of the 1920s, when Japan started to take the course towards militarism, flagrant violations of individual rights began to occur frequently. Especially after the Law on the Maintenance of Public Security was enacted in 1925, those who were suspected of being communists or anarchists could be tried by summary procedure and convicted for their political beliefs. The Special Division of the police, which was primarily in charge of controlling political dissidents, resorted to various illegal means to suppress dissidents and non-conformists. Freedom of conscience and freedom of expression were severely limited until the end of the Second World War.

One of the primary goals of the reforms which took place after the Second World War was to strengthen long neglected guarantees of individual rights. The present Constitution was enacted in 1946 and took effect a year later. At the drafting stage of this Constitution, there was a conflict of views between the American advisors and the Japanese members of the drafting committee. While the former supported radical constitutional reforms, the Japanese members attempted to preserve the then existing system as much as possible. The Japanese drafting committee produced a draft constitution, but this was rejected by the Allied Forces as being undemocratic. The SCAP, despairing of the reluctance of the Japanese for reforms, worked out their own draft, which became the basis of the present Constitution.

The present Constitution is based upon the principle that the sovereign power belongs to the people and not to the Emperor. The Emperor was made a symbol of the State and the unity of

---

2 The Law on Administrative Litigation (Law No. 48, 1890; repealed by Law No. 59, 1947).

the people and his power was limited to ceremonial matters. Concerning individual rights, the Constitution declares as follows (Art. 11):

> The people shall not be prevented from exercising any of the fundamental human rights. These fundamental human rights guaranteed by this Constitution shall be conferred upon the people of this and future generations as eternal and inviolable rights

Thus, human rights guaranteed by the present Constitution are regarded as inherent rights of individuals, rather than granted by the Emperor.

Judicial review was introduced in order to safeguard these individual rights. Unlike Germany, Japan does not have a special constitutional court. The Japanese system is based on the American system, where all courts, from the Supreme Court to the district court, may judge the constitutionality of laws, ordinances, and administrative decisions. It is not rare for lower courts to render a judgment finding certain laws or acts of government unconstitutional.

Since the wording of the Constitution is general and often vague, the role of the judiciary in interpreting the Constitution is particularly significant. Vested with the power of judicial review over the constitutionality of laws as well as governmental acts and administrative actions, it is not an exaggeration to say that Japanese Constitutional Law has developed on the basis of judicial precedent.

The Constitution has a fairly long list of fundamental rights. It is generally acknowledged that the list of rights and freedoms explicitly provided in the Constitution is not exhaustive. Some other rights and freedoms are guaranteed on the basis of a general provision of the Constitution, which provides that all people shall be respected as individuals, and that their right to life, liberty, and the pursuit of happiness should be the supreme consideration in legislation and in other governmental action (Art. 13). This provision is occasionally used to guarantee those freedoms and rights not explicitly provided by the Constitution. Because the present Constitution has never been amended, the social changes which have taken place since the enactment have required the expansion of the guarantees provided by the Constitution.

One example of these rights, which were not foreseen at the time of enactment of the Constitution but gained significance in the last three decades, is the right to privacy. In one celebrated case, a novelist published a fictional account based upon the life of a politician, vividly depicting the relationship between the politician and his mistress. The politician sued the author for infringement of his right to privacy and the district court upheld his claim. The parties reached a compromise after the death of the plaintiff and the case was terminated. In this judgment, the right to privacy was acknowledged for the first time as having a basis in Article 13 of the Constitution, which provides for the protection of the dignity of individuals.[3]

The Supreme Court has acknowledged that the right to privacy comes within the guarantee of Article 13, and this includes the right to one's own portrait. In this case, the constitutionality of photographing a political demonstration by the police was at issue. Although the Court acknowledged that this right came under Article 13, in this particular case the Court found that the activities of the police were justifiable.[4]

Furthermore, in cases involving the environment, a concept of the 'general rights of personality' based upon the same provision has developed, and some lower courts have explicitly adopted this concept. There was a case where inhabitants living near an airport sought an injunction to limit the time during which planes could land and take off. The appellate court granted an injunction on the basis of a 'general right to lead a peaceful, free and dignified life.' The Supreme Court did not allow the injunction to stand, but found the State liable for damages for past loss caused by plane movements, on the basis of the Law on Government Liability.[5]

Traditional concepts such as freedom of expression have also been expanded to cover some rights and freedoms which had not been foreseen at the time the Constitution was enacted. One such example is the right to know or the right to have access to information. In the era of rapid technological progress, in which information tends to be concentrated in the hands of governmental agencies and powerful private entities such as banks, the possibility of individuals having access to such information has increasingly become limited. Furthermore, it is necessary to control the use of information on individuals by the government and private corporations. Therefore, the right to know or the right to have access to information has received growing

---

3 Judgment of the Tokyo District Court, 28 September, 1964 (*Kaminshū* 15–9–2317 : *Utage no Ato* case).

4 Judgment of the Supreme Court, 24 December, 1969 (*Keishū* 23–12–1625). See also Judgment of the Supreme Court, 14 February, 1986 (*Keishū* 40–1–48).

5 Judgment of the Osaka Appellate Court, 25 November, 1975. Judgment of the Supreme Court, 16 December, 1981 (*Minshū* 35–10–1369 : Osaka *Kūkō kōgai* case).

attention. These rights are now considered to be covered by the Constitution, which guarantees freedom of expression (Art. 21). Some local authorities have enacted regulations allowing access to information, but at the national level such a law is yet to be adopted. In 1988 the Law on the Protection of Computer Information on Individuals was enacted. This law provides for the handling of information on individuals processed and stored in computers by government agencies.[6] According to this Law, government agencies are prohibited from using information on individuals for purposes other than the original purpose for which files were compiled. Any person may require a government agency to disclose the information concerning himself which is stored in the computer and, if necessary, demand its alteration.

The right to know becomes particularly vulnerable when State secrets are involved. Japan does not have a comprehensive law to punish the divulgence of State secrets, such as the Official Secrets Act of the United Kingdom. Regarding state employees and local government employees however, the leaking of information obtained in office is punishable.[7] In one case, a reporter obtained information from a female clerk at the Ministry of Foreign Affairs. When this reporter was prosecuted with the employee, he claimed that he had merely exercised his right to know and the right to collect information and materials for the press. The Supreme Court ruled that the freedom of the press in collecting information should be appropriately respected, and that soliciting a government employee to disclose a secret is not in itself illegal. However, in this particular case, the Supreme Court ruled that the means employed to obtain information was unjustifiable and the reporter had exceeded the scope of permissible activities.[8]

2. Criteria for the protection of human rights

1) Diversity of human rights

The Constitution provides that the freedoms and rights guaranteed by the Constitution should not be abused (Art. 12). Moreover, it provides that the right to life, liberty and the pursuit

6 Law No. 95, 1988.
7 Article 100, Law on Government Employees (Law No. 120, 1947).
8 Decision of the Supreme Court, 31 May, 1978 (*Keishū* 32–3–457 : Nishiyama Reporter case).

of happiness shall be guaranteed in so far as it does not contradict public welfare (Art. 13). The Supreme Court initially resorted to this public welfare clause in order to justify government actions and legislation. However, in the following years, a more sophisticated approach, primarily imported from the United States, became widely adopted in the judgments of the Supreme Court as well as the lower courts.

It is characteristic of Japanese judicial decisions on constitutional cases to be influenced by the judgments of the United States Supreme Court. The judgments of the Warren Court in the 1960s have had an especially significant influence on Japanese constitutional cases. Since the present Constitution resembles the U.S. Constitution in various ways, constitutional lawyers study American cases and doctrines, and the courts often rely on doctrines developed in the United States. For example, the provision of the Japanese Constitution on the right to a speedy trial is modeled after the Sixth Amendment of the U.S. Constitution. When the Supreme Court of Japan rendered a judgment on this issue, it apparently based its judgment on *Barker v Wingo*.[9] This borrowing of doctrines also applies to the standards adopted by the Supreme Court in deciding whether a particular restriction on fundamental rights is constitutional or not.

The way the fundamental rights and freedoms are guaranteed may differ, depending on the nature of each right or freedom. The realisation of social rights, such as the right to minimum standards of life, largely depends on the policy of the government. The supreme court has maintained that this provision does not grant an individual a specific right on which to base a claim to require certain measures to be taken by the government.[10] In one case, a person living on social benefits sued the government for not providing a minimum standard of living. This person argued that her benefits were insufficient to lead a 'minimum civilised life' as guaranteed by the Constitution. The District Court upheld this claim, but the Supreme Court ruled that whether a specific measure met the standard of 'cultural and healthy life' as provided by the Constitution was to be primarily judged by the Ministry of Health and Welfare and unless it exceeded the scope of discretion, the court may not interfere. This judgment was based upon the view that this particular provision of the Constitution was a 'programmatic' provision generally obligating the government to adopt certain measures,

9 407 US 514 (1972).
10 Judgment of the Supreme Court, 29 September, 1948 (*Keishū* 2–10–1235).

but not necessarily giving citizens a specific right to a claim against the state.[11]

Additionally, some rights and freedoms are guaranteed less than others, perhaps because the wording of the provisions differ. Thus, Article 29 which guarantees the right to ownership provides that it will be guaranteed in so far as it is not against public welfare. In contrast, Article 21, which guarantees freedom of expression, does not have such a reservation. Restrictions on individual economic rights are inevitable and in the contemporary social state, economic rights have lost their priority, and the necessity to limit them for the sake of public welfare has increased. Therefore, the right to private ownership is not regarded as an absolute right anymore, as it used to be under a *laisser faire* State. It can be limited by way of legislation enacted by the Diet, the representative of the people. Private ownership over land, for instance, is limited in various ways, such as by planning controls, acquisition of property for public purposes, etc.

In contrast, other rights and freedoms such as the freedom of expression and freedom of conscience need more guarantees than economic rights. It is inevitable that the exercise of freedoms or rights come into conflict with other interests and that under certain circumstances, these rights and freedoms may have to be restricted. Nevertheless, due to their significance, it is generally agreed that the restriction of these rights and freedoms should be kept to a minimum. Thus, the doctrine of double standard, or preferred doctrine, is generally supported in Japan. The essence of this doctrine is that a higher standard should be applied to judge the constitutionality of measures which restrict individual rights, such as the freedom of expression, freedom of conscience and other related rights. The rationale behind this doctrine is that these rights and freedoms are indispensable prerequisites to democracy and constitute the basis of the Constitution, and therefore should be given almost absolute guarantees.

The freedom of expression enjoys the highest of guarantees, since it forms the basis of democratic society. Admittedly, there may be cases where freedom of expression must be limited for the benefit of other interests. For instance, when press coverage is likely to damage someone's reputation or degrade his dignity, such coverage may be restricted in one way or another. Also the government may want to limit freedom of expression for various reasons. The problem here is how to maximise guarantees of

---

11 Judgment of the Supreme Court, 24 May, 1967 (*Minshū* 21–5–1043 : Asahi *soshō* case).

freedom of expression while minimising the negative effect it may have on other legally-protected interests.

2) Freedom of expression as an example

In order to see how fundamental rights and freedoms are realized by the courts in Japan, it is useful to take the example of the freedom of expression. The Constitution guarantees the freedom of expression as follows:

> Freedom of assembly and association, as well as freedom of speech, press and all other forms of expression are guaranteed.
> No censorship shall be exercised. Secrecy of communication is guaranteed.

The scope of this provision is fairly broad. It includes the freedom of press and broadcasting, freedom of publication, as well as the right to know (access to information) which is regarded as a prerequisite to the freedom of expression.

There have been a number of cases where the extent of the guarantees of the freedom of expression was at issue. The courts have attempted to work out functional criteria to demarcate the boundaries of permissible and impermissible restrictions on the freedom of expression.

Initially, the Supreme Court resorted to a general principle when judging the constitutionality of restrictions on individual rights. In the 1940s and early 1950s, the Supreme Court tended to refer to the 'public welfare clause' and rather easily acknowledged the permissibility of restrictions imposed on freedom of expression. Thus, the Supreme Court found an act of the Tokyo Metropolitan government which prohibited the use of a park surrounding the Imperial Palace for a May Day assembly, as constitutional, since this act served public welfare, i.e. the maintenance of the park.[12] In theory, it is generally acknowledged that some fundamental rights are not immune from certain kinds of limited restrictions. However, whether it is appropriate or not to use a vague and general term such as 'public welfare' in order to restrict fundamental rights is questionable. After all, most laws can be construed as promoting public welfare in one way or another, so excessive reliance on this clause gives the government *carte blanche* to restrict fundamental rights. It has been suggested that a more specific and workable standard for judging the legality of restrictions on fundamental rights should be developed.

12 Judgment of the Supreme Court, 23 December, 1953 (*Minshū* 7–13–1561).

Perhaps influenced by the criticism against this approach, the Supreme Court adopted a balancing of interests approach. Here, the value of the freedom or right in question and the value which can be achieved by restricting it are compared and weighed. The Supreme Court, in a case where the rights of government employees were at issue, ruled that the necessity of guaranteeing fundamental rights of workers and the necessity of enhancing and promoting the interests of citizens as a whole should be weighed and balanced to determine the constitutionality of restrictions on the workers' rights.[13]

However, there is a risk that such a test can lead to the justification of almost all government measures which the government claims are for the benefit of the majority. If the balancing is made at an abstract level, such as weighing national security in general against the right to know, it may invariably end in favoring the interests of the public at the cost of individual rights.

One case involved the constitutionality of the general prohibition against government employees' involvement in political activities. The Supreme Court ruled that if the purpose of the prohibition is justified and the value of the interests lost by this prohibition does not unreasonably exceed the value of the interests protected by this ban, then such a prohibition is not unconstitutional.[14]

In another case, the constitutionality of a court order requiring a television company to produce a film reporting a riot was at issue. The court intended to use the film as evidence in a case where members of the riot police were being prosecuted for abuse of power vis à vis the students. The television companies argued that this order was against the freedom of collecting news material, since if the film was used as evidence for the prosecution at trial, it may affect the relationship between the mass media and the people and make the future collection and reporting of information difficult. The Supreme Court acknowledged that freedom of the press is part of the freedom of expression and that freedom of collecting materials and information for the press is guaranteed by the Constitution. However, the Court proceeded to point out that such a freedom was naturally limited, and if there is a need to have a fair and just trial, it can be limited to a certain extent. The Court weighed the

13 Judgment of the Supreme Court, 26 October, 1966 (*Keishū* 20–8–905 : Zentei chūyū case. The Supreme Court overruled this precedent in 1973).
14 Judgment of the Supreme Court, 6 November, 1974 (*Keishū* 28–9–393 : Sarufutsu case).

evidential value of the film and its necessity for securing a fair criminal trial on one hand, and the extent to which the freedom of collecting information and material for the press would be harmed, and the effect it may have on this kind of freedom on the other. The Supreme Court ruled that the disadvantage to the press which may occur in the future, namely the loss of trust by citizens, should be tolerated by the television companies.[15] Thus, as a result of the 'balancing of interests,' a restriction on the freedom of the press was justified in this case.

As seen from these examples, the balancing of interests approach does not necessarily mean better safeguards for individual rights. When weighing freedom of expression against the interest of the public or the State, a mere balancing of interests may lead to an overemphasis on the latter. Therefore, a more sophisticated standard had to be worked out in order to mediate conflicting interests and to safeguard individual rights as much as possible. Thus, the clear and present danger test, the less restrictive alternative test, or the void for vagueness test, etc. were introduced in Japan by academics and some of them have found the support of the courts.

In some cases, courts resorted to the 'clear and present danger' test. This was originally conceived by Justice Holmes of the U.S. Supreme Court. According to this standard, a person is punishable by law for exercising freedom of expression only when there is a clear and present danger that the harm which the law intends to prevent is likely to occur. Some lower courts in Japan have adopted this standard, but the Supreme Court seemed to be against it. In one case, the constitutionality of a provision of the Public Election Law was at issue. The Japanese Public Election Law imposes various restrictions not found in other countries on election campaigns. In this case, the defendant was prosecuted for visiting over 40 homes of voters and handing out pamphlets in violation of the Public Election Law. The defendant argued, *inter alia*, that it was unconstitutional to generally prohibit door to door campaigning and election campaigning before the notice of election, since there was no clear and present danger to a fair election. The Supreme Court expressly rejected the application of the clear and present danger test in this case.[16]

Another standard often used is whether the provision of the law which restricts freedom of expression is vague or not. This

15 Decision of the Supreme Court, 26 November, 1969 (*Keishū* 24–6–280 : Hakata Station case).
16 Judgment of the Supreme Court, 21 November, 1967 (*Keishū* 21–9–1245).

was also introduced from the United States. The rationale behind this test is that ambiguous provisions restricting the freedom of expression may entail abuse in implementation and, as a result, are likely to discourage people from exercising their freedom of expression. The Supreme Court acknowledged this test in 1954. In this case, the constitutionality of a local regulation which required prior permission of the local government when organising a mass assembly or procession was at issue. The Supreme Court ruled that, although it was unconstitutional to subject such assemblies and processions to the permission of the authorities in general, it was not unconstitutional to require a prior permission as to the place or method of assembly or procession under a reasonable and accurate standard. However, the court concluded that the local regulation was sufficiently clear and accurate.[17] This standard, if it had been applied with due consideration to the superior status of freedom of expression. might have contributed to guaranteeing freedom of expression. However, the Supreme Court has rather too easily found restrictions to be accurate and clear, and thus invariably found the restriction on freedom of expression by law or regulation to be constitutional.

There also have been instances where the less restrictive alternative test, which developed in the United States, was used. According to this test, when restricting fundamental rights and freedom by law, if a less restrictive alternative had been available, the restriction should be regarded as unconstitutional. This test was widely used by lower courts in judging the constitutionality of laws which prohibit political activity of government employees under the threat of criminal sanctions. In one case, a post office employee prosecuted under these laws had taken part in an election campaign in his spare time. The law provides for a maximum of three years' imprisonment for such violations and the defendant argued that this restriction on political activity was unconstitutional. The district court, taking into account the importance of the right to take part in political activity, ruled that restrictions on such activities of government employees should be kept to a minimum. In this regard, the provision of the law which imposes criminal sanctions exceeds the limit of reasonable and maximum necessary restriction as applied in this particular case. Therefore, the court found this provision to be against Article 21 of the Constitution. The conclusion was upheld by the appellate court. However, on appeal from the

17 Judgment of the Supreme Court, 24 November, 1954 (*Keishū* 8–11–1866: Niigata *Kōan Jyōrei* case).

prosecutor, the Supreme Court explicitly rejected the application of the less restrictive alternative test and quashed the judgment of the appellate court. According to the Supreme Court, whether an act should be punished or not is a problem of legislative policy which is to be decided by the legislature. The Supreme Court found that the legislature did not exceed the limit of its discretionary power in this particular provision.[18]

3.   Rights and freedoms guaranteed by the Constitution

1)   Equal treatment

The list of fundamental rights and freedoms guaranteed by the Constitution is fairly long. The Constitution guarantees equal treatment regardless of race, religion, sex, social status or origin (Art. 14). In one celebrated case, the provision of the Criminal Code punishing homicide of one's direct ascendant was found unconstitutional by the Supreme Court. The provision of the Criminal Code had provided for only the death sentence or life imprisonment for patricide, while ordinary homicide was punishable by death or a minimum three years' imprisonment. However, in a case where a provision of the Criminal Code which punished the injury of an ascendant more severely than ordinary injury was at issue, the Supreme Court ruled that the difference of penalties (life or a minimum three years' imprisonment as compared with a maximum ten years' imprisonment) was not unreasonable.[19]

The problem of whether the provision on equal treatment has a direct effect on discrimination by private bodies was at issue in a case where a company refused to promote a trainee to full employee because of his past political activities. In this case, the Supreme Court, in theory, acknowledged that unreasonable discrimination by private bodies can be invalidated through the general provisions of private law, such as the provision on public order and good morals in the Civil Code.[20] Furthermore, in a case concerning sexual discrimination, the Supreme Court found

---

18 Judgment of the Supreme Court, 6 November, 1974 (*Keishū* 28–9–393 : Sarufutsu case).
19 Judgment of the Supreme Court, 26 September, 1974 (*Keishū* 28–6–329).
20 Judgment of the Supreme Court, 12 December, 1973 (*Minshū* 27–11–1536 : Mitsubishi Jushi case).

an office regulation which provided for a different retiring age for men and women to be unreasonably discriminatory and void by virtue of this provision of the Civil Code.[1]

Another important case related to this equality clause is where the inequality in the value of votes in a general election was contested. The Supreme Court has accepted that the inequality amounting to a ratio of 1 to 4.4 was unconstitutional.[2]

Freedom of thought and conscience is also guaranteed by the Constitution (Art. 19). This is followed by a provision which guarantees freedom of religion, and prohibits religious acts and education by the State (Art. 20). A very controversial issue is the separation of state and religion under this provision. Before the end of the Second World War, the political system was ultimately based upon the religious authority of the Emperor, and Shintoism was regarded as the national religion. After the War, the Supreme Commander of Allied Powers' policy was to separate religion from the State. However, in recent years, there have been cases where this principle seems to be undermined. One such example is the practice of Prime Ministers to visit a Yasukuni Shrine, a particular Shinto shrine built before the Second World War, in order to commemorate Japanese soldiers who fell in war. The constitutionality of such a visit is questionable and this practice is now being contested in court.

In one case, a city authority conducted a Shinto ceremony designed to ensure the safety of workers before starting construction of a gymnasium. The Appellate Court found this ceremony to be unconstitutional, but the Supreme Court overruled this judgment. The majority argued that a complete separation of State and religion was impossible, and the Constitution should not be construed in the sense that any kind of relation between the State and religion was impermissible. The purpose of the allegedly religious activity, place of the ceremony, intention of the organiser, and its effect on the general public should be taken into account, and only when the relationship is unreasonable from the view point of the social and cultural background of the country, should the act be found to be impermissible. Five dissenting opinions argued that the act was nothing less than religious and therefore unconstitutional.[3]

Additionally, the separation of State and religion was high-lighted on the occasion of the enthronement of the present

---

1 Judgment of the Supreme Court, 24 March, 1981 (*Minshū* 35–2–300).
2 Judgment of the Supreme Court, 17 July, 1985 (*Minshū* 39–5–1100).
3 Judgment of the Supreme Court, 13 July, 1977 (*Minshū* 31–4–533 : Tsu *jichinsai* case).

Emperor in 1990. The ceremonies which took place as part of the Emperor's public acts had a strong Shintoist imprint, which were not compatible with the secular status of the Emperor as provided in the Constitution.

2)　Freedom of expression

As mentioned above, freedom of expression as guaranteed by the Constitution covers a wide range, including freedom of assembly, association, speech and press. Censorship is explicitly prohibited. The constitutionality of public security regulations enacted by local governments had once been a much controversial issue in relation to freedom of assembly. These regulations require permission from the relevant local authority for assemblies and processions and violations of these requirements are punishable. Although many cases reached the Supreme Court, without exception, the Supreme Court recognised the constitutionality of these regulations.[4]

One significant exception to the freedom of association and the freedom of assembly is the Law on the Prevention of Destructive Acts, which was enacted in order to cope with violent political turmoil in the early 1950s.[5] This Law is intended to control the activities of groups and organisations involved in violent and destructive acts, listing a wide range of such acts, from treason to distribution of leaflets and publication of documents for specific purposes (Art. 4). The Public Security Review Board is empowered to prohibit processions and public assemblies involving these organisations and the publication and distribution of their literature. Under certain conditions, the Board may order dissolution of such organisations (Art. 7). The Board is attached to the Ministry of Justice and its members are appointed by the Prime Minister with the consent of both Houses. So far, there has not been a case where the activities of an organisation have been restricted by a decision of the Board.

As for freedom of expression, two issues were recently decided by the Supreme Court. The first is the constitutionality of the provision of the Criminal Code which punishes the distribution, sale or public display of obscene photographs, pictures and other material (Art. 175). In 1957, the Supreme Court upheld the judgment of the appellate court, which convicted the publisher

---

4 For instance, see the judgment on Niigata Prefecture public security regulation case, Judgment of the Supreme Court, 24 November, 1954 (*Keishū* 8–11–1866).
5 Law No. 240, 1952.

and the translator of *Lady Chatterley's Lover*. The judgment pointed out that the maintenance of a minimum sexual ethic was part of public welfare.[6] A decade later, in a case concerning the work of Marquis de Sade, the District Court acquitted the defendants on the ground that the artistic and ideological content of the work reduced the obscenity of the sexual content. The Supreme Court overruled the judgment, but with five dissenting opinions.[7] While the defendants argued that the artistic and philosophical value of the work reduced its obscenity, the Supreme Court ruled that the artistic and philosophical value of the work does not in itself make the publication legal. In contrast, one dissenting opinion acknowledged that the standard of obscenity is variable, and whether the work is obscene or not should be judged by taking into account changes in people's perception of obscenity as well as the artistic and philosophical value of the work. Another dissenting judge argued that a balancing test should be applied, weighing the harm which will be caused by publication against the value the work may have to the public. Ten years later, the Supreme Court rejected the argument that Article 175 of the Criminal Code was vague and therefore unconstitutional. On the other hand, the judgment set forth detailed standards to judge the obscenity of the publication.[8]

In a more recent case, in which the Supreme Court found a publication to be obscene, one concurring justice proposed a different approach. When judging the obscenity of the work, hardcore pornography and soft pornography should be distinguished. Hardcore pornography is almost worthless to the society, and therefore is not protected by the Constitution, while some types of soft pornography are covered by the Constitution.[9]

The Constitution explicitly prohibits censorship (Art. 21). This provision is also understood to prohibit other forms of prior restriction on the freedom of expression. In this regard, the constitutionality of customs control over importation of foreign pornography was contested in the court. Japanese Customs Tariff law prohibits importation of items which are likely to offend public morals. A person who was refused importation of films and magazines from Europe filed a suit. The Supreme Court ruled that censorship was impermissible without exception, but

---

6 Judgment of the Supreme Court, 13 March, 1957 (*Keishū* 11–3–997 : Lady Chatterley case).
7 Judgment of the Supreme Court, 15 October, 1969 (*Keishū* 23–10–1239).
8 Judgment of the Supreme Court, 28 December, 1980 (*Keishū* 34–6–433 : *Yojyōhan fusuma no shitabari* case).
9 Judgment of the Supreme Court, 8 March, 1983 (*Keishū* 37–2–15).

customs control did not amount to censorship. Four dissenting opinions found the relevant provision of the Customs Law to be excessively vague and therefore unconstitutional.[10]

Concerning the prohibition of censorship, another relevant issue is the system of reviewing text books for schools by the Ministry of Education. Text books are subject to screening by the Ministry of Education, and only those books which have been cleared by the Ministry can be used in schools. In one case, a text book written by a professor of history was rejected by the Ministry, for, *inter alia*, 'describing the Second World War in excessively negative terms.' The author was advised by the Ministry, for instance, to omit the phrase 'reckless War', and replace 'invasion of China' by 'advancement to Asia'. The author sued the government for revocation of the decision.

The district court found that the screening system itself does not amount to censorship insofar as the system is administered adequately and does not extend to the appropriateness of the author's thought as expressed in the publication. In this particular case, the court found that the screening had gone too far and constituted a violation of freedom of education as guaranteed by the Constitution.[11] The appellate court upheld this judgment, but the Supreme Court reversed the case and remanded it to the appellate court on procedural grounds. The appellate court again ruled the action of the Ministry unconstitutional. In the meantime, the Ministry of Education's guideline for the screening of textbooks has been substantially altered.

In some cases, an expression may result in the infringement of another person's rights. A typical case is where expression constitutes libel, which under Article 230 of the Criminal Code is punishable by a maximum of three years' imprisonment. However, following the adoption of the Constitution, a new provision was added in order to safeguard freedom of expression. Thus, Articles 230–2 provide that when a libellous act concerns matters of public interest, and the act is primarily intended for the benefit of the public, then whether the asserted fact is true or not should be judged and if the defendant proves that the statement was true, he shall not be punished.

In one example of this policy, a magazine published articles criticising a large religious organisation. In one article, the private life of the head of this organisation was examined. The article asserted that he had used his influence to make his

---

10 Judgment of the Supreme Court, 12 December, 1984 (*Minshū* 38–12–1308).
11 Judgment of Tokyo District Court, 17 July, 1970 (*Gyōsaireishū*, 21–7 special issue 1 : The Second Yanaga *kyōkasho* case).

mistresses members of the Diet. The district court and the appellate court found the defendant guilty, but the Supreme Court quashed the judgment of the appellate court. The Supreme Court ruled that behavior of a private person can also be a matter of public concern, depending upon his social activities and the power he wields in society. Therefore, Articles 230–2 of the Code applied and the defendant should be allowed to prove the truth of his statement.[12]

In another case, the Supreme Court found that even when the defendant failed to prove the truth of the statement concerning public interest, if he had mistakenly believed that the statement was true and had reasonable grounds in believing so, then there is no libel.[13]

A related problem is whether civil interlocutory measures, when used as a means to prevent publication of a slanderous publication, are constitutional or not. Such measures could have the same effect as a prior restriction on freedom of expression. In one case, the district court granted an interlocutory injunction sought against the publication of a periodical containing libellous statements against a candidate in an election for prefectural governorship. This decision of the court was upheld by the appellate court. The publisher appealed to the Supreme Court, arguing that an injunction in this case was unconstitutional.

The Supreme Court examined, among other issues, whether an injunction in such a case constituted prior restriction on freedom of expression or not. The Court pointed out that as a prior restriction is likely to be broader in effect than a restriction after the event, this may entail abuse. Therefore, prior restrictions on freedom of expression are only allowed under strict and clear conditions derived from the Constitution. Furthermore, when the expression concerns the public interest, such as criticism of government officials or candidates for election to public office, such an expression requires special protection by the Constitution and in principle an injunction should not be granted. As an exception, the Supreme Court ruled that when the statement is not true, or it is evident that the statement is not primarily intended for the benefit of the public, and at the same time, the victim is likely to suffer serious and irrecoverable loss, an injunction will be granted. The Supreme Court found that in this

---

12 Judgment of the Supreme Court, 16 April, 1981 (*Keishū* 35–3–84 : *Gekkan Pen* case).
13 Judgment of the Supreme Court, 25 June, 1969 (*Keishū* 23–7–975 : *Yūkan Wakayama Jiji* case).

particular case, such an exception should be applied and granted the injunction.[14]

3)   Due process of law

One of the provisions of the Constitution which has close affinity with the United States Constitution is the provision on the due process of law (Art. 31). This Article provides that no one shall be deprived of life or liberty or face a criminal sanction without recourse to procedures established by the law. It evidently has its origins in the Fifth and Fourteenth Amendments of the United States Constitution. However, it differs from the American model in that the provision requires observance of procedures established by law, but does not explicitly require the procedures to be 'due.' Also, property rights are not explicitly covered by the provision. Despite the differences in wording, the courts and academic opinion in Japan have broadly interpreted this provision. Firstly, it is generally agreed that this provision covers substantive due process as well as procedural due process. Secondly, the procedure and the substance of the law restricting fundamental rights should be fair, although the provision does not explicitly require fairness. In this regard, notice and hearing are required for limiting fundamental rights on the basis of this provision. Thirdly, the provision is not limited to life, liberty or imposition of criminal penalties. Restrictions on property rights are also understood to be covered by this provision.

The Supreme Court once found a confiscation of property without providing the owner an opportunity to defend his rights to be unconstitutional.[15] Some lower court judgments extend the application of this provision to administrative procedures, for instance, to licensing procedures for taxi business. The Supreme Court has not explicitly ruled on this, but has upheld the judgments of the lower courts.[16]

4)   Other rights and freedoms

The Constitution guarantees the rights of suspects and defendants in criminal procedure (Arts. 33–39). After the adoption of the Constitution with these provisions, the Code of Criminal

---

14 Judgment of the Supreme Court, 11 June, 1986 (*Minshū* 40–4–872 : *Hoppō* Journal case).
15 Judgment of the Supreme Court, 28 November, 1962 (*Keishū* 16–11–1593).
16 See for example, Judgment of the Supreme Court, 28 October, 1971 (*Minshū* 25–7–1037).

Procedure was totally amended in 1948.[17] While the previous Code was primarily based upon German Law, the present law is influenced by American Law. It should be added that cases decided by the United States Supreme Court have inspired the development of research into Japanese criminal procedure. On the other hand, although the American adversarial system has been introduced by the new Code, the influence of the previous 'inquisitorial' system still remains strong in practice.

According to the Constitution, no one should be arrested without a warrant issued by a competent judicial officer, except in cases where the arrest is *in flagrante delicto*. Similarly, no one shall be arrested or detained unless he is notified of the grounds of arrest or detention immediately and given a right of access to legal advice. Furthermore, a person cannot be detained without justifiable reason, and upon the request of any person, such grounds shall be shown in an open court with the presence of defense counsel (Arts. 33 and 34). In this regard, the Law on *Habeas Corpus* was enacted in 1948.[18]

In addition to the provision on freedom of expression, which also guarantees the secrecy of means of communication, homes and other property are protected from unlawful search and seizure (Art. 35). This also applies to administrative procedure, such as search and seizure by tax officers.[19]

The use of torture and cruel punishment by government employees is strictly prohibited (Art. 36) and in one case, capital punishment was tested against this provision. The Supreme Court ruled that when the crime committed by the offender is extremely serious, and considering the purpose of general deterrence, requires an extreme penalty, then the death penalty is justified.[20]

Defendants have a right to a fair and speedy public trial (Art. 37, para. 1). In cases where all judges agree that an open trial is likely to damage public order or public morals, a closed trial is allowed. However, if the issue is a political crime, crimes involving the publication of information, or fundamental rights guaranteed by the Constitution, the trial must be in open court.

Defendants have a right to legal representation, and if they can not afford it, the State has the responsibility to provide a lawyer

17 Law No. 131. 1948.
18 Law No. 199, 1948.
19 Judgment of the Supreme Court, 22 December, 1972 (*Keishū* 26–9–554 : Kawasaki *Minshō* case).
20 Judgment of the Supreme Court, 8 July, 1983 (*Keishū* 37–6–609 : Nagayama case).

(Art. 37, para. 3). In more than 50% of criminal cases handled by the district courts, defendants are assisted by counsel assigned by the court.[1] Defendants are also guaranteed the right to cross-examine all witnesses (Art. 37, para. 2). Cross examination was introduced into Japan after the Second World War. As a rule, hearsay evidence is not allowed in court, but the exceptions to this rule are fairly wide. Documents which contain statements recorded during the investigation still play a significant role at trial.

The Constitution also guarantees that no one should be forced to make incriminating statements (Art. 38, para. 1). This provision has its origin in the Fifth Amendment of the U.S. Constitution, which guarantees the right against self-incrimination. This also extends to administrative procedures. Concerning this provision, the constitutionality of the Road Traffic Law, which requires those who caused a traffic accident to report to the authorities under the threat of criminal penalty, was found constitutional by the Supreme Court.[2]

Confessions made under compulsion, torture, or threat, or when made after unduly prolonged arrest or detention, shall not be admitted as evidence. No one should be convicted when the only proof against him is his confession, i.e. corroborative evidence is required (Art. 38, paras. 2 and 3).

The principle of *nulla poena sine lege* is not explicitly set out in the Constitution, but there is no doubt that this is also guaranteed by the Constitution which commits itself to safeguarding fundamental rights and freedom. Some court judgments presupposed that the due process provision includes this principle. The Constitution does explicitly guarantee some related principles. Thus, no one shall be held criminally liable for an act which was lawful at the time it was committed or for an act of which he has been acquitted. The Constitution also prohibits double jeopardy.

Finally, the Constitution provides for property rights. It declares that property rights are inviolable, but in the following paragraph, provides that the contents of property rights are to be defined by law. Therefore, although the system of private property itself is safeguarded by the Constitution, the legislature is empowered to restrict property rights by way of legislation. Furthermore, private property may be used for public purposes with appropriate compensation. The Law on Acquisition of Land

1 Supreme Court of Japan ed., *Outline of Criminal Justice in Japan*, Tokyo 1985, pp. 40–41.
2 Judgment of the Supreme Court, 2 May, 1962 (*Keishū* 16–5–495).

for Public Purposes, for example, provides for the procedure of compulsory acquisition of land and the payment of compensation.[3]

All in all, the system of judicial review has been functioning properly in the sense that citizens who have felt their constitutional rights have been infringed by government action are able to challenge such action in open court. There are a number of cases where citizens have contested the constitutionality of laws, ordinances or government action.

However, the Supreme Court has become more reluctant in recent years to rule against restrictions imposed by the government on individual rights. Some judgments in the last decade show a tendency to return to the approach which the Supreme Court took in an earlier period, i.e. the public welfare approach. This tendency to uphold the constitutionality of laws and acts by simply juxtaposing public welfare and individual rights may, in the long run, lead to a mistrust of the system of judicial review on the part of the citizens.

In one case, the Supreme Court even reversed itself only seven years after a previous judgment, which found a provision of the Law on Government Employees to be unconstitutional. This involved the constitutionality of the provision which punished government employees for being involved in political activity. The 1966 judgment of the Court ruled that the restrictions on basic rights of the workers should be kept to a necessary minimum, that the imposition of criminal sanctions should be especially limited, and that the provision at issue exceeded this limit and was thus unconstitutional.[4] This judgment was followed by two judgments of the Supreme Court which took a similar approach. However, in 1973, when an identical case reached the Supreme Court, the court explicitly reversed the previous judgment, and found that the rights of the workers should be limited by taking into account 'public welfare'. A change in the composition of the Bench between these two judgments may have affected the latter judgment, which was reached by an eight to seven vote.[5]

4. International treaties and human rights

Japan has ratified the International Covenants on Human Rights, although with a few reservations. Japan is not bound by Article 8, paragraph 1(d) which provides for workers' rights to industrial

---

3 Law No. 219, 1951.
4 Judgment of the Supreme Court, 26 October, 1966, *supra* note.
5 Judgment of the Supreme Court, 25 April, 1973 (*Keishu* 27–4–547 : *Zennōrin Keishokuhō* case).

action. This right is generally acknowledged in relation to workers in the private sector, but certain categories of government employees are not given this right.

Although the Covenant was ratified and promulgated, it is regarded rather as a program, and is rarely used as a basis for actions to protect human rights. This may be due to the long and open-ended list of fundamental rights provided by the Constitution, which seemingly makes it unnecessary to resort to the Covenant. However, the Covenant was cited in court in a case where the Law on Aliens' Registration, which requires foreigners to have their fingerprints taken at the time of registration renewal, was at issue.[6] The plaintiff, who was a resident of Korean origin, claimed that this requirement was against the equal treatment clause of the Constitution and the International Covenant on Human Rights. He argued that this was a 'degrading treatment' prohibited by the Covenant (International Covenant on Civil and Political Rights, Art. 7). The appellate court acknowledged that the Covenant was directly applicable, but did not accept this argument.[7]

In accordance with the Covenant, the Japanese government submits a regular report on the state of human rights to the United Nations Secretary General to be discussed at the Economic and Social Council. At the Human Rights Committee, the Japanese practice of long pretrial detention and restrictions on the rights of suspects in criminal procedure as well as the discrimination of minorities are said to have attracted the attention of the members.

6 Law No. 125, 1952.
7 Judgment of Tokyo Appellate Court, 25 August, 1986 (*Hanji* 1208–66).

7 General principles and rules of civil law

1. The Civil Code

The Japanese Civil Code is a comprehensive Code which covers Property, Contract and Tort law, Family law and the Law of Succession. The Civil Code is divided into five Books. The first Book is the General Part, which provides for basic principles and rules of Civil Law. These include the Civil Law capacity of natural and juridical persons, juristic acts, and agency. The second Book which is entitled 'real rights' covers property and real security. The third Book is the Law of Obligations. Tort is considered to be one of the sources from which an obligation emerges, and therefore, is included in this part along with Contract. The fourth Book deals with Family Relations, while the fifth Book concerns Inheritance.

The present Civil Code was enacted in 1896. While Books One to Three have not been substantially amended since the enactment, Books Four and Five which deal with Family Law and Inheritance Law respectively were almost totally amended after the Second World War to democratise family relationships and ensure equality of the sexes.[1]

There is other relevant legislation in the field of private law together with the Civil Code. Some laws are supplementary to the Civil Code and were enacted at the end of the last century. These include the Law on the Registration of Real Property (1899) and the Law on Deposits (1899).[2] Other laws, such as the Law on Hypothec of Factory and laws on hypothec of a company and some movable properties, including cars and ships, were adopted at a later stage as the economy developed.[3]

Modernisation had a by-product: the emergence of socially deprived people – workers and tenant farmers. In order to

---

1 Y. Kawashima, 'Americanisation of Japanese Family Law, 1945–1975', *Law in Japan*, Vol. 16, 1983, pp. 54–68.
2 Laws No. 15 and 24, 1899.
3 Law No. 54, 1905, No. 106, 1958, No. 187, 1951.

protect those who were in socially weak positions, laws were enacted to modify the provisions of the Civil Code. Thus, the Law on the Protection of Buildings (1907), the Law on the Lease of Houses (1921), and the Law on the Lease of Land (1921) were enacted.[4] In 1991, these three Laws were merged into a new Law – the Law on Lease of Land and Houses.[5]

In recent years, with increased risks accompanying advances in technology, some new laws in the field of tort law have been enacted. These include the Law on Compensation for Nuclear Damage which provides for strict liability (1961) and the Law on the Compensation of Losses caused by Pollution which provides for a sophisticated mechanism of compensating victims of pollution (1971).[6] In addition, the Law on Compensation for Losses arising from Car Accidents was enacted in 1955 in order to cope with growing number of traffic accidents.[7]

The Commercial Code is a special law in relation to the Civil Code and is applied to merchants. It modifies and supplements the provisions of the Civil Code and sets forth special provisions. When there is no applicable provision in the Commercial Code, commercial custom is applied. Only when there is no such custom, is the Civil Code applied.

The first attempt to codify a Civil Code started under the initiative of the Minister of Justice, Shinpei Etoh, soon after the establishment of the Emperor's government in 1867. In 1870, a commission for the preparation of the civil code was formed and started to translate the French Civil Code with the help of a French advisor. The initial intention of the commission was to transplant the French Code Civil into Japan as soon as possible. The draft which came out in 1878 was almost a total copy of the French Code. The translation was very poor in quality, and what was more, the draft had not paid due attention to the issue of transplanting the French Code to a very different soil – preindustrial Japan.

The government soon realised this problem and decided to draft a code based upon European legal principles, but which was also 'practical and appropriate'.[8] Gustave Boissonnade, who was invited as a government advisor from the University of Paris, was commissioned for this formidable task. Most of the draft, except

4 Law No. 40, 1909 and Laws No. 49 and 50, 1922.
5 Law No. 1991.
6 Law No. 111, 1973.
7 Law No. 97, 1955.
8 For the influence of French law on the Japanese Code, see E. Hoshino, *Minpō-ronshū* (*Treatise on Civil Law*), vol. 6, Tokyo 1950, pp. 90–149. Translated in H.Tanaka, *The Japanese Legal System*, Tokyo 1976, pp. 229–235.

for Family Law and Succession, was worked out primarily by Boissonade on the basis of the French Code Civil and, to a certain extent, German law, although some innovations were added by Boissonade. The Japanese members of the drafting committee were those who had studied French law. Simultaneously with the drafting of the Civil Code, a Commercial Code was being drafted – though this time the leading role was given to a German advisor. The draft Civil Code was discussed at the Senate and the Privy Council, and the parts on property, the acquisition of property, obligation, securities and evidence were promulgated in 1890.

This Code, which is referred to in Japan as the old Civil Code, adopted the system of the French Code, although in some provisions, the influence of Italian, Belgian, and Dutch Codes can be seen. Although the parts on Family Law and Inheritance had been drafted by Japanese specialists, these parts also have been inspired by the European concept of a family based upon the equality of husband and wife, rather than that of the traditional Japanese family dominated by the male head.

This Code was subjected to barrage of criticism from various quarters. It was true that the Code, being the first major legislative work by the Japanese, had shortcomings and ambiguities. It was not surprising that the Code was criticised from these technical points. The criticism, however, was more deeply rooted. First, the Code was claimed to have been drafted almost entirely on the basis of French Law and did not pay due attention to other jurisdictions such as English or German Law. This led to factional criticism from lawyers trained in German or English Law. This rivalry between French specialists and German and English specialists was not merely a struggle for hegemony. The French specialists had been inspired by the theory of natural law, while German and English specialists had studied historical jurisprudence. The former acknowledged the universal applicability of legal principles, while the latter emphasised the historical and social environment within which a particular legal system developed. Therefore, the latter were skeptical of the possibility of transplanting the French Code in Japan.

The latter were also associated with those who were against rapid modernisation and who stressed that the traditional virtues of Japan should not be replaced by a Christian ideology and European individualism. From this viewpoint, the Family Law and Succession parts of the Code were especially anathema. In an opposition tract published at the time, it was pointed out that the Civil Code destroyed traditional morals and underrated the role of the state. Some people asserted that the concept of natural rights was against the Constitution. The criticism was primarily concentrated in the Family Law part. For example, one provision of the Code provided that the father exercised parental rights. If the father died, the mother was to take over these parental rights. However, this was said to be against Japanese tradition, because in such cases a guardian was always appointed.[9]

After a long and fierce debate, the Imperial Diet in 1892 decided to postpone the implementation of the Code, as well as the Commercial Code. Although formally, the Diet merely decided to amend the Code, in fact, the government set up another commission and instructed it to draft another Code. This Code was eventually adopted in 1898. This is the present Civil Code. It should be noted that this was adopted two years earlier than the German *Bürgerliches Gesetzbuch* (BGB) and nine years earlier than the Swiss Civil Code.

The new Civil Code has long been considered to be based upon German law. It is true that the Code was strongly influenced by the second draft of the German BGB and the Saxon Civil Code. The Code was composed on Pandekten lines starting with the General Part which is to be applied to the rest of the Code, followed by Property and Securities Rights and the Law on Obligations. There are many provisions which resemble the German BGB. For example, the concept of juristic acts, i.e. *Geschäftshandlung* evidently came from Germany. Taking into account that the new Code was enacted after the previous code had been scrapped for its strong French inclination, it was not surprising that the new Code was regarded as a rehash of the German Code. A German commentator pointed out at the time the Code was enacted that the new Code was almost entirely based upon German law and was much clearer and simpler than the previous Code. 'It does not look like a translation (as was the case with the previous code), but can be read as an original work'.[10]

Because of the belief that the new Code was based upon German law, Japanese scholars and lawyers have worked hard on digesting German Civil Law theory. The most common destination of scholars travelling abroad was Germany, especially before the Second World War.

However, recent research shows that the influence of French Law was still predominant in the new Code. In order to enact a

9 T. Hoshino, *Minpōten Ronsō-shi* (*The History of the Debates concerning the Civil Code*), Tokyo 1942, p. 234.

10 L. Loenholm, *Das Bürgerliche Gesetzbuch für Japan*, erster Band, Tokyo 1896, iii–iv.

new Code in a short time span, the drafters had to rely on the abortive previous Code. Many provisions of the old Code have been inherited by the new Code. For example, the provision which requires registration of title in order to claim a property right over an immovable against a third party in the new Code can already be found in the previous Code. Incidentally, in German law, registration is a requirement for transfer of immovables to take effect, while in French law, the transaction is valid without registration, although the parties may not claim their rights against a third party without registration. In this sense, the present Code has clearly adopted the French approach.[11]

Thus, while maintaining the facade of being strongly influenced by German law, the legislature at that time kept certain parts of the previous Code influenced by the French Code. It is more correct to say that the drafters intended to produce an ideal system by taking the best of German and French Codes.

It should be added that some of the Civil Law doctrines and institutions came from sources other than French or German Law. For instance, the doctrine of *ultra vires* originally came from English law, probably via French Law.

2. Basic principles of Civil Law

It is one of the characteristics of the German Pandekten system that general principles and rules not specific to particular institutions are singled out and put at the beginning of the Code.[12] The General Part of the Civil Code begins with a general provision on the exercise of private rights. Article one of the Code provides as follows:

> Private rights shall conform with public welfare.
> The exercise of rights and the performance of obligations shall be effected in a fair way and in good faith.
> The abuse of rights is not permitted

This provision was added to the Civil Code after the promulgation of the present Constitution. The first paragraph coincides with the provision of the Constitution which provides that the contents of property rights are to be regulated by law in accordance with public welfare (Art. 29, para. 2). Various laws, such as the Law on Agricultural Land, provide for restrictions on

11 Hoshino, *supra* note 8, p. 99.
12 N. Horn, H. Koetz and H. G. Leser, *German Private and Commercial Law*, (translated by T. Weir), Oxford 1982, pp. 66–67.

private property. This provision symbolises the rejection of the sanctity and absolute inviolability of property rights, but is seldom applied in practice. One of the rare cases involved the claim of a landowner who let his land for use as a U.S. military base. When the term of lease elapsed, he claimed the return of his property. This was turned down by the Supreme Court as an excessive demand and therefore, against public welfare. The term was thus renewed.[13]

The second and the third paragraphs, in contrast, are often referred to in court judgments where an equitable solution cannot be reached by relying on specific provisions of the Civil Code. It should be added that the provision on public order and good morals which is in the General Part (Art. 90) is also used together with these two sections.

The doctrine of good faith and fair dealing had long been recognised by the court before it was formally incorporated in the Civil Code in 1947. French and German Codes have similar provisions.[14] This doctrine is applied in various circumstances, including cases which in England would be covered by collateral estoppel. For instance, there was a case where a lessee of a piece of land – a company – was sued by the lessor for failing to pay the rent. The chairman of this company established another company with a similar name in order to avoid such claims. However, he contested the case in the court as a defendant against this claim. Then, after a year, while the case was still pending, the chairman claimed that his company was a different entity from the one which had been sued and therefore, the plaintiff should have sued the new company. The court rejected this argument as being against good faith and fair dealing.[15]

The courts often resort to this provision in order to protect the lessee of a house or land from eviction. According to the provisions of the Civil Code, the lessor is entitled to rescind the contract of lease when the lessee sublets the property, or assigns his interest to a third party without the consent of the lessor (Art. 612). The contract can also be rescinded when the lessee fails to pay the rent. However, the court limits the rescission of the contract by the lessor to cases where the act of the lessee amounts to a destruction of mutual trust. Thus, in one case, the court refused to rescind a contract of lease on the ground of this doctrine; the court pointed out that the amount of arrears was small and that the lessee was entitled to a claim for repair, and

---

13 Judgment of the Supreme Court, 9 March, 1965 (*Minshū* 19–2–233).
14 Horn et al., *supra* note, pp. 86–87.
15 Judgment of the Supreme Court, 26 October, 1973 (*Minshū* 27–9–1240).

therefore, the lessee cannot be regarded as having acted against good faith and fair dealing.[16]

Sometimes, a claim that a certain right has been extinguished by prescription is turned down by the courts on the ground that it is against good faith and fair dealing. There was a case where a widow who had obtained a piece of land from the eldest son (the only heir under the pre-War family law) failed to have it registered in her own name. She was not on good terms with the eldest son and brought up other children by farming this piece of land. Some 20 years later, she asked the eldest son to cooperate in registering the property in her name. The latter refused, and as a defence at the court, claimed that her right to demand cooperation in registration had already been extinguished by prescription. The Supreme Court found that this defence was against fairness and good faith.[17]

While the doctrine of good faith and fair dealing is used in cases where a particular relationship – such as a contract – exists between the parties, the prohibition on the abuse of rights is generally used in cases where there is no such relationship. This had also been acknowledged by the court before it was incorporated in the Civil Code. Exercise of one's right can be regarded as abusive, if it unreasonably infringes upon other persons' rights. An intention to harm on the part of the holder of the right is not needed.

In a leading case, there was a pipeline which came from a hot spring and went through a small piece of land which belonged to another person. The plaintiff purchased this piece of land and required the owner of the pipeline to purchase it at a high price. When this was not accepted, he brought an action against the owner of the pipeline, demanding that the pipeline be removed. The court rejected the claim as an abuse of rights.[18]

This provision is sometimes used in cases of public nuisance. In one case, the construction of a two-storied building was found to be an abuse of rights, since it seriously affected the sunshine and ventilation of an adjacent house. In this case, the building did not meet the standard required by the Law on Architectual Standards.[19] However, these kinds of cases can be dealt within the framework of tort law or property law, and the reasonableness of resorting to this provision is being questioned.

---

16 Judgment of the Supreme Court, 28 July, 1964 (*Minshū* 18–6–1220).
17 Judgment of the Supreme Court, 25 May, 1976 (*Minshū* 30–4–554).
18 Judgment of the Supreme Tribunal, 5 October, 1935 (*Minshū* 14–1965 : Unazuki *Onsen* case).
19 Judgment of the Supreme Court, 27 June, 1972 (*Minshū* 26–5–1067).

3. Legal Capacity

1) Natural persons

The first chapter of Book One of the Civil Code deals with the capacity of natural and juridical persons. The term 'legal capacity' was introduced from Germany (*Rechtsfähigkeit*). It denotes the capacity to be a subject of rights and duties. Distinguished from legal capacity is the capacity to act (*Handlungsfähigkeit*), which means the capacity to obtain rights, assume duties, and incur liabilities. Natural persons have legal capacity without exception. They are entitled to hold private rights from the moment of their birth (Arts. 1–3). These rights are also extended to a child in the womb in relation to tort and inheritance. Thus, an unborn child is regarded as being born and is entitled to a claim for damages (Art. 721). The same applies to inheritance (Art. 886).

A natural person has legal capacity until his or her death. When several people have died and the order of death is not known, it is presumed that they have died simultaneously (Arts. 32–3). When it is not known whether a person is dead or alive for seven years, the family court may declare this person to be missing (Art. 30, para. 1). In cases of a war or a shipwreck, a person can be declared missing one year after the incident (Art. 32, para. 2).

Foreign citizens are also entitled to be subjects of private rights in so far as such entitlement is not prohibited by law or ordinance (Art. 2). In some cases, for instance, in government tort liability, instead of equal treatment of Japanese and foreign citizens, the principle of reciprocity is applied. The Law on Government Liability provides that when the victim is a foreign citizen, the Law is applied only when the law of his home country provides for equivalent treatment (Art. 6).[20] The same applies to foreign lawyers. There are also laws which restrict the rights of foreign citizens to obtain specific rights or operate certain business in one way or another. For instance, foreign citizens are not allowed to be shareholders of the International Telecommunication Company (KDD). Foreign citizens are also excluded from operating certain categories of businesses, including telecommunication.[21]

Not every person with legal capacity can act on his own and

---

20 Law No. 125, 1947.
21 See M. Dōgauchi, '*Keizai no Kokusaika to Hō-kisei* (Internationalisation of the Economy and Legal Regulations)', *Jurist*, No. 875, 1987, pp.238–244.

acquire entitlement and assume duties. The Civil Code provides for persons who do not have this capacity to act, or have only limited capacity to act. They are: incompetents, quasi-incompetents and minors. Until 1947, wives were considered to be legally incompetent.

An incompetent denotes a person who is mentally disturbed chronically (Art. 7). A court order is needed to declare a person incompetent. An incompetent person is not capable of acting on his own and so can only act through his guardian (Art. 8). When he has acted on his own, that act is voidable – i.e. it can be rescinded unconditionally (Art. 9).

Quasi-incompetents are those who are mentally unstable – but not totally disturbed, or spendthrifts (Art. 11). Until 1979, blind, deaf or dumb persons have been treated by the Code as quasi-incompetents, but following criticisms, the Code was finally amended. As is the case with incompetency, quasi-incompetency is also a matter for the family court. A quasi-incompetent has limited capacity to act, and is required to obtain consent of his curator when performing certain acts listed in the Civil Code. These acts include: borrowing money or becoming a guarantor, transactions concerning real property or movables of significance, receiving or investing funds and initiating litigation (Art. 12, para. 1). If one of these acts was done without the consent of the curator, it is voidable and can be rescinded (Art. 12, para. 2).

Minors have a limited capacity to act. A person acquires majority at the age of 20, or by marriage (Arts. 3 and 753). A minor is required to obtain consent of his legal representative to acquire entitlement or assume duties (Art. 4, para. 1). Usually, those who have parental rights over a minor become the minor's legal representative. Acts done without the consent of the legal representative can be rescinded (Art. 4, para. 2).

Although there is no statutory provision to the effect, it is considered that an act of a person who is incapable of understanding the meaning and effects of his action is void. For instance, if a person who is suffering from serious mental disease but has not yet been declared incompetent by the court, concludes a contract, this contract is void.

2) Juridical persons

As in other major jurisdictions, juridical persons have legal capacity together with natural persons. The Civil Code provides for two types of juridical persons: corporations by membership (associations) and foundations.

A corporation by membership is a group of persons who

 selves to achieve a certain purpose. The assembly
s its decision-making body. Articles of association
by the members as the fundamental rules governing
tion and activities. In contrast, a foundation is a set of
endowed for a certain purpose. Foundations have no
s. They are administered in accordance with their act of
nent.

s two-tiered system of corporations by membership and
foundations comes from the German Civil Code, which distinguishes *Verein* and *Stiftung*. However, there is a significant difference between Japanese and German Law. While German law divides *Verein*s into economic associations and non-economic associations, the Japanese Civil Code divides corporations by membership into profit-making associations and public interest associations.

Public interest associations are those concerning religion, charitable purposes, science or art and which do not have profit-making as a purpose (Art. 34). It should be noted that these juridical persons are not required to have the public interest *as their purpose*; it is sufficient if they 'concern' public interest. Corporations by memberships can be either profit-making or public-interest associations, although profit-making associations are primarily regulated by the Commercial Code. On the other hand, profit-making foundations are not permitted.

Once a corporation by membership is founded, its assets are separated from those of the members. Therefore, creditors of the members cannot attach the assets of the corporation by membership, and by the same token, creditors of the corporation by membership cannot attach the assets of the members. Assets of a foundation are treated in a similar way.

Since the Japanese Civil Code does not recognise an association which is neither profit-making nor public interest, non-profit organisations which do not concern public interest, such as social clubs and alumni associations, are not entitled to juridical personality. Also some organisations refrain from applying for juridical personality in order to avoid the cumbersome procedures, cost and supervision by the administrative agency.

Under certain circumstances, these organisations also should be treated as juridical persons and have relevant provisions of the law applied to them. As for capacity to sue and to be sued, the Code of Civil Procedure allows these organisations such status (Art. 46). It is considered to be appropriate to deny attachment of the assets of the organisation by the creditors of the members, when the assets of the organisation are effectively separated from those of the members. In a similar way, there are organisations without juridical personality, whose creditors may attach only the assets of the organisation and not the assets of the members. There was a case where a director of an association, which does not have juridical personality, abused his power, incurred debts and disappeared. The creditor sued the members of the association for repayment. The District Court found that the liability of members should be limited to the amount of the assets of the association and should not extend to their individual assets. The Supreme Court upheld this judgment.[1]

Juridical persons are established in accordance with the Civil Code and other laws (Art. 33). Public-interest juridical persons can be established only with the permission of the relevant administrative agency (Art. 34), while profit-making corporations by membership can be established without such permission. In either case, registration is needed in order to claim juridical personality against others.

Since the procedure for establishing a public-interest foundation is rather cumbersome, trusts for public-interest purposes governed by the Trust Law have begun to be used in recent years.[2]

Actually, juridical persons established on the basis of the Civil Code are relatively small in number – approximately 20,000. On the other hand, there are more than two million companies – profit-making corporations by membership – established in accordance with the Commercial Code and the Law on Limited Companies. Furthermore, since the Second World War, a number of separate laws, for instance, the Law on Religious Organisation and the Law on Private Schools, have been enacted. These laws have special provisions as to the procedure for establishing and organising these entities. Juridical persons established on the basis of these separate laws amount to almost 200,000.

The Code provides that a juridical person acquires entitlement and assumes duties in accordance with laws and ordinances, and 'within the scope of its purposes' as provided by the articles of association or the act of endowment (Art. 43). Thus, transactions which exceed the scope of purposes set out by the articles of association are void. This provision evidently has been influenced by the doctrine of *ultra vires*. However, as is the case with companies (which will be discussed later), a strict implementation of this provision may result in disadvantage to those who deal with juridical persons.

In cases concerning profit-making juridical persons, the courts

1 Judgment of the Supreme Court, 9 October, 1973 (*Minshū* 27–9–1129).
2 Law No. 62, 1922.

tend to interpret the 'purpose' of the articles of association broadly and acknowledge the validity of transactions which are claimed to be *ultra vires*. There was a celebrated case where a major steel company made a donation to the ruling political party. A shareholder of this company brought an action against the representative manager of this company. The Supreme Court repeated the precedents in that 'acts within the scope of purposes' in the sense of Article 43 includes not only the purposes explicitly stipulated in the articles of association, but also includes acts needed directly or indirectly to achieve these purposes. In this particular case, the court ruled that donations of a reasonable amount are not *ultra vires*, in so far as they are needed to fulfill the social role expected of the company.[3]

In comparison, in cases involving public-interest juridical persons, the courts tend to interpret the scope of purposes narrowly. In one case, an agricultural cooperative extended a loan to wholesale grocers; the articles of association did not provide for extending loans to non-members. However, the Supreme Court found this transaction to be within the scope of the cooperative's 'auxiliary business' and therefore valid.[4]

Public-interest juridical persons are supervised by the relevant agencies (Art. 67). In the late 1970s, in response to mounting criticism of such public-interest juridical persons for allegedly abusing their status and being involved in profit-making activities, some provisions were added to the Civil Code. The administrative agency which supervises public-interest juridical persons is empowered to give orders to these entities (Art. 67, para. 2). In an extreme case, where a public-interest juridical person is involved in businesses beyond the scope of its purposes, violates the conditions of incorporation, defies any order of the supervising agency or acts against the interest of the public, the competent agency may rescind the grant of incorporation (Art. 71).

Juridical persons have one or several directors who represent them (Art. 52). Together with directors, juridical persons may have an auditor whose duty is to supervise the state of assets and the administration of affairs (Art. 58). Juridical persons are liable for tortious acts of directors and other representatives done in the course of their business (Art. 44, para. 1).

In some cases, a juridical person is established as a veil, or is used as an instrument to avoid attachment. In recent years, a

---

3 Judgment of the Supreme Court, 24 June, 1970 (*Minshū* 24-6-625: Yawata Steel case).
4 Judgment of the Supreme Court, 18 September, 1958 (*Minshū* 12-13-2027).

theory which denies juridical personality to these entities has developed under the influence of similar developments in the United States and Germany. In Japan, there are a number of small companies limited by shares, which have only one shareholder and are actually an individual business. The Supreme Court ruled that when the juridical personality is abused in order to avoid the law or the juridical personality is merely a veil, the juridical person status can be ignored by the creditor. In this case, A ran a shop for home appliances which was incorporated as a company limited by shares (Company Y). The shop premises were let by X. X wanted to evict A and Company Y from the property and eventually X and A reached a compromise in court; A agreed to move out. However, A failed to comply with the agreement, claiming that Company Y was not a party to the compromise and part of the premises used by the Company need not be returned to X. X sued Company Y. The Supreme Court ruled that although Y was a company limited by shares, in reality, it was nothing other than A as an individual. Therefore, the compromise reached between X and A in court should be regarded as an act between X and Company Y, and was binding on Y as well.[5]

4. Juristic acts

1) The concept of a juristic act

The General Part of the Civil Code further provides for juristic acts. This term came from the German term *Rechtsgeschäft*. It is a product of the German Pandekten jurisprudence, which has a penchant for abstractism. The General Part of the German Civil Code has provisions concerning juristic acts which is a concept formulated out of common characteristics of contracts, wills, acts of incorporation and other legal acts. The Japanese Code has followed this model. A juristic act is defined in Japan as an act directed towards a specific legal effect, i.e. an act aimed at obtaining, relinquishing or otherwise altering a right, which can be enforced through the judicial system. Legal relationships between the subjects of law, as well as the subjects and objects of

---

5 Judgment of the Supreme Court, 27 February, 1969 (*Minshū* 23–2–511). K. Egashira, '*Kigyō no Hōjinkaku* (Juridical Personality of Corporations)', in A. Takeuchi & M. Tastuta eds., *Gendai Kigyō-hō Kōza* (*Contemporary Corporate Law*), vol. 2, Tokyo 1985, p. 57ff.

law emerge as a result of a juristic act.[6] A typical juristic act is a contract, but it also covers unilateral acts such as gift, wills, and joint acts such as an act of incorporation.

As the renowned German lawyer Savigny elaborated in his 'Theory of Will', the core of the juristic act is the declaration of will, which is an expression of the will of a person directed at a specific legal effect. Specific legal effects result from the will of a person. This presupposes the principle of private autonomy (*Privatautonomie*); where there is no freedom of will, there are no grounds for juristic acts to have any legal consequences.

The relationship between a juristic act and the declaration of will has long been an issue of controversy. In the early period, Japanese lawyers did not distinguish these two concepts. The influence of German theories in the following period led to the distinction being made between the two concepts. A declaration of will is an element – indeed, the core – of a juristic act, but it is not the juristic act itself. This is because juristic acts require elements other than a mere declaration of will. Bilateral juristic acts require two declarations of will to coincide and therefore, are more than a declaration of will; besides, there are some acts which require other elements such as the license of an official body to be effective. Thus, juristic act is understood to be a broader concept than the that of declaration of will.

2)   Juristic acts against public order and good morals

The Civil Code provides that juristic acts whose purpose are against public order or good morals are null and void (Art. 90). Together with Article 1, the Code gives a broad discretion to the judges by this general provision. The courts have been fairly active in applying this provision in order to reach fair and equitable solutions.

For instance, immoral contracts or contracts which infringe upon the integrity of a person are null and void by virtue of this provision. There was a case before the Second World War where Y borrowed money from X and in return, sent his daughter to work under X as a barmaid. Half of her salary was deducted in order to repay her father's debt. The daughter fled, and X claimed repayment from Y. The Supreme Court found the employment contract between the daughter and X, as well as the loan contract between X and Y void on the ground of Article 90.[7] By the same token, a contract of payment for being a

---

6 H. Brox, *Allgemeiner Teil des Bürgerliches Gesetzbuchs*, zweite Auflage, Köln 1987, S. 43–54.

7 Judgment of the Supreme Court, 7 October, 1955 (*Minshū* 9–11–1616).

mistress is null and void. Also a loan contract for gambling money is null and void when the creditor knew the purpose of the loan.[8]

Furthermore, contracts concluded where one party is in a strong bargaining position and which contain excessively disadvantageous clauses as regards the other can be null and void on the basis of this provision. For example, there was a case where a loan contract was concluded in which the debtor had to transfer to the creditor a piece of land worth eight times as much as the amount he had borrowed in case he failed to repay the debt on time. The creditor had thus abused his dominant position over a person in economic difficulty. The Supreme Court found this contract to be against public order and good morals.[9]

Juristic acts are required to comply with laws. The Code provides that the parties may deviate from provisions of laws and ordinances, unless these provisions concern public order (Art. 91). Thus, there are two kinds of legal provisions: mandatory and optional. Juristic acts should not contradict mandatory provisions. Whether a given provision is mandatory or optional is not always explicit in the Code. Parts Four and Five – Family Law and Inheritance, as well as Part Two – Property Law – have more mandatory provisions than Part Three – Law on Obligations.

However, it should be noted that juristic acts which are against the law are not always null and void. This is especially significant in relation to administrative law. In some cases, violations of the laws in this field do not necessarily make an act void, although they may result in criminal or administrative penalties. For instance, a person who sells goods without the necessary license may incur administrative penalty, but the contract itself is valid.[10] This problem is also discussed in relation to the Anti-Monopoly Law – whether acts against Anti-Monopoly Law are void or not under the Civil Code or the Commercial Code. There was a case where the Supreme Court ruled that an act in violation of the Anti-Monopoly Law is not necessarily null and void in terms of Civil Law.[11]

3) Defective declaration of will

It is the role of the court to interpret the will of the parties. More emphasis is placed on the objective expression as the other party

8 Judgment of the Supreme Court, 4 September, 1986 (*Hanji* 1215–47).
9 Judgment of the Supreme Court, 18 January, 1963 (*Minshū* 17–1–25).
10 For example, Judgment of the Supreme Court, 18 March, 1960 (*Minshū* 14–4–483).
11 Judgment of the Supreme Court, 20 June, 1977 (*Minshū* 31–4–449).

would have understood it, rather than the internal will, in order to safeguard those who had relied on the objective expression. Normally, the intention of the declarant and his expressed will should coincide in order to bring about the intended legal effects. However, in some cases, there is a gap between these two. For instance, a person may be under duress or be mistaken. These instances are denoted as defective declaration of will (*Willensmaengel*).

Following the model of the German Civil Code, there are provisions dealing with the effects of defective declaration of will. Here, the Code endeavours to balance the interests of the declarant, recipient and any third party.

The first of such defects is 'mental reservation' (*geheimer Vorbehalt*). The Code provides that a juristic act should not be invalidated when a party knowingly declares a will which does not coincide with his genuine will. This does not apply when the other party had known, or should have been aware that this was not the declarant's genuine will (Art. 93), since in such cases, there is no need to protect the interest of the opposite party at the cost of the declarant. For instance, a person who sold his property as a joke is nevertheless bound by his words. However, if the opposite party was aware that this was a joke, or should have been aware of this, the act is null and void.

The second instance of defects of will is fictitious declaration of will by collusion (*Scheingeschäft*). A fictitious (or sham) juristic act made in collusion with the other party is null and void, because the act does not coincide with the parties' genuine intention. However, the interests of a third party who relied upon this false declaration of will have to be protected. Therefore, the parties may not claim that the act is void against a *bona fide* third party (Art. 94). Such fictitious acts are often seen when the parties intend to avoid attachment – for example, a husband registers his property under his wife's name in order to avoid attachment from his creditors. It may happen that a person entrusted with property resells it to a third party thus abusing his position. Let us assume that a person X colludes with another person B and fictitiously sold him a piece of land. Between X and B, the sales contract is null and void, because this does not coincide with their genuine intention. B is not entitled to claim the property against X. However, if B abused X's trust and sold the land to a third party Y, who had believed without fault that B was the genuine owner, X may not claim his rights against Y. After all, X had contributed to create an appearance that B was the owner and Y has relied on it; X should accept the outcome of his act.

The Supreme Court has extended the application of this provision to some other cases, where the protection of a *bona fide* party was needed. For instance, there was a case where a man A registered in his name a piece of land which belonged to his mistress X. X soon found this out, but left the registration unchanged. Some time afterwards, A, who had married X, sold the land to a *bona fide* third party Y without the permission of X. Although there was no explicit collusion of will between X and A, the Supreme Court found that X could not claim her ownership against Y, since she had left the registration unchanged and created the appearance that A was the owner of the property.[12]

The third instance of defective declaration of will is mistake (*Irrtum*). A juristic act is null and void when there is a mistake in any essential elements. However, when there is gross negligence on the part of the declarant, he is not entitled to claim that the act is null and void (Art. 95). The courts distinguish between mistakes as to element and mistakes as to motive. An example of the latter is a case where a person purchases a piece of land, believing that there is a hotspring there. While the former is considered to be void, the latter does not affect the validity of the act, unless the motive is made explicitly known to the opposite party.[13] However, recent academic opinion is of the view that the demarcation between mistakes as to element and mistakes as to motive is ambiguous and that there is no justifiable ground for requiring the motive be made known to the opposite party. It is now agreed that even when the motive is not explicitly stated, there are cases where the transaction should be made void.

Finally, juristic acts made by fraudulent means or under duress can be rescinded. While the declarant may claim rescission of an act made under duress against a third person, he may not do so against a bona fide third party in cases of acts made by fraudulent means (Art. 96, paras. 1 and 2).

4) Invalidity of juristic acts

The Civil Code distinguishes between acts which are null and void on the one hand, and voidable acts – acts which can be rescinded – on the other hand. Acts which are null and void have no legal effect whatsoever even without a claim to that effect advanced by someone, and cannot be made valid by ratification (Art. 119). In contrast, voidable acts are valid until an entitled

12 Judgment of the Supreme Court, 22 September, 1970 (*Minshū* 24–10–1424).
13 Judgment of the Supreme Court, 26 November, 1954 (*Minshū* 8–11–2087).

person rescinds the act. On rescission, the act is regarded as having been void *ab initio* (Art. 121). When the act is null and void, one can claim its nullity any time, whereas when the act is merely voidable, the right of rescission lapses five years after ratification became possible or twenty years after the act (Art. 126).

A typical act which is null and void is an act against public order and good morals (Art. 90). Here, the act is null and void, independent of the will of the declarant or others. Acts of mental reservation, fictitious declaration and mistake are also null and void. In contrast, acts made by fraudulent means or under duress are merely voidable. However, as was mentioned above, voidness of juristic acts provided from Article 93 to Article 95 are limited in one way or another. In the case of mental reservation, it can not be claimed against a *bona fide* third party. Theoretically, any person may claim that an act is null and void, but in the case of mistake, although the act is supposed to be null and void, there is an established precedent that no one may claim that the act is void, if the declarant who made the mistake does not intend to so claim.[14]

Rescission or ratification is effected by a unilateral act. If a person who is entitled to rescind a juristic act performs the act fully or partly, demands performance of the opposite party, renews the act or furnishes surety, he is deemed to have ratified the voidable act (Art. 125).

5.   Agency

Juristic acts can be performed by an agent. When an agent is authorised by a principal to perform juristic acts on his behalf with a third party, the legal effect of such acts are attributed to the principal. General rules concerning agency are provided in the General Part of the Civil Code. Furthermore, the Commercial Code has provisions for commercial agency.

Agents can be divided into two types: agents created by agreement and statutory agents. In the case of statutory agents, agency arises directly from provisions of the law. For instance, minors are represented by a legal representative (Art. 4). Parents are expected to act on behalf of minors (Art. 818). Curators are appointed in order to represent those without capacity to act, including minors who do not have a person with parental rights (Art. 838). The Code also provides for administrator of an

---

14 Judgment of the Supreme Court, 10 September, 1965 (*Minshū* 19–6–1512).

inherited property (Art. 952), executor of will (Art. 1015) and administrator of a property of an absentee both appointed by the family court (Art. 25). In addition, a juridical person is represented by a representative.

As for agency created by agreement, the relationship between the principal and the agent varies. Agency arises from mandate or employment contracts, work contracts and partnership contracts. These contracts are regulated in Part Three of the Code – the Part on the Law of Obligations.

In order to create an agent, no specific form is required. A letter of attorney is often issued, but this is not mandatory. An agent does not need to have full legal capacity (Art. 102).

Agents created by agreement may not appoint a sub-agent unless the principal has given permission or an unavoidable reason exists (Art. 104). If an agent appoints a sub-agent in accordance with these requirements, he is responsible to the principal as to the selection of, and supervision over, the sub-agent. If the agent appoints a sub-agent upon instructions from the principal, the agent is not responsible for the wrongdoing of the sub-agent, unless he knew that the sub-agent was unfit or untrustworthy but has nevertheless failed to inform the principal or remove the sub-agent (Art. 105). In contrast, statutory agents have broader power to appoint sub-agents, but are responsible for the acts of the sub-agent (Art. 106).

Agency comes to an end when the principal and the agent agree to terminate the relationship. In addition, agency is terminated by the death of the principal. Death, total loss of capacity, or bankruptcy on the part of the agent also end the relationship (Art. 111).

In order to avoid a conflict of interests, an agent is not allowed to represent a person in a transaction in which he is the other party. For instance, a seller's agent may not conclude on the seller's behalf a sales contract with himself as a buyer. A person may not act as an agent of both parties in the same transaction (Art. 108). A similar provision exists for representatives of a juridical person. Where there is a conflict of interests, a special representative has to be appointed (Art. 57).

An agent is required to disclose that he is acting on behalf of the principal (Art. 99, para. 1). If the agent fails to do so, the transaction has no effect upon the principal, and the agent is deemed to have acted on his own behalf. This, however, does not apply when the opposite party was aware, or should have been aware that the agent acted on behalf of the principal (Art. 100).

The Commercial Code provides an exception for commercial transactions; in such transactions, even when the agent failed to reveal that he was acting on behalf of a principal, the act is binding on the principal (Art. 504).

Where the validity of a juristic act is affected because of defective declarations of will, such defects are to be determined by reference to the agent's position and not the principal's (Art. 101, para. 1). For instance, when the principal A purchases a painting through his agent B, who had known that this painting was a fake, A may not claim that he had acted out of mistake, even when he had not known that this was a fake.

In cases of agency arising from agreement, the scope of the agent's authority is defined by the agreement between the principal and the agent. If a person without authority acts ostensibly on behalf of the principal, then, as a rule, the act has no effect on the principal. However, the scope of authority given to the agent is not always apparent from outside. It is often not even precisely defined by the principal. This may confuse the third party, and therefore, a safeguard to protect those who had mistakenly believed that an agent was acting within his authority is needed. This can be justified in so far as the principal had contributed in one way or another to the creation of such an appearance. Therefore, under certain circumstances, a principal may be bound by the act of his agent, although the agent has exceeded his authority.

Firstly, when a person declares to others that he has granted another person authority to act on his behalf, he is liable for the acts of that person (Art. 109). Therefore, once a principal has made known to others that he has given authority to another person, he may not deny the effect of the act done by the agent, in so far as it is within the scope of authority ostensibly granted to the agent. For instance, when Y allows A to use his name or signet in a transaction without intending to allow him to act on his behalf, nevertheless, Y may be bound by A's actions against a third party X. The court applied this provision in a case where A issued promissory notes in the name of Y, using Y's signet. X mistakenly believed that A was authorised by Y to do so. The Supreme Court found the promissory notes to be valid on the ground of Article 109.[15]

In another case, Tokyo District Court was held liable for a transaction concluded by an organisation. This organisation was an association of court employees which had an office in the court building and used the name of 'welfare department' of the District Court. The plaintiff had sold stationary to this organisation, but the latter failed to pay. Therefore, he brought a suit

15 Judgment of the Supreme Court, 7 February, 1957 (*Minshū* 11–2–227).

against the State, arguing that the District Court, and ultimately the State, was liable. Although there was no formal relation between the Court and this organisation, the Supreme Court found that the District Court had created the appearance that this organisation was part of the court and therefore, was liable for the transaction.[16]

It is common commercial practice for a person to allow another person to use his or his company's name in a commercial transaction in order to increase the second person's credibility, or to do business which is subject to license without one. In such cases, the Commercial Code provides that the principal and the person who uses the principal's name are jointly liable in any related transaction (Art. 23).

It should be noted that the provision of the Civil Code does not explicitly require that a person who has had dealings with an unauthorised agent should have been *bona fide*. However, those who were or should have been aware that an agent was not authorised need not be protected at the cost of the principal. There is now case law to the effect that such a person should be *bona fide* and not negligent in believing that the person was indeed authorised.[17]

The second safeguard applies in situations where an agent who has actually been granted authority by the principal exceeds the scope of that authority. Such an act in excess of the authority is nevertheless binding on the principal provided that the third party had a justifiable reason to believe that the agent had acted within his power (Art. 110). It is necessary that at least some authority was granted to the agent. For example, there was a case where the principal Y authorised an agent A to register a piece of land which he owned. A was given the title deed and Y's signet. Instead of registering the property, A sold it to a third person X. X filed a suit against Y in order to have the property transferred. The Supreme Court acknowledged that Article 110 was applicable in such a case.[18]

A blank power of attorney is often issued in Japan. This can also be regarded as a grant of authority, and if the person who received such a wide power has abused it, this is a matter to be decided by this provision. When a representative of a juridical person exceeds his power, this provision is also applicable.

The third safeguard is that the lapse of an agent's authority can not be claimed against a *bona fide* third party, unless the latter

16 Judgment of the Supreme Court, 21 October, 1960 (*Minshū* 14–12–2661).
17 Judgment of the Supreme Court, 22 April, 1966 (*Minshū* 20–4–752).
18 Judgment of the Supreme Court, 3 June, 1971 (*Minshū* 25–4–455).

knew, or should have known, that it had expired (Art. 112). Therefore, even after a termination of agency, when the former agent acted as if he was still authorised, the former principal may be held liable for the former agent's act. In order to avoid this, the principal has to let it be known that the agency has been terminated.

When a person acts ostensibly on behalf of the principal, but without authorisation, such an act is not binding on the principal, unless it is covered by the three above-mentioned provisions. Where the transaction is not supported by apparent authority, the principal may ratify the act (Art. 113, para. 1). Ratification should be addressed to the other party, not to the agent. The other party may give notice to the principal and ask him to decide whether he wishes to ratify the act or not within a fixed period of time (Art. 114). Until the principal ratifies the act, the other party is entitled to rescind the transaction (Art. 115). An agent who acts on behalf of another person, but fails to prove his authority and also fails to have the principal ratify the act, may be required to pay damages or effect performance at the option of the other party (Art. 117, para. 2).

6. Prescription

The General Part provides for extinctive prescription together with acquisitive prescription. This arrangement is in common with French law and differs from German Law. In this book, acquisitive prescription will be dealt with in the chapter on property law. Rights arising from an obligational relationship expire if not exercised for ten years. Rights other than those arising from obligational relationship and ownership expire if not exercised for twenty years (Art. 167, paras. 1 and 2). Apart from this general provision, the Code provides for short term prescription of three years, two years, and one year for some categories of rights arising from obligational relations (Arts. 170–174). Prescription can be interrupted or suspended under certain circumstances (Arts. 147, 158–161).

The *raison d'être* of extinctive prescription is first, those who do not exercise their rights for a long period do not necessarily deserve protection, and second, after a long period, it becomes difficult for the debtor to prove that he had performed his obligation, and such obligors need protection.

8 The law of property

1. The concept of real rights

Part Two of the Civil Code provides for 'real rights.' This arrangement comes from the German BGB, where *Sachenrecht* (the law of property) and *Schuldrecht* (the law of obligation) are contrasted. The latter is dealt with in Book Three of the Japanese Civil Code.

Real rights are rights of a person over a thing, i.e. a relation *in rem* (in contrast to a relation *in personam*). They are distinguished from rights arising from obligational relationships in two ways. Firstly, real rights are rights which allow one to take control of, use, and make profits from a specified thing, while rights arising from obligational relationships are rights to require another person to do or not to do something. Secondly, real rights can be claimed against any other person, whereas in rights arising from obligational relationships, usually only two parties are involved, and the relationship exists only between them. Therefore, the former is often termed an absolute right, while the latter is termed a relative right.

The distinction has some practical consequences, because in cases of infringement, a holder of real rights is entitled to demand cessation of such infringement by any person, while a holder of rights arising from obligational relationships, as a rule, does not have such power against a third party. For instance, rights of ownership can serve as a basis for an action to remove obstruction to the property, but a lessee may not initiate such action on the basis of his right arising from a lease. Furthermore, if a real right and a right arising from an obligational relationship coexist on the same property, the former has priority. If, for example, the owner of a piece of land sells it, the lessee of the property may not claim his rights against the new owner unless his right is registered.

The distinction, however, cannot now be strictly maintained. Some rights arising from obligational relationships are protected in a way similar to that of real rights, due to the enactment of separate laws after the Civil Code and case law which has accumulated since then. Thus, for example, lessees of a piece of land may claim rights against a new owner under certain conditions. Lessees may also protect their interests from infringement by a third party in the same way as owners by substituting the owner-lessor.[1]

The General Part of the Civil Code defines a thing as a corporeal thing (Art. 85). Things are divided into immovables and movables. This distinction is somewhat different from that of real and personal property. Immovables are land and 'things firmly attached to it' (Art. 86, para. 1). Houses and buildings are examples of immovable things. Houses and buildings are treated separately from the land to which they are attached. This is one of the peculiarities of the Japanese property law. Trees used to be traded separately from the land, but the Civil Code does not specifically refer to trees. By virtue of the Law on Trees of 1909, trees which are registered, or which have signs indicating the name of the owner are treated as separate immovables.[2] Everything other than immovables are movables (Art. 86, para. 2).

The distinction between immovables and movables has practical effect in that firstly, in transactions involving the former, registration or other means of publicity are needed. Secondly, a person may obtain ownership of a movable instantly by commencing possession peacefully and openly with an intention to own. Immovables cannot be obtained in such a way. Thirdly, some rights, such as hypothec, may exist on immovables only although some exceptions are provided by separate laws.

One of the attributes of real rights is that whenever the exercise of real rights is infringed by someone, the holder of the right is entitled to initiate an action in order to eliminate such infringement. Historically, this has developed out of the *rei vindicatio* and *actio negatoria* of Roman Law as modified by the German *Gemeinesrecht*. The current Civil Code does not have general provisions concerning actions based upon real rights. The closest provisions are those concerning actions on the basis of possession (Arts. 197–202). However, it is understood that the Civil Code presupposes such actions based upon other real rights, namely ownership.

The three types of action based upon real rights against

---

1 Judgment of the Supreme Court, 18 December,1953 (*Minshū* 7–12–1515).
2 Law No. 22, 1909.

infringement are an action for recovery, an action for elimination of infringement and an action for preventing infringement. In recent years, the latter two types of actions are sometimes used in disputes concerning the protection of environments, particularly against noise, vibration and odour. Real rights which serve as a basis of such actions are primarily ownership, but such actions can also be taken by secured creditors.

The Civil Code lists ten kinds of real rights; no rights other than those provided by the Code or other laws may be created (Art. 175). The Code first provides for right of possession, which emanates from actual possession of a thing. This arrangement of the Code is problematic, because possession is not a right in itself, but merely a state of affairs. In any case, the Code gives protection to actual possession in various ways. Second, the Code provides for ownership. There are also four types of real rights which allow one to use another person's property: superficies, emphyteusis, servitude and commonage. Superficies is a right to use the land of another person for the purpose of owning a building or trees and plants (Art. 265). Emphyteusis is a right to cultivate or raise livestock on other person's land by paying a rent (Art. 270). Servitus praedorium denotes a right to use another person's land for the convenience and benefit of his own land, such as using the adjacent land for passage (Art. 280). Finally, commonage is a traditional right which belongs to a collective body, for instance, a village community, to use a forest, field, fishery zone, or irrigation system. Commonage under the Civil Code primarily concerns forests and fields.

Finally, there are four types of real security rights: rights of retention, preferential rights, pledge and hypothec. In pledge, the possession of the collateral is transferred to the creditor, and in case of default, the creditor may secure repayment from the proceeds of auction. In hypothec, the creditor does not have possession of the collateral, but if the debtor is in default, the creditor may secure repayment in the same way as pledge.

The principle that only those real rights provided by law should exist, and that one may not change the contents of a real right arbitrarily, is justified by the 'absolute' character of real rights, i.e. real rights affect not only the other party but anyone else in the world. If one can freely change the content of a real right or create new rights, this will harm the predictability and stability of transactions. This principle was also needed to eliminate some traditional rights which did not fit into the scheme of a modern Code in the late 19th century. However, since the enactment of the Code, some new real rights have developed either out of separate laws or out of practice. Firstly, laws such as the Mining

Law, Fishery Law and the Law on Hypothec of Factories have created new types of real rights.[3] The Civil Code itself was amended and a new type of hypothec, i.e. base hypothec, was introduced. Secondly, various atypical security rights have developed out of practice, sometimes against explicit provisions of the Code. Some of them have later found a legal basis. The Law on Contracts of Security by Provisional Registration serves as an example. Case law played a significant role in shaping these rights and ensuring fairness in their realization.

2. Registration

The Code provides that the establishment and assignment of real rights take effect by the declaration of will of the parties (Art. 176). No formalities such as registration or transfer of possession are needed. This arrangement follows the pattern of French law in which property transactions are completed *par l'effet des obligations*. In contrast, the German Civil Code requires registration or actual transfer of the object for the transaction to be effected. There, ownership of immovables, for instance, is not assigned by a mere agreement; entry into the *Grundbuch* (Land Register) is needed.[4]

A problem which arose in relation to this provision is whether the establishment or assignment of a real right takes effect merely by an agreement such as a sales contract, or whether a separate agreement specifically aimed at establishing or assigning a real right is needed. German law has adopted the latter system; two different agreements, obligational and real, are required, whereas the French system requires a single agreement. Scholarly opinion in Japan is divided on this matter, but since both schools allow exceptions, the practical outcome does not differ.

Although registration or other means of publicity are not a prerequisite for the transaction to take effect in Japan, it is needed to claim the rights against a third party. Thus, the Code provides that the acquisition, loss, or alteration of a real right cannot be set up against a third party unless it is registered when it involves an immovable (Art. 177), or delivered when it involves a movable (Art. 178). For example, if seller A sold a house to buyer B, the latter may claim his ownership against the

3 Laws No. 289, 1950, No. 267, 1949, No. 54, 1907.
4 N. Horn, H. Koetz and H. G. Leser, *German Private and Commercial Law: An Introduction*, Oxford 1982, pp. 179–182.

former without registration. However, if A had afterwards sold the same house to a third party C who then registered his acquisition, B can not claim ownership against C. Naturally C may claim damages from A in such cases.

Land, buildings and trees are registered in accordance with the Law on the Registration of Immovables at the local legal bureau.[5] A register is organised in a manner in which each piece of land, building, or tree is assigned a separate section. Ownership as well as other real rights are entered on the register in chronological order. Most rights which can be registered are real rights, but a lease of immovables, which is a right arising from obligational relationship, can also be registered.

Registration must be made jointly by the current holder and the prospective holder of the right concerned. Thus, when A sells a house to B, A and B jointly apply for registration. B has a right to demand that A cooperate and where A refuses, he may seek a court order.

There are two major issues with regard to registration. First is the scope of 'acquisition, loss and alteration of real rights' which require registration. There is no doubt that alteration resulting from sale, gift and other juristic acts must be registered. In addition, alteration caused by rescission of a juristic act also must be registered under certain circumstances. For instance, A sells his house to B. A later rescinds the sales contract because of fraud on the part of B. However, after the rescission but before A restores his registration, B sells the house to C who registers it in his name. In such a case, A is not entitled to assert his ownership or rescission against C because he has failed to register the return of property in time.[6]

The second problem is the scope of 'third parties' in the context of Article 177. The Code does not limit the scope of the third parties against whom registration is needed in order to claim alteration in real rights. For example, if A sells his house to B, while C, knowing that the house was sold to B, nevertheless purchases the house from A and registers it in C's name, B cannot claim his ownership against C because he failed to register. Thus, even a third party who was aware of the fact that the seller was not the real owner is entitled to claim the lack of registration on the part of the genuine owner. The problem is whether or not any kind of third parties, for instance, a third party who had acted against fairness and good faith, should be protected in this way. It should be noted that the Law on

5 Law No. 24, 1891.
6 Judgment of the Supreme Tribunal, 30 September, 1942 (*Minshū* 21–911).

Registration of Immovables provides that those who obstruct registration by fraudulent means or by extortion are not entitled to take advantage of the lack of registration (Art. 4). The Supreme Tribunal, the predecessor of the present Supreme Court before the end of the Second World War, limited the scope of third parties as provided in Article 177 soon after the adoption of the Code. In a leading case, the Supreme Tribunal ruled that a third party against whom no right can be claimed without registration meant those who have a justifiable interest in claiming the lack of registration.[7] Therefore one may claim his ownership against a person, for instance, who is illegally occupying the property, without registration. Also when the third party has absolutely no right whatsoever over property, such as a person who forged the Register and registered property in his name, he is not entitled to claim the lack of registration for his advantage.

The Supreme Court further limited the range of third parties covered by this provision. This concerns 'third parties in bad faith'. In a leading case, A sold a forest to Y; part of the forest had been left out of the register and therefore was not registered even after this change in ownership. X became aware of this and also found out that A still had the deed, so he purchased this in order to sell it to Y at a high price. Y refused to buy, so X sold this to B. When B brought suit against Y, X repurchased the property from B, registered it in his name and joined the suit. The Court ruled that X had acted in bad faith, and was not entitled to claim the lack of registration on the part of Y.[8]

Similarly, when the third party acts against his previous words or acts, or acts with the intention of harming the person who has not registered, the court has ruled that these third parties may not take advantage of the lack of registration. This conclusion can be justified by estoppel or the doctrine of fairness and good faith.[9]

Unlike the German *Grundbuch* in which registration has a constitutive effect, Registry in Japan does not always reflect the true state of property relations. People often fail to register transactions concerning immovables because of tax ramifications, or simply because of the cumbersome procedure. Therefore, when A, for example, purchases a piece of land from its

---

7 Judgement of the Supreme Tribunal, 15 December, 1908 (*Minroku* 14–1276).
8 Judgment of the Supreme Court, 2 August, 1968 (*Minshū* 22–8–1571).
9 For example, Judgment of the Supreme Court, 16 January, 1969 (*Minshū* 23–1–18).

registered owner B, there is no guarantee that B is the genuine owner and that A acquires ownership over the land. A must check in advance of transaction whether or not an unregistered transaction involving the property had taken place before.

In some cases, the court has interpreted the law flexibly and protected those who relied on registration. There was a case where an owner of a piece of land, X, had registered the property in A's name without the latter's consent. X had no intention of transferring the property to A. A found out later that the property was registered in his name, and, taking advantage of this, sold the property to Y, who registered it in his name. X brought suit against Y to have his ownership confirmed. The Supreme Court applied Article 94, para. 2 which provides for declaration of will by collusion (sham transactions, see Chapter 7), although there was no collusion between X and A, and ruled that X was not entitled to claim his ownership against Y. In this case, X was responsible for creating the appearance that A was the genuine owner. Instead of protecting A, who, according to the register, was the owner, the court chose to protect Y, who had relied upon the Register.[10]

3.   Ownership

The Civil Code protects possession of property without questioning whether or not the possessor has a genuine right to the property in question. The possessor of an object is presumed to have a lawful claim over the object (Art. 188). A possessor in good faith acquires the fruits of the thing in his possession (Art. 189, para. 1). If his possession is infringed, he is entitled to claim recovery of the object, elimination of infringement or the prevention of further infringements (Arts. 197–200).

The Code defines ownership as a right to use, make profit from and dispose of a thing, subject to such limitations as may be imposed by law (Art. 206). One should note the provision of the Constitution which provides that the contents of property rights are to be defined by law in accordance with public welfare (Art. 29, para. 2). Private property may be taken for public purposes with just compensation (Art. 29, para. 3). Ownership is no longer considered as something absolutely inviolable as it used. As the Germans say, *Eigentum verpflichtet* (ownership is accompanied by duties).

10 Judgment of the Supreme Court, 24 July, 1970 (*Minshū* 24–7–1116).

There are various limitations on ownership arising from different policy considerations. Particularly, the ownership of land and houses is subject to various restrictions. For instance, the Law on Agricultural Land provides that agricultural land may not be transferred or sold without the permission of a governor of the prefecture government (Art. 3).[11] The City Planning Law imposes restrictions on the use of land in order to ensure the 'healthy development and orderly maintenance' of cities (Art. 1).[12] Moreover, the Law on Acquisition of Land for Public Purposes allows private land to be expropriated with just compensation (Art. 1).[13]

Another important development concerning the ownership of land and houses is the gradual move towards strengthening protection afforded to tenants of land and houses. Laws such as the Law on the Lease of Land and Law on the Lease of Houses provide protection to tenants by limiting the rights of the owners.[14] For instance, a lease contract for a piece of land is automatically renewed unless the lessor objects to it without delay and with justifiable reasons, insofar as there is a building on it. The courts, too, have contributed to increasing the protection afforded to tenants by finding the claim of landlords to be an abuse of rights or by resorting to the doctrine of fairness and good faith as provided by the Civil Code (Art. 1).

Ownership of a thing can be acquired by different means; most commonly by agreement or by inheritance. Movables can be acquired by taking into possession things without an owner (Art. 239, para. 1) or a lost article (Art. 240). Also in cases of accession, consolidation and processing, ownership may be acquired (Arts. 242–246). For example, if a lessee of a house fixes a window in a rented house, the owner of the house acquires ownership of the window, because it is unreasonable to separate it when the lease ends. The rights of parties can be adjusted by the provisions concerning unjust enrichment (Arts. 703 and 704); the lessee is entitled to reimbursement.

Movables can also be acquired through immediate acquisition. The Civil Code provides that a person who has peacefully and openly started to possess a movable with an intention to exercise a right over it shall acquire that right immediately. The person must act in good faith and without negligence (Art. 192). A

---

11 Law No. 229, 1952.
12 Law 100, 1968.
13 Law No. 219, 1951.
14 These laws were replaced by a new comprehensive law in 1992.

typical example is where A purchases a watch from B, who had acted as the owner. A acquires ownership of the watch, provided he believes that B was the genuine owner, and is not negligent in believing so. Even when the genuine owner C demands recovery, A can assert his ownership interest against him. However, if the watch had been stolen or lost, the genuine owner has two years to claim recovery (Art. 193). In addition to ownership, rights which can be obtained by immediate acquisition include the right to pledge.

Immediate acquisition is designed to protect those who deal in movables, because unlike immovables, rights over movables are not manifested easily. Possession serves as the primary means of manifesting ownership, and therefore, those who believe that the possessor is the genuine holder of the right must be protected if they acquire the apparent interest. As a corollary, movables which can be registered, such as cars, ships, and airplanes cannot be acquired in this way, although some court judgments acknowledge immediate acquisition of unregistered cars and ships.[15] Similarly, immediate acquisition is not possible when the transaction is void or voidable for want of capacity to act, defects in declaration of will, or through acts of an unauthorised agent.

Ownership may be acquired through acquisitive prescription. Acquisitive and extinctive prescriptions are both provided for in the General Part of the Civil Code. As for acquisitive prescription, the general rule is that a person who, with an intention to own, has peacefully and openly possessed a thing which belongs to another person for 20 years acquires ownership. If a person has possessed a property peacefully and openly and this person had started possession in good faith and without negligence, he acquires ownership in ten years (Art. 162, paras. 1 and 2).

Good faith in the context of Article 162 means that the possessor was not aware that the immovable in question belonged to another person. In both cases, 'intention to own' on the part of the possessor is required. Thus, a lessee of a piece of land will not acquire ownership of the land, insofar as he possesses the property with the intention to use it as a lessee and not to own it.

Prescription is interrupted by acknowledgement on the part of the possessor, or by demand, attachment, provisional attachment or disposition by the genuine holder of the title (Art. 147). A reminder (extra-judicial) must be followed by legal process within six months in order to have an effect of interruption (Art. 153). The *raison d'être* of prescription has been an issue of

---

15 Judgment of the Supreme Court, 4 December, 1970 (*Minshū* 23–14–1987).

controversy among specialists of Civil Law. The prevailing view is
that acquisitive prescription is needed, first, in order to protect
those who deal with possessors of a property in the belief that the
present state reflects the genuine legal relations. The Register of
Immovables in Japan does not necessarily reflect the true state of
affairs; there is no guarantee that the registered owner is the
genuine holder of the title. Therefore, parallel with immediate
acquisition for movables, the Code provides for acquisitive
prescription of ten years for immovables, requiring good faith
and the absence of negligence. If, for instance, A has purchased a
piece of land from B, believing that B was the genuine owner, A
acquires ownership after ten years of peaceful and open
possession.

Twenty years' acquisitive prescription is needed, for instance,
in cases involving the boundary of two adjacent pieces of land. If
A mistakenly believes that a strip of his neighbour's land was his,
and has used it as his own property peacefully and openly for 20
years, A acquires the ownership of this strip of land. The reason
behind this is that after a long lapse of time, it is difficult for any
one out of possession to prove that he is a genuine holder.
Therefore, the fact that a party has continued to possess the
property openly and peacefully should serve as a basis for
establishing his ownership. It may be the case that there is a
genuine owner other than the possessor, but he should have
claimed his right in 20 years' time, and since he has not done so,
the possessor is protected.

Furthermore, when someone intends to purchase a piece of
land, naturally he should check the Register. Let us assume that
property is registered in A's name. This does not necessarily
mean that A is the genuine owner. A may have purchased the
property from C, who was not a genuine owner. Or A may have
abused his power as an agent and registered the property in his
name. Therefore, a prospective buyer B of the piece of land
cannot be certain whether A is the genuine owner or not.
However, if B checks the past record of the property and
ascertains that A has occupied the property peacefully and
openly with the intention to own for more than 20 years, B may
rest assured that A is the owner without inquiring into his title.[16]

Incidentally, a possessor may assert his own possession only, or
may choose to have the period of his predecessor's possession
added (Art. 187). Therefore, if A purchased a piece of land from
B, who had occupied it for 15 years, A may claim that he has

---

16 E. Hoshino, *Minpō Gairon* (*An Outline of Civil Law*), vol. 1, Tokyo 1971,
pp. 249–254.

acquired ownership by prescription in 5 years, if other conditions are met.

4. Joint ownership

Ownership can be held or shared by several persons. The Civil Code has general rules for joint ownership, and in addition, some special rules concerning the property of a cooperative and inherited property. On the other hand, scholarly opinion recognises indivisible joint ownership (*gōyū*), and collective joint ownership (*sōyū*) along with ownership in common. In indivisible ownership, the right of each owner to dispose of his share is limited. As for collective ownership, each party does not have a divisible share at all, and is merely entitled to use and profit from the property together with other owners. The property itself is administered not by the parties jointly, but by a representative selected according to custom or tradition. It is more accurate to say that it is an ownership by a collective.

Classification of joint ownership into these three types originally came from German theory. The German Civil Code categorises cooperative property, matrimonial property and jointly inherited property as *Eigentum zur gesamten Hand*. However, taking into account the fact that provisions of the Japanese Civil Code on cooperatives and inherited property are sufficiently clear, it is now being questioned whether this concept is really necessary in Japan. As for collective joint ownership, the customary right of commonage is the closest. The right of commonage is held by a village as a whole and members do not have a specific share. The property is administered in accordance with the communal rule. However, in recent years, commonage has gradually lost its original meaning and has become more individualistic.

In joint ownership as provided by the Civil Code, each owner has a share, and is entitled to make use of the whole property in proportion to his share (Art. 249). Each joint owner may dispose of his share, but is not entitled to change the state of property without the consent of other owners (Art. 251). The administration of the property is determined by a majority vote of the joint owners whose votes are related to the value of their shares (Art. 252). There are some special provisions concerning cooperatives and inheritance (Arts. 676, 906–911).

In recent years, joint ownership has gained significance in relation to housing. Due to the concentration of population in the cities, a large number of people now live in blocks of flats, which are often jointly owned by the inhabitants. However, provisions of joint ownership in the Civil Code were unable to cope effectively with these types of buildings. For instance, the Civil Code requires the consent of all joint owners when altering the state of the property (Art. 251). Therefore, if a block becomes old and needs refurbishment, or needs to be rebuilt, the unanimous support of the owners is necessary. This, however, is very difficult to obtain in a large block of flats where people with different interests live together.

The Law on Divided Ownership of Buildings was enacted in 1962 to deal with jointly-owned buildings. This Law was extensively amended in 1983 after the rapid growth in the number of blocks of flats and other buildings in urban areas.[17] It applies to buildings which are divided into separate flats, shops, or storage rooms owned by different persons (Art. 1). These buildings have individual as well as communal parts. The individual part is owned and used exclusively by the individual owner, while communal parts are jointly owned by all or some of them. The term 'divided ownership' is used in this Law to denote the rights of individual owners over the part exclusively owned by them (Art. 2, para. 1). Although the relationship involving such kind of buildings is basically joint ownership, provisions of this law have priority over the provisions of the Civil Code on joint ownership.

An owner may not do anything against the common interest of owners in using or administering the building, such as harmful acts against the preservation of the building (Art. 6, para. 1). In cases where such acts have taken place, or are likely to take place, other owners may take such action as is needed to prevent or terminate such acts, or remove the result of such acts (Art. 57, paras. 1 and 2). In extreme cases, other owners may request the court to auction the part owned by a particular owner or order him to surrender it (Arts. 58 and 59).

The decision-making body of the owners is the general meeting. Each owner has votes in proportion to the size of his share, unless it is provided otherwise by the charter (Art. 14, para. 1). Decision of the general meeting and the charter are binding on the owners as well as their successors in title (Art. 46, para. 1). The owners may also form a cooperative to administer the building and its site. The communal part of the building can be altered by a three-quarters majority of the vote, provided that the alteration does not involve excessively high costs (Art. 17, para. 1).

17 Law No. 69, 1962, as amended in 1983 and 1988.

5.   The right to use another person's property

There are four types of real rights which allow a person to make use of property – immovable – which does not belong to him. These are: superficies, emphyteusis, servitus praediorum, and commonage. Holders of superficies is entitled to use other persons' land for the purpose of owning a building or trees (Art. 265). Provisions of the new Law on Lease of Land and Houses are also applied to superficies. By the 1966 amendment to the Civil Code, superficies for owning installations underground or above the land has been introduced (Art. 269–2). In Emphyteusis, a farmer rents land and farms it or use it for raising livestocks (Art. 270). However, most farmers now own the land, and therefore, this right is no longer relevant.

Commonage denotes a traditional right of the collective (village) to use land. Provisions of ownership in common or servitude are applied to commonage, depending on the nature of the commonage in question. Also local custom is expected to supplement the Code (Arts. 263 and 294).

Today, the lease is the primary form of using other persons' property in built-up areas. A large proportion of housing in major cities is comprised of either rented flats or houses. Buildings are often built on rented property. Legally, such arrangements can be either lease or superficies, but owners prefer lease, because a holder of superficies has more rights against the owner than a lessee.

Rights based upon a lease are not real rights in terms of the Civil Code. Leases are provided for in Book Three of the Civil Code (Law of Obligations) as a typical contract. Lease in the Code covers not only the lease of immovables but also the lease of movables. It is not surprising that these provisions in the Civil Code gave insufficient protection for lessees of houses and land. Therefore, since the enactment of the Civil Code, in the wake of industrial action and social unrest, separate laws were adopted to supplement the Code and to strengthen protection of lessees of houses and land. These are the Law on the Protection of Buildings, the Law on the Lease of Land and the Law on the Lease of Houses.[18] Finally, a new law which integrates all three laws with some amendments was adopted in 1991.

The first problem with the provisions for lease in the Civil Code concerns the means of notice. The Code provides that if a lease of immovables is registered, the lessee may claim his right

---

18 Law No. 40, 1909, Law No. 49 and No. 50, 1921.

against persons who subsequently acquired real rights over the property (Art. 605). This differs from the arrangement in the German Code which entitles the lessee to claim his rights if he had taken possession of the property. In practice, registration of a lease is difficult, since the lessor has no obligation to cooperate with the lessee in registering the lease. Only real rights can serve as a basis for requiring cooperation and a lease is not one of them.

The Law on the Protection of Buildings had a provision which strengthened the lessee's position. It enabled a lessee or a holder of superficies who owns a registered building on the land to assert his rights against a new owner of the land without registration (Art. 1). It should be noted here that the ownership of the land and the building can belong to different persons. This provision is now incorporated in the new Law on the Lease of Land and Houses (Art. 10, para. 1). Further protection was provided by the Law on the Lease of Houses. If a lessee of a house was actually given possession of it, he is entitled to assert his right as a lessee against a new owner of the house without registration. This provision is also incorporated in the new Law (Art. 31, para. 1).

In reality, owners of houses on other persons' land often fail to register despite the arrangements set down by the Law on Protection of Buildings and, therefore, are not entitled to assert their interests against a new owner of the land. Still, the courts sometimes have provided protection to these lessees. In one case, Y owned an unregistered building on A's land by lease. X purchased this land at an extremely low price and attempted to evict Y. The Supreme Court ruled that X's act was an abuse of rights.[19]

A second problem is the term of lease. The Code sets the maximum term at 20 years (Art. 604). This was considered to be insufficient for a lease of immovables and therefore, the Law on the Lease of Land set the maximum at 60 years if solid buildings are to be built and 30 years for other buildings (Art. 2, para. 1). A related problem is the renewal of a lease contract. In this regard, the law imposed restrictions on the lessor's freedom to refuse renewal. The Law on the Lease of Land provided that when the lessee required renewal of lease, the lease contract was deemed to have been renewed under the same conditions as before, provided that the building owned by the lessee is still there. If the lessor had a justifiable reason to refuse renewal, such as the personal need to use the land, he was required to

19 Judgment of the Supreme Court, 3 September, 1968 (*Minshū* 22–9–1817).

object the renewal without delay (Art. 4, para. 1). If the lease was not renewed, the lessee was entitled to require the lessor to purchase the building at the current market price (Art. 4, para. 2). As for the lease of houses, a lessor was not allowed to refuse renewal or propose rescission of the lease agreement, unless he has a justifiable reason (Arts. 1–2).

Furthermore, the Law on the Lease of Land provided that if, after expiration of the lease, the lessee of the land continues using the land, the contract is deemed to have been renewed unless the lessor objects to it without delay. He is not entitled to object unless he has a justifiable reason (Art. 6). A similar arrangement was also available to lessees of houses (Art. 2).

These two Laws and the Law on the Protection of Buildings was replaced by the new Law on the Lease of Land and Houses in 1991, but these basic arrangements remain the same, except for the newly introduced fixed-term lease.

The courts have discussed the difficult issue as to whether reasons asserted by the lessors are justifiable or not. Despite the wording of the Law, the mere fact that the lessor needs the property for himself is not sufficient; various factors relating to the lessor as well as the lessee, such as their financial status, the possibility of finding an alternative house or land, whether the lessor offered compensation, etc., are relevant to the issue of justifiability.[20] In one case, the lessor intended to sell the house to gain income and asked the lessee to leave. He offered the lessor another house, and a sum of money to cover removal expenses. However, the house offered was not as desirable as the one in which the lessee was living. The lessee had a family of five including one who was ill. The Court did not accept in this case that the lessor had a justifiable reason to refuse renewal.[1]

In another case, the lessor offered three million yen (approximately 13 thousand pounds) or a similar amount determined by the court to the lessee to leave his house. He intended to demolish the house which was rather old and build a modern, taller building. The Supreme Court ruled that an offer of money does not in itself constitute a justifiable reason, but in this case, decided in favour of the lessor, on condition that he pay five million yen to the lessee.[2]

---

20 For lease of land, see K. Kamata and N. Yamada, '*Shakuchi-hō Yon-jyō Roku-jyō no Seitōka-riyū* (Justifiable Reasons in relation to Articles 4 & 6 of the Law on Land Lease)', *Jurist*, No. 828, 1985, pp. 222–229.
1 Judgment of the Supreme Court, 23 October, 1953 (*Minshū* 7–10–1114).
2 Judgment of the Supreme Court, 25 November, 1971 (*Minshū* 25–8–1343).

The new Law on the lease of Land and Houses lists the following factors which should be considered in such cases; 1) the reason why the lessor and lessee need the property; 2) circumstances and facts relevant to the agreement (e.g. the amount of rent); 3) the purpose and form of the use of property (e.g. whether it is for housing or business, whether the property is in good shape or not); and 4) financial offer made by the landlord (Arts. 6 and 28). There was a proposal by property developers to include the necessity of using the land in a more effective way (e.g. for the redevelopment of the area) as one of the justifications, but this was not accommodated in the final draft.

The new Law did not broaden the scope of justifiable grounds for refusal. It merely incorporated the existing court practice. On the other hand, the new Law, based on the view that an excessively strict control over the lessors' refusal to renew lease agreements may inhibit the effective use of land and supply of housing in urban areas, introduced a fixed term lease which is not renewable (Arts. 22 and 38, para. 1). For instance, if the owner of a house is unable to live there for a certain period because he has been transferred abroad by the company, but it is apparent that he would want to live there on return, he may enter into lease which is not renewable.

A third problem is the assignment of the lessee's interest. The Civil Code requires the consent of the lessor when the lessee wants to assign his rights or sublet the property to another person (Art. 612, para. 1). The Law on the Lease of Land introduced a significant change to this arrangement by the amendment of 1966, which applies typically to a case where a lessee of a piece of land owns a building on it and wants to sell it to a third party. The third party either needs to sublet the land from the lessee, or have the lessee's right assigned to him. The Civil Code requires the consent of the landlord to effect this. By the amendment to the Law on the Lease of Land, if the lessor refused to give permission in such a case even if the subletting or assignment of lessee's rights would be unlikely to cause him disadvantage, the court may give permission in lieu of the lessor (Article 9–2). Thus, the lessor's permission can be substituted by a decision of the court. The lessee may also choose to require that the lessor purchase the building (Art. 10). These provisions have been replaced by Art. 19 of the new Law.

Such a system of substitute consent does not exist for lease of houses. Here, it is thought that the identity of the lessee is more important than in the lease of land. The courts have made efforts to protect the lessee who sublets or transfers his interest to another person without the permission of the lessor. If the court finds the act of the lessee not to be in particularly bad faith, the lessor may not rescind the lease on the ground of unauthorised subletting or transfer.[3]

6. Real securities

Book Two of the Civil Code also includes provisions on real security. The four types of real security are the right of retention, preferential rights, pledge and hypothec. There are also some separate laws which provide for real security, for instance, the Law on Security over Companies and the Law on Hypothec over Factories.[4] There are also some types of real security which have developed out of practice and are upheld by the courts. These real securities, which are denoted as atypical real securities, include, *inter alia*, proprietary securities and retention of title clauses. Some of them have later found legal basis in the Civil Code and some other laws.

A possessor of another person's property may retain possession of that property until the latter performs an obligation owed to the possessor which concerns this property (Art. 295). The right of retention arises only in cases where the creditor already has possession of the property. Unlike a possessory lien, the object is not limited to movables. The obligation which is secured by the right of retention must have arisen in relation to the retained property. For instance, if A repaired B's watch, A may retain it until B pays for the repair. However, A may not retain B's watch to secure B's payment for a camera which B had purchased. The relation between the obligation and the property retained is not required in the Commercial Code. Merchants are entitled to retain property received in a commercial transaction between them in order to secure payment of any debt arising from such transactions (Art. 521).

In certain cases provided by the Civil Code or other laws, a creditor is granted a preferential right to secure payment, either from a specified property or the assets of the debtor in general, in preference to other creditors. Such preferential rights arise automatically when certain conditions are met. A person who has a preferential right may demand that the property be auctioned and have his right arising from the obligational relationship satisfied from the proceeds of the auction. For example, salaries

---

3 Judgment of the Supreme Court, 25 September, 1953 (*Minshū* 7–9–979).
4 Law No. 106, 1958 and Law No. 54, 1905.

of employees are secured by a preferential right over the company's entire assets. Therefore, when the company goes bankrupt and its assets are being auctioned, employees may exercise a preferential right to six months' salary payable out of the proceeds (Art. 306).

In contrast to preferential rights and the right of retention, a pledge and hypothec are created by agreement of the parties. A pledgee is entitled to hold possession of the property which has been pledged to him, and in case of the pledgor's insolvency, the pledgee may have the property auctioned (Art. 342). An actual transfer of possession to the pledgee is needed to create pledge (Art. 344). The object of a pledge is not limited to movables; immovables, securities and intellectual property rights can be pledged (Arts. 356 and 362).

Although pledges over immovables are rarely used today, pledges over movables and property rights are widely used to provide credit to individuals, and especially in the case of the latter, to small and medium sized companies.

A pledgee is entitled to demand auction of the property, but on the other hand, he is prohibited from acquiring ownership over the property without having had recourse to the formal enforcement procedure (Art. 349). This is to prevent the pledgee from obtaining an excessive profit. However, this restriction is removed in the Commercial Code (Art. 515). Further, the activities of pawn shops, which are regulated by a separate law, are not covered by this provision.

Whereas in pledge, the pledgee has possession of the property, in hypothec, possession of the property is not transferred to the obligee. The title as well as possession of the property remain with the person who hypothecated the property (Art. 369). Unlike mortgage, the title is not transferred to the creditor. Therefore, the hypothecary debtor may borrow money and, at the same time, continue using the property. Another difference with mortgage is that hypothecary creditor may not repossess the collateral without recourse to court.

The Code limits the object of hypothec to ownership of immovables and superficies and emphyteusis over land. This is because there is no way to give notice of the existence of a hypothec on movables, and therefore, if a hypothec over movables was allowed, the interests of those who purchase movables could be harmed. However, since the enactment of the Civil Code, the necessity of hypothec over certain categories of movables, or a group of movables and immovables, have increased. This led to the enactment of laws such as the Law on Hypothec over Automobiles, the Law on Hypothec over

Factories,[5] and the law on Securities over Companies. Corporate bonds can be secured by the entire assets of the company.[6]

A creditor who has a hypothec over the property will receive payment from the proceeds of an auction in preference to other creditors should the debtor becomes insolvent. The existence of a hypothec is made known by way of registration and without registration, the creditor who has a hypothec cannot assert his rights against other creditors with a hypothec or anyone who has purchased the property. Situations where several hypothecs exist over one property are not rare. In such cases, the priority of hypothecs is decided in accordance with the order of registration, i.e. a creditor who registered earlier has priority over others. For example, A borrows five million yen from B and three million yen from C. A hypothecates his property worth six million yen to B and C. B registers the hypothec before C. In case of insolvency, if the proceeds of an auction were six million yen, B takes five million and C takes the rest, one million. It should be noted that when a hypothec which has priority is extinguished, the hypothec of the next rank is upgraded. If A had repaid debt to B, B's hypothec extinguishes and C obtains priority. C will receive full repayment from the proceeds.

In Japan, it is common for land and the buildings attached to land to be treated as different things. Hypothec over land does not cover buildings on it, nor does hypothec over a building have effect over the land. This causes a problem when either the land or the building is hypothecated and then, through an auction, sold to a third party. For instance, A owns a house on his land. A hypothecates the house to B, but fails to repay the debt. The house is auctioned, and C purchases it. However, C does not have a right to use A's land without a special arrangement.

In order to avoid such a situation, the Code provides for a statutory superficies, which is unique to Japanese Law. When a piece of land or a building attached to it, both of which belong to the same person, is hypothecated and then purchased by a third person in an auction, a statutory superficies is deemed to have been created for the building (Art. 388). Therefore, in the above-mentioned example, C is deemed to have a superficies over the land. The rent is determined by the court if the parties fail to reach agreement.

Real rights to use immovables, which were registered after a hypothec, will extinguish once the hypothec is enforced. However, there is an exception. Short term leases, i.e. a lease of

---

5 Laws No. 187, 1951, No. 54, 1895, No. 106, 1958.
6 Law No. 52, 1905.

less than five years for land and three years for buildings, are not extinguished by auction, even though registered after the hypothec (Art. 395). For example, if B concludes a lease contract with the landlord A in respect to a piece of land which has already been hypothecated, B is entitled to assert his lease against C, who acquires this land by auction. This system was intended to protect the right to use immovables. However, in practice, this is abused by the owner of the immovable in order to obstruct the obligor in the exercise of his rights, and is therefore criticised.

Another controversy regarding hypothec is the right of a third party who obtained ownership, superficies, or emphyteusis over a hypothecated property to discharge the hypothec. These persons are entitled to offer the hypothecary creditor a sufficient amount of money to discharge the hypothec. If the hypothecary creditor considers this amount to be insufficient, he may demand auction within a month. However, the creditor must purchase the property himself, unless the property is sold at auction at a price more than 10% higher than the price offered by the third party (Arts. 378–387).

This right of a person who acquired the hypothecated property to discharge the hypothec comes from French law. In France, it is designed to protect those who have purchased property and later found an unregistered hypothec on it. However, in Japan, this institution has much broader application. By this institution, hypothecary creditors are forced to initiate the auction procedure at a time which is not always desirable for the creditor or else accept a relatively low price. This is often unfair to secured creditors, and therefore its abolition is being proposed. As a result, some of the laws providing for specific hypothecs no longer incorporate this system of discharge.[7]

A special kind of hypothec which had developed in practice and was acknowledged by the courts in the pre-War period was incorporated into the Civil Code in 1971. This is called the floating hypothec or base hypothec (*ne-teitō*), which secures unspecified obligations within a fixed limit. In ordinary hypothec, when the obligation is fulfilled, the hypothec is extinguished, while in floating hypothec, it does not extinguish, but covers future obligations whenever they arise. It is designed primarily to secure payments relating to a long-term supply contract between merchants and also current account agreements between a bank and a customer, both within a fixed limit.

---

7 E. Hoshino, *Minpō Gairon (An Outline of Civil Law)*, vol. 2, Tokyo 1976, p. 287.

7. Atypical real security rights

The Civil Code provides for only the above four real securities. However, some other types of securities denoted as atypical real securities have developed in practice. A special law was adopted in 1978 for security rights by way of provisional registration, but others remain without such a statutory basis.[8]

These atypical securities have developed in order to fill the gaps in the Civil Code which were thought to be impractical for commercial transactions. A major shortcoming of the Code is that it does not provide for means of security on movables, allowing its owner/debtor to use the property until he repays the debt. Hypothec on movables is not acknowledged by the Code while pledge is possible, but in pledge, the owner is deprived of the possession of the collateral. Atypical security rights are designed to secure loan and at the same time, allow the debtor to continue using the property.

Another shortcoming of real security rights is the cumbersome and often costly enforcement procedure provided in the Civil Code. By using atypical securities, creditors may avoid the formal enforcement procedure, and secure payment by selling the object or acquiring it himself. Furthermore, if there are many creditors, atypical security rights may provide a better and easier way of ensuring priority of payment ahead of others.

On the other hand, atypical security rights have disadvantages in that they often unfairly benefit the creditor at the expense of debtors and other persons involved. Therefore, the courts have tried to avoid such unfair results by developing a body of case law.

The first type of atypical security rights involves the sale of the property to the creditor. By this arrangement, the parties do not intend to effect an out-and-out sale, although by appearance, there is only a contract of sale. The debtor sells a property to the creditor, who promises to let the debtor repurchase the property once he repays the debt (option to repurchase). Alternatively, the creditor may also agree to redemption, i.e. if the debtor repays the debt, the debtor is entitled to rescind the original sales contract and have the property returned.

The second type of atypical security rights is security by of conditional assignment of ownership. This is combined with a loan agreement. The assignment of ownership becomes final, when the debtor becomes insolvent. As a variation, the parties may agree to substitute performance. Thus, if the debtor fails to

8 Law No. 78, 1978.

repay the debt, he is obliged to assign the ownership of the collateral to the creditor.[9]

The option for repurchase and substitute performance of immovables can be registered as provisionary. Securing a debt by way of provisionary registration developed out of practice, and was embodied in law by the Law on Contracts of Security by Provisional Registration.[10]

Technically, some atypical security rights seemingly contradict provisions of the Civil Code. For instance, security by way of assigning ownership over a movable is against the provision which prohibits the pledgee from agreeing in advance to acquire ownership of the collateral (Art. 349). Furthermore, only those real rights which have a basis in the Code or other laws are acknowledged (Art. 175). However, the courts felt it desirable to overcome these limitations and give legal substance to atypical security rights.

Atypical securities may cause problems when either of the parties disposes of property without the knowledge of the other. For example, A borrows money from B and as a security, assigns ownership of a piano to B. By taking the opportunity of still being in possession of the piano, A may sell it to C. On the other hand, B may abuse his position as the holder of title, and sell the piano to D. In both cases, the third party, C and D, will acquire ownership by immediate acquisition (Art. 192). In the second case, D may not acquire, since he does not have possession of the piano.

If the property in question is not a piano but an immovable, for instance, a house, C, who purchased it from the original owner A may assert his rights against B, provided that he has registered his ownership. This is a typical case where Article 177 of the Civil Code is applied. If C purchased the property from B, who abused his position, A, the original owner may not claim his right against C. The court based this conclusion on the concept of collusion of declaration of will (sham transaction) between A and B. After all, A and B created an appearance that B was the genuine owner, and therefore, A may not claim his rights against C, provided that C was a *bona fide* third party.[11]

Previously, a creditor whose right was secured by an atypical real security right was entitled to receive full ownership of the property, regardless of its value. Hence, the creditor could

---

9 For details, see R. Suzuki, *Bukken-hō Kōgi* (*Lectures on Property Law*), Tokyo 1985, pp. 256–285.
10 Law No. 78, 1978.
11 Judgment of the Supreme Tribunal, 25 March, 1921 (*Minrokū* 660).

acquire ownership of a property with a much higher value than that of the loan. However, this was thought to be unfair by the courts. It is now established case law that the difference between the amount of the secured loan and the price of the property should be returned to the debtor.[12]

In addition to the above-mentioned atypical securities, in order to secure payment in sales of goods by installments (hire purchase in English Law) retention of ownership is commonly used.

---

12 For instance, see the judgment of the Supreme Court, 25 March, 1971 (*Minshū* 25–2–208).

9 The law of obligations

1. General rules of the Law of Obligations

1) An overview

The Law of Obligations deals primarily with the effects and enforcement of obligations. Obligations arise not only from contracts but also from non-contractual matters such as tort or management of affairs without mandate. Book Three of the Civil Code, which covers the law of obligation, begins with a chapter containing general rules applicable to all kinds of obligations. It is followed by a chapter on contracts. Then come chapters on management of affairs without mandate, unjust enrichment and tort. For the purpose of this book, tort will be discussed in a separate chapter. It should be noted that the rules concerning declaration of will set out in the General Part of the Code are also applicable to contracts.

Book Three starts with a voluminous chapter on the General Rules of the Law of Obligations. It contains provisions on the effects of obligations, statutory interest rates, non-performance, damages, obligations with multiple parties, as well as assignment and extinction of obligations. On the other hand, issues such as capacity to act, agency, prescription, public policy, and defective declaration of will, are dealt with in the General Part of the Civil Code.

The Code provides that matters which cannot be valued in terms of money can still be a subject matter of obligation (Art. 399). There are several classifications of obligations; it can be either money debt or non-money debt. It can be an obligation to do something (*obligation de faire*), or to give something (*obligation de donner*). Some obligations have a specified thing as an object, while other obligations have a non-specified generic thing as an object. An obligation to sell a Ming porcelain vase is an example of the former, and an obligation to sell a case of beer is an example of the latter. It is the duty of the obligor to perform the obligation in accordance with the terms of the obligation and in good faith (Art. 1, para. 2). Unlike the German BGB, the provision on good faith and fair is found at the beginning of the Code, instead of the Law on Obligations. This principle is considered to be applicable throughout the entire Code. If the object of the obligation is to give a specified thing, the standard of care required of the obligor is that of a good manager (Art. 400).

2) Irregularity of performance

Irregularities may occur in the performance of an obligation. These are delayed performance, defective performance and impossibility of performance.

1. Delayed performance

The Code provides that if the obligation was with a fixed time of performance, the obligor will be in delay after the obligation becomes due. If there is no fixed time for performance, the obligor is in delay after the obligee required performance (Art. 412). Performance of some obligations requires the cooperation of the obligee. If the obligor tenders performance and the obligee fails to accept it, the obligee is in delay (Art. 413). However, in principle, the obligor is not entitled to rescind the contract in such circumstances.[1] If there is a justifiable reason for the delay, for instance, in a sales contract where goods were to be delivered against payment and the buyer failed to tender payment, the obligor (seller) is not in delay.

In cases of delay, the obligee may apply to the court for enforcement, execute real security rights if the obligation is secured. If the obligation emerged from a contract, the obligee is entitled to rescind the contract and claim damages. Existence of fault on the part of the obligor is a prerequisite to the claim for damages. In the case of delay in payment of a monetary debt, the obligor is not required to prove loss and the obligee is not entitled to claim *force majeure* (Art. 419, para. 2). The obligor has to pay interest for the delay (Art. 419, para. 1).

2. Impossibility of performance

There are instances where the performance of obligation becomes impossible after it came into effect. Obligations which

---

1 Judgment of the Supreme Court, 3 December, 1965 (*Minshū* 19-9-2090).

were already impossible to perform at the time they came into effect are null and void. This is not a matter of impossibility of performance. An example is a contract concluded after the destruction or loss of the subject matter, the parties being unaware of such circumstances. However, the obligor may be held liable for damages in such cases if he was at fault in not knowing of the loss of the subject matter.

In one case, Y, who was leasing a property from A, assigned the lease to X. However, A did not give consent to the assignment. This was considered to be impossibility of performance.[2] A textbook example of impossibility of performance is a sales contract of a specific house which was destroyed by fire after the conclusion of the contract. Here, not only the obligation to give possession, but also the obligation to transfer ownership is considered to be impossible to perform.

Whether or not an obligation is impossible to perform is decided by common sense. Although performance may be physically possible, there are cases where the obligation is practically impossible to perform.[3]

In cases of impossibility of performance, the obligor is liable for damages, but only when he was at fault (Art. 415). This rule, however, does not apply if, at the time when the obligation became impossible to perform, the obligor was already in delay. In such cases, the obligor is liable, even though he was not at fault for the impossibility of performance itself. The burden of proof lies with the obligor.

It is generally acknowledged that *force majeure* releases both parties from their obligations, except in cases of monetary obligation. Naturally, non-existence of *force majeure* does not mean that either party was at fault. Even when the cause of non-performance is not insurmountable, still, the obligor may be found to be not at fault.

If the obligation had arisen from a contract, the obligee is entitled to rescind the contract on the ground of impossibility of performance, but this is not a precondition of claiming damages (Art. 543). Damages can be claimed without rescinding the contract, provided that the obligor was at fault.

3.   Defective performance

Obligors are liable for the failure to perform the obligation in accordance with its purport and meaning (Art. 415). In cases of

2 Judgment of the Supreme Court, 17 September, 1959 (*Minshū* 13–11–1412).
3 Judgment of the Supreme Court, 21 April, 1960 (*Minshū* 14–6–930).

defective performance, the obligation is performed, but not in an appropriate way. An example is a delivery of defective goods. Cases where performance of obligation has caused loss to the obligee also fall within this category. An example of the latter case is a situation where the obligor delivered poultry infected with disease, which later spread to the obligee's farm. German theory categorises such improper performances as positive breach of obligation (*positive Vertragsverleztung*). As for defective goods, there are other provisions of the Civil Code in the part on contracts, which can be concurrently applied together with this provision.

Defective performance is not considered as a valid performance. The obligee is entitled to refuse acceptance of such a performance and claim damages. If a proper performance can be expected, the obligee may demand such performance within a reasonable period. Only when the obligor fails to make such performance, is the obligee entitled to claim damages. If a proper performance is impossible or impractical, the obligee may claim damages immediately. In order to claim damages, fault on the part of the obligor is a prerequisite.

It should be noted that, although the Code does not explicitly require fault on the part of the obligor for the delay in performance and improper performance, the courts have acknowledged that fault is a prerequisite of establishing the obligor's liability for damages.[4]

4. Breach of duty to care for safety (*obligation de securité*)

Since the mid–1970s, another type of non-performance of obligation emerged in a series of judgments of the Supreme Court. In one case, a member of the Self Defence Force was killed in a car accident in a base. His family brought the case to court and claimed damages from the State four years after the accident. A claim for damages based on tort had already become barred by prescription, whereas a claim on the basis of general rules of obligation was still possible. The Supreme Court ruled that the employer had an obligation on the basis of good faith and fair dealing to take such steps as necessary in order to protect the life and health of employees, and that this applied to the State as well.[5]

In another case, a security officer was killed on duty. The Supreme Court ruled that the employer was liable, since he failed

---

4 Judgment of the Supreme Tribunal, 22 November, 1922 (*Minrōkū* 27–1978).
5 Judgment of the Supreme Court, 25 February, 1975 (*Minshū* 29–2–143).

to take sufficient measures to protect the employee. [6] This 'duty to care for safety' is considered to be one of the effects of obligations and is based upon the same provision which covers impossibility and defective performance (Art. 415). This concept was devised to deal with cases where remedy by tort is not available or is inappropriate. It was influenced by developments in Germany (BGB Art. 618) and France. It has developed as a doctrine in employment contracts, but it is not necessarily limited to these kind of contracts.

3)   Refusal to accept a performance

There may be cases where the obligee unreasonably refuses to accept performance, or it becomes impossible for him to do so. The Code provides that the obligee is in delay once he refuses acceptance or it became impossible for him to accept performance; however, it does not specify the effect of such delay (Art. 413). At least, the obligor will not be in delay in such instances.

If the obligee refuses to accept performance tendered by the obligor, the latter may deposit the subject matter of obligation at the public depository at the local legal bureau. Money and securities are depositable.

If the obligation arises from a contract, whether or not the obligor is entitled to rescind the contract, because of delay or refusal of acceptance by the obligee and claim damages, has been a focus of discussion. Some specialists of Civil Law are of the view that it is a duty of the obligee to accept performance, and his failure to do so will entail the same result as non-performance of obligation on the part of the obligor.

The courts have generally denied such rights to the obligor. However, there was a case where X, a mining company, had concluded a continual supply contract with a company Y for a fixed period. After several deliveries and payments, Y refused to accept further delivery because of the fluctuations in the market. The Supreme Court ruled that in such a contract, Y is obliged to accept the delivery, and by his failure to do so X was entitled to rescind the contract and claim damages. The Court based this judgment on the doctrine of fairness and good faith. [7]

There are instances where the obligor performs his obligation through another person. Where it is a common practice to employ such a person, or it was allowed by the obligee, the obligor is liable for the acts of this person to the same extent as

---

6 Judgment of the Supreme Court, 10 April, 1984 (*Minshū* 38–6–557).
7 Judgment of the Supreme Court, 16 December, 1971 (*Minshū* 25–9–1472).

he would be liable for his own acts. If, however, by law or contract, the obligor was required to perform the obligation himself, but nevertheless, he employed another person to perform it, the obligor is liable for any act of this person.

4) Enforcement of an obligation

When the obligor does not perform his obligation voluntarily, the obligee may go to the court for enforcement. The law which provides for the enforcement procedures is the Law on Civil Enforcement.[8] Method of enforcement varies, depending on the nature of the obligation. If the obligation in question is monetary, the assets (land, building, movables, ships, cars, construction machinery as well as creditory rights and other property rights) of the obligor may be attached and auctioned by the court. The obligee receives payment from the proceeds. If the obligation is to *give* movables to another person, the bailiff takes possession of the object and hands it over to the obligee. If the property in question is an immovable, the bailiff relieves the property from the possession of the obligor and gives it to the obligee.

The method of enforcing an obligation *to do* something differs from that of an obligation to *give* something. It is not possible directly to compel the obligor to perform an obligation to do something. The Civil Code provides that in such cases, the obligee may apply to court for substitute performance, i.e. have a third party perform the obligation at the expense of the obligor (Art. 414). If the obligation is to perform a juristic act, it can be substituted by a decision of the court (Art. 173, Law on Civil Enforcement). If substitute performance is not possible, indirect enforcement is available. In cases of such indirect enforcement, the court orders the obligor to pay a certain amount of money to the obligee until the former performs the obligation. Detention of the obligor in cases of failure to pay like the system in Germany does not exist.

An obligation *not to do* something is also enforced by indirect enforcement (Art. 172, para. 1, Law on Civil Enforcement). If the result of non-fulfillment of such an obligation remains, for instance, when a person has built a house unlawfully on another person's property, the latter may apply for substitute enforcement to remove the house.

The methods of enforcement have been a focus of discussion in two kinds of cases. One is the enforceability of an obligation to

8 Law No. 4, 1979.

transfer custody of a child. There is a controversy as to the problem of whether a bailiff may take possession of the child and hand it over to the person with parental authority, or whether indirect enforcement should be used.

Another problem is the publication of apology in libel cases. The Civil Code has a special provision which empowers the court to order the tortfeasor to take necessary measures to restore the honour of the aggrieved party in cases of libel (Art. 723). The courts often order the tortfeasor to publish an apology in major newspapers. If he refuses to do this voluntarily, the court allows substitute enforcement. There was a case where the tortfeasor argued that substitute enforcement in such a case was against the Constitution which guarantees freedom of conscience. The Supreme Court rejected this argument.[9]

5)   Effects of irregularities of performance

The obligee is entitled to damages in cases of irregularities of performance (delay, impossibility of performance, defective performance) on the part of the obligor. Fault is a prerequisite except in cases of money debts. Damages are calculated on a monetary basis unless the parties choose otherwise (Art. 417).

The Civil Code has a special provision concerning the scope of damages (Art. 416):

> The object of claim for damages is the recovery of loss which would normally arise from non-performance of obligation.
> Damages for loss which has arisen from special circumstances may also be claimed, provided that the parties had forseen, or should have foreseen, such circumstances.

It is generally accepted that non-performance in this context covers all kinds of irregularities in performance, including impossibility and defective performance. Normal loss is recoverable in principle, while loss arising from special circumstances is recoverable only when it was foreseen or should have been foreseen by the obligor. The burden of proof concerning foreseeability lies with the obligee.

The first problem here is what 'normal loss' encompasses. Whether the loss is normal, or has arisen from special circumstances is often difficult to determine. The law protects the expectation and reliance of the obligee, but various factors such as whether the party to the transaction was a merchant or not,

---

9 Judgment of the Supreme Court, 4 July, 1956 (*Minshū* 10–7–785).

the type and nature of the transaction, etc. have to be taken into account.[10]

When, due to the default of the seller, the buyer has to purchase similar merchandise at a higher price, the difference in price as well as the cost of finding an alternative source of supply are normal loss.[11] If the buyer had expected to resell the merchandise for a profit, this will also be normal loss. In one case, a contract of sale was rescinded by the buyer because of the default on the part of the seller. The price of the merchandise was three times as high as the contracted price when the contract was rescinded. The court found that the loss should be calculated on the basis of this higher price, since the increase in the price was the result of inflation which already existed at the time the contract was concluded. Therefore, the difference between the contract price and the price at the time of rescission by the buyer was found to be a normal loss.[12]

On the other hand, the fact that the buyer had promised to resell the goods to a third party at a price three times as high as the buying price was found to be 'special circumstances' and unless it was foreseen by the obligor (seller), the latter was not liable.[13]

Previously, it was generally accepted that this provision required 'adequate causation' between irregularities of performance and the loss. This interpretation demonstrates the strong inclination towards German law in Japan. In fact, recent studies showed that this provision in fact did not come from Germany; actually it came from English law, which in turn, was influenced by French law. The part dealing with loss arising from special circumstances came from the celebrated English case of *Hadley v Baxendale*.[14] However, specialists of Civil Law in Japan had long maintained that this provision had come from German law and interpreted it in a way similar to that of German law.

The difference between German law on one hand and French and English law on the other is that the former presupposes full compensation as a principle – compensation for all loss which is caused by irregularities of performance, while the latter limits the scope of damages. In order to mitigate the requirement of full

---

10 E. Hoshino, *Minpō Gairon* (*An outline of Civil Law*), vol. III (Law of Obligations), Tokyo 1978, pp. 72–73.
11 Judgment of the Supreme Court, 28 April, 1961 (*Minshū* 15–4–1105).
12 Judgment of the Supreme Court, 18 December, 1953 (*Minshū* 7–12–1446).
13 Judgment of the Supreme Tribunal, 5 April, 1929 (*Minshū* 373).
14 [1843–60] All ER Rep 461. See Y. Hirai, *Songaibaishō-hō no Riron* (*The Theory of the Law on Compensation*), Tokyo 1971. G. H. Treitel, *An Outline of the Law of Contract*, London 1984, pp. 321–324.

compensation, the Germans had to introduce the concept of 'adequate causation'. However, there was almost no use for such a concept in Japanese law, since the scope of damages was already limited in French and English law.

Another problem related to this provision is the reasonableness of applying this provision to tort cases. Since tort is part of the Law of Obligations and regarded as one of the causes from which obligations arise, this provision was intended to be applicable also to tort. The Supreme Court has ruled once that this provision is applicable with modifications to tort cases.[15] Recently, there are views which cast doubt on the applicability of this provision to tort cases. It is natural to require foreseeability of the consequences of the tortious act as one of the constituent elements of tort; fault is a prerequisite to tort liability. However, it is theoretically questionable to determine *the scope* of compensatable loss on the basis of foreseeability. Furthermore, by requiring foreseeability of special circumstances, it is argued that the scope of loss may be excessively narrowed.

In the case of monetary debt, there is no room for impossibility of performance. The Code provides that damages for delay of money debt should be calculated on the basis of statutory interest rate of 5% (Art. 404). For obligations arising from commercial transactions, the rate is 6% (The Commercial Code, Art. 514). The parties may agree to a different interest rate, but this rate should not exceed the rate provided by the Law on the Limitation of Interest Rates.[16]

In determining the amount of damages, the fault on the part of the obligee which contributed to the loss is also taken into account by the court (Art. 418).

6)   Assignment

Rights arising from obligational relations can be assigned to a third party unless the nature of the relation does not allow it (Art. 466). Assignment can be restricted between the parties, but this cannot be claimed against a *bona fide* third party. Assignment of an ordinary debt i.e. where the obligor is specified (which are contrasted to securities) can be effected between the assignor and the assignee. However, it cannot be claimed against the obligor or any other third party unless the assignor notifies

---

15 Judgment of the Supreme Court, 7 June, 1973 (*Minshū* 27–6–681). See also Judgment of the Supreme Tribunal, 22 May, 1926 (*Minshū* 5–386 ; known as Fukimaru case).
16 Law No. 100, 1954.

the obligor or the obligor gives consent to the assignment (Art. 467, para. 1). Consent in this context means that the obligor recognises the assignment. Notification or consent has to be made by a document with fixed date such as a notarised document or registered and certified mail.

Assignment of a securitised obligation such as promissory notes, bills of exchange, cheques, as well as bearer claims cannot be claimed against the obligor and other third parties unless the assignor endorses the assignment in writing on the security and hands it to the assignee (Art. 469). Although there is no explicit provision in the Code, an obligor may assign his obligation to a third party under certain conditions (assumption of debt). Assumption of debt is commonly used in cases where a person intends to purchase real property which is already hypothecated. If the obligor, obligee and the third party all agree, then the debt can be assumed by the third party. If the obligor and the third party agree that the latter perform the obligation in lieu of the obligor, unless the obligee agrees, the obligor is still required to perform obligation. However, if the obligee demands performance of this third party, the latter must perform the obligation. If the obligee agrees to the assumption of debt, whether the original obligor is totally exempted from performance or he is still liable with the third party has to be determined.

2. The rights of the obligee to secure the assets of the obligor

In cases of non-performance of obligations, especially monetary obligations, obligees may want to attach the assets of the obligor. It is in the interest of the obligee to ensure that the assets of the obligor do not decrease below the amount owed and thus endanger the performance of an obligation. The Civil Code provides two devices to safeguard the obligee's expectation: the right of subrogation (*action subrogatoire*) and the right to rescind the act of the obligor which is against obligee's interest (*action révocatoire*). The German Law provides for only the latter (*Gläubigeranfechtungsrecht*), while the French Code provides for both devices.

An obligee may exercise a right which belongs to the obligor in order to ensure the performance of a monetary obligation by the latter (Art. 423, para. 1). For example, A lent one million yen to B and the repayment is due. B, in turn, had lent half a million yen to C some years ago, but failed to remind C, since he was aware that once he receives the money from C, he has to repay it to A. B does not have any other assets. In such a case, A may exercise B's right against C, and thus prevent prescription.

This right of substitute exercise of rights was designed to ensure performance of monetary obligations. It was supposed to be a stage preceding civil enforcement, but today, by substitution, the same effect as civil attachment can be achieved in some cases. In the above example, obligee A has two alternatives. First, he may sue B and obtain an enforcement judgment against B, attach B's right against C and then demand payment from C. Second, he may simply substitute B and claim payment directly from C. Initially, C was required to repay the debt to B, not A. However, by the judgment of the Supreme Court in the 1930s, obligees were allowed to claim performance directly from the third party (in this example, C).[17]

In order to justify such substitution, it is required that the obligor does not have sufficient assets to repay the debt. However, the courts have gradually relaxed this requirement and broadened the applicability of this provision. Firstly, this right is now used in order to secure transfer of a specific property. For instance, A purchases a house from B, who had originally purchased it from C. However, B has failed so far to register his ownership and therefore, A is also unable to register the property in his name. In such a case, A may exercise B's right against C to demand him to cooperate in registering the property. In order to make things simpler, A is actually allowed to demand directly that C cooperate in registering the house in A's name.[18]

Secondly, in cases of lease of land or houses, the status of the lessee is fairly weak, since the lessee's interest is not a right *in rem*, but a right *in personam*. However, in some cases, lessees are entitled to exercise those rights which belong to the lessor-owner. For example, A owns a house on a piece of land owned by B on a lease contract. C is obstructing the use of this land, but B does not take necessary measures to terminate this, although he is entitled to do so on the basis of his ownership. On the other hand, A, as a lessee is not entitled to take action directly against C. Therefore, the court has acknowledged that B, as a lessor, has obligations against A to enable him to use the property, and therefore, A may exercise B's right to terminate obstruction against C. Whether B has sufficient assets to cover the debt to A is irrelevant in both cases.[19]

---

17 Judgment of the Supreme Court, 12 March, 1935 (*Minshū* 14–482).
18 Judgment of the Supreme Tribunal, 6 July, 1910 (*Minroku* 16–537).
19 Judgment of the Supreme Tribunal, 16 December, 1929 (*Minshū* 8–12–944).

Another device designed to safeguard the assets of the obligor for the benefit of the obligee(s) is the latter's right to rescind an act of the obligor which is harmful to the interests of the obligee(s). When an obligor knowingly effects such a juristic act, the latter may request the court to rescind this act (Art. 424, para. 1). Unlike the right to substitution, the obligee's right has to be exercised through the court. For example, X lends one million yen to Y. Y does not want to repay the debt, so he gives away his only property – a house, to Z. In such a case, X may apply to the court to rescind the transaction between Y and Z.

It should be added that once bankruptcy proceedings have started, obligees are entitled to deny the validity of the acts of the obligor performed after his financial status has become critical. This right of disclaimer is provided in the Law of Bankruptcy.[20] The right of subrogation is often resorted to when several obligees (creditors) fight for priority. In the above example, Z and X are both an obligee against Y, but they do not have collaterals. Therefore, if Z secures repayment in one way or another from Y, X will try to anull the transaction by resorting to the right of subrogation.

The right to subrogation is designed to safeguard the interests of 'all obligees' by preventing a decrease in the obligor's assets below the value of the debt (Art. 425). Unlike the right of substitution, the obligation does not have to be due when the obligee exercises his right. Acts which can be rescinded are those which harm the interests of the obligee and make full performance of an obligation impossible. A sale of property at an unreasonably low price or giving away of property are examples. As a rule, if the remaining assets are sufficient to perform the obligation, such acts cannot be rescinded. The courts have even found a sale of a real property at a reasonable price to be harmful, since cash is more easily spent, and therefore, the likeliness of the decrease in the assets is more acute, although the nominal amount of the assets has not changed.[1]

The act of the obligor which harms the interests of the obligee may involve a third party. If invalidation of such an act is without limitation, it may affect the interests of those who unwittingly entered into a transaction with the obligor. Therefore, the Code provides that the obligee may not exercise this right of rescission when the beneficiary of the obligor's act was not aware at the time of transaction that the act was harmful to the obligee (Art. 424, para. 1). Thus, if an obligor Y sold his only property to Z at

---

20 Law No. 71, 1922.
1 Judgment of the Supreme Tribunal, 5 February, 1906 (*Minroku* 12–136).

a low price, obligee X may not revoke the sales contract between Y and Z insofar as Y had not known that the sale was harmful to the interests of Z. The burden of proof lies with the beneficiary Z. The same applies where there is a *bona fide* purchaser from Z.

3.   Obligations with multiple parties

1)   Divisible and indivisible obligations

The General Part of the Law of Obligations also includes provisions concerning obligations involving several obligees or obligors. There are three different kinds of obligations with several obligees or obligors: divisible obligations, indivisible obligations, and joint and several obligations. In cases where there are several obligees or obligors, the obligation is considered to be divisible in equal proportions unless the parties have agreed otherwise (Art. 427). Thus, in cases where the obligation is divisible, e.g. when Y and Z have an obligation of 100,000 yen to X, Y and Z are liable for 50,000 yen each if there is no other agreement. This presumption of divisible obligation may be against the expectation of the obligee, since if Y pays 50,000 yen, Y is discharged regardless of whether Z has repaid his debt. Therefore, scholarly opinions attempt to narrow the application of this presumption. For instance, where the joint financial status of obligors has been taken into account when the contract was made, such an obligation should not be regarded as divisible. Furthermore, when the obligation has arisen in return for a benefit which all obligors share, this obligation should not be considered to be divisible.[2] However, the courts maintain that without a special agreement or particular circumstances, obligations are divisible.[3]

The second type of obligation with several obligees or obligors is an indivisible obligation. The Code provides that an obligation is indivisible when the parties has agreed as such, or when the object of obligation is indivisible by its nature (Art. 428). An obligation of joint lessees of the same property to pay the rent is an example of the latter.

When there are several obligors under an indivisible obligation, the obligee may demand full performance from any or all of the obligors. For instance, if Y, Z and W are liable under an indivisible obligation of 900,000 yen against X, X may demand

---

2 R. Suzuki, *Saiken-hō Kōgi* (*Lectures on the Law of Obligation*), Tokyo 1986, p. 307.
3 Judgment of the Supreme Court, 13 October, 1970 (*Hanji* 614–46).

payment of 900,000 yen from either Y,Z, or W or all of them. A change in relationship between the obligee and one of the obligors does not affect the relationship between the obligee and other obligors, except for discharge and novation. For example, if Z's obligation is extinguished because of prescription, it does not affect Y or W's obligations against X.

On the other hand, when there are several obligees, the obligor may effect performance against any of the obligees. A change in circumstances between any of the obligees and the obligor does not affect the others, except where novation or discharge is involved.

The third type of obligation with multiple obligees is joint and several obligations. In joint and several obligations, the obligee may demand performance from any or all of the obligors. If the amount of the debt is three million yen, the obligee may demand all obligors to repay this amount or ask any of them to repay the same amount. If the debt is repaid by any of the obligors, the obligation is extinguished and the obligors who repaid the debt can be indemnified by other obligors.

In joint and several obligations, circumstances between one of the obligors and the obligee affect the relationship between the other obligors and the obligee less than that in the case of a divisible obligation but more than that in indivisible obligation. However, as compared with German law, circumstances affecting others are broader in Japan.[4] Prescription, discharge, merger and novation affect other parties (Arts. 435–439). For example, Y, Z, and W are jointly and severally liable in respect of three million yen to X. When Y agrees with X to novate the original contract and to give X a property worth one million yen as a substitute for repayment of the debt, not only Y's but also Z and W's obligation is extinguished and their liability will be reduced to two million yen. Similarly, if Y's obligation is extinguished by prescription, if his share in the obligation was one million yen, W and Z are jointly liable only for the remaining two million yen.

Indivisible obligations are more advantageous to the obligee than joint and several obligations, since in the latter, there are more instances where circumstances arising between the obligee and one of the obligors affect the other parties. In practice, joint and several obligation is not so widely used. In order to gurantee an obligation, suretyship with joint and several liability is more common.[5]

---

4 Hoshino, *supra* note 10, pp. 156–157.
5 Y.Hirai, *Saiken Sōron* (*The Law of Obligation, General Part*), Tokyo 1985, pp. 252–254.

Along with these three types of obligations with multiple obligees or obligors, some lawyers contend that there is a fourth type in which circumstances pertaining to one of the obligors and the obligee do not affect the others, except for repayment. The obligor is not entitled to indemnity from other obligors. This is called quasi-joint and several obligations. It is claimed to be applicable in cases involving joint tort liability and employer's vicarious liability. In one case, A was hit and killed by a car which belonged to a local authority. A's heir X sued the chauffeur Y1 and the local authority Y2, but later reached a compromise with Y1 and discharged him. Y2 claimed that his obligation too was extinguished by X's discharge in relation to Y1. If the obligation of Y1 and Y2 is joint and several, discharge against Y1 has an effect on Y2. The Supreme Court found that the obligation was not joint and several in a strict sense, but quasi-joint and several, and denied that discharge against Y1 affected Y2.[6]

In this kind of tort case involving an employee, the victim often reaches a settlement with the employee and opts to seek damages from the employer. Therefore, a strict application of provisions on joint and several obligations in such cases is likely to be unfair to the victim. However, recent scholarly opinion is sceptical of the necessity of using the concept of quasi-joint and several obligation, which came from Germany. The legislature was already aware of the concept of *obligatio in solidum*, and the Code has presupposed this concept.[7] Besides, the application of provisions on joint and several obligation can be limited by way of interpretation.

2) Suretyship

The Civil Code also provides for suretyship as a type of obligation with several obligees or obligors. A surety is liable if the principal obligor does not perform the obligation. Suretyship arises from a contract between the obligee and the surety, without the consent of the principal obligor. However, in practice, it is a tri-partite contract of the obligee, obligor and the surety. When the principal obligation is extinguished, the suretyship extinguishes as well. When the principal obligation is assigned, suretyship follows.

6 Judgment of the Supreme Court, 21 April, 1970 (*Hanji* 595–54).
7 Hirai, *supra* note 25, pp. 266–267.

Suretyship covers the principal obligation as well as the interest, liquidated damages and penalty. When the contract between the principal obligor and the obligee is rescinded, the suretyship secures the obligor's duty to recover the *status quo ante*. For instance, when a sales contract is rescinded, the surety of the seller guarantees the return of the money to the buyer.[8]

There are two kinds of defence which the surety may employ when an obligee demands performance. First, the surety may ask the obligee to demand performance from the principal obligor (Art. 452). Second, the surety may refuse performance if he proves that the principal obligor has sufficient financial capacity to perform the obligation, and that enforcement of the obligation would be easy (Art. 453).

From the viewpoint of an obligee, these two defences are disadvantageous. Therefore, instead of ordinary suretyship, joint and several suretyship is utilised more frequently. The above-mentioned two defences are not allowed and the provisions of joint and several obligations are applied (Art. 454).

Another variation of suretyship is floating suretyship. In a continuing relationship such as that between a bank and its customer, or between a trading house and a manufacturer, it is necessary to secure an unspecified number of obligations the amount of which is not identical. The Code does not have a special provision for this kind of suretyship, but the courts have long acknowledged this. There is a possibility that such a suretyship would be too harsh on the surety. It is generally acknowledged that when there is a significant change of circumstances, for example, when the financial status of the principal obligor rapidly deteriorates, or when the status of the principal obligor has changed, the surety may rescind the contract of suretyship and be released from further obligation.

It is common for Japanese companies to require a surety when employing someone. The surety is expected to guarantee payment of compensation which may arise from the acts of the employee in the future. However, sureties were often unexpectedly made liable for large amounts of money. Therefore, the courts tried to limit the liability of the surety. Also in 1933, a Law on Suretyship for Employment was enacted.[9] According to this Law, the term of a suretyship cannot exceed five years, although it is renewable (Arts. 1 and 2). A surety may rescind suretyship and be discharged from further obligations under certain conditions (Art. 4). When deciding the amount of damages, fault

8 Judgment of the Supreme Court, 30 June, 1965 (*Minshū* 19–4–1143).
9 Law No. 42, 1933.

on the part of the employer and other relevant circumstances are to be considered (Art. 5).

4.   Extinction of obligations

Obligations may become extinguished for various reasons. The Code lists the following: performance, set-off, novation, discharge and merger. Performance can be effected by a third party, unless the nature of the obligation does not allow it, or the parties expressed a different intention (Art. 474, para. 1). Those who do not have any legal interest with the obligation may not perform the obligation (Art. 474, para. 2).

Performance is valid in some cases where it was not made to the genuine obligee. The Code provides that the performance of obligation to a person who appears to be an obligee is valid, insofar as the obligee was not aware that the obligor was not genuine and was not at fault in believeing so (Art. 478). This provision is designed to protect those who relied on the appearance. For instance, if a bank lets a person who turned up with a certificate of deposit and a signet withdraw money from the account, the bank is normally exempted from liability, provided that the bank has exercised the required standard of care. The Supreme Court acknowledged the validity of payment by a bank to a person who turned up with a certificate of deposit and a forged signet and claimed to be the depositor.[10]

An obligor may effect substitute performance with the consent of the obligee (Art. 482). For instance, the obligor may repay the debt by giving the obligee a car instead of cash with the latter's consent. This has the same effect as a performance. This is contrasted with novation, in which parties agree to alter essential elements of the original contract, and as a result, the original obligation is extinguished and a new obligation emerges (Art. 513).

In cases where the obligee either refuses to accept performance or is unable to accept it, the obligor may deposit the subject-matter of the obligation at a depository and be exempted from liability. The same applies where the obligee cannot be identified or found without any fault on the part of the obligor (Art. 494).

Among the causes of extinction of obligations, set-off and substitute performance also function as a means of security. Real security rights by means of substitute performance are covered by the Law on Contracts of Security Rights by Provisional

---

10 Judgment of the Supreme Court, 4 October, 1966 (*Minshū* 20-8-1565).

Registration.[11] Usually the obligor promises the obligee to effect performance of his obligation via his property if he fails to repay the debt. In this way, the obligee is able to secure repayment in priority to other creditors.

Set-off is also commonly used as a means of security in banking transactions. The Code provides that when two persons have obligations against one another, each of them may be relieved of his obligation by a set-off to the extent corresponding to their obligation (Art. 505, para. 1). In order to set-off an obligation, both obligations have to be of the same kind and due. Set-off is effected by a declaration of will by one of the parties. The effect of set-off is retrospective, i.e. it goes back to the time when both obligations became mature for set-off (Art. 506). Set-off is not possible when the parties agreed otherwise, or the nature of the obligation does not allow it. However, the agreement between the parties cannot be claimed against a bona fide third party. In obligations arising from tort, the obligor may not set off his obligation against the obligee (Art. 509).

Banks use set-off in the following way. When a bank lends money to a customer, the latter is asked to open a fixed time deposit account. It is agreed in advance between the parties that if the customer's creditor attaches this account, the bank will set-off its obligation against the customer's obligation. In this way, the bank manages to secure at least the amount of the fixed deposit in priority to other creditors. The lawfulness of this practice was contested before the Supreme Court. The Court upheld the validity of such an arrangement.[12]

There are other causes of extinction of obligations such as discharge and merger. If the obligee discharges the obligor, the obligation is also extinguished (Art. 519). Merger denotes a situation where the right and obligation come to belong to the same person (Art. 520). This happens, for example, when the obligor inherits the status of the obligee.

5. The Law of Contract

1) The Civil Code and Commercial Code

Japanese contract law is not embodied in a single piece of legislation. It is found in parts of the Civil Code and the

---

11 Law No. 78, 1973.
12 Judgment of the Supreme Court, 24 June, 1970 (*Minshū* 24–6–587).

Commercial Code. The second chapter of Book Three of the Civil Code, following the first chapter on the General Rules of the Law of Obligation, deals with contracts. Chapter Two is divided into a general part and provisions on individual contracts. In addition, the Commercial Code has provisions on commercial transactions which are applicable to contracts. There are transactions which are regarded as commercial *per se* and also transactions which are treated as commercial only when they are conducted as business (Arts. 501 and 502). Moreover, transactions which merchants enter into in the course of their business are regarded commercial (Art. 503).

The provisions of the Commercial Code are special rules in relation to the Civil Code and, therefore, have priority whenever they are applicable. In the absence of relevant provisions in the Commercial Code, commercial custom is first applied, and only when there is no such custom, is the Civil Code applied.

Since contracts are juristic acts, provisions in the General Part (Book One) of the Civil Code on juristic acts are applied to contracts. Thus, a contract, which is an outcome of a declaration of will, can be null and void, or voidable on various grounds, such as fraud, mistake, duress etc. as provided in the General Part. Furthermore, agency is also covered in the General Part.

Freedom of contract is of course recognised in Japanese law, despite the absence of an explicit provision in the Code. Freedom of contract includes freedom to conclude a contract as well as the freedom to decide the content of a contract. As is the case with other industrialised countries, this principle which emerged in the 19th century *laisser faire* state cannot be maintained without modification in a modern age. For example, if employment agreements or lease agreements of immovables were to be entirely left to the contracting parties, it might lead to unfairness and injustice to employees and lessees.

Therefore, some modifications have had to be made to this principle in the light of contemporary developments. In the field of housing law, for example, the right of the lessor to decide the content of a contract is limited in various ways. Under certain conditions, the court may substitute its own views for the will of the lessor. Clauses of a lease agreement of land and buildings which are against the law and against the interests of the lessee are void. Similarly, in the field of labour law, employment agreements are subject to strict control by labour legislation. Furthermore, due to the growing necessity to safeguard the interests of consumers, laws concerning consumer protection, which impose further restrictions on the freedom of contract, are developing.

2) The role of contracts in Japan

A contract comes into effect when the intentions of the parties coincide, i.e. when offer and acceptance correspond. The concept of consideration does not exist in Japan. Gift is also considered to be a contract. A contract is concluded without any formality. It does not have to be in writing. There are, however, exceptions. For instance, some contracts, such as a contract to sell arable land, require permission from an administrative agency. In a contract of pledge, actual transfer of the collateral is needed to give rise to the contract. The Law on Sale by Instalments requires a contract to be made in writing. Furthermore, the Anti-Monopoly Law requires the notification of some kinds of transnational agreements.

The fact that the Code does not require a contract to be made in a written form does not mean that, in Japan, contracts are generally made orally. On the contrary, the written form is usually adopted in business transactions as well as transactions among ordinary people. The issue of whether or not there is a unique Japanese approach towards contracts has been discussed in Japan and abroad for some time. A distinguished specialist of sociology of law in Japan has once pointed out that the necessity of concluding a formal contract is not fully recognised in Japan, and that the binding force of contract is not as strict as in Europe and in the United States. The Japanese prefer not to form a relationship based on contract, since this presupposes the possibility of conflict.[13]

This notion of the limited role of contracts in the Japanese society is now being questioned. In contemporary Japan, contracts do play a significant role in various areas. Contracts which major companies conclude with foreign companies have little difference from contracts seen in Europe or the United States. Ordinary citizens also have to sign contracts from time to time; for instance, agreements of employment, loan agreements and lease agreements.

These kinds of contracts are often standard form contracts, which contain clauses disadvantageous to those in a weaker bargaining position. Although the parties feel bound by a contract, the validity of some clauses has been contested in the court. The courts have invalidated some of them out of considerations of fairness. Incidentally, if one of the parties to such a contract is a major company, they usually do not invoke

13 T. Kawashima, 'The Legal Consciousness of Contract in Japan', *Law in Japan* vol. 7, 1974, pp. 1–21.

those clauses against ordinary citizens. Neither do they sue citizens for breach of contract, but instead, prefer to settle the case out of the court, since it will affect the company's reputation, and in the long run, will be harmful to the company.[14]

On the other hand, contractual relationships between companies within Japan are somewhat different, and perhaps this is the reason why Japanese contracts are considered to be unique. These contracts, especially those between trading partners, are often very short – in some cases, only a few pages. They define the rights and duties of the parties in broad terms and leave the rest to negotiation between the parties should a conflict arise. When a difficulty arises, the parties do not necessarily stick to the clauses of the contract, but instead, try to reach a mutually acceptable compromise.

According to a foreign observer, in Japan, parties to a contract are not seen as entities with conflicting interests; they are considered to have entered into a mutually beneficial and cooperative relationship to achieve a common purpose. In this sense, a contract represents a relationship of mutual trust and therefore, it is sometimes considered to be a sign of distrust if either party attempts to cover every possible contingency in the contract.[15]

There is some truth in this observation. However, it should be noted that flexible and simple contracts are not necessarily a characteristic unique to Japan. A survey conducted in the United States showed that even there, contracts between companies with continuing relationships are simple and flexible.[16]

It is also misleading to state that the Japanese feel less bound by a contract than the nationals of other countries. Studies indicate that Japanese may disregard standard contracts, but once a formal contract has been concluded in a written form, they observe it faithfully.[16]

3)   Doctrine of good faith and fair dealing

Contracts are to be performed by the parties in accordance with the doctrine of good faith and fair dealing. One corollary of this doctrine is the effect of a change in circumstances. There may be cases where due to a change in circumstances, it is no longer fair

---

14   E. Hoshino, *supra* note 10. For detailed discussion, see Société de legislation comparée, *Etudes de droit japonais*, Paris 1989, pp. 391–491.
15   E. J. Hahn, *Japanese Business Law and the Legal System*, Westport 1985, pp. 10–11.
16   W. Gray, 'Use and Non-Use of Contracts', *Law in Japan*, vol. 17, 1984, pp. 98–99.

to require a party to perform his obligations. Although there is no explicit provision in the Code, it is generally recognised that under certain conditions, such obligations should not be enforced. In a leading case, the Supreme Tribunal acknowledged that when, due to circumstances such as the enactment of a new law regulating prices, the contract becomes impossible to execute at the price which had been agreed, and when this impossibility of performance is likely to continue for a considerable time, it is not reasonable, taking into account the doctrine of good faith and fair dealing, to bind the parties to such a contract.[17]

After the end of the Second World War, confronted with steep inflation, the Supreme Court held in *obiter dicta* that the seller may rescind a contract on the ground of change in circumstances.[18] However, the Supreme Court has not applied this doctrine in a concrete case so far. In recent years, the price of land has risen sharply and there still are cases where this doctrine can be applied. Some lower court judgments have upheld a claim for revision of a contract or its rescission in certain cases.[19]

In a contract, in which both parties have an obligation to do or give something, a party may refuse to perform until the other party offers to perform his obligation (Art. 533). When, for example, a seller A concludes a contract with a buyer B, A may refuse payment until B offers to transfer possession to A, or vice versa. This defence, which is referred to as a defence of simultaneous performance, can be invoked also in cases where a contract has been rescinded and both parties mutually have an obligation to restore the *status quo ante*.

The special part of contract law lists various types of contract: gift, sale, exchange, loan for consumption, loan for use, lease, employment, work contract, mandate, bailment, partnership, life annuity and compromise. For the sake of convenience, the following will focus on sales.

6. Contract of sales

1) General rules

In order to conclude a contract, an offer should be made by one party and accepted by the other. In transactions with foreign

---

17 Judgment of the Supreme Tribunal, 6 December, 1944 (*Minshū* 23–19–613).
18 Judgment of the Supreme Court, 6 February, 1951 (*Minshū* 5–3–36).
19 See K. Igarashi in *Minpō Hanrei Hyakusen* (Hundred Selected Cases in Civil Law) , vol. II 1982, pp. 100–101.

counterparts, Japanese companies often make inquiries and exchange letters of intent. However, these enquiries and letters of intent by no means constitute offers.

In Japanese law, the offeror is not necessarily free to retract his offer. When the offeror asks that acceptance be made within a fixed period, he may not retract the offer (Art. 521, para. 1). Even when the period of acceptance is not set by the offeror, he may not retract his offer for a reasonable period necessary for him to receive the acceptance (Art. 524). In commercial transactions, if the offeree failed to accept the offer within a reasonable period, the offer loses its effect (Commercial Code, Art. 508, para. 1).

Sometimes, earnest money is paid in a sales contract. The Code provides that a buyer may rescind the contract, provided that he waives any claim to money he has paid. On the other hand, the seller may also rescind the contract if he returns twice the amount of the earnest money. In both cases, rescission has to be made before either party initiates performance (Art. 557). There are also cases where earnest money is meant to be liquidated damages, i.e. the parties have agreed on the maximum amount of damages in advance. The courts are of the opinion that unless it is expressly stated otherwise, the earnest should be regarded as money for the retention of the right to rescind the contract.[20]

Ownership – title – of the goods is transferred in accordance with the terms of the contract, i.e. it depends on the intention of the parties. The problem of *when* the title is transferred to the buyer has been a controversial issue in Japanese Civil Law for a long time. Recently, some people suggest that the answer to this question has little practical effect. There are provisions in the Code which regulate the transfer of risk and the rights and duties of the parties, and these provisions can be applied without determining exactly when title is transferred.[1]

The Code provides for the transfer of risk in the following way: 1) when a specified thing is an object of a contract, if the object is lost or damaged by a cause not attributable to the seller, the risk is born by the buyer (Art. 534); 2) otherwise, when the performance of an obligation became impossible due to a cause attributable to neither of the parties, the seller is not entitled to performance (Art. 536, para. 1).

If, however, the first principle is applied strictly, it may be

---

20 Judgment of the Supreme Court, 21 January, 1954 (*Minshū* 8–1–64).
 1 R.Suzuki, *Bukken-hō no Kenkyū* (*Treatise on Property Law*), Tokyo 1976, pp. 126–143.

unfair to the buyer. For instance, if A concludes a contract to purchase a painting from B, but before the painting is handed over to A, it is damaged by an earthquake, under this principle, A, the buyer, has to bear the loss and therefore still has to pay the agreed price. This can hardly be considered as an appropriate solution. Scholarly opinions maintain that in such cases where the object has not been handed over to the buyer, nor the price paid, this provision should not be applied on the ground that this was against the intention of the parties, or there is a different trade practice.

In cases of non-performance of contractual obligations, provisions in the general part of the Law of Obligation (Arts. 412–422) as well as special provisions included in the part dealing with contracts (Arts. 540–548) are applied. If it is a sales contract, provisions concerning sale are further applied (Arts. 560–578).

2) Liability of the seller

The Chapter on Contracts includes provisions on the liability of a seller where he does not have full legal rights over the property, or where the object is defective. Firstly, when the object of sale belong to a third party and not to the seller, unlike French law, the contract itself is valid. The seller is obliged to obtain rights over this object and transfer them to the buyer (Art. 560). If he fails, the buyer may rescind the contract and claim damages (Art. 561).

Secondly, there are cases where some of the rights over the object belongs to a third party. This happens, for example, when a joint owner sells property without the consent of other owners. In such a case, if the seller is unable to transfer the entire object to the buyer, the latter may ask for a reduction of the price in proportion to the part which is unavailable. If the buyer would not have purchased the object had he known that only part of it was available, he may rescind the contract. The seller is liable in both cases (Art. 563).

Similarly, when the amount of the object delivered is less than that agreed in the contract, or when a part of the object is lost, the buyer is protected in the same way (Art. 565). The same applies to cases where superficies, emphyteusis, servitude, or registered lease etc. exist on the property; the buyer may rescind the contract and demand compensation (Art. 566).

Thirdly, there are cases where the object of sale has been hypothecated or there is a preferential right over it. When, as a result, the buyer loses the property, the buyer may rescind the contract and claim damages. Furthermore, if the buyer pays money and discharges the hypothec or preferential right, he may demand reimbursement from the seller (Art. 567).

Finally, the most contentious issue concerning the liability of the seller is his liability for objects with latent defects. The Code provides that when any latent defect is found in the object of sale, the buyer may rescind the contract, provided that he is unable to achieve the purpose of the contract with such a defect (Art. 570). The defect has to be latent, i.e. it should be a defect which an ordinary buyer is unable to find with normally required care. The seller bears the burden to prove that the buyer knew or should have known, by exercising due care, the existence of the defect, in order to avoid liability. The buyer has to exercise this right within one year of his discovering the defect (Art. 566, para. 3).

It should be noted that the Commercial Code has special provisions for sales between merchants. The Code provides that a buyer should inspect the object of sale without delay after he has received it, and if he fails to inform the seller immediately of any defect found at that time, he is not entitled to make a claim against the seller. Even when the defect was of a nature which could not be found at the time of this initial inspection, the buyer has only six months after receiving the object in which to enforce his rights (The Commercial Code Art. 526, para. 1).

The defect does not have to be physical. The Supreme Court has acknowledged a latent defect in a case where a buyer purchased a piece of land destined to be part of a planned road and to be demolished. The plan to build a road had been officially announced, but it was more than ten years before the contract was concluded.[2] There was a similar case where a seller sold a forest which was designated as a preservation area.[3]

There is a controversy over the relationship between the provision on seller's liability in the Chapter on Contracts (Art. 570) and the provision on incomplete performance in the General Part of the Law of Obligation (Art. 416). When a defective item is sold, seller's liability based upon Article 570 can be pursued, but it can also be considered as a defective performance on the part of the seller, and Article 416 may possibly be applied.

Practical differences between applying Articles 416 and 570 are; first, the buyer may claim danages, but not replacement by Article 570. Second, claims based on Article 570 have to be made within one year, while claims on the ground of Article 416 can be made for ten years. Third, Article 416 presupposes fault

2 Judgment of the Supreme Court, 14 April, 1966 (*Minshū* 20–4–649).
3 Judgment of the Supreme Court, 8 September, 1981 (*Hanji* 1019–73).

on the part of the seller, while Article 570 presupposes strict liability.

While there are different views among specialists of Civil Law, the court seems to be of the view that the buyer may freely choose between those two provisions. In one case, Y purchased broadcasting equipment from X. X required payment, which Y refused on the ground that the equipment was defective. Y also claimed that the contract was rescinded on the basis of Articles 416 and 570, and demanded replacement. X argued that since Y had accepted the equipment, he had no right to claim replacement because of defective performance. The Supreme Court ruled that the buyer Y was entitled to invoke either provision and was still entitled to replacement.[4]

This view is shared more or less by scholarly opinion. It is also asserted that in such cases, the claim based upon Article 416 should be subject to the same time limit as Article 570 – one year – by reason of the doctrine of good faith and fair dealing.

3.   Consumer protection

In recent years, people have become increasingly aware of consumers' rights, and calls for better protection of consumers have gained support. Incidents where consumers suffered from fraudulent business such as a pyramid business scheme occurred from time to time. Consumers also became conscious that they were sometimes compelled to accept disadvantageous terms in standard form contracts. There is also a move to provide better protection against defective goods by enacting a law on product liability. This will be discussed in the next chapter.

Significant changes to the law of contract have been made in recent years by amendments to the Law on Installment Sales and the enactment and subsequent amendments of the Law on Door-to-Door Sales.[5] The former mandates the seller to explain to the buyer relevant terms of sale, such as the cash price or the price payable by instalments, terms of payment and the rate of commission. After the conclusion of the contract, the seller is required to issue a written statement to the buyer which specifies these terms and the time of the transfer of title as well as conditions for rescission (Arts. 3 and 4). This is an exception to the general rules of Japanese contract law which does not require any formality for concluding a contract. Similar arrangements can

---

4 Judgment of the Supreme Court, 15 December, 1961 (*Minshū* 15–11–2852).
5 Laws No. 159, 1961 and No. 57, 1976.

be found in the Law on the Regulation of Credit and Loan Business.[6]

Another innovation resulting from the increased protection of consumers is the 'cooling-off' period for some kinds of contracts. The cooling-off period is designed to protect consumers, who have been unfairly persuaded by the seller to make an unnecessary purchase. The Law on Installment Sales and the Law on Door-to-Door Sales provide that when a seller concludes a contract or accepts an offer in a place other than his sales office, the buyer or the offeror may rescind the contract or retract the offer respectively in a written form within eight days after he had been informed of his rights by the seller (Law on Installment Sales Arts. 4–3, Law on Door to Door Sale Art. 6). The seller is not entitled to compensation in such cases. A similar provision can be found in the Law on Investment Advisory Business (Art. 17).[7]

There are also problems concerning standard form contracts. In a modern society, ordinary people usually do not have a say in forming contracts concerning various goods and services, such as transportation, supply of gas and electricity, telephone services, insurance and banking. They merely have a choice whether to enter into a contractual relationship or not, but even this choice is very limited, since these services or items are indispensable to normal living.

In standard form contracts, where one party is an ordinary person and the other is a major company, there is a possibility that the latter may abuse its bargaining power and force the former to accept unfair or unjust contract terms. Some standard form contracts are so specialised and complicated that ordinary people find them unintelligible.

There are various provisions in standard form contracts which have led to controversy. Exclusion clauses are particularly problematic. For instance, in banking transactions, a provision which exempts the liability of the bank when it repays money to the possessor of the account book and signet has been contested in the court. A clause in a transportation contract which limits the liability of the company has often been a focus of dispute.

Although a special law on this issue, such as the one in Germany (*Gesetz zur Regelung des Rechts der Allgemeinen Geschäftsbedingungen*) and the Unfair Contract Terms Act of the United Kingdom, is yet to be enacted, some laws have been amended in order to exercise more control over such standard

6 Law No. 32, 1983.
7 Law No. 74, 1986.

contracts. For instance, the Law on Insurance Business has made standard form contracts used by insurance companies subject to the approval of the relevant ministry (Art. 10). Furthermore, the Law on Installment Sales specifies the terms which should be incorporated in such a contract and sets minimum criteria (Art. 3).

Apart from these measures adopted by administrative and economic law, methods of controlling these standard form contracts have also been discussed in civil law. Some experts propose that the public order and good morals provision of the Civil Code (Art. 90) should be broadly applied in order to invalidate unfair terms, while others propose to resort to the doctrine of fairness and good faith. Furthermore, there is another approach which denies the validity of an unreasonable clause in a standard contract because of the lack of consent. In support of this latter approach, there have been cases involving house or land lease standard form contracts where lower courts found some clauses to be *clauses de style* under which the parties had no intention to be bound.

8. Management of affairs and unjust enrichment

Book Three of the Civil Code also deals with obligations arising without any contract. There are three such categories; management of affairs without mandate, unjust enrichment and tort.

A typical textbook case of management of affairs without mandate is a case where a person repairs the roof of the neighbour's house in the owner's absence when the area is hit by a storm. There are also cases where a person repays the debt of another person without being asked.

The Code provides that those who started to manage affairs for the benefit of another without having any obligation should manage the affairs in accordance with the nature of the affairs and by means which most suit the interest of the latter. If the person who is managing the affairs is able to presume the will of the principal, he must manage the affairs in accordance with his will (Art. 697). The necessary expense incurred for the benefit of the principal can be reimbursed (Art. 702, para. 1).

A person shall not be allowed to enrich himself at the expense of another. The Code provides that those who benefited from another person's assets or service without any legal ground and thus caused loss to this person are liable for restitution insofar as the benefit remains (Art. 703). For example, a landlord who had lost the title, but still kept receiving rent from the tenant, has enriched himself without legal ground and is obliged to reimburse the rent to the new owner.

In one case, X repaired a bulldozer for M, who had rented it from Y. M went bankrupt and the repaired bulldozer was returned to Y. X sued Y in order to recover the fee for the repair on the ground of Y's unjust enrichment. The Supreme Court acknowledged unjust enrichment on the part of Y in this case.[8]

There are cases where a person gives something to another person, but later, it turns out that this person was under no obligation to do so. For example, after the buyer paid the price, the sales contract may be rescinded. In such cases, the seller is under the obligation to return the money he has received as a payment, plus interest.

However, there may be cases where the absence of the obligation has been known to the obligor, but he still proceeds to perform the obligation. In such cases, he is not entitled to claim restitution (Art. 705).

Those who gave something on illegitimate grounds, i.e. against public policy and good morale, are not entitled to restitution. For instance, money which is due from gambling cannot be claimed (gambling is prohibited in Japan); the winner is not entitled to claim against the loser. On the other hand, once the money has been paid, there are cases where restitution is possible. The Code provides that if the ground for illegitimacy is primarily on the part of the benefactor, restitution is possible (Art. 708).

---

8 Judgment of the Supreme Court, 16 July, 1970 (*Minshū* 24-7-909).

10   The Law of Torts

1.   The development of Tort Law

In the Civil Code, provisions for tort liability are found in Part Three, the Law of Obligations. This is in common with the German and French Codes, where tort falls under the law of obligations. However, in academic research and teaching, tort is often regarded as a separate and independent sphere of civil law, along with the law of contracts, the law of property, family law and the law of succession.

The part of the Civil Code which deals with tort liability starts with a general provision. The Code provides as follows (Art. 709):

> A person who intentionally or negligently violates the rights of others shall be liable for the loss caused by the act.

Provisions concerning nonpecuniary loss, liability of minors, vicarious liability, contributory negligence, and other matters follow this general provision.

This way of setting out tort law is common in Continental legal systems. In fact, the Japanese Code is close to the French Code, since it has a single general provision on tort liability, while the German Code has three basic provisions which define the grounds for tort liability.

At the time when the Civil Code was enacted, tort liability was mostly limited to acts between individuals. However, social change which took place since then led to the emergence of new types of torts. There are pollution cases and product liability cases, where tortfeasors are major companies and the loss is widespread. The development of technology made atomic energy and various highly hazardous materials available. Even between individuals, the growth in motorised transport has resulted in an increase of tort cases.

In 1990, out of 112,140 civil cases accepted at the district court level, 11,448 involved claims for damages. 6,159 traffic accident cases were accepted in the same year. In 1987, there were 314 pollution cases, 356 medical malpractice cases, and four cases involving faulty cars. The number of cases involving traffic accidents has sharply decreased in the last two decades. Only a small portion of cases is handled by the courts and the Centre for Settling Traffic Accident Cases. The remaining cases are settled mostly through negotiation between the victim and the insurance company.[1]

Despite the social changes that occurred after the enactment of the Civil Code in 1896, provisions regarding tort liability in the Civil Code have remained unchanged. These provisions, especially the general provision of Article 709, were made intentionally abstract in order to give sufficient discretion to the courts in their interpretation. This enabled the courts to cope with newly emerging problems such as pollution. In fact, it is not an exaggeration to state that court judgments, not only of the Supreme Court, but also of the lower courts, have played a major role in forming the modern Japanese law of tort. One such example is the judgments of the lower courts in the celebrated 'four major pollution cases' where victims who have suffered from water pollution sued the companies which emitted toxic substances. These judgments, although given by lower courts, introduced some new concepts, such as 'epidemiological causality', which in fact reduced the burden of proof falling on the plaintiff.[2]

There are some special laws pertinent to tort which should be mentioned here. The first is the Law on the Compensation of Loss arising from Car Accidents which was enacted in 1955. This Law provides for liability of the owner or possessor of the car which was involved in the accident, regardless of whether he was the driver or not. This almost amounts to strict liability. Furthermore, it introduced the system of compulsory insurance. Secondly, laws concerning pollution control, which were enacted in the late 1960s and early 1970s are relevant in that they incorporated provisions for strict liability. Thirdly, the Law on the Compensation for Loss caused by Atomic Energy also introduced strict liability. Finally, the Law on the Remedy of Harm Caused to Human Health by Pollution which was enacted

1 Supreme Court of Japan, *Annual Judicial Statistics; 1990*, Civil Cases, Tokyo 1991, p. 123. '*Fuhō-kōi Seido to Higaisha-kyūsai* (The System of Tort Liability and the Redress of Victims), *Jurist*, No. 926, 1989, pp. 18–21.
2 J. Gresser et al, *Environmental Law in Japan*, Cambridge, Mass., 1981, pp. 128–130.

in 1973 is of significance.[3] This Law has introduced a system whereby those who suffer from designated diseases caused by air or water pollution in specific areas may have their hospital costs, the cost of supporting the family, and some other expenses paid from a general fund supported by the government as well as the companies considered to have caused pollution. Victims do not individually have to prove the liability of the companies. It is sufficient if they are certified as victims of a designated disease by the governor of the prefecture.

Academic opinion has also played a major role in shaping tort law. Initially, academics turned to Germany and France to analyse tort law, but after the Second World War, the American law of tort has been extensively studied. Recently, the cost-benefit approach, favoured by American lawyers, is finding support among Japanese scholars.

2.   General rules of Tort Law

Traditionally, it has been considered that there were four factors which constitute tort. First, the tortfeasor should be at fault: i.e. either he acted with intent or negligently. Second, the act has to be unlawful. Third, causality should exist between the tortious act and the loss. Fourth, loss should have occurred.

These elements of tort are almost parallel to the elements which constitute a crime under the theory of criminal law in Japan as well as in Germany. In criminal law, an act is punishable when one is at fault, the act is unlawful, causality exists between the act and criminal damage, and the person is capable of bearing responsibility. However, whether it is appropriate to transplant this framework into tort law is now being questioned. Moreover, some academics maintain that these four elements are not really independent. For example, if negligence is considered to be not a psychological state of mind but a breach of duty to foresee or to avoid the outcome of one's act, it may not be different from the concept of unlawfulness; a breach of duty is the main component of unlawfulness.

In principle, fault is a prerequisite of tortious liability. The problem lies not with intentional acts, but with acts arising out of negligence. Academic opinion was divided as to whether negligence is a state of mind – lack of attention – or a breach of duty. The latter seems to be the prevailing view today. Basically,

3 Law No. 111, 1973.

there are two approaches to defining negligence. One school of thought asserts that a person should be considered negligent for his failure to foresee the loss which is likely to occur from his act. The other school maintains that a person is negligent if he fails to take measures needed to avoid and prevent the loss. In their view, foreseeability is a prerequisite, but in addition to the breach of the duty to foresee the outcome of his act, there should be a breach of the duty to avoid the outcome.

The courts have adopted the second approach, considering negligence to be a failure to avoid the occurrence of the result which was foreseen or should have been foreseen. In one case, inhabitants who lived near a chemical plant sued the company for air pollution, which caused damage to the crops. The Supreme Tribunal ruled that insofar as the company had taken adequate measures to prevent loss likely to occur in the course of operations, even if, by chance, loss had been caused, the company was not liable. In this case, the result was foreseeable, and since the company had taken measures to avoid the result, it was not held liable.[4] In a more recent case, the Supreme Court ruled that a driver does not have a duty to foresee that a car running parallel to him would act against traffic rules *and* accordingly take action to prevent an accident.[5] Thus, a majority of court judgments takes the position that even if the tortfeasor had foreseen or should have foreseen the result of his act, he is not liable, provided that he had fulfilled his duty to take measures to prevent and avoid loss.

At first sight, this approach of the courts may seem to narrow the liability of the tortfeasor. However, the difference between the two approaches – one stressing foreseeability and the other focusing on avoidability – can be very small, if the duty to prevent or avoid the result is interpreted broadly. In cases involving pollution in the 1960s and 70s, the courts imposed a stricter duty on companies to avoid and prevent the results of their actions and thus held them liable. In one case involving serious loss of life by a toxic substance discharged into a river, the district court ruled that if damage to human health is likely and unavoidable even though the most advanced technology is used, it is the duty of the company to curtail or suspend the operation of the plant.[6] It should be noted that even in the above-cited case involving air pollution, after the Supreme

---

4 Judgment of the Supreme Tribunal, 22 December, 1916 (*Minroku* 22–2474: Osaka Alkali case).
5 Judgment of the Supreme Court, 24 September, 1968 (*Hanji* 539–40).

Tribunal had reversed the case, the lower court again ruled in favour of the plaintiff and acknowledged the negligence of the company.

In some cases, the court expects a person to do a specific act to avoid causing loss, and if he fails to do so, he will be found liable. This often happens in medical malpractice cases. In one case, a doctor administered a blood transfusion with blood which was infected by syphilis. The doctor asserted that since he was shown certificates stating that the donor was healthy and was not infected with syphilis, he had good reason to proceed. The Supreme Court ruled that the doctor should not have used the blood unless he had personally questioned the donor about the possibility of his being infected.[7] In another case where a baby suffered from the after-effects of an influenza vaccination, the Supreme Court ruled that the doctor had a duty to question the state of health of the patient in a clear and concrete way.[8]

The standard of care required is that of the reasonable man. While the Code does not expressly provide for the standard of care, a concept similar to the reasonable man is found in the General Part of the Law of Obligation (Art. 400). Thus, a person who is under a duty to deliver an item is bound to look after that item with a standard of care equivalent to that of a 'good manager'. Naturally, a higher standard of care is required of those who are engaged in a profession which needs expertise, or in some areas of industry such as pharmacy and food processing. Thus, the Supreme Court in the above-mentioned blood transfusion case ruled that people engaged in a profession which deals with the life and health of others are required to exercise the highest standard of care that is empirically proved to be necessary. In a case where a toxic substance – PCB – was mixed into rice oil in a food processing plant, the court acknowledged that the producer of the substance, as a supplier to a food processing plant, was also under a high duty of care.[9] A similar standard of care was required of a chemical company which discharged waste water into a river.[10]

On the other hand, if a doctor has taken sufficient care in the light of scientific research and surgical experience concerning a

6 Judgment of Niigata District Court, 29 September, 1971 (*Hanji* 642–96 : Niigata Minamata case).
7 Judgment of the Supreme Court 16 February, 1961 (*Minshū* 15–2–244).
8 Judgment of the Supreme Court, 30 September, 1976 (*Minshū* 30–8–816).
9 Judgment of Fukuoka District Court, Kokura Division, 29 March, 1982 (*Hanji* 1037–14: *Kanemi Yushō* case).
10 *Supra* note 2.

given disease, i.e. the state of the art, and has satisfied the medical standards of the time, he will not be liable. For example, in a case where a premature baby suffered from retinal disease caused by oxygen treatment, the Supreme Court ruled that the doctor was not liable, since his treatment was in accordance with the current standard of academic opinion and surgical knowledge.[11] However, in a similar case ten years later, the Supreme Court held that the hospital was liable, presumably taking into account the advances made by medicine in the meantime.[12]

The burden of proof that the tortfeasor has acted negligently or with intent lies with the plaintiff. However, in practice, if the plaintiff proves the existence of certain relevant factors, fault on the part of the tortfeasor can be presumed, and the defendant has to prove that he was not at fault. Thus, in the above-mentioned case involving after-effects of an influenza vaccination, the Supreme Court ruled that the breach of the duty on the part of the doctor can be presumed by his failure to question the state of health of the patient properly.[13]

Since fault is a prerequisite of tortious liability, it presupposes the ability on the part of the tortfeasor to make certain judgments. The Civil Code provides that in cases where a minor has caused damage to another person, he is not held responsible for the act provided that he was not capable of recognising his responsibility for the act (Art. 712). The court has found a boy of twelve years old who discharged an air gun into the face of another boy not liable.[14] Furthermore, a person, who, while mentally unsound, causes loss to another person is not liable (Art. 713). In both instances where the person who perpetrated the act or omission is not liable, then the person who is responsible for overseeing that person is liable, unless he proves that he had not neglected his duty (Art. 714).

A problem arises when a minor is found responsible and thus liable for his tortious act. Does this mean that the persons who are in charge of overseeing him are exempted from liability? The wording of the relevant provision seems to be in the affirmative. If so, however, the victim will be confused as to whether he should sue the minor or the person in charge of overseeing him, since it is up to the court to decide whether the minor was liable or not. Therefore, scholarly opinion has taken the position that

---

11 Judgment of the Supreme Court, 13 November, 1979 (*Hanji* 952–49).
12 Judgment of the Supreme Court, 26 March, 1985 (*Minshū* 39–2–124).
13 *Supra* note 8.
14 Judgment of the Supreme Tribunal, 30 April, 1917 (*Minroku* 23–715).

the victim is entitled to claim damages either from the tortfeasor or from those in charge of overseeing those people (a minor or a person who is mentally unsound) on the general ground of tortious liability (Art. 709). According to the proponents of this view, the essence of Article 714 lies in that the person in charge of overseeing the minor is exempted from liability when he has proved that he had not neglected his duty. It is not designed to exclude the possibility of claiming damages against a person in charge of overseeing a minor or mentally unsound person on the general ground of tort liability.

The Supreme Court accepted this argument in a case where a paperboy was killed by a minor of 15 years of age and was robbed of the money he had collected. The mother of the boy sued the minor and his parents as co-tortfeasor, and claimed damages for the anticipated earnings the victim might have brought in and non-pecuniary loss. In this case, the parents failed to teach him basic rules of social life and allegedly to take action when he was caught for shoplifting. The Supreme Court ruled that even in cases where the minor can be held liable, if there is an 'adequate causality' between the loss on one hand and the neglect of duty on the part of those overseeing him on the other hand, they are liable on the general grounds of tort liability.[15]

The second requirement for tort is the unlawfulness of the act. The Code provides that tort is a violation of the rights of a person. The prevailing view among scholars is that in interpreting this provision, one should not be concerned as to what extent the right in question is recognized. Instead, they assert, 'unlawfulness' of the act is decisive. This 'unlawfulness' is not explicitly provided by the law. It is not equivalent to illegality or breach of law, although they may overlap. The unlawfulness of the act is decided by 'balancing' the nature of the interest which was violated and the mode of the tortious act. For example, in cases where pollution or public nuisance exceeds the tolerable limit of the victims, it is regarded as 'unlawful'.[16] If the infringed interest is serious, even a slight contravention of law or breach of duty may result in liability, while if the interest is not so serious, a serious violation of law is required. In essence, the remedy is not to be limited to cases where a right in the strict legal sense has been infringed.

The court took the position initially that an infringement of a certain right had to exist, and rejected a claim for the violation of an author's rights as regards a traditional story teller, since it was

---

15 Judgment of the Supreme Court, 22 March, 1974 (*Minshū* 28-2-347).
16 I. Kato, *Fuhō-kōi-hō* (*Tort Law*), supplemented edition, Tokyo 1980, p. 36.

not covered by copyright law.[17] However, the court changed its position ten years later and ruled that the 'rights' in the context of Article 709 do not have to be rights in a strict sense. It is sufficient, if such an interest is considered as appropriately deserving protection under tort law.[18] Since then, the courts have been interpreting the violation of rights fairly broadly. Remedies were provided in cases such as the breach of common law marriage, deprivation of sunshine by an adjacent building, defamation, breach of privacy, and other cases where 'interests' which cannot necessarily be regarded as rights in a strict sense have been infringed.

Scholarly opinion which replaced the concept of infringement of rights with the concept of unlawfulness was instrumental in making remedies available to a broader range of acts. It has also contributed to the development of tort law by avoiding an all-or-nothing approach by a rigid interpretation of the law by taking into account various factors relevant to a specific case and balancing them. However, whether this concept of unlawfulness is really needed in order to achieve equitable results is now being questioned. It is pointed out that if the concept of 'rights' in the context of Article 709 can be interpreted broadly, there is no need to resort to the concept of unlawfulness. Actually, the concept of unlawfulness has come from the doctrine which developed in Germany. However, the composition of the provision is different in the German Code, and the appropriateness of resorting to this doctrine in interpreting the Japanese Code may be questionable. Furthermore, the courts do not necessarily resort to the concept of unlawfulness to reach a conclusion. It is pointed out that in practice, this concept is not used as a positive element of tort.[19]

The third requirement is a causal link between the tortious act and the loss. Until recently, at least two different matters were discussed in this respect. One was the causal relation between the act and the loss, while the other was the scope of loss to be compensated. The latter will be examined in the next section.

As to the first problem, the plaintiff bears the burden of proof in demonstrating the existence of a causal relation between the tortious act and the result. This arrangement seldom causes a problem in cases where the causal link is fairly evident, such as in

17 Judgment of the Supreme Tribunal, 4 July, 1914 (*Keiroku* 20–1360: Tōchūken Kumoemon case).
18 Judgment of the Supreme Tribunal, 28 November, 1925 (*Minshū* 4–670: Daigaku-yu case).
19 See E.Hoshino in I. Kato ed., *Nihon Fuhō-kōi-hō no Restatement* (*The Restatement of Japanese Tort Law*), Tokyo 1988, pp. 37–39.

a typical traffic accident. However, in pollution cases, cases involving medical malpractice or product liability, this may result in disadvantage of the plaintiff, who lacks the highly technical knowledge which is required to prove causality. In some cases, the loss may accrue gradually, taking more than decades, and it is almost impossible for the victim to prove that the loss has been caused by a specific act. Therefore, theories have been developed to make it easier for victims in such cases to prove causality. It was proposed, for example, that in pollution cases, it should not be necessary to prove that a causal link existed with high probability, but a mere probability is sufficient.

In fact, there are cases where the court have alleviated the burden of proof. One such example is the judgment of the district court in the celebrated *Itai-itai* case, which involved a number of victims suffering impaired health through effluent discharges from factories into the river. In this case, the court ruled that the causal link between the toxic substance and the disease did not have to be proved beyond any possible doubt. It is sufficient to prove the epidemiological causality between the damage to health and the discharge. More specifically, the court ruled that the following factors had to be proved: 1) discharge of the polluting substance has preceded the outbreak of the disease; 2) increased exposure to the substance has resulted in increased occurrence of the disease; 3) areas where pollution was not serious were associated with low occurrence of disease; 4) epidemiological data do not contradict the clinical or experimental evidence.[20] In a similar case, a district court ruled that if the substance causing the disease is specified and can be traced from the victim to the factory and supported by circumstantial evidence, it is for the company to prove that its factory had not created the substance in its production process or emitted the substance.[1]

However, it was not necessarily clear how the alleviation of the burden of proof in a limited categories of cases could be legally justified. Therefore, another theory which is called a doctrine of indirect counter-proof, based upon a doctrine of civil procedure, has developed. According to this theory, if the victim proves the existence of some facts which are regarded as 'indirect facts', and if the causal link between the act and the loss can be presumed

---

20 Judgment of Toyama District Court, 30 June, 1971 (*Kaminshū* 22–5/6–1). For epidemiological causality, see J. Gresser et al. eds., *supra* note 2, 1981, pp. 128–130.
 1 Judgment of Niigata District Court, 29 September, 1971 (*Kaminshū* 22–9/10–1: Niigata Minamatabyō case).

empirically from these facts, the existence of a causal link should be confirmed, unless the defendant proves the existence of facts indicating otherwise.

The Supreme Court appears to have adopted this approach. In one case, a child who suffered from bone-marrow disease was injected with penicillin. The child had a convulsive fit and suffered from after-effects. The parents sued for damages. The district court rejected the claim on the ground that the doctors were not at fault, and the appellate court supported this conclusion, since it was not certain whether the after-effects were caused by the bone-marrow disease itself or by the injection. However, the Supreme Court quashed the judgment of the appellate court and reversed the case.

In this judgment, the Supreme Court discussed the standard of proof as regards the link between the act and the loss that must be met. Unlike a proof in natural science, in the court, it is sufficient to prove the causality to the extent of a high probability that a specific fact had caused a specific loss in the light of experience. It is satisfactory if the causality is proved to the extent that no ordinary man would cast doubt on the conclusion. Concerning this particular case, the Supreme Court acknowledged the existence of causality, since the convulsion happened suddenly a short while after the injection and the possibility of this bone-marrow disease recurring is normally low, while there was no other special circumstance which could explain its recurrence.[2]

Even when the above-mentioned requirements, i.e. fault, unlawfulness of the act, causality and the existence of loss are fulfilled, there are instances where the perpetrator of the act or omission is not held liable. Firstly, when a person has acted in defence of his or another person's rights against a tortious act of a third person, he is not liable for the loss caused (Art. 720, para. 1). Secondly, when a tortious act was committed against the property of another person out of extreme necessity to avoid imminent danger arising from this property, the perpetrator is not liable for the loss caused to this property (Art. 720, para. 2).

In addition to self defence and extreme necessity, in some cases, the consent of the victim exempts a person from liability. Also where an act is a legitimate exercise of a right, naturally, the perpetrator is not held liable. As for an example of the latter, the Law on the Trade Union provides that the workers are not liable for losses caused by industrial action provided that it was within the limit of law (Art. 8).

---

2 Judgment of the Supreme Court, 24 October, 1975 (*Minshū* 29-9-1417).

3. The scope of loss

The scope of loss to be compensated has also been discussed in conjunction with the problem of causality. It was maintained that out of the infinite variety of losses which are caused by a tortious act, only those losses linked by an 'adequate' causal relation with the act will give rise to damages. Thus, when a car hits and injures a shopowner, his family will suffer, his shop may have to be closed, and therefore the employees may also suffer. Also the wholesale trader dealing with this shop may be affected if the shop is to close. However, it is not always equitable to require the tortfeasor to compensate all the consequential losses caused by the act. Therefore, it is necessary to limit, to a reasonable extent, the scope of loss to be compensated. The doctrine of 'adequate' causal relationship limits the scope of loss to be compensated to those which normally result from a given tortious act.

This doctrine was based upon Article 416 in the General Part of the Law of Obligations in the Civil Code, which provides as follows:

> The object of claims for damages is the recovery of loss which would normally arise from the non-performance of obligation.
>
> Damages for a loss which has arisen from special circumstances may also be claimed, provided that the parties had foreseen, or should have foreseen, the circumstances.

Logically, it is not impossible to apply this provision to tort, since the provisions of this part are generally designed to apply to all kinds of obligation. However, the current prevailing opinion is that this provision should not be applied to tort, since, first, it is inappropriate to require foreseeability of specific circumstances in tort cases. Article 416 was originally designed to cope with contractual relationships, where it is natural to require foreseeability of the obligors. In contrast, in tort cases, there are instances where the tortfeasor has to compensate for loss, although he could not foresee the circumstances causing such special loss.

In addition, a study of the origin of this provision shows that this provision comes from French law via English law. On the other hand, the doctrine of 'adequate' causal relationship has been influenced by German law. German law, in principle, mandates the tortfeasor to compensate for all loss caused by his act. Since this may result in an excessive burden on the tortfeasor, a theory for limiting the scope of damages had to be invented, and this was the role of the doctrine of 'adequate' causal relationship. In Japan, however, the Code does not expressly make the tortfeasor liable for all losses caused by his act. Therefore, according to the recent prevailing view, this doctrine is not as useful in Japan as in Germany, and may even be misleading.

Instead, some lawyers suggest using the concept of the 'scope of protection'. They maintain that the scope of loss to be compensated is not determined by foreseeability, but depends on the extent to which the law intends to protect the given right or interest. The matter does not have to be linked with the problem of causality.[3]

Although there is not that much difference in the actual outcome of these two approaches, the traditional view demonstrates the way foreign legal doctrines have been introduced into Japan. Since it was believed at the initial stage that German law was the model of the present Code, academics at that time often introduced German doctrines regardless of the actual differences which existed between German and Japanese Code.

The courts have held that Article 416 should be applied *mutatis mutandis* to tort. The court normally uses the 'adequate' causality doctrine, and decides whether a particular loss was in 'adequate' causal relation with the act. In one case, a close relative of a person injured by an accident returned from a foreign country to take care of him. When the victim sued for the travel expenses, the court ruled that if the need to return from foreign countries was justified in the light of common sense, this was a normal loss, and the defendant should meet such costs within the limits of a normal fare.[4]

Actually, the scope of compensatable loss is a value judgment on the part of the court as to who, either the defendant or the plaintiff, should bear the loss. It is judged by taking into account various factors, such as the significance of the right infringed, the amount of loss, and the mode of the tortious act. For example, if the act was intentional and reckless, the amount of damages can be extended to almost all loss, while if the damage was a result of mere carelessness, the scope of damages may be more limited.

Loss can be divided into pecuniary and non-pecuniary loss. As for pecuniary loss, positive (actual) loss, for example, a loss of property or a decrease in the value of the property, as well as negative loss, i.e. a loss of anticipated profit, are both covered.

As regards positive loss incurred on property, the courts have held that damages should be computed on the basis of the market

---

3 Y. Hirai, *Saiken-kakuron (Special Part of the Law of Obligations)*, Tokyo 1992, pp. 111–129.
4 Judgment of the Supreme Court, 25 April, 1974 (*Minshū* 28–3–447).

price at the time the object was lost or damaged, unless there are special circumstances which should be taken into consideration.[5] In cases of physical loss, hospital expenses, costs for medicine etc. are covered insofar as they are reasonable and appropriate.

As for negative loss, the following leading case is pertinent. X, a merchant, lost his merchandise by a tortious act of Y. X sued Y and claimed that since the price of the merchandise had gone up after the act, he had lost the opportunity to resell it and profit from the sale, and Y should compensate for the anticipated profit. The Supreme Tribunal applied Article 416 with necessary modifications. The court ruled that such anticipated profit should be compensated only when the victim has proved that there was a special circumstance where, had not the tortious act occurred, the victim would have certainly made a profit from resale or other means, and that these circumstances were foreseen or should have been foreseen at the time of the act by the tortfeasor.[6]

Anticipated profit is also at issue when physical harm or death is caused by a tortious act. For example, if a person is disabled in a car accident, he is entitled to claim damages for his lost anticipated income. If the annual income of the victim was P yen, and his income after the accident fell to p yen, his annual loss of anticipated profit is P − p yen. The total anticipated profit, presupposing that this person will live the average life span, will generally be as follows:

$$\sum \frac{P - p}{(1 + r)^{n - x}}$$

(r = annual interest rate, n = expected year of retirement, x = current age of the victim)

Heirs are entitled to claim damages for the anticipated loss of income of the victim. As for the anticipated loss of the deceased, two basic methods of calculation are adopted by the court. At the Tokyo District Court, in cases where the victim has died from a tortious act, the difference between basic income and living costs is multiplied by the years which the victim was expected to work, i.e. the difference between the age the victim would have retired and the age when the victim died.[7] There are some adjustments such as rises in income in accordance with age and an increase in prices.[8]

---

5 Judgment of the Supreme Court, 31 January, 1957 (*Minshū* 11-1-170).
6 Judgment of the Supreme Tribunal, 22 May, 1926 (*Minshū* 5-386: Fukimaru case).
7 Y. Fukuoka, '*Kōtsu Jiko ni kansuru Songai Baishō Soshō* (Claims of Damages for Traffic Accidents)', *Jurist*, No. 833, 1985 pp. 29–30.
8 Judgment of the Supreme Court, 27 August, 1968 (*Minshū* 22-8-1404).

Loss of anticipated income on the part of the deceased is also relevant when the victim is a minor without a job, or a housewife without an income. If, for example, the victim was a baby, heirs may receive damages for the loss of anticipated income from the age he is expected to start working. The Supreme Court has acknowledged that on the death of a small child, parents are entitled to damages for the loss of anticipated earnings. The Supreme Court ruled that the anticipated income of a child can be calculated by using statistical methods, and therefore, compensation for the anticipated income of the deceased child should not be unconditionally ruled out.[9] As for housewives, the Supreme Court ruled that damages should be calculated on the basis of the average income for female workers until the age of retirement.[10]

Compensation is generally paid in a lump sum. In cases of disability, there are suggestions that compensation should be paid annually, since the calculation is based upon various assumptions such as average life span. On the other hand, it is burdensome for the victim to make sure that the compensation is actually paid annually. Therefore, at present, payment by lump sum is a rule and annual payment is an exception.

Together with pecuniary loss, non-pecuniary loss is also compensated. The Civil Code provides as follows (Art. 710):

> A person, who, on the basis of the preceding provision, is liable for damages of non-pecuniary loss, irrespective of whether he has harmed the other person physically, prejudiced his freedom, his honour or his property rights.

There are no statutory guidelines as to the amount of non-pecuniary loss. Damages are decided solely by the court. In traffic accident cases, however, in some district courts, there is a standardised practice for calculating non-pecuniary damages. According to the practice of the court, damages for non-pecuniary loss in the case of breadwinner's death was, at the maximum, 24 million yen (approximately 100 thousand pounds), while in the case of a housewife's death, it was around 20 million yen (80 thousand pounds) in 1991. Non-pecuniary loss covers not only physical harm itself, but also its after-effects.[11]

It is often pointed out that since the amount of damages for non-pecuniary loss can be flexible, the court supplements

---

9 Judgment of the Supreme Court, 24 June, 1964 (*Minshū* 18–5–874).
10 Judgment of the Supreme Court, 19 July, 1974 (*Minshū* 28–5–872).
11 Joint Committee of the Tokyo Bar Associations on the Settlement of Traffic Accident Cases ed., *Songai-Baishō Santei-Kijun (Guideline for the Calculation of Damages)*, Tokyo 1991, p. 24.

compensation for pecuniary loss with that for non-pecuniary loss in order to reach a fair solution. This happens especially in cases where the victim is a child or a housewife, since in these cases, compensation for pecuniary loss can be very low.

A related problem is the inheritability of the right to claim compensation for non-pecuniary loss. The problem here is on what basis should the family and relatives of the person who was killed by a tortious act receive compensation. The Code provides as follows (Art. 711):

> A person who has caused the death of another person shall be liable for damages for non-pecuniary loss to the parents, spouse and children of the victim, although their property rights were not affected.

In addition to the right to damages based on this provision, the court has maintained that the victim's right to claim compensation for non-pecuniary loss is inherited by the heirs. In a leading case, A was injured in a car accident, and later died. A's brother X, being one of the heirs, sued the culprit claiming that he had inherited the right to compensation for non-pecuniary loss. The Supreme Court ruled that since the right to compensation is a monetary right, it could be inherited. It should be noted that X was the brother of the deceased and was not entitled to compensation on his own right on the basis of Article 711 ; only parents, spouse or children are entitled to damages by this provision.[12]

The appropriateness of this solution which acknowledges that the claim for compensation of non-pecuniary loss can be inherited is being disputed. The primary aim of the above-mentioned solution is to protect the dependents of the deceased who are not covered by Article 711 from economic difficulty. If this is so, the aim can be also achieved by simply acknowledging the heirs' own right to compensation.

This solution may be more reasonable and fairer than the position taken by the court, since it is not always reasonable to give compensation, especially for non-pecuniary loss, to all heirs regardless of their relation to the deceased. It is far better to decide whether the rights of a specific person are infringed or not and whether the general requirements of tort are met or not.[13]

The Supreme Court has applied Article 711 flexibly in a case where a sister of the deceased – she was disabled and was totally dependant on him – was granted compensation on the basis of

---

12 Judgment of the Supreme Court, 1 November, 1967 (*Minshū* 21–9–2249).
13 I. Kato, *Minpō ni okeru Ronri to Rieki Kōryō* (*Logic and the Balancing of Interests in Civil Law*), Tokyo p. 289.

this provision.[14] Furthermore, despite the wording of Article 711, which limits compensation to cases where the victim has died, it was held by the Court that this provision should be applied with necessary modifications to cases where the victim has suffered a severe injury. This is an example of flexibility in the application of private law. The court sometimes does not refrain from deviating from a provision when it is necessary to achieve an equitable result.

Another problem is the loss to a company by the death or disability of an employee. The Civil Code does not have a provision defining the range of persons entitled to sue, except for Article 711. A problem arises when the owner or a senior employee of a company is killed or becomes disabled by a tortious act. If the company collapses after the loss of the owner or a manager, are the employees entitled to damages? In one case, the owner of a pharmacy was injured by a motorbike and as a result, his eyesight was severely damaged. The pharmacy was a limited company, owned by the victim; his wife was the sole member of the company. The victim sued the defendant for non-pecuniary loss, while the limited company, the pharmacy, sued the defendant for pecuniary loss, i.e. the decrease in sales resulting from the injury suffered by the victim. The defendant argued that the company was not entitled to damages, but the Supreme Court rejected this argument. The Court ruled that since the pharmacy was an extremely small company run primarily by the victim and economically, the victim and the company were one and the same, there was a causal link between the tortious act and the loss to the company.[15] So far, liability has been acknowledged by the court in similar cases where the company was small and could be considered in economic terms to be identical to the victim. This approach is supported by a majority of academics, since it is too harsh for a negligent tortfeasor to compensate for loss inflicted upon larger companies.

The Civil Code has a provision for contributory negligence. It is provided that when the victim is at fault, the court may take this into account when assessing the amount of compensation. Since contributory negligence is a device to achieve a fair distribution of loss, fault in this sense does not have to be strictly interpreted. The victim does not even have to be capable of responsibility. The court maintains that it is sufficient if the victim had the ability to distinguish between what is wrong and what is right. For instance, in one case, the court took into account the

14 Judgment of the Supreme Court, 17 December, 1974 (*Minshū* 28–10–2040).
15 Judgment of the Supreme Court, 15 November, 1968 (*Minshū* 22–12–2614).

contributory negligence of an eight-year-old boy in a traffic accident.[16]

When considering contributory negligence, not only the negligence of the victim himself, but also the negligence of those who are 'on the side of the victim' such as those who are responsible for overseeing the victim, are to be taken into account. Thus, when a toddler was hit by a car while his mother was looking away, the mother's negligence was taken into account in assessing compensation.

4. Special provisions concerning tort liability

Although the general provision on tort – Article 709 – is based upon the principle of fault, there are some provisions in the Civil Code which are close to strict liability. Provisions concerning the liability of parents and persons who have a duty to oversee the mentally unsound, which have already been mentioned, are examples. A person who is in charge of a minor is held liable for the latter's acts, unless he proves that he had not been negligent. In practice, the courts seldom accept that they have not neglected their duty.

Another provision pertinent to this issue is the provision on the liability of the employer for the act of employees. The Code provides as follows (Art. 715, para. 1):

> A person who employs another person for his business is liable for the loss caused to a third person by the latter in the course of business. However, if the employer proves that he has taken reasonable care in selecting the employee and overseeing his work, or that even with reasonable care, the loss could not have been avoided, he is exempted from liability.

The employer may claim indemnification from the employee after he has paid damages to the victim.

The employer's liability was initially seen as the personal liability of the employer for his negligence in selecting or supervising employees. The current prevailing view is that Article 715 provides for vicarious liability. Generally, the employer is pursuing profit by employing others, and therefore, should be liable for the loss caused in the course of his business. However, 'business' in this provision is not limited to commercial or profit-oriented undertakings and the relationship between the employer and the employee does not have to be onerous, and therefore,

16 Judgment of the Supreme Court, 24 June, 1964 (*Minshū* 18–5–854).

this argument alone cannot serve as a basis of liability on the part of the employer. The fact that the employer has opportunities to adopt effective measures to prevent the loss-causing action is also considered as the basis of this liability.

The liability of the employer presupposes the liability of the employee. The act of the latter has to fulfill the requirements of tort – i.e. he has to be either negligent or have acted intentionally, his act has to be unlawful, and there has to be a causal link between his act and the loss. Recently, there are people who propose that the requirement of fault on the part of the employee is not needed in a certain category of cases. It is pointed out that in cases where companies are involved, for instance in pollution cases, it is often difficult to specify which employee is at fault. Therefore, a strict requirement for proof of negligence on the part of the employee may result in unfair disadvantage of the victims.[17] This view, however, still remains a minority.

In order to pursue the liability of the employer, the given tortious act has to be committed in the course of business. More specifically, the act of the employee which caused loss has to be within his competence or closely related to it. This particularly becomes an issue when an employee has abused his position, acted out of self-interest and caused loss. For example, there may be cases where an employee who is authorised to sign contracts on behalf of the company abuses his position and enters into transaction with a third party out of his own interest. This is usually considered by the courts to be done 'in the course of business'.

Initially, the courts tended to interpret this clause narrowly and limited the liability of the employer to cases where the act of the employee was 'inseparable' from the business of the employer. However, in the 1920s, the courts changed their position and found the employer liable more broadly. The leading case involved a senior executive of the general affairs section who abused his power and issued share certificates. The company was found to be liable for his act.[18] The Supreme Court places weight on the issue of whether the given act appeared to be performed in the course of business. In one case, a manager of the accounting department of a company abused his power, used the signet of the executive chairman and issued a promissory note in the name of the company. The Supreme Court found this act to be done in

---

17 S. Itoh, *Fuhō-kōi-hō no Gendaiteki-kadai* (Current Problems of Tort Law), Tokyo 1980, pp. 124 ff.
18 Judgment of the Supreme Tribunal, 13 October, 1926 (*Minshū* 5–785).

the course of business on the ground that it appeared to a third party to be an act within the employee's power.[19] In such cases, it is required by the court that at least the victim was not aware, and was not seriously negligent in believing that the transaction was done in the course of business.[20] Thus, whether it was reasonable for an average person in business to assume that the employee is acting legitimately or not is the crucial point.

This conclusion is supported by the necessity to balance the interests represented by the employer, who had employed this person for his business, and the third party, who had believed that the tortfeasor had been acting within his power. If the third party had known that the tortfeasor was abusing his power, or was seriously negligent in believing that he was acting properly within the scope of his power, the employer is not liable.

The courts also interpret the 'in the course of business' proviso fairly broadly in cases other than business transactions. In one case, an employee of a car dealer killed a person while he was driving, without permission, a car which belonged to the company. The Supreme Court ruled that from the outside, the act of the employee appeared to be part of the employer's business, when taking into account the type and size of the employer's business, and therefore, should be considered to be performed in the course of the business.[1] However, it is questionable whether the 'appearance' of the act should be crucial in cases other than those involving business transactions, since in cases such as traffic accidents, the victims have not relied on the 'appearance'. It should be added that the Law on Compensation of Loss arising from Car Accidents has a provision on the liability of those who provide a car to the driver.[2] Employers are covered by this Law and are liable for loss caused by the driver even when the latter is not negligent (Art. 3).

In cases involving the liability of the employer, the defence of the employer on the ground that he had not been negligent in selecting or supervising the employee is seldom upheld by the court.

Another provision of the Civil Code which has moved towards strict liability is the provision on the liability of the owner of a building or a structure. Thus, if loss is caused to another person due to defects in the construction or maintenance of a building or structure on land, the person who possesses it is liable. If he proves that he had taken the necessary care to prevent such loss,

19 Judgment of the Supreme Court, 16 July, 1957 (*Minshū* 11–7–1254).
20 Judgment of the Supreme Court, 2 November, 1967 (*Minshū* 21–9–2278).
1 Judgment of the Supreme Court, 4 February, 1964 (*Minshū* 18–2–252).
2 Law No. 97, 1955.

then the owner is liable (Art. 717). The liability of the possessor is based on fault, while the owner bears strict liability. The rationale for this provision is that those who administer, manage or own a building or structure which is potentially dangerous to others should take sufficient steps to prevent the occurrence of harm, and once loss occurs, it is fair to make these people liable.[3]

Structures in this context include bridges, tunnels, roads, dikes, and lifts. The Supreme Court acknowledged that a railway crossing was a structure within the meaning of this provision and found that the owner was liable. In this case, safety devices were considered to be insufficient.[4]

The loss must arise from a defect in the construction or maintenance of the building or structure. If the loss would have occurred even had the object been without a defect, the loss is seen as arising from *force majeure* and this will excuse the possessor or owner from liability.

A similar provision exists in the Law on the Compensation by the State.[5] It is provided that the State or other public entity is liable for damages in cases where loss to others has been caused by a defect in the construction or administration of roads, rivers and other public property (Art. 2, para. 1).

This provision does not require negligence on the part of the State or the public entity. If the property does not meet the normally-required safety standard, it is regarded as defective. In one case, the Supreme Court ruled that the State was liable for improperly maintaining a highway where a driver was killed by a fall of rocks.[6] On the other hand, in a case where inhabitants who suffered from flood sued the State for improper maintenance of the river, the Supreme Court considered various factors including budgetary limits and rejected the claim of the plaintiff.[7]

5.   Joint tort liability

The Civil Code has a provision dealing with torts committed by several persons. The Code provides as follows (Art. 719, para. 1):

---

3 I. Kato, *supra* note 16, pp. 192–193.
4 Judgment of the Supreme Court, 23 April, 1971 (*Minshū* 25-3-351).
5 Law No. 125, 1947.
6 Judgment of the Supreme Court, 20 August, 1967 (*Minshū* 24-9-1268).
7 Judgment of the Supreme Court, 26 January, 1984 (*Minshū* 38-2-53: Daitō Suigai case).

In cases where several persons have jointly caused loss to another person by a tortious act, each one of them is liable jointly and severally with the others. The same should apply when it is impossible to specify which one of the joint perpetrators have actually caused the loss.

The first part of this provision deals with 'joint tort liability'. The meaning of joint tort liability varies, and the terms used here are rather confusing. The most typical case is where several persons injure somebody. Everyone who takes part in the assault is liable, even though not all of them have inflicted damage on the victim. Fault is required of all the tortfeasors. Also causal links should exist between the act of each person and the result, but this latter requirement is somewhat relaxed in the prevailing opinion. Thus, it is sufficient if the act of each perpetrator is 'related' to the joint act which directly causes the loss. After all, if each perpetrator has to fulfill all the requirements of the definition of a tort, there is almost no point in providing for joint tort liability in addition to the general provision on tort.

The court does not require prior agreement, conspiracy, or a common intention among tortfeasors. It is sufficient if the tortious act can be regarded objectively as being committed jointly.[8] Instigators and accomplices are considered to be joint tortfeasors and are jointly and severally liable for the loss.

Joint liability means that each tortfeasor is liable for all the loss. The victim may demand full compensation from any one of the tortfeasors. Thus, the victim does not have to sue all the tortfeasors, nor does he have to decide the proportion of liability among them in order to demand compensation. In this way, the provision of joint tort liability is designed to safeguard the interests of victims. If one of the tortfeasors pays full compensation, he is entitled to demand indemnification from the other tortfeasors in accordance with the extent of liability.

Joint tortious liability became an issue in pollution cases in the 1960s and 1970s. For instance, there was a case where several factories discharged polluted air and caused local inhabitants serious bronchial problems. These factories formed an industrial complex in the area, and were closely connected with one another. The victims sued the companies which constituted the industrial complex. The district court ruled that even when the act of each tortfeasor did not by itself cause loss, if it caused loss in concurrence with other tortfeasors' act, all of them were liable. In this case, it was ascertained that without each party's act, the

8 Judgment of the Supreme Court, 26 March, 1955 (*Minshū* 11-3-543).

loss would not have been caused. The court also acknowledged that the defendants, who formed an industrial complex, were sufficiently related to be made jointly liable.[9]

The latter part of Article 719, para. 1 deals with cases where it is not known which of the persons involved in the act is liable for the loss. It is presumed that those who were involved have jointly caused the damage. A defendant may refute the presumption by proving that there was no causal link between his act and the harm caused. For example, if three persons were smoking and fire broke out afterwards, they are jointly liable even if it is not specified which one of them caused the fire. In one case, a person was injured in a car accident and later died in hospital. The condition of the victim had deteriorated in the hospital due to malpractice on the part of a doctor. However, it was not known whether the accident itself or the malpractice was the real cause of the death. The court found both the driver and the doctor liable for the death of the victim on the basis of this provision.[10]

6.   Available remedies

As a rule, the remedy comprises monetary compensation (Art. 722). Furthermore, the plaintiff may demand the restoration of the *status quo ante* in some cases. For example, in libel cases, the court may order the publication of an apology together with compensation (Art. 723).

As regards injunctions, there is no explicit provision in the Civil Code allowing for injunctions. In cases where a real right has been infringed, an injunction is available. For example, when someone is building a house on another person's property, the owner, on the basis of his right of ownership, is entitled to an injunction. In fact, this is not a remedy based on tort law, but is regarded as an attribute of real rights. Therefore, fault on the part of the trespasser is not required.

In some cases other than the infringement of real rights, an injunction is also available. For instance, when there is an infringement of privacy, honour or reputation, it is asserted that an injunction should be made available on the basis of the general right of personality, despite the absence of an explicit provision in the Code. However, in principle, injunction based

---

9 Judgment of Tsu District Court, Yokkaichi Division, 24 July, 1967 (*Hanji* 672–30: Yokkaiachi Pollution Case).
10 Judgment of Tokyo District Court, 7 June, 1967 (*Kaminshū* 18–5/6–607).

on Tort Law is not available. At least the courts seem to take this view.

As for pollution and public-nuisance cases, an injunctive remedy is needed, but its availability and its legal basis are a focus of discussion. Some broaden the concept of real rights, while others resort to the notion of 'general rights of personality' or 'rights to a proper environment' in order to justify injunctions. In some cases, the courts found that a property right of the plaintiff was infringed and granted an injunction. According to a study of cases between 1950 and 1980, there were 145 cases where injunctions were sought. In 77 cases, the grounds for seeking an injunction were not specified, while in 29 cases, the claim was based upon real rights.[11]

In one case, people living near the Super Express train line sued Japan National Railways for harm caused by the noise and vibration of the trains. In addition to damages, the plaintiffs demanded that the company slow down the trains and so reduce the vibration and noise. The District Court of Nagoya generally acknowledged the availability of an injunction based on 'general rights of personality', but in this specific case, it refused to grant one. This view was upheld by the Appellate Court, but was later reversed by the Supreme Court.[12]

It should be added that interlocutory injunctions are used to achieve a goal similar to that of injunctions. It is possible to ask the court to order a temporary freezing of the situation, or to terminate temporarily the activities concerning the alleged tort. Since the mid–1960s, there have been cases where householders sued a developer to prevent him from constructing a building which could decrease their access to sunlight. In such cases, the courts often order suspension of the construction until the case is decided by the court. This may take some years.[13]

7. Product liability

There is no special law on product liability in Japan. This is in contrast to some other jurisdictions including the European Community where special legislation has come into force in recent years. The number of litigations concerning product

11 For details, see M. Kato, "Sashitome (Injunction)" in *supra* note 19, pp. 75–83.
12 Judgment of Nagoya District Court, 11 September, 1980, Judgment of Nagoya Appellate Court, 12 April, 1985 (*Hanji* 1150–30).
13 T. Ikuyo, *Fuhō-kōi hō (Tort Law)*, Tokyo 1977, pp. 300–301.

liability was fairly small in Japan – less than 100 cases since the Second World War. This is not to say that serious incidents where product liability was at issue did not occur in Japan. On the contrary, there were cases where toxic substances included in food caused serious harm to human health. The case involving powder milk for babies with toxic ingredients and another case involving rice oil intoxicated with PCB have already been mentioned in the preceding sections. There were also cases such as the Thalidomide case where, as a result of side effects of a medicine, newly born babies had to suffer. The problem of defective cars was also highlighted some years ago.

Technically, product liability can be pursued either by contract law (Arts. 415 and 570) or by tort law (Art. 709). Differences are that 1) tort law presupposes fault on the part of the tortfeasor which has to be proved by the plaintiff, while Article 570 provides for strict liability and Article 415 lays the burden of proof with the obligor=defendant; 2) contract law is applicable only between the seller and the buyer; it does not reach the manufacturer.

The liability of those who produced and marketed intoxicated food or medicine with side effects was pursued primarily on the basis of tort law. This was because the manufacturer's, and not the seller's, liability was at issue. However, it is often very difficult for an individual without resources to prove causal links and fault. In the cases cited above, the plaintiffs were successful, but in these cases, the harm was widespread and a number of people were involved. Since the incident drew attention of the general public, some official bodies assisted the plaintiffs in collecting necessary information and providing evidence. The courts endeavoured to alleviate the burden of proof. Even with such support, it took many years to reach the final settlement.

On the other hand, individuals who suffered a loss arising from defective home appliances or cars, find it hard to prove the case against manufacturers. For instance, there was a case where a fire broke out and a television set was suspected to be the cause of the fire. Victims saw flame coming out of the set, but the manufacturer refused to pay damages on the ground that there was no causal links. The parties reached a compromise at the court, on the condition that the name of the manufacturer will not be disclosed.

In order to make matters easier for those who suffered a loss, enactment of a Law on Product Liability has been proposed from time to time. In 1990, an advisory committee to the Economic Planning Agency published a report which stressed the necessity of a new law. Japan Federation of Bar Association published a draft programme of the Law on Product Liability in the same year.[14]

This programme has introduced strict liability. Whereas the European Community Directive of 1985 allows Member States to acknowledge the defence of development risk, i.e. the defence that the manufacturer has exhausted all the safety means in the light of the state of the art, this was denied in the programme. Defect of merchandise is defined as a condition of goods which is likely to endanger life, health, or property of a person in an unreasonable way because of the failure to meet safety standards or to ensure quality which consumers are entitled to expect. If a loss occurred despite the fact that the goods has been used, transported, or disposed of in a normal way, it is presumed that it was defective and the loss was caused by such a defect.

Persons who are liable for defective goods are not limited to manufacturers; importers as well as those who allowed the goods to be marketed in their name are equally liable. Agreements which limit the liability in advance are null and void. As for damages, pecuniary and non-pecuniary losses are both covered. In addition, in cases where the manufacturer was at serious fault, they are liable for punitive damages of maximum twice the amount of normal damages.

This move towards the enactment of the law on product liablity has generally been favourably accepted. However, there are those who are cautious since, in their view, this law, once enacted, may give rise to a flood of litigation and excessive demand for damages.

14 M. Asaoka, 'Nichibenren Seizōbutsu-Sekinin-Hō Yōkō Dai-ichiji Shian no Kaisetsu' (*Commentaries on the First Draft of the Law on Product Liability by the Japanese Federation of Bar Associations*), *New Business Law*, 1991, No. 464, pp. 32–40.

11 Family law and succession

1. The development of Japanese family system

Family Law in Japan is embodied in Part Four of the Civil Code. Together with Part Five which deals with succession, this part of the Code has undergone a total change in the course of post-War Reform.

In the pre-War period, the family was dominated by the head of the family, and was considered to be the basic unit of the entire social system. While authority was concentrated in the head of the family, other members of the family were 'protected' by the head, but had no formal rights against him. The head of the family had the power to designate the place where family members should live, to control their choice of marriage-partner and to expel them from the family when necessary. He had exclusive rights of control over the property of the family. The family relationships were strictly hierarchical. Thus, children were subordinated to their father and the eldest son, expected to succeed his father as the head of the family, enjoyed a privileged status. Female members were considered to be inferior to male members and even the mother was ranked below the eldest son. The wife had no legal capacity at all and was listed as an 'incompetent' in the Civil Code. The Criminal Code had a provision punishing adultery, but it applied only to wives.

It should be noted that this Confucian, male-dominated hierarchical 'house' was considered to be a reflection of the entire social system, at the top of which reigned the Emperor. After the seventh century, even the imperial throne was tied to the male line. The idea that the Emperor was the benevolent father and the head of the entire Japanese family was promoted by the rulers in the period of modernisation in order to ensure national unity.

The reform of family law was thought to be a priority after the War, because the family system in the pre-War period had helped to support the Emperor-centred political system. Preparations for amending the Civil Code started almost simultaneously with the drafting of the new Constitution. The reform of the family system did not proceed without opposition. Some Japanese conservatives who took part in the drafting process defended the previous 'house' system.[1]

The Constitution preceded the amendment of the Civil Code by a year. The Constitution incorporated a provision on family relations. Thus, Article 24 (para. 2) provides as follows:

> With regard to choice of spouse, property rights, inheritance, choice of domicile, divorce and other matters pertaining to marriage and the family, laws shall be enacted from the standpoint of individual dignity and the essential equality of the sexes.

Family relations as provided by the amended Civil Code are entirely different from those in the pre-War period. Firstly, members of the family are now treated as equals instead of being dominated by the head of the family. The chapter of the Code on the 'house' and the head of the family have been deleted. Secondly, the inequality between the sexes has changed. Husbands and wives, fathers and mothers now have equal rights to property as well as in the upbringing of the children. Thirdly, while the eldest son enjoyed privileges under the previous system (he was the sole heir), the amended Code provides for equality of children. Finally, provisions concerning the lack of legal capacity of wives were removed from the Code.

2. Marriage

Part Four of the Civil Code is divided into five chapters, which are the General Part, Marriage, Parents and Children, Parental Rights, and Guardianship.

While under the 'house' system, the consent of the head of the family was required for marriage, marriage under the present law is solely based upon the agreement of the parties. Marriage is effected by registration in accordance with the Law on the Civil Status.[2] Naturally, registration has to coincide with the intention of the parties to marry. Thus, registration for a marriage in which the parties intended to marry merely in order to make their child legitimate was found to be void.[3] Registration is accepted when the requirements set out by the Civil Code are met.

---

1 T. Kawashima, 'Americanisation of Japanese Family Law', *Law in Japan*, vol. 16, 1983, p. 55.
2 Law No. 224, 1947.
3 Judgment of the Supreme Court, 31 October, 1969 (*Minshū* 23–10–1894).

The age requirement for marriage is 18 for males and 16 for females (Art. 731). However, for those who are below 20 years of age, parental consent is needed. If the views of the parents differ, consent of either of the parents is sufficient (Art. 737). These minors are given full legal capacity upon marriage (Art. 753). Those who are already married may not marry (Art. 732). Such an act is an offence under the Criminal Code. Marriage between lineal relatives by blood, or between collateral relatives by blood of up to the third degree of relationship is prohibited (Art. 734, para. 1). Thus, for instance, an uncle may not marry his niece, while cousins may marry. Furthermore, marriage between lineal relatives by affinity is banned (Art. 736). For instance, a man may not marry his mother-in-law, even after the marriage has been dissolved.

The Civil Code does not have explicit provisions regarding engagement, but it is an institution protected by law. The courts have maintained that a breach of engagement without a justifiable reason entails compensation on the ground of contract law or tort law.[4] On the other hand, engagement with a married person in the expectation that the marriage will be dissolved is void, since it is against public order and good morals.[5]

The husband and wife must have a common family name. Under the previous Code, wives had to use the husbands' family name. In contrast, now the couple may chose which family name they are to use (Art. 750). This arrangement of a common family name is criticised because it is disadvantageous for the spouse which has to change his/her name. When the marriage has been terminated by the death of a spouse, the remaining spouse may choose to use the previous family name. Also in cases of divorce, the spouse may choose to continue using the family name before the divorce.

A married couple have mutual obligations. They have a duty to live together, although not enforceable, and to support each other and cooperate. A breach of the duty to live together, cooperate and to support each other without justifiable reason is a ground for divorce. In practice, due to the gap in the living and educational standards between Tokyo and other parts of Japan, it is not unusual for businessmen to lead a solitary life while their family lives in Tokyo.

The property of a married couple belongs separately to the husband and wife. Property which has belonged to the spouse from before the marriage, or which the spouse has obtained in his

---

4 Judgment of the Supreme Court, 11 April, 1958 (*Minshū* 12–5–789).
5 Judgment of the Supreme Tribunal, 28 May, 1920 (*Minroku* 26–773).

or her own name during the marriage belongs to this spouse during the marriage (Art. 762). Property whose ownership cannot be determined is presumed to be jointly owned by the couple. This contrasts with the previous system where the husband had control over the wife's property.

The husband and wife may conclude a contract as to their property relationship before marriage (Art. 756). This contract cannot be altered after the marriage has taken effect (Art. 758). In practice, pre-nuptial arrangements are seldom made.

A problem arises when property is obtained in the name of the spouse, but the other party has contributed to obtaining it. Such contribution is to be taken into account when determining the distribution of property. This was contested in a case where a husband and wife ran an inn, which had been inherited from the husband's mother but was managed and registered in the name of the wife. When the wife was divorced for infidelity, she claimed that the land on which the inn was built belonged to her, since it was registered in her name. The Supreme Court rejected this argument and ruled that registration itself is not sufficient to determine whether the property belonged to the wife.[6] This judgment has been criticised since it failed to take into account the contribution made by the wife in running the inn.

Expenses incurred during the marriage are shared by the husband and wife by taking into account their assets, income and other circumstances (Art. 760). When either a husband or a wife has incurred debts in relation to daily household matters, they are jointly liable (Art. 761). Daily household matters include purchase of daily goods, contracts for medical treatments and domestic rent.

Marriage is dissolved by death of either party, declaration of disappearance or divorce. Divorce is possible upon agreement by the parties (Art. 763) and there is no restriction on the ground for such divorce. Divorce is effected by registration. When the parties fail to reach agreement, a conciliation procedure is available. Even when the parties intend to contest the case in a formal procedure, the case must first go through the conciliation procedure. Conciliation is conducted by the conciliation committee of the family court. The committee is composed of a conciliation officer, who is a judge of the family court, and two conciliation councillors. Even when conciliation fails, the committee is entitled to grant divorce by taking into account all the circumstances of the case. This happens, for example, when the

6 Judgment of the Supreme Court, 14 July, 1959 (*Minshū* 13–7–1023).

marriage has actually broken down beyond repair, but the parties fail to agree because of emotional reasons. The unsatisfied party may file an objection which nullifies the award. When there is no objection, the award has the same effect as a formal judgment.

Divorce can be effected by a court judgment. In Japan, most divorce cases are settled by conciliation or adjudication and it is rare that a divorce case is settled by formal civil procedure. The Civil Code lists five grounds for divorce by court procedure: infidelity or malicious desertion, the death or life of the spouse being unknown for more than three years, serious mental disease of the spouse which is irrecoverable, and other grounds which makes it impossible to continue marriage (Art. 770, para. 1). Divorce on a ground which makes the continuation of marriage impossible, i.e. where the marriage has irretrievably broken down, includes cases such as the conviction of the spouse, alcoholism, severe incompatibility and maltreatment by parents-in-law. It is considered to be impractical to force a couple to continue marriage in spite of its actual breakdown.

The court may refuse to grant divorce even when there are grounds for divorce as provided in the Code (Art. 770, para. 2). Since the grounds on which the court may refuse to grant divorce are not explicitly stated in the Code, the courts have developed a body of case law on this issue. Thus, the court has refused to grant divorce in a case where the spouse was suffering from mental disease. In this case, the Supreme Court ruled that unless certain arrangements are made for medical treatment and the future life of the spouse, divorce should not be allowed.[7]

Furthermore, there is a controversial line of cases to the effect that divorce cannot be claimed by the party responsible for the breakdown of the marriage. The rationale is that an unlimited divorce on the initiative of such a party may result in unfairness to the other party or children. In a leading case, the Supreme Court refused to allow divorce claimed by a husband who left his wife and chose to live with a pregnant mistress.[8] The precedent has been relaxed to a certain extent since then. The Supreme Court ruled that in some cases, the party which was 'primarily' responsible for the breakdown of the marriage was entitled to seek a divorce.[9] It is considered to be inappropriate to force the continuation of a marriage which has already broken down. Therefore, the courts came to grant divorces even when sought

7 Judgment of the Supreme Court, 25 July, 1958 (*Minshū* 12–12–1823).
8 Judgment of the Supreme Court, 19 February, 1952 (*Minshū* 6–2–110).
9 Judgment of the Supreme Court, 24 November, 1955 (*Minshū* 9–12–1837).

by the responsible party, provided that sufficient financial arrangements are made for the other party and that there are no children under 20.

Finally, the Supreme Court explicitly changed its approach in 1987. In this case, a couple had adopted two daughters. The husband actually had relations with the real mother of these two adopted daughters, and when this was revealed he began to live with her. The couple lived separately for more than 30 years. The husband was well-off but failed to support the abandoned wife, who had no property. The husband sought a divorce procedure, but the lower courts refused to grant a divorce. The Supreme Court set out general guidelines for granting divorce to the responsible party and reversed the decision of the lower court. Thus, the Supreme Court ruled that when the couple had been living separately for a sufficiently long period, had no young children, and there were no special circumstances making the claim from the responsible party unjust, such a claim for divorce should not be rejected.[10]

When divorce is granted, issues concerning the property of the parties and the welfare of the children must be settled. The couple also must discuss the problem of which person should take custody of the children. If the parties fail to reach agreement, the family court decides (Art. 766, para. 1 and Art. 771). After divorce, either party may claim distribution of property (Art. 768, para. 1, Art. 771). This claim includes redistribution of matrimonial property and payment of alimony, as well as damages for non-pecuniary loss. It is generally accepted that the party which was responsible for the breakdown of the marriage is liable for compensation based on tort law. Whether the damages can be claimed together with redistribution of matrimonial property and alimony has been a focus of discussion. The Supreme Court allows the party to choose whether to claim damages together with other claims or not.[11]

Distribution of property is made through conciliation proceedings, but if the parties fail to agree, the family court decides by taking into account 'the amount of property which has been obtained with the assistance of the spouse and all other circumstances' (Art. 768, para. 3). The Code has only two provisions concerning matrimonial property and its distribution. Therefore, a wide range of issues are left to the practice of the family courts.

10 Judgment of the Supreme Court, 2 September, 1987 (*Minshū* 41–6–1423).
11 Judgment of the Supreme Court, 23 July, 1971 (*Minshū* 25–5–805).

The contribution of a spouse in obtaining matrimonial property is often difficult to assess, especially when only one member of the couple had an income. The contribution of the wife through housework is generally taken into account by the courts. In some cases where only the husband had an income, the house which the couple had acquired during the marriage was acknowledged to be joint property by taking into consideration the contribution of the wife.[12]

Common-law marriages were not uncommon in the pre-War period, especially because of the 'house' system which inhibited free marriage. The Supreme Tribunal had extended some protection to such marriages. Thus, the Tribunal acknowledged that a common-law wife who was deserted by the husband was entitled to compensation for breach of contract.[13] Furthermore, a common-law wife was allowed to claim damages in tort resulting from the death of the husband. Since the Second World War, the Supreme Court has treated common-law marriage as a quasi-marriage which should be treated in a similar way to formal marriage. The court ruled, for instance, that desertion without justifiable ground in a common-law marriage constituted a tort.[14] In financial arrangements also, common-law marriage is treated in a similar way to that of formal marriage. Thus, spouses have the same mutual duties as in formal marriage. Matrimonial property is distributed in the same way.[15] In one case, a common-law wife who had run a cloth shop with her husband claimed rights over pieces of land which the couple obtained during the marriage. The land was registered in the husband's name. The court acknowledged the contribution of the common-law wife and ruled that the land belonged jointly to the wife and husband.[16] It should be added that in insurance claims and pension rights, common-law marriage is treated equally with formal marriage.

A problem arises in common-law marriage where one of the parties is formally married to a third party. Initially, the courts ruled that this kind of relationship had no legal effect. Later, the courts changed their views and acknowledged such common-law marriage, provided that the extant formal marriage has irretrievably broken down.[17]

---

12 Judgment of the Sapporo Appellate Court, 19 June, 1986 (*Hanta* 614–70).
13 Judgment of the Supreme Tribunal, 26 January, 1915 (*Minroku* 21–49).
14 Judgment of the Supreme Court, 11 April, 1958 (*Minshū* 12–5–789).
15 Decision of Hiroshima Appellate Court, 19 June, 1963 (*Kōminshū* 16–4–265).
16 Judgment of the Osaka Appellate Court, 30 November, 1982 (*Kagetsu* 36–1–139).
17 Judgment of the Supreme Tribunal, 8 April, 1937 (*Minshū* 16–418).

3. Family and the children

A child born between a married couple is a legitimate child. There are 'presumed' legitimacy and 'non-presumed' legitimacy. A child conceived by the wife during the marriage is legally presumed to be legitimate (Art. 772, para. 1). A child conceived after 200 days of marriage or within 300 days of the dissolution of marriage is presumed to be conceived during marriage (Art. 772, para. 2). The presumption of legitimacy can be reversed only by a court order sought by the father (Art. 775). The father may initiate proceedings against the mother to deny the legitimacy of the child.

Legitimacy is not limited to children conceived after 200 days of marriage. The Supreme Tribunal acknowledged a child which was born on the day of marriage to be legitimate where a common-law marriage preceded the formal marriage, although it is not presumed to be legitimate.[18] In registration practice, a child born within 200 days of the marriage is also treated as a legitimate child.

An illegitimate child can be legitimised either by the father or mother (Art. 779). The child may initiate an action against the father for legitimacy. This action cannot be brought more than three years after the father's death (Art. 787). A legitimised child has the same rights as other children, except that the portion of inheritance is half that of other children.

Family relationships are also created by adoption. There are only three legal requirements for adoption. The adopter has to be over 20 years of age, the person who is to be adopted must be younger than the adopter, and should not be his lineal ascendant (Arts. 792 and 793). A married person must adopt a child jointly with the spouse. Adoption of a minor must be approved by the family court. The court decides the matter from the viewpoint of whether or not the adoption is appropriate for the welfare of the child. The motives and purposes for adoption, the suitability of the adopter and family relations are taken into account. In one case, adoption of a baby with the view of making him the successor of an abbot was rejected by the family court.[19]

When the child is less than 15 years old, a legal representative may agree to adoption on behalf of the child. However, if there is

---

18 Judgment of the Supreme Tribunal, 23 January, 1940 (*Minshū* 19–54).
19 Adjudication of the Niigata Family Court, 10 August, 1982 (*Kagetsu* 35–10–79).

a person who has custody over the child, this person's consent is also needed (Art. 797).

It is not rare that a married couple adopts a baby from the cradle and registers it as their legitimate child. The courts have denied the legitimacy of such a child.[20] Some people maintain that such an arrangement should be considered as a valid adoption.

The amendment of the Code in 1987 introduced a system of 'special adoption'. This system is applicable to children below six years of age, whose parents have serious difficulties in bringing up the child and where the adoption is particularly needed for the welfare of the child. The family court, after six months' trial period, may approve adoption. With the adoption, the relationship between the real parents is severed, and the child becomes a legitimate child of the adopters. It is not apparent from the registry that the child has been adopted (Arts. 817-2 – 817-11).

Parents have rights and duties to care and bring up the child. A child who has not yet attained majority is subject to parental power, which is exercised jointly by the parents. The parents have the right to designate the child's place of residence and give consent to the choice of occupation (Art. 821, Art. 823, para. 1). Those with parental power have the right to administer the property of the child and act on the child's behalf in financial matters. In cases of conflict of interests, for instance, transfer of the child's property to the parents, a special legal representative must be appointed by the family court (Art. 826, para. 1).

In cases where a father or mother abuses parental rights, or has committed gross misconduct, the family court may deprive the person of parental rights on appeal from the public prosecutor (Art. 834).

When a minor is left without both parents, or when there is no one to exercise parental power for other reasons, a guardian is appointed. Unless the person who last held parental power had designated a guardian, the family court makes the appointment. A guardian is also needed for those who are declared to have no legal capacity. If either of a married couple is declared incompetent, the spouse becomes a guardian. Guardians are supervised by the family court. In practice, when there is no person to exercise parental power over a minor, the relatives care for the child without formally selecting a guardian.

---

20 For example, judgment of the Supreme Court, 8 April, 1975 (*Minshū* 29-4-401).

4.   The law of succession

The law of succession also underwent a significant change after the Second World War. In the pre-War period, the 'house' and all the property contained in it were inherited by the eldest son. The younger sons and daughters had no rights whatsoever to the estate. This system was totally changed in the post-War reforms. The estate is distributed to the spouse as well as to younger sons and daughters.

There are two kinds of succession: testate and intestate. In practice, the former is rather exceptional.

The rules concerning the distribution of inherited property are set out in the Code in detail. A surviving wife or husband is, without exception, an heir. Children of the deceased are heirs of the first rank, lineal ascendants (parents and grandparents) are heirs of second rank, and brothers and sisters come third. Thus, where there is a wife and several children left, the heirs of the second and third rank have no share in the estate. In such cases, half the estate is distributed to the surviving spouse, while the remaining half is divided equally between the children. If there are no children, but a spouse is left, the estate is divided among the spouse and the lineal ascendants. The former takes two-thirds of the estate. If the latter have already died, the spouse and the sister or brother divide the estate. The surviving spouse takes three quarters of the property (Arts. 887, 889, 890, and 900). Previously, the spouse's share was smaller, but an amendment of 1980 increased it. Common-law wives and husbands are not entitled and children of half blood have half the share of those with whole blood.

If a prospective heir (a child, a sister or a brother) dies before the deceased, this person's lineal descendant (grandchildren, a niece or a nephew) becomes the heir (Art. 887).

A person may apply to the family court for disinheritance of the prospective heir (Art. 892). Disinheritance can also be effected by will. The grounds for disinheritance are maltreatment or a serious insult to the testator, or gross misconduct on the part of the prospective heir.

An heir can also be disqualified on the grounds specified by the Code, which cover instances where the heir has killed or attempted to kill the deceased or other heirs who have priority, failed to report the death of the deceased while knowing that he has been killed, or forged the will or forced the deceased to alter his will (Art. 891). Disqualification is effected without any formality.

A prospective heir has a choice to accept or renounce succession. The heir may also accept succession with reservation by declaring that he is liable for the debts of the deceased only to the amount of the inherited estate (Arts. 920, 922, and 938). Renunciation or acceptance with reservation has to be done within three months after the person has become aware of the death of the deceased and of the fact that he is to inherit the estate. He must prepare an inventory of the estate and declare renunciation or acceptance at the family court in order to effect renunciation or acceptance with reservation. When an heir fails to renounce or accept inheritance with reservation within three months, he is deemed to have accepted inheritance.

By succession, the estate of the deceased as well as his or her debts are passed directly to the heirs. The Code provides that until the estate is distributed among the heirs, it belongs to them jointly (Art. 898). The system of personal representatives is unknown in Japan. Administrators are rarely appointed in practice. The distribution of the estate takes effect retrospectively to the time when the succession took place (Art. 909, para. 1). Since the estate passes to the heirs immediately after succession, there are cases, for instance, where one of the heirs sells part of the property without the consent of the other heirs before the division of the estate. Also one of the heirs may want to pay his debt out of the estate. In such cases, the distribution of the estate does not affect the third party who emerged before the distribution (Art. 909, para. 2). Thus, if one of the heirs sold part of the inherited land to a third party before distribution, this transaction is valid, provided that the third party was not negligent.[1]

If there is a will, the estate is distributed accordingly. If there is not, the heirs are to discuss the way the estate should be distributed. When this fails, an heir may apply to the family court for distribution. The court will try to conciliate, but when this attempt fails, the case will be adjudicated. Distribution of the estate is made by taking into account the nature of the property, age of the heirs, their occupation, mental and physical health, the state of their life and all other circumstances (Art. 906). Distribution of the estate does not have to coincide with the share of each heir as provided by the Code or the will insofar as all parties agree.

An heir whose right to inherit the estate has been ignored may claim recovery of his share within five years after this person or his legal representative has become aware of the fact (Art. 884).

1 Judgment of the Supreme Court, 22 February, 1963 (*Minshū* 17–1–235).

The scope of an inherited estate is disputed in some cases. Firstly, whether a lease of a flat or a house is inheritable or not has been discussed. For instance, in cases where the deceased has been living with a common-law wife, she, after his death, may be evicted by the heirs, if the status of lessee is to be inherited by the heirs. Scholarly opinions deny that the lease may be inherited, in order to safeguard the wife's right to live in the matrimonial home. Regarding the claim of eviction from a landlord, the Supreme Court has acknowledged that a common-law wife may exercise the right of the heir against the landlord.[2]

Secondly, whether insurance payments should be counted as an inherited estate has been a focus of debate. Generally, when one of the heirs has been designated as a beneficiary of insurance, it is considered not to be included in the estate. The same applies to a death allowance paid by a company where the deceased had worked. The beneficiary is to receive such allowances separately from the sums inherited.

Among the heirs, those who by providing labour, service or financial support to the business of the deceased, or by nursing him, made special contributions for maintaining or increasing property of the deceased, receive an additional share from the estate. When the heirs fail to agree, the family court is to decide on the matter (Art. 904–2). This system was formally introduced by the amendment of the Code in 1980, but in practice family courts had invariably taken into account the contribution of the heirs in dividing the estate even before the amendment. In a typical case after the amendment, the second wife of the deceased, her daughter, the daughter of the former wife and her husband who was later adopted by the couple claimed that they were entitled to an additional share. The second wife had worked for 40 years on a pig farm on behalf of the deceased who has been busy somewhere else. The adopted son has also worked for eight years and contributed to the assets. Their contribution was found to warrant an additional share by the court. The daughter had helped her mother, but it was not enough to be acknowledged as a special contribution. The other daughter had left the family after she was grown up and was found not to deserve an additional share.[3]

Testate succession is fairly uncommon in Japan. Any person over 15 years of age is capable of making a will. Persons who lack lack legal capacity may also make a will. A will can be retracted any time by the testator.

2 Judgment of the Supreme Court, 28 April, 1967 (*Minshū* 21–3–780).
3 Adjudication of Maebashi Family Court, 14 July, 1986 (*Kagetsu*, 38–12–84).

A will must follow the formalities set out in the Code. There are three kinds of ordinary wills: a will by his own hand (holographic will), a will by notary and a secret will (Arts. 968–970). There are also extraordinary wills such as a deathbed will and a will at a remote place, for instance, on a ship.

A holographic will must be written by the testator with the date of the will and the name of the testator and must have his or her signet on it. Witnesses are not needed. In order to have effect, it requires probate by the family court. A notarial will is made by dictating the will to a notary in the presence of two witnesses. It is signed and sealed by the testator, witnesses and the notary. In a will by a secret deed, the testator makes a will or has someone write the will on his behalf, signs and seals it, puts it in an envelope. The envelope is then sealed and signed by the testator, two witnesses and the notary. This also needs probate by the family court.

The deceased may dispose of his property in his life time or in his will as a testamentary disposition. If the deceased has given property to one of the prospective heirs during his life time or by testamentary disposition, this is counted in the distribution of the estate. A certain category of heirs have a secured portion in the estate which cannot be deprived even by a will. This is intended to safeguard the family from arbitrariness on the part of the deceased. Heirs entitled to this secured portion are children, spouse and lineal ascendants (Art. 1028). When the lineal ascendants are the only heirs, one third of the estate is reserved for them. Otherwise, a half of the estate is reserved. Therefore, if a wife and two children are left, they are entitled to a half of the estate regardless of the will of the deceased.

12 Intellectual property law

1. Patent law

1) The Development of Patent Law

An embryonic form of the patent system emerged in Japan in 1871 in the form of the Summary Rules of Monopoly. This Rule was in force for only a year. Then in 1885, the Patent Monopoly Ordinance, which was influenced by French and U.S. law was enacted. After three years, this Ordinance was replaced by the Patent Ordinance of 1888. A new Patent Law was enacted in 1899 together with the Design Law and the Trade Mark Law in order to pave the way for the accession to the Paris Convention. Japan became a signatory to the Paris Convention on the Protection of Intellectual Property in the same year.

The Patent Law of 1899 was replaced by a new Law in 1922. This Law, which laid the basis of the present patent system, marked a shift from the previous system where, similar to U.S. law, priority of invention was determined by the date of invention. The new Law gave priority to the invention which was first filed.

The present Patent Law was adopted in 1959 together with the Law on Utility Models. Some provisions of the Patent Law are applied with necessary modifications to utility models. The Patent Law has undergone various amendments since then. The 1970 amendments introduced an early disclosure system and examination-on-requirement system. In 1975, product patent was acknowledged and pharmaceutical products came to be covered by the Patent Law. By a 1987 amendment, a multi-item claim system, which is similar to the English and French system, was adopted.

Japan is a signatory to the Paris Convention and ratified the Stockholm amendments in 1975. Japan has also ratified the World Intellectual Property Organisation Treaty, Patent Cooperation Treaty, and the Strasbourg Treaty on the Classification of Patents.

2) Patentability

Invention is defined by the Patent Law as a highly advanced creation of technical ideas by utilising the law of nature (Art. 2, para. 1). It must be a result of the application of the *law of nature*. Therefore, mathematical theories, methods of ciphering, and computer programmes etc. are not patentable. Whether it is a 'highly advanced' creation or not is relevant when distinguishing a patentable invention from an invention suitable for protection as a utility model. There are three basic requirements for an invention to be patentable. These are novelty, inventive step, and industrial applicability (Art. 29).

The Law does not give any definition of novelty. Instead, it lists grounds by which novelty is lost (Art. 29, para. 1). Thus, if the invention was publicly known or implemented in Japan, or was published in Japan or abroad before application, it is not patentable. In one case, the invention was disclosed in the specification for a utility model in Germany. Copies of the specification were available on request. The Supreme Court found this to be a 'publication' in the meaning of Article 29, paragraph 1 and denied the novelty of the invention.[1]

There are some exceptions to this provision. For example, if the inventor tests the invention and discloses it in a publication or at a research conference, the invention is patentable, provided that the patent application is filed within six months from the date of disclosure (Art. 30, para. 1). Evident abuse is also considered to be an exception.

As regards inventive step, the Law provides that if a person who has standard knowledge in the given area of technology (a person skilled in the art) before the application could have easily made such an invention, it is not patentable (Art. 29, para. 2).[2] A mere aggregation of known technologies,[3] easily accomplished conversion of the existing technology, a mere replacement of a known technology etc. are not considered to have made an inventive step. On the other hand, inventive step may be acknowledged in an invention on the use of a known technology. A well-known example is an insecticide DDT, which had previously been used for a different purpose. This kind of invention is common in the pharmaceutical industry.

The third requirement of patentability is industrial

---

1 Judgment of the Supreme Court, 4 July, 1980 (*Minshū* 34–4–570).
2 Y. Hashimoto, *Tokkyo-hō* (*Patent Law*), revised edition, Tokyo 1988, p. 195.
3 Judgment of Tokyo Appellate Court, 17 October, 1967 (*Gyōsai-reishū* 18–10–1307).

applicability. Methods of curing a disease or diagnosis fail to meet this requirement and are not patentable. However, inventions concerning a gene or cell line may have industrial applicability.

The Law lists two grounds on which a patent cannot be granted. Firstly, invention of a substance which is produced by atomic nuclear transformation is not patentable. However, the method of producing such a substance is patentable. Secondly, an invention which is likely to harm public order, good morals, or public health is not patentable (Art. 32). Chemical substances, food, and medicine were delisted in 1975 and became patentable.

3) Patent procedure

Japan has adopted a system in which the first applicant, not the first inventor, is granted a patent in cases where there are competing inventions (Art. 39, para. 1). If there is a person who made the same invention independently and is exploiting the invention as a business or preparing to do so, he may continue exploiting the invention on a non-exclusive basis even after a patent was granted to the first applicant (Art. 79).

Any person who has made an invention is entitled to apply for a patent. If an employee makes an invention which falls within the scope of the employer's business and the acts which led to the invention was part of the duty of the employee, still, the employee has the right to apply for a patent. If the employee is granted a patent, then the employer has a non-exclusive licence to exploit this invention without payment of royalty (Art. 35, para. 1). It is possible for the employer and the employee to make a prior agreement as to the assignment of the patent or the right to apply for a patent.

Foreign citizens who are not domiciled or resident in Japan, are not entitled to patent and other related rights, unless there is a reciprocal arrangement with the home country of these persons, or an international treaty provides otherwise (Art. 25). Since Japan is a signatory to the Paris Convention and various bi-lateral treaties, this requirement of reciprocity is generally met.

The applicant may claim priority based upon Article 4 of the Paris Convention. If a person applies for a patent in the second country within 12 months of the application in the first country, he still has priority. The Director General of the Patent Office must be informed of the date and country of the first application in writing simultaneously with the patent application in Japan

(Art. 43, para. 1). The applicant is also obliged to submit a copy of the priority document within 16 months (Art. 43, para. 2).

By virtue of the Patent Cooperation Treaty, residents and nationals of the member countries are entitled to international patent application. The application has the same effect as an application within the designated countries. Thus, if there is an international application for a patent in England, which is a signatory to the Patent Cooperation Treaty, and Japan is one of the countries designated by the applicant, the date of international application is regarded also as the date of application in Japan (Art. 184–3, para. 1). This also applies to utility models. Patent Offices of countries concerned may not proceed with examination for 20 months from this date, while the procedure goes ahead at the international level.

Patent applications are filed with the Director General of the Patent Office. The Patent Office is an agency which is attached to the Ministry of International Trade and Industry. Its activities cover examination of patent applications and the registration of utility models, industrial design and trademarks.

Application can be filed via patent attorneys (*benrishi*), but it is not mandatory. However, those who do not have domicile or residence, or in case of juridical persons, which do not have an office, in Japan must apply via an agent who is either domiciled or resident in Japan (Art. 8, para. 1).

Application must be accompanied by a specification, drawings and a summary (Art. 36, para. 2). Previously, an application was needed for each invention. The scope of claim used to be narrow as compared with that in other industrialised countries. However, in order to join the Patent Cooperation Treaty, a multiple claims system was introduced in 1975 and then expanded in 1987 (Art. 36, paras. 4 and 6, Art. 37).

After the application is made, applications are disclosed to the public. Previously, applications were disclosed only at the later stage, when it was confirmed that there was no ground for refusal of patent. However, since it takes time to reach that stage, it was considered appropriate to disclose the application earlier. Without knowing other persons' applications, there might be an overlap of research and investment. Therefore, after one-and-a-half years from the date of application, the Director General of the Patent Office publishes the specification and the drawings in the Patent Gazette (Art. 65–2, paras. 1 and 2).

If someone exploits the invention as a business on the basis of the information published in the Patent Gazette while the patent application is pending, the applicant is entitled to compensation provided that he had issued a warning (Art. 65–3, para. 1).

Japanese patent law presupposes examination of a patent application on its merit. Until 1970, all patent applications were fully examined by the Patent Office. However, it became clear that not all applicants want full examination. For example, there are those who do not want to obtain a patent, although their inventions are patentable. They simply apply in order to prevent others from obtaining a patent on the same invention. Some people are not certain whether the invention is patentable, but just to make sure that others do not obtain a patent, they apply for a patent. Since the number of applications was steadily increasing, it was thought to be better to reverse the principle and the exception. Under the current system, only those applications for which the applicant or any other person has required examination are examined (Art. 48–2). Thus, any person may demand examination of the application within seven years of patent application. If there was no request for examination within this period, the patent application is deemed to be withdrawn (Art. 48–3, para. 4).

Patent applications are examined by a patent examiner. Examiners are guaranteed independence in the same way as administrative judges (*shinpankan*) of the Patent Office. They can be excluded on the grounds provided by law, but they cannot be challenged by the applicant (Arts. 139, 48). Applications are normally examined by a single examiner without a hearing.

Article 49 lists grounds for refusal of a patent. These include instances where the invention does not meet the requirements of patentability, where the invention is identical to another invention which has been filed earlier and was disclosed before examination or published upon examination, or when another person has filed application earlier. Also when the applicant is not the inventor and has not been assigned the right to application from the inventor, the application will be turned down. If the examiner finds a ground for refusal, the applicant is informed of the decision and the reason of refusal.

If the applicant does not agree with the decision of the examiner, he may present his opinions in writing and amend the application. Amendments to the specification and the drawings is also possible when the application is accepted, but the changes are deemed not to have affected the core of the specification (Art. 41).

If there is no ground for refusal, the application is published in the Patent Gazette. Documents are available for public inspection at the Patent Office for two months. While the early disclosure of the application in the Gazette merely has an effect of disseminating information, at this stage, publication of the application is aimed at inviting the public to file an objection if the invention should not be patented. At the same time, the applicant is given an exclusive right to exploit the invention as a business (Art. 52, para. 1). This right extinguishes retrospectively if eventually, a patent was not granted.

Any person may file an objection to the application which was published in the Gazette within three months of publication (Art. 55, para. 1). Grounds for objection are basically the same as the grounds for refusal of applications (Art. 49). The objection procedure is handled by an examiner. The applicant is invited to present a counter-statement.

When the examiner finally comes to the conclusion that a patent should be granted, he will render a decision in writing. Upon payment of the patent fee, a patent is granted by registration (Art. 66, para. 3). The duration of patent is fifteen years from the date of publication of application in the Patent Gazette. However, it may not exceed 20 years from the date of application (Art. 67, para. 1). In 1987, a new system of patent term extension (restoration) was introduced. In some industries like the pharmaceutical industry, it takes time to market a patented product, since it is subject to government licence. It so happens that when the manufacturer obtains a licence, only six-seven years are left for the patent. In such cases, maximum five years' extension is possible (Art. 67, para. 3).

Decisions of the examiner can be reviewed by the Patent Office by examiners designated by the Director General of the Patent Office. Refusal to grant a patent can be contested in this way, but the appeal must be made within 30 days of the notice of the decision. The examiners' decision is subject to judicial review.

The validity of a patent can be contested by an interested party exclusively in this way (Art. 123). Defendants in an infringement action cannot claim invalidity, unless the patent is invalidated by the Patent Office.

4) Infringement

A patent holder as well as those who have an exclusive licence are protected from infringements. Infringements are not limited to direct infringement. Indirect infringements, such as a sale, as a business, of a set of parts and components exclusively used for a patented product are covered. Patent litigation is time-consuming. It is sometimes difficult to demarcate the boundary of a particular invention, and a 'gray zone' is left. Therefore, people often make efforts to settle the case out of the court.[4]

Injunction is available, if there is a likelihood that a patent or a licence may be infringed (Art. 100, para. 1). Fault is not a prerequisite to injunction. Demands can be made to destroy things which constituted the act of infringement, to remove the equipment which has contributed to such an act, and to take other measures to prevent infringements (Art. 100, para. 2). Since injunction takes time, patent holders or licensees often file a petition for provisional disposition under the Law on Civil Interlocutory Measures.

Damages are claimed on the basis of general tort law (Civil Code, Art. 709). It should be noted that the fault on the part of the infringer is presumed by the Patent Law (Art. 103). The amount of loss is presumed to be the profit which the infringer made out of the infringement (Art. 102, para. 1). Patentees and licensees may also claim damages equivalent to the amount which they would normally have received for the exploitation of the invention (Art. 102, para. 2). In addition to tort, claims based on unjust enrichment can also be made.

If, by infringement, the credibility (business goodwill) of the patentee or the licencee was harmed, the court may order the infringer to take necessary measures to restore their credibility (Art. 106). This normally takes the form of publishing a statement of apology in a newspaper.

Infringement is subject to penalties (Art. 196).

2. Copyright law

1) An overview

The first copyright law in Japan was enacted in 1899, when Japan was about to sign the Berne Convention for the Protection of Literary and Artistic Works. Japan signed the Convention in 1899 and since then, has ratified the Brussels Act and Paris Act of the Berne Convention. Under the 1899 Law, copyright subsisted for 30 years after the death of the author. No formality was required for the copyright to take effect. This Law was replaced by the present Copyright Law in 1970. The term of subsistence was extended to 50 years by the new Law. Furthermore, the moral rights of the author were expanded and neighbouring rights came under the protection of the Copyright

---

4 Hashimoto, *supra* note 2, p. 271.

Law. The Law has undergone various amendments since then. Major amendments took place in 1985 and 1986 respectively, when copyright protection was extended to computer programmes and data bases.

Japan also ratified the Universal Copyright Convention in 1956. Other international treaties to which Japan is a signatory include the Rome Convention on the Protection of Performers, Producers of Phonograms and Broadcasting Organisations (1989) and the Geneva Convention on the Protection of Phonogram Producers from Unlicenced Copying (1978). On the other hand, Japan is yet to sign Vienna Treaty on the Protection of Typeface and the Brussels Treaty on Satellite Broadcasting.

2)   The scope of copyright protection

Works which are entitled to copyright protection are defined by the Law as a creative expression of thoughts or emotions which fall in the literary, scientific, artistic, or musical domain (Art. 1, para. 1). This includes literary and musical works, performing works, artistic works, architectural works, maps and drawings, cinematographic works, photographs as well as computer programmes (Art. 10, para. 1). However, copyright protection is not extended to programming languages, rules, or argorythms. Layout of semi-conductor circuits is protected by a separate law, i.e. the Law on the Layout of Semi-Conductor Circuits of 1985.[5]

The means of protection for computer programmes has been a focus of debate since the 1970s. At one stage, the Ministry of International Trade and Industry considered enacting a special (*sui generis*) law for the protection of computer programmes. It was planned to introduce a special right for computer programmes with shorter term of subsistence (15 years) and a fairly broad compulsory licence system. However, United States, Germany, and France chose to protect computer programmes by copyright law. Also Japanese courts acknowledged that computer programmes were 'a creative expression of an original scientific thought of the author' and therefore, should be protected by copyright.[6] The Copyright Law was amended in 1985 in order to extend protection to computer programmes.[7] A system of

5 Law No. 1985.
6 Judgment of Tokyo District Court, 6 December, 1982 (*Hanji* 1060–18; Space Invader Part II case).
7 T. Doi, 'The Role of Intellectual Property Law in Bilateral Licencing Transactions between Japan and the United States', in G. R. Saxonhouse and K. Yamamura eds., *Law and Trade Issues of the Japanese Economy*, Tokyo 1986, pp. 170–178.

registration of the date of creation of computer programmes was introduced in the same year.

Derivative works are protected independently of the original work, but it should not affect the protection of the original work (Art. 11). A derivative work is defined as a work created by translating, arranging musically, modifying, dramatising, cinematising or otherwise adapting an existing work (Art. 2, subpara. 12). Edited works are also protected, in so far as the selection or the arrangement of materials is original (Art. 12, para. 1). Data base is protected, provided that the selection or the systematic organisation of the information is original. However, this does not affect the copyright over individual works which comprise the data base (Art. 12–2).

3) Rights of the author

The author of a work has a right to reproduce, to perform, to broadcast or to diffuse by cable network, to recite, to exhibit the work, to show a cinematographic work to the public and distribute copies of the work (Arts. 21–26). The author also has a right to present the work to the public by lending copies (Art. 26–2) and a right to translate, musically arrange, modify, dramatise, cinematise, or otherwise adapt the work (Art. 27).

The present Copyright Law protects moral rights of the author. Thus, an author has the right to publish the work, the right to be identified, and the right of integrity (the right to object to derogatory treatment of work) (Arts. 18–20). As regards the right of integrity, the Law provides that authors have the right to maintain the identity of the work and its title, and these should not be altered, cut, or otherwise modified against his intentions (Art. 20, para. 1). In one case, a parody work was produced out of a photograph. The author added a photograph of a huge car tire to the original photograph which featured snow mountains. This was found to be an infringement of the moral rights of the original photographer.[8]

There was controversy over the authorship of cinematographic works. This covers films as well as videos. The present Law explicitly provides that the author of a film is the person who, by producing, supervising, directing, filming, or art-directing the work, contributed to the overall creation of the work (Art. 16). Usually, the director, producer, cameraman, and the art director are co-authors of the film. However, if the film was produced by

8 Judgment of the Supreme Court, 28 March, 1980 (*Minshū* 34-3-244; The Parody case).

employees in the course of business on the initiative of a juridical person, this juridical person is the author (Art. 15, para. 1). Authors of the original novel, scenario, music, etc. have a copyright, but are not regarded as co-authors of the film itself. The copyright of a film belongs to the person (usually a juridical person) who has taken the initiative and was in charge of producing the film, provided that the author has agreed to take part in the production (Art. 29, para. 1). The copyright holder of a cinematographic work has a right to present the work publicly, to distribute copies, and to offer copies to the public by rental (Arts. 26 and 26–2).[9]

Authors in the context of the Copyright Law include juridical persons and associations without juridical personality. A person who is identified in the work as an author is presumed to be an author (Art. 14). Works which were created by an employee in the course of business on the initiative of the employer and published in the name of the employer belongs to the latter. Publication is not required for computer programmes (Art. 15).

Works of foreign citizens are protected under the Copyright Law. Works of foreign citizens which are first published in Japan are protected as a work originating in Japan. If the work was first published abroad, it is not regarded as a work under the Japanese Copyright Law, but by virtue of international treaties, is eligible to protection in Japan. If the work was first published abroad, but was published in Japan within 30 days of the first publication, the work is treated as a work originating in Japan (Art. 6).

Copyright takes effect when the work was created. As a rule, copyright subsists for 50 years after the death of the author (Art. 51). If the author is not known or used a pseudonym, the copyright subsists for 50 years after publication. Despite using a pseudonym, if the author is known, then the general rule applies. Works of a juridical person or any other organization subsists for 50 years after the publication (Art. 53). The same rule applies to cinematographic works and photographs. If these works were not published within 50 years of their creation, the copyright cease to exist (Arts. 54 and 55).

The Copyright Law provides for various types of fair use of a work. These include reproduction for private use, reproduction of part of the work in libraries, reproduction at educational institutions, quotation, reproduction in school text books, reproduction as examination questions etc. In the last two instances, a fee must be paid. Published works can be performed,

---

9 M. Handa and N. Monya eds., *Chosaku-ken no Know-How* (*The Know How of Copyrights*), Fourth edition, Tokyo 1990, pp. 73–78.

recited, and presented to the public on a non-profit making basis (Arts. 30–47–2).

4) The protection of neighbouring rights

As regards neighbouring rights, Japan has ratified the Rome Convention for the Protection of Performers, Producers of Phonograms and Broadcasting Organisations. The present Law covers the rights of performers, producers of phonograms, broadcasting companies and cable broadcasting companies. Performers have an exclusive right to have their performance recorded or fixtured, to broadcast their performance either by wireless or cable (Arts. 91 and 92). If a broadcasting organisation (either wireless or cable) uses for broadcasting a phonogram on which the performance was recorded, the performer is entitled to fees for secondary use (Art. 95, para. 1). Performers also have a lending right, i.e. a right to present his performance to the public by lending phonograms (Art. 95–2, para. 1). On the other hand, producers of phonograms have an exclusive right to reproduce a phonogram and the right to fees for secondary use of the phonogram in broadcasting (Arts. 96 and 97).

Broadcasting organisations are given a right to reproduce the broadcast by sound or visual recordings and by photographs. They also have a right to rebroadcast, to diffuse by cable, and to communicate television broadcasts to the public (Arts. 98–100).

The duration of the protection of neighbouring rights is 30 years from the next year of the performance (Art. 101).

5) Infringements

In cases of infringements of copyright, moral rights, publication rights and neighbouring rights, injunction is available. Demand for the destruction of the object which constituted infringement, objects produced by the infringement, and machinery and equipment used solely for infringement can be made simultaneously (Art. 112). Infringements include importation into Japan for distribution, of articles made by an act, which would have constituted an infringement, it if was committed in Japan at the time of importation. Also knowingly distributing, or possessing for distribution, items which were produced by an act of infringement is considered to be an infringement (Art. 113, para. 1). As regards moral rights, after the death of the author, relatives are entitled to injunction (Art. 116, para. 1).

Damages can be claimed on the basis of general tort law. However, fault on the part of the infringer is not required. There is a provision concerning the presumption of the amount of loss, similar to that in the Patent Law (Art. 114). Criminal sanctions are also provided for infringement (Art. 119–124).

3.   Protection of trade marks

The first Trade Mark Law of Japan was enacted in 1899 together with the Patent Law. It was replaced by the present Trade Mark Law in 1959. The Law only covered trade marks; service marks were protected by the Law against Unfair Competition. However, by the 1991 amendment, service marks also came to be covered by the Trade Mark Law.

A trade mark is defined by the Law as characters, letters, figures or signs, or a combination of those, or combination of those with colours which are used on merchandise or for services as a business (Art. 2, para. 1).

An exclusive right to use a trade mark is created by registration with the Patent Office (Art 18, para. 3). The duration of registration is ten years, but it can be renewed.

Trade marks which lack distinctiveness cannot be registered. For example, a trade mark which primarily consists of the common name of the goods or services expressed in an ordinary way or a trade mark which is extremely simple and common cannot be registered. In addition, marks which resemble a well-known mark of various entities, such as the Red Cross, United Nations, etc. are not allowed to be registered (Art. 4). Furthermore, a trade mark which resembles a trade mark broadly recognised by consumers as representing another entrepreneur's goods or service is not registrable if it is used on similar goods or services (Art. 4, para. 10). The same applies to trade marks which may be misleading concerning the quality of the goods or services (para. 16). In addition, trade marks similar to an already registered trade mark upon earlier application cannot be registered (para. 11).

Applications for registration are filed with the Director General of the Patent Office. Goods or services to which the trade mark is attached must be designated. A document which shows the trade mark with an explanation must be submitted together with the application. The application is examined by an examiner of the Patent Office and is published in the Patent Gazette if there is no ground for refusal. Any person may file an objection to the trade mark within two months of the publication. If there is no objection or objections turned out to be groundless, the final decision to register the trade mark is rendered. The decision of the examiner is subject to appeal to Tokyo Appellate Court.

In addition to direct infringement of trade marks, the Law provides for acts which are deemed to be an infringement. Acts such as the use of a trade mark similar to the registered mark on designated goods or services, the use of a registered trade mark or a similar mark on goods or services similar to designated goods or services, the production and importation of items which incorporate a registered trade mark or a similar mark on them for the purpose of using such a trade mark on designated goods or services or similar goods or services, are all regarded as infringement. Furthermore, importation of items which are solely used for producing things which incorporate a registered trade mark or a similar mark as business constitutes an infringement (Art. 37).

It should be noted that the Customs Tariff Law lists as items prohibited from importation, among other items, goods which infringe patents, utility model rights, design rights, trade mark rights, and copyright (Art. 21).

As is the case with patent and copyright infringement, injunction is available and damages can be claimed. Similar arrangements are made concerning the amount of loss and the presumption of fault on the part of the infringer. Criminal sanctions are also provided for in the Law (Arts. 78–82).

4. Protection of trade secrets

The basic law which protects trade secrets is the Law against Unfair Competition.[10] This Law, which should not be confused with the Anti-Monopoly Law (Competition Law) of 1947, emanates from the Paris Convention. It was enacted in 1934 when Japan ratified the Amsterdam Act of the Convention which was designed to control 'all kinds of act which are against unfair practice in commerce and industry'. Although the German Unfair Competition Act of 1896 served as a model, provisions on trade secrets which were contained in the German Act were dropped at the drafting stage. It was only in 1990 that the Law was amended in order to provide protection to trade secrets.[11]

The Law lists various types of acts which comprise unfair competition and are subject to injunction. These included the use

---

10 Law No. 14, 1934.
11 For the background of the Law, see H. Oda, 'Protecting Trade Secrets in Japan', *Financial Times*, 6 September, 1990.

of name, trade name, trade mark, or package, identical or similar to another person's, false statement of origin, and misrepresentation of quality, methods of production, content of the merchandise (Art. 1, para. 1). By the 1990 amendment, infringement of trade secrets was added to this list. The amended Law defines trade secrets as production formulae or methods, methods of sales and other technical or commercial information relevant to business activities which are not known to the public and are treated as a secret (Art. 1, para. 3). The actual scope of protected trade secrets is expected to become clearer by accumulation of case law.

Thus, information must not be known publicly if it is to be protected as a trade secret. This means that the information should not be available to unspecified persons unless one resorts to unfair means. The information must have an economic value and has to be treated as a secret by the holder. The holder must have made sufficient efforts to keep the information secret. Therefore, access to the information must have been limited to a certain number of people. Furthermore, the holder must make clear that the information is restricted, for example, by designating it as 'secret' or 'restricted'.

The Law basically covers two types of infringements. The first is the unauthorised acquisition of trade secrets by theft, fraud, or extortion. If a third party acquires, uses or discloses trade secrets knowing that they had been obtained by such means, or was at serious fault in not knowing it, his act is subject to injunction. If a person, who has obtained trade secrets by legitimate means, later becomes aware of the fact that the secrets have been obtained in an unauthorised manner, he is not entitled to use or disclose such information. A person who, by serious fault, failed to find out such a fact, may face injunction if he uses or discloses such trade secrets.

The second type of infringement is the use or disclosure of trade secrets, which had been disclosed by the original holder, for the purpose of unfair competition or of harming the interests of the original holder. Those who knowingly obtain, use or disclose such trade secrets or those who were at serious fault in not knowing the facts also face the risk of injunction. The same applies to those who later became aware of the relevant facts, but nevertheless use or disclose trade secrets and to those who, by serious fault, fail to recognise such facts.

Holders of trade secrets (entrepreneurs) whose interests are affected or are likely to be affected are entitled to seek an injunction. In addition, they may require the destruction of items incorporating trade secrets as well as end-products, and any equipment used for infringement. They are also entitled to damages and other measures to restore their credibility. However, criminal sanctions are not available.

It is not uncommon for companies to sign an agreement with the employees for protecting trade secrets. Employees are bound by agreements not to work in a competing company for a certain period. Such agreements are considered to be valid if the restriction is reasonable and arrangements are made to compensate the employees for the restrictions on the choice of business.[12]

5. Other types of intellectual property

1) Utility models

Japan has a two-tier system of patent and utility models. The Law on Utility Models of 1959 protects 'petit inventions (devices)' which concern the shape, structure, or combination of things (Art. 1). Invention in this context means a creation based on technical ideas by using the law of nature. Inventions concerning the use or methods are not covered.

Any person who has made such a petit invention which is industrially applicable may register it as a utility model. Novelty, industrial applicability, and non-obviousness are required. Application for registration is filed with the Patent Office. The process of examination is similar to that of a patent and various provisions of the Patent Law are applied with some modifications to utility models.[13]

2) Protection of designs

The Design Law of 1959 is the primary law protecting industrial designs. Design is defined as the shape, pattern, or colour or the combination of these which is visually perceived as aesthetic (Art. 2, para. 1). There are three basic requirements for registration: novelty, industrial utility, and creativeness (Art. 3). Applications for registration are filed with the Director General of the Patent Office. If there are competing applications, the first applicant is entitled to registration (Art. 9, para. 1). Rules concerning an employee's invention are applied with modification to designs.

---

12 Judgment of Nara District Court, 23 October, 1970 (*Kaminshū* 21–9/10–1369).
13 T. Doi, *The Intellectual Property Law of Japan*, Alphen aan den Rijn 1980, pp. 68–75.

The Design Law has a peculiar system of registration under seal (secret registration). Thus, an applicant may require the Patent Office to keep the design secret for a maximum of three years after registration. Drawings and other materials are kept under seal.

Once registered, the holder of the design right has an exclusive right to exploit the design and similar designs as a business. The duration of the right is fifteen years (Art. 21).

3)   New plant varieties and bio-technological products

Japan ratified the Paris Convention on the Protection of New Plant Varieties in 1981. Accordingly, the Law on Seeds and Plants was amended. New plant varieties are protected for fifteen years after registration. On the other hand, with the advance of technology, some new species which may fulfill requirements of patent protection have emerged. The Patent Office published a guideline concerning the patentability of these new plant varieties in 1975.

As regards bacteria, patent is available. Japan is a signatory to the Budapest Convention on the International Recognition of the Depositing of Bacteria in the Patent Procedure.

13 Company law

1 The commercial code and related laws

The present Commercial Code is divided into the General Part, Company, Commercial Transactions, and Merchant Shipping and Insurance.[1] The part on company law covers joint stock companies as well as general partnership and limited partnership. There is a separate law for limited liability companies (the Law on Limited Liability Companies).[2] The Commmercial Code is also supplemented by various laws such as the Law on Cheques, the Law on Bills, and the Law on Commercial Registration.

The first Commercial Code of Japan was promulgated in 1890. It was based upon a draft prepared by a German adviser, Herman Roesler, who consulted German, French and English Law in the course of preparation. The composition of the Code was similar to that of the French Commercial Code of 1807, although in substance, it could be described as a blend of German and French law. However, the Code was caught in a crossfire, as was the Civil Code, and it was some years before it took effect. A revised Code, which is still in effect to date, was finally adopted in 1899. This was primarily modeled after the German Commercial Code (*Handelsgesetzbuch*) of 1897.[3]

The Code has undergone some major changes since its enactment. Japan ratified the Geneva Conventions on the Unification of the Law of Bills and the Law of Cheques in 1930 and 1931 respectively, which resulted in the separation of the part of the Commercial Code on bills and cheques from the rest of the Code. The part concerning company law was totally amended in 1938. The power of the general meeting of the shareholders was expanded and the liability of directors was increased by this amendment.

---

1 Law No. 73, 1911.
2 Law 74, 1938.
3 Law No. 48, 1899. For the history of the Commercial Code, see The Codes Translation Committee, The League of Nations Association of Japan, *The Commercial Code of Japan*, vol. 1, Tokyo 1931, pp. xlvii.

After the Second World War, amendments based on U.S. law were made to the part dealing with company law. In 1947, the Anti-Monopoly Law was enacted, followed by the Securities and Exchange Law the next year.[4] These laws were modelled after U.S. law and necessitated the reform of the accounting and disclosure systems in the Commercial Code.

Part Two of the Code (company law) was substantially amended in 1950. Firstly, the system of authorised capital was introduced together with non-par shares. Secondly, powers of directors were expanded, reducing the powers of the general meeting of shareholders. At the same time, the board of directors was introduced and the liability of directors was increased. Thirdly, the rights of the shareholders were expanded so that they could exercise control over the management of the company. Thus, by the post-War reform, American institutions were introduced into the primarily German framework set up by the Code.

The necessity of a major reform of company law has been acknowledged for a long time because of a considerable gap between the law and reality in this field. While provisions of the Commercial Code of joint stock companies presuppose large corporations, these companies, exceeding one million in number, are in fact mostly small or medium sized companies. The legislature had expected these companies to take the form of a limited company rather than a company limited by shares. A majority of these small and medium-sized joint stock companies do not issue shares, hold shareholders meeting or a board meeting.

Preparations for reform began in the early 1970s, and the process was facilitated by several celebrated cases of window-dressing on the part of large companies. The general public expected closer monitoring and proper regulation of large joint stock companies. Although preparations for a total reform of the company law had not been completed yet, it was decided to proceed with the part which had already been drafted. Thus, a major amendment to the Code took place in 1974. Companies were split into three categories: large, medium and small sized. For large corporations with capital of 500 million yen, a new Law on the Special Measures concerning Auditing of Joint stock companies strengthened auditing requirements.[5] These corporations are now required to have their books audited by a certified

---

4 Law No. 25, 1948.
5 Law No. 22, 1974.

public accountant or an accounting firm. The power of the auditor was expanded to cover not only accounts but also administration of business in general.

In 1981, another major amendment took place which primarily concerned regulations on shares, improvements in the administration of the annual general meeting of shareholders, strengthening the power of the board of directors at the expense of individual directors' power, and further revisions of the audit system.[6] It should be noted that the issuing of warrant bonds was made possible by this amendment. This has greatly facilitated the financing of major Japanese corporations in Europe.

The latest amendment to the Commercial Code and the Law on Limited Liability Companies took place in 1990. This amendment was intended to cope with the situation where the law designed for larger companies was ill-fitted for small and closed companies, which represent the majority of joint stock companies and limited liablity companies. Thus, the minimum capital for joint stock companies was increased from 350 thousand yen to 10 million yen. The minimum capital is three million for limited liability companies. On the other hand, the procedure to set up joint stock companies and limited liability companies was streamlined and made simple.

2. The types of companies

The Commercial Code defines a company as an association established for the purpose of conducting commercial transactions as a business (Art. 52). It provides for three types of companies: general partnerships (*gōmei-gaisha*), limited partnerships (*gōshi-gaisha*), and joint stock companies (*kabushiki-gaisha*). In addition, there are limited liability companies (*yūgen-gaisha*), which are regulated by the Law on Limited Companies.[7] Some provisions of the Commercial Code are applied with necessary modifications to limited liability companies.

In general partnership, investors bear unlimited liability, whereas in limited partnership, there are two classes of members (Arts. 80, 146, and 157). Some bear unlimited liability while others are liable to the extent of their investment. The company

6 See '*Kaisha-hō no Kaisei* (The Reform of Company Law)', *Jurist* No. 747, 1981.
7 Law No. 74, 1938.

is run by members with unlimited liability unless there is a special arrangement in the articles of association.

General partnerships and limited partnerships are often characterised as personal companies and are considered to be suitable for small companies. In the past, these two forms of companies were used, for instance, for holding companies of major business conglomerates. The credibility of general and limited partnership is based upon the identity of partners and their personal assets. In contrast, joint stock companies and limited liability companies are characterised as capital companies, since their credibility comes from their assets. Investors assume liablity to the extent of paying in the capital. At present, newly set up companies seldom take the form of partnership. However, with the introduction of the basic capital requirement for joint stock companies by the 1990 amendment to the Commercial Code, it is likely that small companies which fail to meet the requirement will have to be converted to partnership in five years' time.

Limited liability companies are designed to be a format for medium size business. The minimum capital used to be 100,000 yen (approximately 400 pounds), but was increased to 3,000,000 yen by the 1990 amendment (Art. 9, Law on Limited Liability Companies). Limited liability companies resemble joint stock companies in many respects, but instead of shareholders, there are members. The number of members is limited to fifty (Art. 8). They roughly correspond to private companies in the U.K. and closed companies in the United States. Members have shares which are counted by units. The minimum amount of a unit is 50,000 yen. These share units may not be converted to securities, since this form of a company is intended to be a closed company (Art. 21). Assignment of shares is free among the members, but in order to assign the share to a third party, the approval of the general meeting of members is required. In such cases, any non-members who had shares assigned are entitled to ask the company to approve the assignment. If the company does not approve it, then it has to designate a person, who is to purchase the shares from this assignee. Also, the assignor may require the company to designate an alternative assignee (Art. 19).

This is in contrast to joint stock companies in which shares are transferrable in principle. However, it should be noted that assignment of shares of joint stock companies can be limited by the articles of association. Joint stock companies may make assignment of shares subject to the approval of the board of directors. In fact, most companies which are not listed in the stock exchange have such restrictions on assignment of shares to outsiders. Thus, joint stock companies in Japan are not always public companies, or rather, a majority of them are closed companies.

Procedures for incorporation and administration of limited liability companies are simpler than joint stock companies. Governing bodies are also simplified. The general meeting of members is the supreme body of the company. The director(s) is appointed by the general meeting, but there is no requirement for the number of directors. The conduct of business is decided by the majority of directors (Art. 26). Each director is, in principle, entitled to represent the company (Art. 27). There is no board of directors. The appointment of an auditor is not mandatory. Another important feature of limited liability companies is that their means of financing is limited. They are not allowed to issue bonds.

The law was designed to encourage large companies to adopt the form of joint stock companies and smaller companies to incorporate in the form of limited liability companies. However, in reality, this is not the case. In 1988, 52.7% of companies in Japan (in total there were 1,851,673 companies) were joint stock companies, 44.8% were limited liability companies, 0.3% were general partnerships and 1.6% were limited partnerships. Of these joint stock companies, 57.5% had capital of less than five million yen (approximately 20,000 pounds). Apart from 2,000 listed companies, most companies are of medium or small size. The large number of joint stock companies is striking. Although the Code had presupposed that the form of joint stock companies would be used only by large companies, in fact, even small local shops are incorporated as joint stock companies. In most cases, shares are held entirely by family members. This happens because joint stock companies are believed to have advantages in taxation, employment and the securing of loans from financial institutions. It is also claimed that joint stock companies carry a certain credibility.

Thus, there is a considerable discrepancy between the written law and the law in practice. Small and medium sized companies often ignore statutory regulations, such as the requirement for registering changes of directors, taking minutes of board meetings, and holding general meetings of shareholders. A series of amendments to the Commercial Code and the Law on Limited Liability Companies outlined above have been taken in response to this problem.[8]

8 Law No. 22, 1974.

Under the Commercial Code, the three types of companies are all juridical persons. Unlike partnerships in English law, Japanese partnerships are given juridical personality. The Law on Limited Companies also has a similar provision.

The capacity of companies is limited by law in several aspects. Firstly, the Commercial Code and the Law on Limited Companies prohibit a company from becoming a partner with unlimited liability in other companies. However, the reasonableness of this prohibition is being questioned. Secondly, there are restrictions by the Anti-Monopoly Law. Holding companies are not allowed because they were the core of business conglomerates which monopolised the economy before the Second World War. There is also a ceiling on the amount of shares large companies may hold. Thus, companies may not acquire or hold shares of a domestic company when it substantially restricts competition in a particular area of trade. Financial institutions may not hold more than five percent of the issued shares of a domestic company (for insurance companies, the ceiling is 10%).

Finally, the Civil Code provides that a juridical person enjoys the rights and bears liability within the scope of its objects as specified in the articles of association (Art. 43). Transactions beyond the scope of the specified objects are void. This provision has its origin in the doctrine of *ultra vires* in English law.[9] It is a much debated issue whether the provision, originally intended to be applied to public interest juridical persons, should be applicable to companies.

The Supreme Court and its predecessor have long maintained that this provision of the Civil Code should be applied with necessary modifications to companies. Actually this provision had been used often as a defence by the company to avoid claims against it. In one case, a partner of a limited partnership company which ran warehouses and transport businesses purchased oil from X in a transaction designed to further his own interests, intending to resell it and profit privately from the deal. X sued the company for payment, but the company claimed that the transaction was not within the scope of purposes prescribed by the articles of association. The court did not accept this argument and found the company liable.[10] In practice, the courts have broadly interpreted the objects clauses in the articles of association and virtually removed this restriction. The court is of the position that not only transactions within the scope of objects

9 G. Morse, *Charlesworth's Company Law*, 13th edition, London 1987, pp. 75–92.
10 Judgment of the Supreme Tribunal, 7 February, 1938 (*Minshū* 17–50).

expressly specified in the charter, but also transactions which are needed to achieve the object are *intra vires*.[11]

3. Joint stock companies

Since in Japan more than 50% of companies are joint stock companies, the following discussion will be focused on these companies.

In order to form a joint stock company, it is necessary to have a promoter who prepares the articles of incorporation (Art. 165). Before the 1990 amendment, seven promoters were needed. This created a problem when a company wanted to set up a 100% subsidiary. It had to find six other promoters and then, after the incorporation, have the shares assigned back to the company. This requirement was considered to be excessive and has been removed by the latest amendment.

The Commercial Code has detailed provisions as to the formation of joint stock companies. As a rule, if the requirements set forth by the Code are observed, the company which has been formed acquires juridical personality. Permission of administrative agencies and other formalities is not required. Exceptions include the requirement for the Minister of Finance's license for banks, trustee banks, securities companies, investment advisory companies and insurance companies. Incorporation is completed by registration (Art. 57). The registration officer examines whether the rules of incorporation were observed or not, but he does not examine the substance of the matter.

A joint stock company may be formed either by private incorporation or incorporation by offering shares. In private incorporation, a promoter (or promoters) prepares articles of association (articles of incorporation) and has them certified by a notary public. He subscribes to all shares issued at the time of incorporation and makes decisions concerning the issue of shares. After the promoter has paid in the capital, directors and auditors are selected by the promoter. The director is required to ask the court to appoint a comptroller, who checks if proper procedures of incorporation were observed (for instance, whether payment in kind was properly made or not), or whether there is a special benefit which is due to the promoter and reports the result to the court. By the 1990 amendments, this requirement to apply to the court for the appointment of a comptroller was relaxed. If the

11 Judgment of the Supreme Court, 29 November, 1955 (*Minshū* 9–12–1886).

amount of payment in kind does not exceed 5 million yen and one fifth of the capital, appointment of a comptroller is not needed. The same applies when the capital is paid in kind by securities, insofar as they are evaluated at market price (Art. 173). When this procedure is completed, the company is registered. Details of registration are regulated by the Law on Commercial Registration.[12]

In cases of incorporation by offering of shares, after preparing articles of association and the certification by a notary, the promoter makes decisions concerning the issue of shares and subscribes part of the shares, then offers the remaining shares to others. The offer can be made either to the public, or to a certain group of people. After the subscribers pay in, an incorporation meeting is convened by the promoter. The meeting has two primary functions: the appointment of directors and auditors, and the verification of the incorporation process. In certain cases, for example, where part of the capital is paid in kind, a comptroller has to be appointed by the court. Finally, when the registration is complete, the company is formed.

Originally, the former procedure, i.e. private incorporation was designed to cope with the incorporation of smaller companies in which promoters knew each other fairly well. In fact, most companies incorporated today are not large companies. In most cases, incorporation takes place either when an enterprise run by an individual wants to become a joint stock company, when an existing company splits and sets up a subsidiary, or when several companies form a joint venture. Nevertheless, instead of private incorporation, the second procedure, i.e. incorporation by offering of shares, is often used. This is because companies preferred to avoid the interference of the court in the incorporation process, and thus avert delay. Furthermore, in practice, in incorporation by offering shares, instead of offering shares to others as envisaged by the legislature, a majority of shares are subscribed by promoters, and the remaining small number of shares are offered to others. The 1990 amendment liberalised the requirement to apply to the court for the appointment of a comptroller and it is expected that private incorporation will be used more often in the future.

There is no requirement as to who is entitled to be a promoter. A juridical person may also become a promoter. Those who have signed the articles of association as a promoter are treated as such even if they were not actually promoters. The Code

12 Law No. 125, 1963.

provides that those who allowed their name to be used and their consent and support to the incorporation of a company to be publicised in documents concerning the issuing of shares bear liability identical to that borne by a promoter, even though they were not a genuine promoter (Art. 198).

Articles of association are drafted by the promoter(s) in the course of incorporation. The Code enumerates matters which are needed to be included in the articles of association (Art. 166). These include objects of business, trade name, total number of shares issued (authorised capital), par value of the share, total number of shares issued on the occasion of incorporation and the number of par value shares and no-par value shares, the address of the main office, the method of public notification adopted by the company, and the names and addresses of the promoters.

Regulations on trade names are found in the Commercial Code (Arts. 16–33). Companies are free to choose a trade name. The type of the company, such as joint stock company, limited liability company, has to be indicated in the trade name. A trade name which has been registered by another company may not be registered for another company in the same city, town or village for an identical business. If somebody uses a registered trade name for the purpose of unfair competition, the holder of the trade name is entitled to injunction and claim of damages.

It is required to issue at least a quarter of the shares at the time of incorporation (Art. 166, para. 3). As regards par value shares, the minimum price is now set at 50,000 yen (approximately 200 pounds) (Art. 168–3). However, this does not apply to shares of companies which were founded before the 1981 amendment. Therefore, many companies still have shares with par value of 50, 100, or 500 yen. In a majority of compamies, dividend is calculated on the basis of the par value, which makes it rather modest. The number of shares issued at the time of incorporation should not be less than a quarter of the shares to be issued by the company (Art. 16, para. 3). The amount of capital is, in principle, the aggregate of the issue price of shares and the number of issued shares regardless of whether the share is par value or non-par value (Art. 284–2, para. 1).

If the articles of association fail to provide for any of the above-mentioned matters, it is null and void.

There are also matters which are required to be included in the articles of association in order to have effect, although a failure to include them does not make the articles of association void. For example, the company may require the transfer of shares to be subject to the approval of the board of directors, but this must be specified in the articles of association (Art. 204, para. 1). Also, issues related to incorporation, such as special benefits which the promoters are to receive, remuneration of promoters, the name of those who are to contribute in kind, their contribution and the value, the number and types of shares to be allocated in return to these investors etc. are to be specified in the articles of association (Art. 168, para. 1). Normally, in addition to those, matters such as the timing of the general meeting of shareholders, the number of directors and auditors, powers of the chairman, representative director and other directors and the like are included in the articles of association.

In offering of shares, the Securities and Exchange Law is applicable. The Law provides that when an offer is made to an unspecified public and the amount of the issued share exceeds 500 million yen, the offer cannot go ahead unless it is reported to the Minister of Finance (Art. 2, para. 3, Art. 4).

When the offer was made and accepted, the promoters allot shares to those who have accepted the offer. The Code provides that by allotment, the allottees are legally bound to pay the price of the share (Art. 176). Payment can be made only through banks or trustee companies (this also applies to private incorporation). In practice, especially in cases where a small enterprise initiates the procedure of incorporation, disguised payment is not uncommon. The promoter secures a loan from a bank which is designated for the payment of shares. The loan is deposited in the prospective company's account. An agreement is made with the bank that the promoters will not draw the money from the account until the loan is repaid. In some cases, promoters secure a loan from a bank and pay for the shares, and afterwards, transfer the money from the account of the incorporated company to the bank. In order to prevent this kind of practice, the Code provides that the bank designated for the payment of shares should issue a certificate of custody. The bank is not entitled to claim that there is a restriction on the withdrawal of the money from the account in such cases (Art. 189, para. 2).

Directors and auditor are to be selected by promoters in private incorporation. A founding meeting is needed in cases of incorporation by offering of shares. The meeting also checks whether the process of incorporation has been carried out in accordance with law.

The company is incorporated and obtains juridical personality with registration. Since incorporation is not completed until registration, the legal nature of the company in the course of incorporation has to be questioned. Taking into account the fact that a company is gradually formed through various stages and finally completes the process by registration, some people use the concept of a 'company in the course of incorporation'. This 'company' is regarded as an association without juridical personality, but otherwise basically identical to the company incorporated later. This concept is used in order to explain the transfer of rights and duties of the prospective company which emerge in the course of incorporation.

The promoter is liable in ensuring that the capital of the company is actually formed. If part of the shares issued at the time of incorporation are not subscribed, they are deemed to be subscribed jointly by the promoters. The same applies when the subscription is withdrawn after the company has been founded (Art. 192, para. 1). If there are shares which are not paid in after the company is formed, the promoters are jointly and severally responsible for paying in the amount (Art. 192, para. 2). Secondly, the promoters are obliged to perform their task in good faith as 'good administrators'. Promoters are jointly and severally responsible for the breach of this duty. Thirdly, promoters are jointly and severally liable to third persons where they act in bad faith or are seriously at fault (Art. 193, para. 2, Art. 195). They may also be liable under the general provisions of tort law. Fourthly, promoters are jointly and severally liable for acts they have performed in relation to incorporation, if the company eventually failed to be incorporated (Art. 194, para. 1). These arrangements are intended to ensure that money or assets equal in amount or value specified in the articles of association are received by the company, and thus protect the creditors.

In addition to the above-mentioned liabilities, the Commercial Code provides for criminal sanctions. Promoters are penalised for breach of duty for the purpose of benefiting themselves or a third party, making false statements to the court or the founding meeting, acceptance, demand or promise of bribes, etc. (Arts. 486, 489, para. 1, Arts. 490, 491, 493).

4. Shares

Prior to the amendment of the Commercial Code in 1950, the total amount of capital specified in the articles of association was divided into shares with equal value. Thus, the total amount of the shares and the capital coincided. The 1950 amendment introduced a system of authorised capital and no par value share, similar to the American system. Dividends on no par value shares are not given as percentage of the nominal value, but instead in a fixed amount of money per share. With this amendment, the link between capital and shares was severed. In some cases, an increase in capital does not require the issuing of new shares (Art. 293–3). A decrease in the number of shares does not necessarily result in the decrease of capital (Art. 212, para. 1).

In Japan, par value share is the normal type of share and only a few listed companies issue no par value shares. With par value shares, it is prohibited to issue a share at a price below the face value, which should be the same for all shares (Art. 202, paras. 1 and 2). In a majority of companies, the face value of a share is 20, 50, or 500 yen. When the minimum face value of the share was increased in 1950 to 500 yen, companies in existence were not forced to adopt this minimum value, and therefore, companies whose shares have a face value of less than 500 yen are still common. However, these prices, which can be traced back to the 19th century, are considered outdated. Also from the viewpoint of the cost involved in administering the shares, these nominal values were too low. Therefore, the amendment of the Code in 1981 introduced a minimum par value of 50,000 yen for shares issued at the time of incorporation (Art. 166 para. 2, Art 168–3). Also, for no par value shares the minimum price of issue is now set at 50,000 yen. This restriction on the minimum face value of a share, however, is applied only to shares issued at the time of incorporation.

As for those companies already in existence, a new system of a share unit was introduced in 1981. It was intended to compulsorily merge the shares some time in the near future with a face value of minimum 50,000 yen. As a transitional measure until the shares of the companies in existence are merged into a larger share, a unit share system has been introduced. In this system, shares below 50,000 yen in face value are combined into a unit, which has a total value exceeding 50,000 yen. It is these combined shares that are treated as the basic unit. The share unit system is mandatory for all listed companies. Other companies may also adopt this system by specifying the basic unit of shares in the articles of association. This system is not without shortcomings, since the rights of the shareholders with shares less than a unit of 50,000 yen are limited, and this results in some inequality between share-holders.[13]

The amount of capital is, in general, the total of the issuing price of the issued shares. It is possible not to capitalize up to

13 E. Hattori, '*Kabushiki-seido Kaikaku no Igi* (The Significance and Problems of the Reform of Share System)', *Jurist* No. 747, 1981, pp. 102–103.

50% of this amount (Art. 284–2, para. 2). In cases where par value shares are issued, the amount of capital always has to exceed the total amount of the par value of issued shares. Par value shares and no-par-value shares are convertible by the decision of the board of directors (Art. 213). Currently, there are only ten listed companies which issue no par value shares. The reliance on par value shares creates some problems. For instance, the dividend paid out is calculated on the basis of par value and is usually meagre. This is particularly unfair when taking into account that in recent years, companies issue shares not at par value, but at market price, which is significantly higher than the par value.[14]

In addition to ordinary shares, there are shares which carry a preferential right or a deferred right to receive dividends or interest (Art. 291). The former is called a preferred share, while the latter is called a deferred share. A holder of preferred shares receives a fixed rate or fixed amount of dividend in preference to other shareholders.

Preferred shares can be divided further into participatory or non-participatory preferred shares depending on whether the shareholders are also able to receive dividends with common shareholders. Preferred shares can also be divided into cumulative and non-cumulative shares. In the former, if the dividend of a certain year does not reach the fixed rate, the shareholder may receive the shortfall the next year. There are also redeemable shares, which the company may buy back. In most cases, a company issues redeemable preferred shares when it needs money quickly, but after a certain period, it buys back the issued shares.

Preferred shares can be made non-voting by articles of association. However, the number of non-voting shares may not exceeed one third of issued shares (Art. 242, para. 2). Non-voting shareholders are still entitled to vote on certain issues specified by law, for example, when preferential dividends stipulated in the articles of association have not been paid (Art. 242, para. 1).

When several classes or kinds of shares are to be issued, companies were required to specify the types of the shares and the amount to be issued in the articles of association. This proved to be too cumbersome, and therefore, the amendment of 1990 relaxed the requirements in this regard. For preferred shares,

14 H. Maeda, *Kaishahō Nyūmon (Introduction to Company Law)*, Second Edition, Tokyo 1991, pp. 87–92.

only the ceiling of the preferred dividend has to be specified in the articles of association, and other matters can be left to the decision of the board.

When several kinds of shares have been issued and the alteration of the articles of association is likely to harm holders of a certain class of shares, the approval of the meeting of the holders of this class of shares, in addition to the approval of the general meeting of shareholders, is mandatory (Art. 345).

It is possible for a company to issue convertible shares, allowing a holder of a certain class of shares to convert it into another class of shares.

A share certificate represents the status and the rights of the shareholder and is one of the securities provided for in the Securities and Exchange Law (Art. 2). The rights of a shareholder are assigned by transferring the certificate. The certificate specifies matters such as the name of the company, the date of incorporation, value of the share if it is a par value share, the date of issue of the shares after incorporation, conditions for conversion and to what kind of share it is to be converted if they are convertible shares, the fact that the transfer of shares requires the approval of the board of directors if there is such a requirement, and the amount of shares already issued (Art. 225, Commercial Code).

The Commercial Code used to provide for bearer's share certificates and ordinary share certificates. In practice, the latter was common in Japan and therefore, the bearer's certificate was abolished by the 1990 amendment. A company must keep a record of shareholders, which is significant in that first, in order to exercise rights of a shareholder vis à vis the company, it is necessary to make an entry in the record of shareholders. Second, the transfer of registered share certificates can not be claimed against the company unless it is registered in the record (Art. 206, para. 1). Third, notices or reminders by the company to the shareholders are valid when sent to the address of the shareholder as registered in the record (Art. 224, para. 1).

The assignment of shares is effected by the transfer of the share certificate. The holder of a share certificate is legally presumed to be a shareholder. If a person acquires a share certificate in good faith, i.e. believing that the seller was the legitimate shareholder, and was not at serious fault in believing so, he acquires the rights of a shareholder (Art. 229).

Shareholders who do not intend to assign shares for the time being may not want to hold the certificate. In such cases, shareholders may inform the company that he does not want to hold a certificate. The company may either enter in the list of shareholders that certificates are not issued to this particular shareholder, or deposit the certificate to a bank or a trustee company. The shareholder may later ask the certificate to be issued or the deposited certificated to be returned.

In 1984, the Law on the Custody and Clearing System of Share Certificates was enacted. Based upon this Law, an organisation for the custody and clearing of share certificates started operation in 1991. In this system, holders of eligible share certificates may deposit them with securities companies. Securities companies which are participants of the system, in turn, will deposit the certificates with the central depository run by this organization. Transaction of shares can be effected henceforth merely by entering the transaction in the accounts without actual transfer of certificates.[15]

As a rule, shareholders are free to assign shares. However, it is possible to limit the assignment of shares by requiring the approval of the board of directors in the articles of association (Art. 204, para. 1). Almost 90% of the joint stock companies are small or medium-sized companies run by an individual or a family. Such companies often prefer to limit the assignment of shares and prevent 'undesirable' persons from becoming share-holders. Such a restriction on assignment has to be indicated on the certificate.

When such a restriction of transfer is stipulated in the articles of association, a shareholder who intends to assign a share is entitled to demand that the company designate a person to whom he should assign the shares if the company does not approve the assignment. In such cases, the shareholder is required to specify in writing the number and the kind of shares as well as the name of the person to whom he intends to assign the shares (Art. 204-2, para. 1). The company is required, by a decision of the board of directors, to designate an appropriate person to whom the shares should be assigned and notify the shareholder within two weeks, unless it approves the assignment. Within ten days after the notice, the person designated may request the shareholder to assign the shares to him. A contract between the shareholder and the designated buyer comes into effect with this request.

Assignment of shares without approval of the board when such an approval is required does not make the transaction void between the parties. It is void only in relation to the company.[16]

---

15 Japan Securities Research Institute, *Securities Market in Japan 1992*, Tokyo 1992, pp. 146–150. M. Kishida, *Seminar: Kaisha-ho Nyumon* (*Introduction to Company Law*).
16 Judgment of the Supreme Court, 15 June, 1973 (*Minshū* 27–6–700).

If the company refuses to endorse the transaction, the purchaser of the share is entitled to require the company to designate an assignee (Art. 204–5).

In some cases, the assignment of shares is prohibited by law. For example, a company is prohibited from obtaining its own shares unless otherwise specified by the law (Art. 210). Infringement of this ban is punishable by criminal sanction (Art. 489, para. 2). This is intended to keep capital intact and also to prevent directors from being involved in manipulation of the stock market or insider trading. Prior to the 1981 amendment, a company was unable to accept its own share as a pledge, but now it is allowed to accept up to 5% of its shares as a pledge. On rare occasions, a company may obtain its own shares when buying back shares, the merger or total assignment of its business, and in a few other cases.

Whether this ban should be maintained is now being questioned. Since the acquisition of the company's own shares was prohibited, the primary means of defending the company against takeover attempts was cross shareholding by 'stable shareholders'. However, this system came under criticism from abroad as a barrier to the entry into the market in bilateral negotiations with the United States and is unlikely to continue in the present form. In turn, there are proposals to allow the companies to acquire their own shares and also to set up a holding company like in the United States.[17]

Another statutory restriction on the assignment of shares is the restriction on a subsidiary acquiring shares of the parent company. Previously, it was understood that obtaining and holding such shares through a subsidiary was against the ban on acquisition of shares by the company which was mentioned above. However, opinions varied as to the scope of subsidiaries covered by this ban. The amendment of 1981 introduced a new provision regarding the acquisition of shares of the parent company by subsidiaries. Thus, if a company holds more than 50% of the shares of another joint stock company or of the capital of a limited company, these companies are regarded as subsidiaries and are prohibited from acquiring or holding shares of the parent company. The same applies when a subsidiary and the parent company jointly, or a subsidiary alone hold a majority stake of another company (Art. 211–2, paras. 1 and 3). It should be noted that criterion for deciding whether a company is a

17 H. Ichiki in 8 April, 1992, *Japan Economic Journal (Nikkei)*.

subsidiary or not is solely based upon the stake the company has in another company.

The Anti-Monopoly law is also a source of restrictions on the acquisition of shares. Companies are prohibited from acquiring or holding shares of a Japanese company if it will substantially restrict competition in a specific area of business (Art. 10). Financial institutions may not acquire or hold shares of another Japanese company in excess of 5% of its issued shares (Art. 11). Further, the Anti-Monopoly Law prohibits the establishment of a company solely for holding the shares of another company, i.e. a holding company (Art. 9). In practice, however, it is common for companies to hold the shares of other companies. Some large trade corporations hold an enormous amount of shares even exceeding their capital. Since these companies have not been set up solely for holding shares, they are not against the Anti-Monopoly Law.

One phenomenon which is prevalent among major companies is the mutual holding of shares (cross shareholdings). Companies form groups whose members mutually hold their shares. Thus, in a typical case, shares of a company are held by the 'main bank' and other banks, insurance companies, as well as trade partners. In turn, the company holds shares of the banks and other companies. Mutual holding of shares was a reaction to the compulsory dissolution of major business conglomerates (*zaibatsu*) after the Second World War. Since it was impossible to have a holding company any more, another method had to be devised to keep the shares within the group. Therefore, instead of a single key company holding all the shares, the mutual holding of shares became a common practice. With the financial liberalisation taking place in the 1970s, mutual shareholding became even more widely utilised, since it was thought to be a suitable device to defend the company from a possible foreign takeover.[18]

In 1977, the Anti-Monopoly Law was amended and a new provision was designed to limit the holding of shares by companies by setting the maximum amount which they may hold. According to this provision, large companies with a capital of more than 10 billion yen, or with net assets exceeding 30 billion yen and engaged in non-financial business, may not hold shares of domestic companies if the total purchase price of shares exceeds the capital or net assets, whichever is larger. However, some exceptions are listed in the provision (Art. 9–2).

18 H. Okumura, *Kabushiki-gaisha* (*Joint Stock Companies*), Tokyo 1986, pp. 31–32.

5. The general meeting of shareholders

The general meeting of shareholders is the supreme body of joint stock companies. The meeting appoints directors (*torishimariyaku*) to form a board, which carries on the management of the company. The board in turn elects representative directors (*daihyō-torishimariyaku*), who represent the company. In addition, auditors are appointed by the general meeting.

In practice, these institutions do not necessarily perform the functions expected by law. The general meeting of shareholders has become almost a ceremonial or rubber-stamping body. A majority of shareholders, who are stable shareholders, hold the shares not for capital gain or dividends, and therefore, are not necessarily interested in the short term performance of the company, unlike in the United States. The board of directors also is not necessarily capable of controlling representative directors, since most members are promoted from among the employees of the company and subordinate to the chairman of the board or the president.[19]

Some amendments to the Commercial Code have been made to introduce closer control over the management since 1950. However, there has been an almost irrevocable transition power from the general meeting to the board, and eventually the representative directors. For instance, by the amendment of 1974, the position of auditors was strengthened and their power was expanded to include the oversight of business. But so far, it is not certain whether these attempts have been successful or not.

The general meeting of shareholders is empowered to make decisions only on issues stipulated by law, or specifically provided in the articles of association (Art. 230–10). Basic matters concerning the company, such as the appointment of directors, auditors, decisions as to the remuneration of directors, auditors, and liquidators, approval of statements of accounts, decisions as to the dividend, are among the issues to be decided by this meeting. Also the alteration of the articles of association, reduction of capital, dissolution, transfer of business, merger are within the competence of the general meeting. Companies may add some issues to the competence of the general meeting by specifying them in the articles of association.

A general meeting is required to be held at least once a year, and in companies with dividends paid more than twice a year, it should be convened at least once every financial term (Art. 234).

---

19 T. Suzuki and A. Takeuchi, *Kaisha-hō* (*Company Law*), second edition, Tokyo 1987, pp. 198–200.

An extraordinary meeting may be convened whenever necessary (Art. 235). The general meeting of shareholders is convened by the representative director based upon the decision of the board. The board decides the date, place, and agenda of the general meeting. A general meeting convened without the decision of the board is not regarded as a legitimate meeting. However, if all the shareholders have taken part in the meeting, the resolution of the meeting is valid, even if a proper procedure to convene the meeting has not been followed.[20]

Shareholders are given certain rights as to the convening of a general meeting. Those shareholders who have held 3% or more of the issued shares for more than six months, may require the representative director to convene a general meeting. The shareholder must specify the purpose of the general meeting and the reason for convening it in writing. If a meeting is not convened without delay, or the date of the meeting is set later than six weeks after the request has been made, the shareholder may convene the meeting by himself with the approval of the court (Art. 237).

Shareholders have a right to attend the general meeting, ask questions, present their opinions, and vote. Shareholders have one vote for each share (Art. 241, para. 1). The company does not have a vote for its own shares. If a shareholder has more than one share, he may vote in several ways (Art. 239–2).

The voting rights of a shareholder can be exercised by taking part in the meeting or through an agent. There is no requirement as to who may be an agent in the Code. The company may, however, stipulate certain requirements in the articles of association, for example, that only the shareholders of the company may act as an agent.

Actually, most of the individual shareholders are not interested in taking part in the general meeting, nor are they interested in finding agents. A practice had developed before the system of voting in writing was introduced in 1981, in which the company sends individual shareholders a blank proxy to be signed by the shareholder, together with the announcement of the meeting. Shareholders are enticed to sign this proxy which empowers the general manager of the company's general affairs department, or the chief of the securities section to vote on their behalf. The rationale of this practice was to ensure that the meeting reaches a quorum. Moreover, in this way, it was easier for the management of the company to obtain support of a majority of shareholders. As a safeguard against abuses, the Securities and Exchange Law

20 Judgment of the Supreme Court, 29 December, 1985 (*Minshū* 39–8–1869).

provides that a proxy statement should be sent to the shareholders of listed shares as a preprequisite to solicitation of proxies. The proxy should be formed in a way which enables the shareholders to express their support or opposition to each proposal separately.

In 1981, the Law on Special Rules to the Commercial Code on Audit and other Matters of Joint Stock Companies introduced a system of voting in writing.[1] This was intended to enable shareholders who do not wish to take part in the general meeting to express their views. This system only applies to large companies with 1,000 or more shareholders with voting rights. The company is required to enclose information materials and a voting form with the notice of general meeting. If a shareholder submits this voting form to the company not later than the day before the meeting, this is regarded as a valid vote (Art. 21–3, para. 1).

Companies which are eligible for voting in writing may also choose to resort to proxy voting. At present, the abovementioned practice of proxy voting is still common in a majority of companies.

Normally, the agenda of the general meeting is decided by the company, and not by shareholders. In large companies, it is almost impossible for small shareholders to have a say in framing the agenda. To rectify this situation, shareholders who have held 1% or more of the issued shares, or 300 shares for not less than six months may require in writing that the director add certain issues to the agenda (Art. 232–2). If the request has been made in accordance with the procedure provided by the law, the director is obliged to include such matters in the agenda. Shareholders may also make a counter proposal, supplementary proposal, or a correcting proposal in relation to the matters included in the agenda prepared by the company and have a summary of the proposal publicised in the notice for the general meeting.

Directors and auditors have an obligation to give explanations at the general meeting on matters raised by the shareholders (Art. 237–3, para. 1). This provision was introduced in 1981 and is part of the attempts to vitalize the shareholders meeting. Prior to the 1981 amendment, the shareholders' meeting was often dominated by 'special shareholders' who hold a small amount of shares and threaten the company to give benefit to them if the shareholders meeting were to end without trouble. On the other hand, companies retained other 'special shareholders' to support

1 Law No. 22, 1974.

the management at the shareholders meeting and counter such extortion. As a 'by-product', questions from small shareholders were often ignored. It was considered a successful shareholders meeting, if the meeting ended as quickly as possible without any question from shareholders.

A provision was introduced in the Code which prohibits offering of benefits to shareholders; violation may result in criminal prosecution of both the offeror and receivor of such benefits (Art. 294-2, para. 1, Art. 497).

Generally, resolutions of a general meeting are adopted if they are supported by a simple majority of votes by shareholders entitled to vote. The quorum for a meeting is met if shareholders with a total of 50% of outstanding shares took part (Art. 239, para. 1). This quorum may be reduced or totally eliminated if the articles of association so provide. However, this does not apply in cases where the appointment of directors or auditors is at issue.

In certain cases, such as the alteration of the articles of association, dissolution of business, dismissal of a director or an auditor, new issue of shares with preferential terms to third parties, or transfer of business, it is necessary to have two thirds of the votes with shareholders holding not less than 50% of outstanding shares present (special resolutions – Art. 245, para. 1, Art. 343). The proportion of votes required in these cases can not be changed even by the articles of association.

There are also matters which require even more votes (extraordinary resolutions). Thus, support of the shareholders with more than two-thirds of the outstanding shares is needed to discharge a director from liability to the company for the loss caused by the transaction between the company and the director or by other acts where there is a conflict of interests (Art. 266, para. 6). A change to the articles of association in order to impose restrictions on the assignment of shares also requires the support of a majority of all shareholders and two-thirds of the issued shares (Art. 348). In some cases, such as the discharge of the liability of directors in cases other than a conflict of interest, discharge of liability of auditors, comptrollers and promoters, consent (not necessarily a vote) of all shareholders is needed (Arts. 266, para. 5, 280 para. 1, 196, 430 para. 2).

Since resolutions of the general meeting are adopted by various forms of a majority vote, it is necessary to protect the interests of those shareholders opposed to the decision. Taking appraisal rights in U.S. Law as a model, minority shareholders are granted a right to require that the company purchase their shares. There are three instances where such a request is allowed: 1) on the transfer of business, either the whole business or a substantial part of it (Art. 245–2); 2) on the alteration of the articles of incorporation for restricting the transfer of shares (Art. 349, para. 1); and 3) on merger (Art. 408–3, para. 1). The purchase price of shares is decided by the court if the company and the shareholder fail to reach agreement. Since the purchase of shares by the company reduces capital, the appropriateness of this system is being questioned.[2]

One of the novelties brought in by the 1981 amendment was the right of shareholders to apply to the court in advance of the meeting for the appointment of a comptroller to check the procedure whereby the general meeting was convened and the way in which resolutions were adopted. The shareholder is required to have held no less than 1% of the issued shares for more than 6 months. The comptroller reports the result of his inspection to the court and, if necessary, the court may order the directors to convene a general meeting in order to rectify the procedural defects of the previous meeting (Art. 237–2).

In practice, the annual general meeting of shareholders often turns out to be a mere formality. According to a survey of the practice of listed companies, the average length of such a meeting is thirty minutes, and in most cases, shareholders attending the meeting do not ask questions or express their views. It is often pointed out that because of the extremely low dividends, small investors are not interested in the management of the company. On the other hand, consent of major shareholders is obtained before the shareholders' meeting.

There are instances where the resolution of the general meeting has been adopted in violation of the procedures provided by law, or is in substance, contrary to law. Recourse to the courts is allowed in such cases. There are some problems which should be given consideration in litigation involving companies. Firstly, legal relations have to be decided uniformly for all who are concerned. As a rule, court judgments have effect only on the parties to the case. Without a special arrangement, there may be instances where the same resolution of the general meeting or other acts of a company is upheld in one case while found void in another case. Therefore, it is necessary to extend the effect of such a judgment to third parties.

Secondly, even if a resolution is found null and void, it is not necessarily desirable to rule that the act was void from the beginning. Before the act has been found null and void, various legal relationships may have emerged, and it may not be appropriate to make them all invalid. Therefore, in cases such as

---

2 Suzuki and Takeuchi, *supra* note 19, pp. 231–232.

a claim concerning the validity of incorporation, the effect of the act is denied only for the future.

Thirdly, for the sake of stability of legal relations, the grounds for making a resolution or an act null and void, *locus standi*, and the time limit for such claims should be clearly specified.[3]

The Commercial Code acknowledges three types of claims against the resolution of the general meeting: 1) claims for the revocation of a resolution; 2) claims for the confirmation of the voidness of a resolution; and 3) claims for the confirmation of the absence of a resolution. In these claims, the effect of the judgment by the court is binding not only on the parties to the litigation; it has a general effect on other parties as well.

Claims for the revocation of the resolution of a general meeting can be made first, when the procedure to convene the meeting or the decision-making process at the meeting was contrary to the law or the articles of association, or was extremely unfair. The court has revoked a resolution of a shareholders' meeting which had been convened without proper notice and a resolution which was made on an issue not included in the notice of the meeting.[4] Other instances where a resolution may be revoked include cases where the resolution is against the articles of association, or where as a result of the vote by a shareholder who had special interests in the issue, the resolution was extremely inappropriate (Art. 247, para. 1). In one case, a resolution of the meeting to approve the accounts was revoked, because a director had voted for this resolution.[5]

In cases where there is a ground for the revocation of the resolution, shareholders, directors, or auditors may have recourse to the courts to claim revocation of the resolution (Art. 247, para. 1). A shareholder may, according to the Supreme Court, even claim revocation on grounds that only concern other shareholders. Thus, in one case, X assigned his shares to Y, but company A refused registration of Y without an adequate reason. Subsequently there were three general meetings, but Y did not receive notice, since he was not registered. X claimed revocation of the resolutions. The Supreme Court upheld the claim and revoked the resolution.[6]

A claim for revocation must be made within three months of the adoption of the resolution (Art. 248, para. 1). A deposit has

---

3 *Ibid.*, p. 86.
4 Judgment of the Supreme Court, 3 October, 1958, 15 November, 1956 (*Minshū* 10–11–1423).
5 Judgment of Tokyo District Court, 9 March, 1953 (*Kaminshū* 4–1–368).
6 Judgment of the Supreme Court, 28 September, 1967 (*Minshū* 21–7–1970).

to be made upon request from the company (Art. 249, para. 1). The district court where the principal office of the company is located has jurisdiction over such claims. If the claim is upheld and the resolution is revoked, the resolution is regarded as having been null and void from the beginning. In such cases, the judgment has effect on third parties too. On the other hand, if the claim is not upheld, the judgment of the court has effect only on the parties (Art. 247, para. 2, Art. 109).

Even if there are grounds for the revocation of the resolution, the court may reject such a claim if the defect was not serious enough and did not affect the resolution (Art. 251). This provision was intended to limit abuse of claims. It was once deleted from the Code, but in theory as well as in court practice, it was considered that the court had some discretion in revoking resolutions. The provision was reintroduced by the 1981 amendment. In a case where a company failed to formally notify a shareholder about the meeting, the Supreme Court rejected the claim for revocation on the ground that the shareholder had been informed by the representative director, and was aware that the meeting was taking place in the building where he lived.[7]

If the substance of the resolution of a general meeting is against the substantive law, such as a resolution to pay an illegal dividend, or a resolution which is contrary to the equal standing of shareholders, anyone may claim that the resolution is null and void. If the claim is upheld by the court, it is binding on parties and non-parties (Art. 252).

When procedural defects concerning the general meeting are so serious that even the existence of the resolution should be denied, anyone may claim that the general meeting did not take place. This has been acknowledged in court practice for some time, but recently an explicit provision was introduced in the Code (Art. 252). Examples of these serious procedural defects include a general meeting convened without the decision of the board but merely by one of the directors, a meeting without notice to a majority of shareholders, and a meeting attended only by some of the shareholders which took place after the general meeting. In one case where the shareholders were not notified of the place and time of the meeting and a minute of the meeting had been made without an actual meeting of the shareholders, the Supreme Court found that the general meeting did not exist.[8] As is the case with the claim for nullifying the resolution

---

7 Judgment of the Supreme Court, 16 June, 1980 (*Hanji* 978–112).
8 Judgment of the Supreme Court, 9 July, 1970 (*Minshu* 24–7–755).

of a general meeting, the judgment of the court which found the meeting non-existent is binding on everybody.

While claims for revocation can be made only by shareholders, directors or auditors, there is no such limitation in claims for the confirmation of voidness or non-existence of a resolution. For instance, creditors of a company may initiate such a proceeding.

6. Duties of directors

Directors are appointed by the general meeting of shareholders and form a board of directors. In practice, when more than one director is to be appointed at the meeting, the shareholders entrust the selection of candidates to the chairman of the meeting, and the shareholders vote for the list, instead of each director. The board appoints representative directors, who carry out business and represent the company.

Cumulative voting, which gives one vote per share for each director, is allowed in order to enable the minority shareholders to send their representative to the board. Each shareholder may cast his vote entirely on one candidate, or may split his vote among several candidates. This system was introduced from the United States after the Second World War. Shareholders may demand, giving notice five days before the general meeting, that the company adopt cumulative voting. A company may eliminate cumulative voting by stipulation in the articles of association; this is fairly common in Japan (Art. 256-3).

A company must have at least three directors (Art. 255). Previously, there were no restrictions on eligibility, but a new provision was added to the Code in 1981. In addition to persons without civil capacity, or with limited capacity, those who have been declared bankrupt and have not been restored, those who have been convicted of offenses provided by the Commercial Code, etc. are ineligible (Art. 254-2). It is understood that a juridical person may not become a director. A company may add more requirements by stipulating them in the articles of association.

A peculiarity of Japanese joint stock companies is that most directors are appointed from among employees of the company and there are few external directors. In Japan, in approximately 60% of companies, more than 80% of directors are appointed from within the company, while in the United States, in more than 50% of the companies, such directors comprise less than

30% of directors.[9] Those who combine the position of a director with an employee, for example, director and general manager, are not uncommon in Japan. The average term for directorship is three terms – six years.

Directors can be dismissed by a resolution of the general meeting on any ground. The resolution of the general meeting must be adopted by a special vote, i.e. shareholders who hold more than 50% of the outstanding shares should be present and two thirds of their votes are needed (Art. 257). If the director has a fixed term contract and was dismissed without justifiable grounds before its expiration, the company must pay compensation.

Representative directors represent the company and carry out its daily business. Where there are several representative directors, each of them represents the company, but the company may make it a rule to represent the company by representative directors jointly (Art. 261, paras. 1 and 2). The chairman and the president of the company are normally representative directors, but in addition, vice presidents, managing directors are often made representative directors.

Directors form a board of directors. The board is the decision-making body of the company on the carrying out of business and is also entrusted to supervise business activities of representative directors and directors (Art. 260, para. 1). The board is empowered, *inter alia*, to appoint representative directors, authorise the act of a director which competes with the company, ratify contracts of directors with their company (conflict of interest cases), and decide on new share issue or floating of bonds. The Code provides that the following issues be within the exclusive competence of the board and should not be delegated to the representative director: 1) the disposal and acceptance of significant assets; 2) the borrowing of large amounts of money; 3) the appointment and dismissal of senior executives; and 4) the creation, change, or abolition of a branch office or other major affiliate which form part of the company.

A board meeting is summoned at least every three months. Each director is entitled to convene a board meeting. In most companies, the chairman or president is the convenor of the board meeting. In cases where a director has acted against the law or articles of association, or is likely to do so, auditors are also empowered to convene a meeting to give a report on such matters (Art. 260–3). Auditors may also attend the board meeting, although they do not have a vote.

9 Kishida, *supra*, pp. 164–165.

The decision of the board meeting is made by a majority vote of the directors who are present. The quorum is 50% (Art. 260–2, para. 1). An interested party may not vote. For instance, if the dismissal of the representative director or a transaction between the company and a director which involves conflict of interest is at issue, the director concerned is not entitled to vote (Art. 260–2 para. 2).

Decisions vitiated by a procedural flaw, or which are against substantive law, are null and void. Unlike the resolutions of a general meeting, there is no special arrangements for a claim of nullity concerning the decisions of a board meeting. However, since the necessity to decide the validity of the decision of the board in a uniform way is no less acute than resolutions of the shareholders meeting, there are views which support the application of some provisions on the resolution of the shareholders' meeting with necessary modification to board decisions.[10]

In the company law of some European countries, there is a system of a supervisory board, which is designed to supervise the conduct of the business. For instance, in Germany, suprevisory boards are mandatory for joint stock companies; it is composed of representatives of shareholders and employees.[11] In the United Kingdom, non-managing directors perform a similar function. However, the board of directors in Japan is basically free from either type of controls.

The relationship between the director and the company is that of mandate, which is one of the typical contracts provided in the Civil Code. On the basis of the provision of the Civil Code, directors are obliged to act as a 'good manager' (Art. 644, Civil Code). Furthermore, the Commercial Code provides that directors owe a fiduciary duty to the company. Directors must perform their duty in accordance with law and articles of association and the resolution of the shareholders' meeting, and must exercise their powers faithfully for the benefit of the company (Art. 254–3). Directors also have a duty to supervise the exercise of power by representative directors and other directors, and if necessary, convene a board meeting and ensure that directors perform their duties properly (Art. 260, para. 1).

In one case, two directors were found liable for the failure by serious negligence to control mismanagement on the part of the representative director. These directors had left the management of the company entirely to the representative director, who ran

---

10 Maeda, *supra*, p. 304.
11 N. Horn, H. Koetz, H. G. Leser, *German Private Commercial Law*, Oxford, 1982, pp. 260–261.

the company without holding a board meeting. Eventually, the company went bankrupt. The Supreme Court ruled that directors should monitor the carrying out of business by the representative director and if necessary, convene the board meeting and ensure that the company's business is carried out in a proper way.[12]

In another case, a director of a computer software company A, who became at odds with the representative director, set up a new company B for competing business. He induced employees of company A to move to company B with him and as a result, they joined company B. This was found by the court to be against the fidiciary duty of the director.[13]

The Code prohibits directors, either for themselves or for a third party, from being engaged in the same kind of business as that of the company, unless authorised to do so by the board. If a transaction falls within the scope of this prohibition, a director must disclose the material facts of the transaction to the board. Without the authorisation of the board, the director may not proceed further. Also, after the transaction, the material facts of the transaction must be reported to the board meeting without delay (Art. 264, paras. 1 and 2).

Even if the director has failed to obtain authorisation for this kind of transaction, the transaction itself is valid. The board may regard the transaction as having been concluded for the company, and demand that the director transfer any profit which he has made out of the transaction to the company (Art. 264, para. 3). If any loss has been caused by such a transaction, the director is liable to the company for such loss, regardless of whether he had obtained prior authorisation of the board.

The Code also prohibits directors from entering into a contract with the company, since there is an obvious conflict of interest in such a case. The Code provides that if a director is either to purchase goods manufactured by the company or other asset of the company, to sell the company his property or goods which he owns, to borrow money from the company, or to enter into other transactions with the company for himself or on behalf of a third party, he is required to obtain approval of the board (Art. 265).

In addition, transactions between a third party and the company which involve conflict of interest between the company and the director are also prohibited. An example is a contract between the company and the creditor guranteeing the director's

---

12 Judgment of the Supreme Court, 22 May, 1973 (*Minshū* 27–5–655).
13 Judgment of the Tokyo Appellate Court, 26 October, 1990 (*Kinyū-shōji hanrei* 835–23).

debt. The director is not a party to such a transaction, but still this is a case of conflict of interest.

In these cases, the director must disclose material facts of the transaction to the board. In cases where these transactions are actually not disadvantageous to the company because of the absence of the conflict of interest, this provision does not apply.

Transactions made without the authorisation of the board are null and void. The Code does not limit the range of persons who may claim that such an act is void. The problem with this arrangement is that this provision has often been invoked not by the company but by the director or a third party as a defence against a claim by the company. In order to avoid this unfair outcome, the courts have followed academic opinion and limited the range of persons who are entitled to claim voidness. Thus, in one case, a company demanded repayment of the money it had lent to its director. The latter invoked Article 265 as a defence and argued that the contract was void. The Supreme Court ruled that the director was not entitled to invoke this provision.[14]

Transactions which fall within the purview of Article 265 are null and void between the parties. However, the interest of a third party who had acted in good faith should also be protected. For example, the company should not be allowed to invoke this provision against a *bona fide* third party who had unwittingly entered into a transaction with a director who acted in the name of the company. Academics are of the opinion that a company may invoke this provision only against the director or a third party who acted in bad faith. The Supreme Court has accepted this argument and ruled that the company may not resort to this provision, unless it proves that the third party was aware that the director had not obtained approval of the board.[15]

A director is liable for the loss caused by such transactions, irrespective of whether it has been authorised by the board or not. Other directors who approved the transaction, as well as the representative director who represented the company in the transaction may also be liable.

The Code sets forth various grounds of liability for directors against the company. These are proposing to the general meeting the payment of illegal dividends, offering of benefits to shareholders to influence the exercise of their rights, extending of loans to other directors, concluding a transaction which involves conflict of interest with their company, and lastly, acting against law, ordinances, or articles of association (Art. 266, para. 1).

14 Judgment of the Supreme Court, 11 December, 1973 (*Minshū* 26–3–373).
15 Judgment of the Supreme Court, 13 October, 1973 (*Minshū* 25–7–900).

One case involved window dressing, where directors agreed to pay dividends by concealing the loss and without the resolution of the shareholders meeting.[16] Those directors who have committed these acts as well as those who supported them at the board meeting are liable. Unless their objection has been entered in the minutes of the board meeting, directors are presumed to have given consent to such acts (Art. 266, paras. 2 and 3).

As a rule, directors are discharged of their liability only with the consent of all shareholders. In cases where transactions involving conflict of interest between the company and the director are at issue, a director may be relieved of liability with the consent of shareholders who hold more than two thirds of the issued shares.

The Commercial Code also provides for criminal penalties up to seven years' imprisonment for directors and others who acted against the interest of the company in various ways (Arts. 486–491, 494–2, 493–498). Directors and others are penalised if they purport to benefit themselves or a third party or to harm the company and, against their duty, cause pecuniary loss to the company.

Normally, a representative director represents the company in litigation. However, in cases where litigation pursuing the liablity of a director is at issue, the representative director may be reluctant to sue. In such cases, shareholders are also given a right to sue the directors on behalf of the company, provided that the company fails to pursue the liability of a director. The company, as well as other shareholders may take part in the proceedings. This right belongs to those individual shareholders who have been shareholders for more than six months. The general view of the academics is that the issues which a shareholder may pursue extend to everything for which the director is liable to the company. In order to exercise this right, the shareholder must first ask the company in writing to sue the director. Only when the company has failed to start proceedings within 30 days, may the shareholder sue the director on behalf of the company (Art. 267, paras. 1 and 2). However, if it is likely that an irrecoverable loss will occur by following the above mentioned procedure, a shareholder may sue the director immediately (Art. 267, para. 3). This system is modelled after the derivative action in U.S. Law. In Japan, it is not so widely used, since the cost to sue is too much for individual shareholders to bear. Incidentally, if the shareholder wins the case for the company, he may claim the cost

---

16 Judgment of Kobe District Court, Himeji Division, 11 April, 1966 (*Kaminshū*, 17–3/4–222, Sanyo Tokushukō case).

from the company. Even if he loses, he is not liable for damages, unless he had knowingly harmed the company.

If a director is likely to cause irrecoverable loss to the company by a *ultra vires* act, or by other acts in breach of law or articles of association, a shareholder of more than six months' standing is entitled to demand that the director terminate such an action (Art. 272).

In addition to the liability of directors to the company, directors are also liable to third parties in certain cases. Generally, when a director causes loss to a third party, the company, and not the director, is liable to the third party (Art. 261, para. 3, Art. 78). However, in cases where a director had acted in bad faith, or was seriously at fault in exercising his power, then he is directly liable to a third party (Art. 266–3, para. 1). Moreover, if a director has made a false entry on significant matters in an application for shares or bonds, certificate for pre-emptive right, prospectus, etc., he is liable to a third party unless he proves that he was not at fault (Art. 266–3, para. 2).

In a majority of cases, the third party means either creditors or shareholders. In one case, A, a representative director of a company purchased steel material on behalf of the company. A used the signet of another representative director and president B, and issued a promissory note to the seller. B had been asked to become a managing director by A to give credibility to the company. B left the management of the company to A and authorized him to issue promissory notes. The seller failed to cash the promissory note and therefore sued B. The Supreme Court acknowledged the liability of B on the ground of Article 266–3.[17]

Sometimes, those who have agreed to have their names registered as directors but are only nominal directors, are made liable under this provision. There was a case where a person, who was appointed an external director, failed to oversee the managing of the company by the representative director, did not ask the board meeting to be convened, and left the company to the arbitrary management of this representative director. In the meantime, the representative director purchased goods which the company could not afford and fell into default. The seller sued this external director. The Supreme Court found this director to be liable to the seller for his failure to oversee the management.[18]

One of the aims of the liability of directors against third parties

---

17 Judgment of the Supreme Court, 26 November, 1969 (*Minshū* 23–11–2150).
18 Judgment of the Supreme Court, 18 March, 1980 (*Hanji* 971–101).

is the protection of creditors of small and medium-sized companies. A majority of Japanese companies are small or medium-sized and are run by a small number of individuals, often a family. Assets of these companies can be very small, and without the provision which enables creditors to make a claim against the directors, it is difficult for them to recover their money from the company itself. The Supreme Court ruled that the loss does not have to be directly caused by the director to the third party. Even in cases where the director caused a loss to the company by neglect of duty and as a result, the third party suffered a loss, this person is entitled to pursue the liability of the director.[19]

7. Audit

The audit system underwent a major reform in 1974, after window-dressing and subsequent bankruptcy involving a major company took place. Auditors were criticised for the failure of checking such misdeeds. The 1974 amendment introduced a new system in which companies are classified into large, medium and small conpamies and have different audit arrangements in accordance with the size. In 1981, there was another reform which strengthened the independence of auditors.[20]

Firstly, for large companies (i.e. companies which have capital exceeding 500 million yen, or which have debts exceeding 20 billion yen), auditors are entrusted to check the accounts as well as the legality of the carrying out of business by directors (Art. 274, para. 1). Their power is limited to the legality of the conduct of directors, and does not, however, extend to its appropriateness. It was made mandatory for large companies to have an audit either by a chartered accountant or an accounting firm in addition to the audit by auditors. These companies are required to have more than two auditors, and at least one of them must be a full time auditor.

Secondly, auditors of small companies (companies with capital of 100 million yen or less) only check the accounts of the company. Audit by a chartered accountant or an accounting firm is not needed.

Thirdly, in medium sized companies (i.e. the rest of the companies), the scope of the auditor's power is the same as large

---

19 Judgment of the Supreme Court, 26 November, 1969 (*Minshū* 23–11–2150).
20 The Law on Special Rules to the Commercial Code on Auditing of Large Companies, Law No. 22, 1974.

companies, but audit by a chartered accountant or an accounting firm is not mandatory.[1]

Auditors are appointed at the general meeting of shareholders. Auditors are entitled to give an opinion as to the appointment or dismissal of themselves (Art. 275–3). They are entitled to take part in the board meeting and present their views. They are not entitled to vote, but if they may seek injunction if they find that the acts of directors to be against the law or articles of association and is likely to cause serious loss to the company (Arts. 260–3, para. 1, 275–2, para. 1). They must report to the board any act of a director which is against the law or the articles of association, and if necessary, convene a board meeting for this purpose and may also report the fact to the general meeting of shareholders. Furthermore, auditors are also entitled to initiate litigation to revoke the resolutions of a general meeting.

Auditors are empowered to investigate the financial status of the company as well as its subsidiaries and require reports from their directors, managers, and other employees (Arts. 274, para. 2, 274–3). Directors must report to the auditor whenever they discover facts which are likely to cause serious loss to the company (Art. 274–2).

8. Mergers and acquisitions in Japan

Mergers are not uncommon in Japan. In 1991, there were 53 cases of merger which involved listed companies. In four cases, a listed company merged with another company, while in the remaining 49 cases, a non-listed company was absorbed by a listed company.[2] According to a survey by a securities company, there were 258 cases of mergers and acquisitions involving Japanese companies in the first half of 1992. Mergers and acquisitions between Japanese companies accounted for 122 cases, while there were 120 cases where a foreign company was acquired by a Japanese company. There were 16 cases of acquisition of a Japanese company by a foreign company.[3]

Mergers and acquisitions are subject to control by various laws. For example, merger of banks, insurance companies, public utilities, etc. require the permission of the Minister in charge. The Anti-Monopoly Law prohibits a merger if it is likely to

---

1 Special Rules to the Commercial Code on Audit of Companies Limited by Shares (Law No. 22, 1974), Articles 2, 7, 8 and 22.
2 Commercial Law Centre, *Zōshi Hakusho 1992 (White paper on the Increase of Capital)*, Tokyo 1992, p. 182.
3 *Japan Economic Journal* (Nikkei), 1 July, 1992.

restrain competition in a substantial way in a given area of trade, or is effected by unfair practice (Art. 15, para. 1).

The Commercial Code provides for two types of mergers: merger by absorption and merger by incorporation. In the former case, one company absorbs another, while in the latter case, both merging companies cease to exist and a new company is set up. Merger by absorption is the primary method used in Japan.

In order to merge, companies must conclude an agreement of merger which are subject to approval at the shareholders meeting of both companies (Art. 408, para. 1). At the shareholders meeting, the total number of shares held by the shareholders taking part in the meeting must exceed half of the issued shares, and the resolution must be supported by more than two-thirds of the voting shares (Art. 408, para. 3). Both companies are required to offer the balance sheet for public inspection two weeks in advance of the shareholders' meeting. There are certain matters which should be included in the agreement, such as the number and types of new shares to be issued on the occasion of the merger, information concerning the allocation of shares to the shareholders of the absorbed company, i.e. the ratio of the shares of the merged company against the absorbed company's shares, the increase in capital and reserves, etc. (Art. 410).

Shareholders who are opposed to the merger are entitled to require the company to purchase their shares at a fair price which the share may have reached, had the merger not proceeded (Art. 408–3). Shareholders must inform the company of their intention and actually oppose the merger at the shareholders' meeting.

Creditors of the merging companies must be informed (Art. 416, para. 1, Art. 100, para. 1). Both companies must make a public announcement and invite those creditors who are opposed to the merger to inform the company. All known creditors must be contacted too. Bond holders may oppose the merger only through the bondholders' meeting. Those creditors who failed to express opposition are deemed to have approved the merger. The company must repay the debt or offer a collateral to these opposing creditors, or place assets with a trust company for their benefit (Art. 100, para. 3).

After the merger, a shareholders' meeting is convened. The merger takes effect by registration after the shareholders' meeting (Art. 414, para. 1). Rights and duties of the absorbed company are succeeded to by the subsisting company (Art. 416, para. 3, Art. 103). The validity of the merger can be contested at court. Those who are entitled to sue are shareholders, directors, auditors, the liquidator, administrator, and creditors who opposed the merger (Art. 415).

Hostile takeovers of a company are rare in Japan, although the number of such takeovers has increased in recent years. Friendly takeovers are often effected by a company issuing new shares and allocating them to another company. Hostile acquisition of a company may take place by purchasing shares either through the stock market or off the market. In such cases, a shareholder who comes to hold more than 5% of the issued shares of a company must file a report with the Minister of Finance (see Chapter 14). Purchase of convertible bonds and warrant bonds issued abroad is also a possible method.[4] The system of tender offer (Take Over Bids) was introduced in Japan in 1971, but until 1990, there were only three cases where TOB was utilised. All of them involved friendly takeovers. The Securities and Exchange Law was amended in 1990 in order to harmonise the TOB system with those of other countries.[5]

---

4 For practitioners' views on these matters, see K. Ishizumi, *Acquiring Japanese Companies*, Tokyo 1988, pp. 151–184.
5 Japan Securities Research Institute, *Securities Market in Japan 1992*, Tokyo 1992, pp. 197–198.

14 Securities and exchange law

1. Corporate finance in Japan

A peculiarity of the financing of Japanese companies is their heavy reliance on external sources. In 1987, 61.4% of the finance came from external sources, i.e. equity and debt offering, and bank borrowing. Among external sources, indirect financing – borrowing from banks – has been the primary source. Between 1965 and 1985, the share of bank borrowing in corporate financing was well over 80%.[1] Heavy reliance on bank borrowing can be attributed to the low interest rates policy of the government and the then relatively underdeveloped state of the securities market. Historically, the modernisation of Japan was financed primarily by banks which were part of the *zai batsu* (business conglomerates) and not by the securities market. Even as late as the 1970s, issuing of bonds was highly restrictive and costly. Bonds had to be secured by a collateral. The number of companies which were eligible for issuing bonds was limited. As regards share issues, it was a common practice of companies to issue new shares at par value which was 50 or 100 yen.

The share of bank borrowing fell in the latter half of the 1980s to 60%, due to a rapid increase in equity finance.[2] According to a survey by MITI, with the listed manufacturing companies, long term borrowings are half of what they were ten years ago.[3] On the other hand, for medium sized and smaller companies, borrowing from a bank is still the primary means of financing. Therefore, the overall percentage of bank borrowing in general is still high.

In the 1970s, major corporations found alternative sources of finance in the securities market in Japan as well as in Europe.[4] Firstly, in the domestic market, instead of rights issues at par

---

1 R.J.Ballon and I.Tomita, *The Financial Behaviour of Japanese Corporations*, Tokyo 1988, pp. 86–96.
2 H. Oda and G. Grice, *Japanese Banking, Securites and Anti-Monopoly Law*, 1988 London, p. 76.
3 Barron and Tomita, *supra* note 1, pp. 84–85.
4 *Ibid.*, pp. 91–92.

value price, public offering of shares at market price became a common practice. Secondly, restrictions on issuing unsecured bonds were gradually lifted and convertible bonds and warrant bonds came to be widely issued. Thirdly, the financial liberalisation enabled Japanese companies to raise funds overseas by issuing shares and floating bonds. In 1982, 6.323 billion yen worth of covertible bonds and 662 million yen of warrant bonds were issued abroad; the amount increased sharply in 1987 to 10.486 billion and 34.715 billion respectively.[5] There was a rush of large and medium sized companies for equity finance (public offer of shares at market price, floating of warrant bonds and convertible bonds) which reached an all-time high in 1989 at 24.8 trillion yen.

The shift from indirect finance to direct finance in Japan, especially heavy reliance on equity finance, resulted in excess liquidity, which was often used to invest in land and stocks. The low cost of raising funds abroad and low interest rates in Japan have made this possible. In this frenzy of equity finance, some companies came to be involved in speculation in the securities market, instead of profiting from their primary business.

However, share prices have fallen drastically in the last couple of years. The Nikkei average of share prices fell from 38,000 to 17,000 in two years. In 1990, public offer of new shares decreased by 96.8%. Equity finance was suspended for six months that year. Since the cost of floating straight bonds in Japan is still high, companies turned abroad to float straight bonds. In 1990, 64.6% of the finance came from abroad, as compared with 41.2% in 1989.[6]

Some large companies are facing the need for refinancing debts, since convertible bonds issued in the late 1980s have so far failed to be converted to shares because of the fall in the market.

It should be noted that the shift from bank borrowing to equity finance in the 1970s and 1980s does not mean that the role of banks in corporate finance has decreased. In fact, it was primarily financial institutions including the banks which purchased these equities in Japan and abroad. As part of the scheme to strengthen mutual shareholding, banks purchased the equities of business companies and in turn, business companies have increased the holding of shares of banks.[7]

---

5 Oda and Grice, *supra* note 2, p. 76.
6 *Commercial Law Centre, Zōshi Hakusho (White Paper on Corporate Finance) 1991*, Tokyo 1991, pp. 3–5, 90, 1992, p. 4.
7 Nikkei ed., *Seminar; Nihon Kigyō Nyūmon (Introduction to Japanese Corporations)*, Tokyo 1990, 282–283.

Another peculiarity of Japanese corporate finance is the limited role of individual shareholders. In 1950, individuals held 61.3% of the issued shares. Since then, the percentage has kept constantly falling, and in 1989, it reached 22.6%. It should also be pointed out that holding of shares by banks and other financial institutions has steadily increased in recent years. Currently, financial institutions hold 42.3% of the shares, while business companies hold 24.8%.[8] This is due primarily to the increase in stable shareholding or mutual shareholding.

This decline in the share of individual shareholders is unhealthy, since 1) mutual shareholding means the erosion of control by shareholders; 2) nominal increase in the capital by mutual shareholding weakens the financial position of the company; 3) the general public may lose interest in the stock market, and 4) since the number of shares which are actually traded in the market decreases with mutual shareholding, the price formation may become distorted.[9] In fact, the limited number of shares traded in the market was partly to be blamed for the fluctuation of share prices in the late 1980s.

2. History of securities legislation

The earliest legislation concerning securities was the Stock Transaction Ordinance of 1874, which was modelled after the London Stock Exchange rules. The first stock exchanges in Japan were founded in Tokyo and Osaka in 1878. Securities firms started their business, dealing with government bonds and later shares. However, the securities market failed to play a major role in the rapid modernisation process. *Zaibatsu*, which were the major force behind the industrialisation, did not have to rely on the securities market for financing. In fact, it was the banks, which were part of *Zaibatsu*, and not the securities market which financed the rapid industrialisation.

On the other hand, shares of these conglomerates were held by holding companies and banks associated with these conglomerates. Therefore, stocks available at the market were limited in number. This made the market speculative, because it was dominated by securities dealers, particularly through futures trading.[10]

---

8 Japan Securities Research Institute, *supra*, p. 68.
9 *Ibid.*, pp. 68–70.
10 *Ibid.*, pp. 14–15.

After the Second World War, Allied Forces sought the democratisation of the economy. As part of the reform, together with the dissolution of *zaibatsu*, shares held by holding comanies were released to the general public. The number of small investors sharply increased and almost reached 70% at one stage. However, since then, the percentage of individual investors has fallen constantly.

In 1948, the Securities and Exchange Law, which was modelled after U.S. Securities Act of 1933 and Securities Exchange Act of 1934, was enacted. The Law on Securities Investment Trusts was enacted in the same year. A new stock exchange was founded and started operation in 1949. The Allied Forces laid down three basic principles of market operation. First, transactions were to be recorded in the order in which they took place; second, transactions were to be concentrated on stock exchanges; and third, futures transaction were not allowed. The Securities and Exchange Commission, which was modeled on the U.S. SEC was founded in order to implement the Law.

Since then, the Securities and Exchange Law has gone through a series of amendments. In 1952, the Securities and Exchange Commission was abolished and replaced by the supervision of the Ministry of Finance. Instead, Securities and Exchange Council, which is an advisory body to the Minister of Finance, was set up.[11]

The internationalisation of the Japanese securities market was facilitated by the liberalisation of the yen-denominated bond issues abroad in 1971. In the same year, the Law on Foreign Securities Firms was enacted.[12] At the same time, the ban on investment in foreign securities was lifted. Then, in 1980, the Foreign Exchange and Foreign Trade Control Law was substantially amended in order to liberalise international transactions.

Internationalisation of the securities market was further accelerated in the wake of the U.S.-Japan Yen-Dollar Committee Report in 1984, which stressed the importance of an open and liberalised capital market and the free movement of capital. Access of foreign companies to the Japanese market was made easier. The Tokyo Stock Exchange admitted 22 foreign securities firms as members by 1988.

Internationalisation of the market was accompanied by a substantial deregulation of the Japanese financial market. The

---

11 Securities and Exchange Law, Law No. 25, 1948. L. Loss, M. Yazawa and B. A. Banoff, *Japanese Securities Regulation*, Tokyo and Boston 1983, pp. 26–32.
12 Law No. 5, 1971.

commercial papers market, which started in 1987, is an example. Restrictions on floating of bonds have been gradually lifted. Issuing of non-secured bonds became more common and issuing of secured straight bonds became possible for a broader range of companies. At the same time, a credit rating system was introduced. In 1985, trading in bond futures started, followed by stock index futures and securities option trading in 1987.

Recent amendments to the Securities and Exchange Law include the introduction of the tender offer system (Take-Over Bids) of 1971 and the subsequent reform in 1990, improvement in the disclosure system in 1988 and tightening of restrictions on insider trading in the same year. Then, in the wake of incidents involving securities companies in 1991, in which these companies guaranteed certain level of return to major customers, guarantee of yield was made explicitly illegal. A new supervisory body was established within the Ministry of Finance.

3. Key actors in the securities market

a) Stock exchanges

There are eight stock exchanges in Japan. Their membership is limited to securities companies. The stock exchange has a decision-making body in the form of the general meeting of the members. The board of governors decides the basic policy of the exchange and enacts rules. There are currently 23 governors, out of which 13 are elected from among the member companies, four non-member governors elected by regular members to represent the general public, and six standing governors who are appointed by the president from among persons other than employees of the member firms. The president is elected by the member governors and non-member governors with the consent of a minimum two-thirds of all the regular members. The president represents the exchange and supervises its management.

The stock exchange is empowered to supervise listed companies in order to ensure fair price formation and trading. Thus, the stock exchange examines periodic reports submitted by the companies as required by the Securities and Exchange Law and also ensures full disclosure of their financial statements. Listed companies are required to give immediate notice to the stock exchange whenever anything having an important effect on the company ocurrs and whenever any important corporate decision is made.

There are around 2,000 listed companies in Japan. Criteria for listing are given in the rules established by the stock exchange. Listing at the Tokyo Stock Exchange requires that 1) listed shares must be more than six million (20 million shares where the main place of business is outside Tokyo); 2) the number of shareholders must not be less than 1,000 and 80% or less should be held by a few specified shareholders; 3) net assets (shareholder's equity) should be one billion or more and 100 yen per share; 4) net profits for the past three years should exceed a certain level; and 5) dividends must have been paid in the past three years and there must be a prospect of maintaining a minimum five yen of dividend.

Stock exchanges of Tokyo, Osaka and Nagoya have two divisions. Newly listed shares are first assigned to the second division and after a certain period, when the conditions are met, they may be transferred to the first division.

Shares can be delisted when, *inter alia*, the number of shares issued falls under six million or the number of shares held by a few specified persons is 80% or more. In one instance, due to the purchase of shares by a greenmailer, the percentage of shares held by a few specified investors exceeded 80% and as a result, the company had to be delisted.

Along with stock exchanges, there is an over-the-counter market, although it is not as developed as in the United States. Anti-fraud provisions of the Securities and Exchange Law were not applied in this market until this year.

b)   Minister of Finance

The Minister of Finance is in overall charge of regulating and supervising securities business. In 1968, a licencing system for securities companies was introduced. The Ministry licences, supervises and gives guidance to securities companies and investment advisory firms. Investment trust companies, foreign securities firms, and securities finance companies also fall within the purview of the Minister of Finance's supervisory power. The Minister also supervises stock exchanges and is empowered to order them to submit reports or information relevant to its financial condition and business. In addition, he may order companies and individuals to submit a report or material for reference, or send officials to inspect accounting books, records and other materials (Securities and Exchange Law, Arts. 26 and 154).

The Securities and Exchange Council is attached to the Ministry of Finance for researching and deliberating on important matters relating to issuing and buying, selling or other transaction of securities as well as trading in futures and options. However, unlike the SEC which existed until 1952, this is not an administrative commission and does not have full-time members; 13 councillors are appointed by the Minister of Finance from among academics and other learned people.

c)   Securities companies

No person other than a joint stock company licenced by the Minister of Finance may engage in securities business. There are licences which cover four kinds of business: 1) buying and selling securities as a dealer; 2) acting as an intermediary, broker or agent with respect to buying and selling of securities or acting as an intermediary, broker or agent concerning entrusted transactions in the securities market; 3) underwriting securities and making public offering of outstanding securities; 4) handling public offering of new and outstanding securities.

In business concerning shares, the primary business of securities companies is brokerage, i.e. trading in shares on behalf of customers at their risk and account. This is supplemented by dealing in shares at the securities company's own account. In the primary market, securities companies have been active in underwriting new share issues in the 1980s. Competition among the securities companies is partly blamed for excess liquidity that followed. In bond business, securities companies are actively involved in underwriting and distributing new bonds, especially in the Euro-market.

Japan has a peculiar practice in that major securities companies combine the functions of an underwriter, broker and dealer. There is a potential conflict of interests here. For example, in a recent case, a major securities company underwrote the new issue of shares and then, as a broker, advised customers on a large scale to purchase these shares.

The Minister of Finance is empowered to order securities companies to submit reports or information relating to the business or financial condition of securities companies, and have the Ministry officials (securities inspectors) inspect books and records of the company, if it is necessary and appropriate for the sake of public interest or the protection of investors (Art. 55). In certain cases, the Minister of Finance may order the securities company to change its method of business operation, suspend its business partly or wholly for a period of up to three months, or deposit its property.

As a rule, only securities companies may engage in securities business. In the pre-War period, banks were allowed to engage in any kind of business; thus, under this universal banking system, banks acted as major underwriters of securities. After the Second World War, Japan followed the U.S. Glass-Steagall Act and strictly segregated securities business from banking business.

Article 65 of the Securities and Exchange Law provides as follows:

> No bank, trust companies or any other financial institutions designated by a cabinet order may be engaged in any of the business listed in Article 2 paragraph 8 of the present Law.

It should be noted that despite the facade of segregation, large banks had a fairly big influence in the bond market as a commissioned bank or investor. Furthermore, Japanese banking institutions are allowed to hold shares within a limit set by the Anti-Monopoly Law.

There has been a longstanding dispute between the banks and securities companies on the demarcation of boundaries. The boundary between the two businesses has become somewhat blurred in the last decade. With the government's heavy reliance on government bonds after the oil crisis, banks, which underwrote these bonds, urged the government to let them trade in government bonds. Under the new Banking Law of 1981, banks were allowed to engage in the distribution and trade of government bonds, local bonds and corporate bonds guaranteed by the government. Article 65–2 was added to the Securities and Exchange Law to accomodate this change. Since 1983, banks have been allowed to deal in government bonds, local government bonds which they have underwritten. Furthermore, the amendment of the Securities and Exchange Law of 1988 made it possible for banks to engage in securities index futures and securities option trading in government bonds.

The system of segregation between banking and securities business became even less strict in recent years. This is primarily due to the fact that with the shift of corporate finance from indirect to direct finance, banks found it more and more difficult to satisfy customers without dealing in securities. Furthermore, profitability of banking business is in decline and new business opportunities had to be sought.

In 1991, two advisory bodies to the Minister of Finance, one for banking system and the other for the securities system, came to an accord on this issue. Banks are to be allowed to buy and sell in stocks while securities companies will be able to deal in foreign currencies.[13] The precise way of rearranging the system is

13 *Wall Street Journal*, 5 June, 1991.

still being discussed. The adoption of the universal banking system which prevails in Europe was considered to be unsuitable, partly because of the potential conflict of interests. Japanese banks hold a substantial number of shares and bonds and therefore, the possiblity of conflict of interests is particularly acute. The universal banking system also met opposition from securities companies which feared that banks might become too powerful. At present, the solution is expected to be a segmented approach, which would allow subsidiaries of the banks and securities companies to engage in each other's business. This has already been implemented with overseas subsidiaries for some years.

d)   Securities investment advisers

The law on Securities Investment Advisory Business was enacted in 1986. The necessity of regulating investment advisory business was felt in the 1980s when investment advisory business started to flourish in Japan. There were some celebrated cases where advisers were involved in fraudulent business. In order to protect investors, a new law was considered to be necessary. Also the opening up of foreign investment advisory companies advising in international capital transactions necessitated such a law.

   According to this Law, any person who intends to start an investment advisory business is required to register with the Minister of Finance. Investment advisers must deposit a business bond. They must make it clear that they do not accept deposits of money or securities from customers. They are prohibited from making exaggerated claims or false statements in advertisements. A document explaining the content of the agreement must be handed to the clients in advance of, and at the time of, signing such an agreement. Customers are entitled to cancel the agreement unconditionally by giving a written notice within ten days after signing the agreement.

e)   Investment trusts

Investment trusts are regulated by the Law on Investment Trusts which was enacted in 1951.[15] Only investment trusts of a contractual type operate in Japan. Under this system, the trust property is invested in securities in accordance with the

---

14 Law No. 198, 1951. For details, Japan Securities Research Institute, *supra* note 8, pp. 179–186.

instruction of the fund management company (trustors); the right of the beneficiary is shared by an unspecified number of people. Trustees must be either a trust company or a bank engaged in trust business.

Japanese investment trusts started with a unit-type trust in 1951. In a unit-type trust, securities companies collect funds from investors at a fixed amount per trust share and deposit the fund with a fund management company. The company, in turn, transfers the fund to a trustee bank and establish a trust. Thus, the trust agreement is concluded between the management company and the trustee bank. Each unit fund is put in the custody of the trustee bank separately. The primary characteristic of this kind of trust is that once the trust fund is established, no new principal may be added.

In an open type trust, the securities company raises funds from investors, and increases the principal if the market condition permits. The term for the trust fund can be either indefinite or definite; in the latter case, cancellation or repurchase of beneficiary certificates is based on the market price.

Since the 1980s, as investors became selective and yield conscious, the investment trust industry devised various types of investment trusts, such as intermediate-term government bond funds. This was followed by domestic and foreign bond funds (1984) and long-term government bond funds (1986).

3. Securities

The Securities and Exchange Law lists the securities covered by this Law in Article 2. This provision is of importance, since if a given financial product falls within the scope of this provision, then disclosure requirements, anti-fraud provisions such as regulations on insider trading etc. will be applied. On the other hand, it may be the case that by virtue of Article 65, banks will not be allowed to handle these products.

Negotiable certificate of deposits and commercial papers which were introduced in Japan in 1979 and 1987 respectively, were not classified as securities in the sense of Article 2. This was because if they were classified as securities, as a rule, only securities companies would be allowed to handle them. Therefore, these products were left outside the Securities and Exchange Law.

Securities listed in Article 2 include government bonds, local government bonds, secured or unsecured corporate bonds, share certificates or subscription warrants, beneficiary certificates of securities investment trusts or loan trusts, and other securities or certificates provided by ordinances (Art. 2, para. 1). Also, securities issued by foreign governments or foreign corporations are covered by this Law. So far, no other securities or certificates are provided for in the ordinances.

The definition of securities is noticeably narrower in the Japanese Securities and Exchange Law than in U.S. law. The former focusses on the legal form of those products and limits itself to regulating traditional securities, while the latter focusses on their economic substance. U.S. law defines securities in a broader sense in order to provide better protection to investors. In addition, U.S. law has a catch-all clause which provides for investment agreements. This enables it to cope with new financial products. With the progress in securitisation, new financial products will emerge and the current definition in the Japanese Securities and Exchange Law is likely to be insufficient to cover them. A report published by the Securities and Exchange Council in 1990 acknowledged the necessity of broadening the definition of securities with securitisation in view. In this regards, the test adopted in *SEC v W J Howey* is often referred to in Japan as a possible model.[16]

4.   Issuing of securities

1)   New issue of shares

Shares can be issued by a decision of the board of directors, unless the articles of association requires the resolution of the general shareholders' meeting (Commercial Code Art. 280–2). In order to issue new shares at a price especially unfavourable to the exisiting shareholders, a special resolution of the general shareholders' meeting is needed (Art. 280–2, para. 2). If a company issues shares against the law or articles of association and is likely that the interest of shareholders will be harmed, an injunction is available (Art. 280–10).

In order to finance the company by a new issue of shares, there are three methods: rights issue, public offer, and allocation of new shares to selected persons. Until the 1970s, rights issue at par value was the primary method of issuing shares. In a rights issue, shareholders listed in the register on the day the book is closed are given a right to subscribe to new shares. However, in the last decade, new issue of shares by public offer at a market

15 328 US 293 (1946).

price or a price between market price and par value became a standard method. Since new share issue waters down the value of the shares already held by existing shareholders, this is often combined with a new share issue without payment to these shareholders.

In 1989, 82.8% of the funds raised by new issue of shares came from public offering. Rights issues counted for 13.7%. However, with the fall in the market, in 1990, public offering fell drastically to 42%, while allocation to selected persons increased to 28.3% from 3.5% in 1989.

Shares can also be allocated to a selected group of people, such as employees and directors, or to companies and banks which are related to the company in one way or another. In 1973, securities companies adopted a policy of limiting this method to extremely exceptional cases where corporate reorganisation is in progress or the company is planning to strengthen links with another company. However, this method became popular again in the 1980s.[16]

By allocating shares to another company, it is possible to consolidate links between the companies. Allocation of shares to other companies and banks is also used when a company is in financial difficulty. In addition, this method is often used as a means to 'strengthen the management basis', i.e. to increase stable shareholders.

In one case, a manufacturing Company A became a target of take over. 47% of the shares was acquired by Company B. As a measure of defence, Company A issued new shares and allocated them to affiliated companies, trade partners, and financial institutions. Company B sued Company A on the ground that the issue price was 'especially favourable to those other than shareholders' and therefore required a special resolution of the general shareholders' meeting (Art. 280–2, para. 2). The court denied that the issue price was unfair.[17]

When a company intends to 'go public', they have two options: registering in the over the counter market or listing in the stock exchange. The issue price of shares is usually set by comparing it with the share price of similar companies. The problem was that prices of shares formed on the first day were always significantly higher than the issue price. Therefore, those who were allotted pre-floating shares most certainly made profits. In a celebrated case, a selected few, including a number of politicians, made a large profit out of pre-floating shares. After this incident, which

16 Japan Securities Research Institute, *supra* note 8, pp. 34–35.
17 Decision of Tokyo District Court, 5 September, 1989 (*Hanji* 1323–48).

took place in 1988, it is now required to disclose the name of third parties to whom the shares were allocated before going public, and those who had actually been allocated pre-floating shares are obligated to hold them for a certain period.

2) Floating of bonds

Joint stock companies may issue bonds by a decision of the board of directors. Issuing of bonds has been and still is strictly regulated. Since the financial crash in the 1920s until the late 1970s, secured bonds were the rule and unsecured bonds were issued as an exception, primarily by public utilities. Restrictions were gradually lifted in the 1980s. More and more companies were allowed to issue unsecured straight bonds. This was partly due to the internationalisation of the securities market, since if a collateral was needed, it would be difficult for foreign companies to issue bonds in Japan. This requirement of collaterals was also too stringent, inhibiting companies with a sound financial basis from issuing bonds. Trading houses which, by nature of their business, do not have large tangible assets like manufacturing companies also found it difficult to issue bonds.

In the latest amendment to the requirements for the issue of bonds, companies with triple B rating may issue straight bonds. With an A rating, bonds can be issued unsecured. In this way, the number of companies eligible for issuing non-secured straight bonds increased from 300 to 400.[18] The Commercial Code has a provision which sets a ceiling to the amount of bonds which can be issued. The amount may not exceed the net assets (Art. 297). However, this ceiling has been doubled by the Law on Temporary Measures on the Ceiling of Issuing Bonds.[19]

With the amendment to the Commercial Code in 1981, issuing of warrant bonds became possible. With this type of bond, the bond holder may require the issuing company to issue new shares at a predetermined price. Usually, the warrant can be detached from the bond and traded separately. Together with convertible bonds, the issuing of warrant bonds became popular in the 1980s, especially abroad. This was primarily because restrictions on issuing these kinds of bonds were still tight in Japan, while it was easier and the cost was cheaper abroad. However, in 1990, equity finance in Japan as well as abroad fell sharply, while issuing of straight bonds abroad increased by 36%.

It should be added that these bonds issued abroad are often

18 Commercial Law Centre, *supra* note 6, p. 297.
19 Law 49, 1977.

purchased by Japanese investors. This indicates that companies actually circumvent cumbersome regulations concerning the issue of bonds by going abroad. In fact, a streamlining and deregulation of the bond market has been discussed for some years. These problems will be addressed in the continuing review of the Commercial Code.

5. Disclosure

The disclosure system has constantly improved in recent years. There are three types of disclosure requirement: disclosure at the time of issuing securities, periodic disclosure, and disclosure for tender offer (TOB).

The Securities and Exchange Law provides that at the time of public offer of new or outstanding securities 500 million yen or more, the issuer is obliged to file a securities registration statement with the Minister of Finance (Art. 4, para. 1). Public offering of securities in the context of this Law means soliciting many and unspecified persons for subscription of securities in uniform terms (Art. 2, para. 4).

The registration statement contains information, *inter alia*, such as the state of business operations, financial status and other relevant matters to the nature of the business (Art. 5, para. 1). Financial statements accompanying registration reports as well as securities reports are required to be certified by a chartered public accountant or an accounting firm.

With the amendment of the Securities and Exchange Law of 1988, companies which meet certain standards may refer to their annual securities report in the registration statement. Furthermore, a 'shelf registration' system was introduced whereby companies are allowed to issue new securities simply by filing additional documents, provided that they have filed a shelf registration statement which specifies the number of securities to be issued in a fixed span of time.

In addition, issuers of new or outstanding shares are obligated to prepare a prospectus for the investors where public offering takes place. Prospectus must contain information relevant for protecting investors which is included in the registration statement (Art. 13, para. 2).

Registration statements and the prospectus are available for inspection at the Ministry of Finance, stock exchange, securities dealers' association and the issuing company for a certain period of time.

Issuers of securities which are listed in the stock exchange as well as companies which have filed a securities registration statement must file with the Minister of Finance a securities report each business year (Art. 24). This is designed to provide investors with updated corporate information on a continual basis. Issuers whose business year runs for a year are required to file a semi-annual securities report with the Minister of Finance. Interim or ad hoc disclosure is required when a fact having material relevance to business of the issuer occurs. Under the recent timely discosure policy, stock exchanges mandated issuers to disclose information, for instance, issuing of bonds abroad, mergers and acquisitions etc., which has material relevance to investors.

Disclosure is also required when a tender offer is made. A registration statement of a tender offer has to be filed with the Minister of Finance by the person offering to purchase shares outside the securities market. A copy of the registration statement has to be sent to the issuing company (Art. 27–3, paras. 2 and 4). The tender offerer is also obligated to place a public notice in a daily newspaper and disclose information such as the purpose of the offer, the price and the number of shares to be purchased (Art. 27–3, para. 1).

Since the tender offer system was introduced in Japan in 1971, there have been only three cases, until 1990, where this procedure was utilised. All three cases involved a friendly take over. In 1990, some changes were introduced in the system in order to make it more accessible to foreign investors. There have been a couple of tender offers since then.

In cases where a registration statement or periodic securities report contains any false statement concerning material information or failed to disclose material information or any fact necessary to make the statements not misleading, persons involved are liable for damages to those who have acquired securities in response to the public offering and incurred loss. Persons who are liable include directors and auditors of the issuing company, certified public accountants or accounting firms, and the underwriter (securities company) (Art. 21).

Furthermore, any person who filed registration statements or periodic securities reports which contain untrue statements with respect to any material fact may be subject to a maximum of three years' imprisonment or a fine of three million yen (Art. 197).

In 1990, a new disclosure requirement for large shareholdings was introduced in order to supply investors with information concerning possible changes in the ownership. This concerns those who came to hold more than 5% of the outstanding shares of a listed company or a company whose shares are traded over the counter. They are required to file a report with the Minister of Finance within five days of their acquisition of the shares (Art. 27–23, para. 1).

There are other changes concerning disclosure which resulted from the U.S. – Japan Structural Impediments Initiative Talks. Improvements were made in the disclosure of *keiretsu* (intergroup) trading and a segment disclosure system.

7. Anti-fraud provisions

The Securities and Exchange Law provides for safeguards against unfair and fraudulent trading practices. Article 58 is a general provision against fraudulent transactions which covers, *inter alia*, employing of a fraudulent device, scheme or artifice with respect to trading in securities. Market manipulation is prohibited by another provision (Art. 125). Acts which create a false or misleading appearance as to the status of a transaction in securities, for instance, a false transaction which involves no change in the ownership or creation of a false active trading, is banned. Spreading a rumour that the price of specific securities will fluctuate because of his or others' manipulation is also prohibited. Furthermore, it is unlawful to effect transactions for the purpose of pegging, fixing or stabilising the price of securities. Furthermore, Art 50 lists unlawful activities of securities companies and their directors and employees. Any person who acted against Articles 58 and 125 is subject to penalties of up to three years' imprisonment.

The Cabinet Order on the Enforcement of the Securities and Exchange Law provides for 'stabilization operation' in cases of public offering of new or outstanding shares. Since it is possible that a large supply of new shares by public offering may disturb the balance of supply and demand, the price may fall as a consequence. In order to stabilize the price public offering of new or outstanding securities, such an operation is allowed under certain conditions.[1]

Only securities companies listed in the registration statement as principal underwriters may effect such transactions, and only directors of the issuing company may entrust these underwriters

---

1 Articles 20–26, Enforcement Order of the Securities and Exchange Law, Cabinet Order No. 321, 1965.

with a stabilisation transaction. The fact that stabilisation operation may take place and the name of the stock exchange where it is to take place have to be stated in the prospectus. The stabilisation operation is limited to the stock exchange and the period during which the operation takes place is designated. A stabilisation statement has to be filed on the first day of the operation and an operation statement each day with the Minister of Finance. The stabilising price is also regulated.

Until the 1980s, there had been no case where a company or an individual was found guilty of having manipulated the market, although there had been instances where such an act was suspected. However, in the mid–1980s, several cases reached the court. In one case, directors of a company which effected a public offering of shares at market price collaborated with executives of a securities company and purchased shares in the market in order to increase the offering price, using funds provided by the company and its affiliated companies. Those involved were prosecuted and the court, by relying on circumstancial evidence, found the defendants guilty.[2] In another case, a managing director of a securities finance company colluded with a sales representative of a securities company and repeatedly bought and sold shares of the same company at the same time through different securities companies. This did not involve any transfer of ownership. In addition, this person actually purchased a large amount of shares at the beginning of these transactions and as a result, the price went up from 500 yen to 1700 yen at the end. He was found guilty for the breach of Article 125.[3]

Until 1988, the Securities and Exchange Law was unable to cope with insider trading in an effective way. It was not even clear whether the existing provisions prohibited insider trading. The closest to such a provision was the above-mentioned Article 58. However, the provision is vague, and it was not clear at first sight whether this provision had something to do with insider trading, although specialists of securities and exchange law agreed that insider trading is covered and punishable by this provision.

Article 58 has its origin in the Securities Exchange Act, § 10-b and Rules 10-b(5) of the United States. Whereas in the United States, this provision of the Act is duly enforced, in Japan, there has never been a reported case where this provision was applied. It can be argued that this provision would also work in Japan if it was properly implemented. However, it should be noted that in

---

2 Judgment of Tokyo District Court, 31 July, 1984 (*Keishū* 16–7/8–556).
3 Judgment of Tokyo District Court, 27 April, 1981 (*Hanji* 1020–129).

the United States, court judgments and the decisions of the Securities and Exchange Commission have produced a body of precedent that has helped to clarify this somewhat vague provision. In contrast, the principle of *nulla crimen sine lege* is strictly applied in Japan, and it was thought to be difficult to sustain a prosecution on the basis of Art 58.

This is not to say that insider trading seldom happens in Japan. Because of the absence of an explicit provision banning insider dealing, it is sometimes pointed out that people fail to perceive insider trading as being unlawful and often engage in such practices. There have been cases where the price of shares has soared immediately before a company increases its capital or announces a new product. Insider dealing was suspected in a number of cases, but it was difficult to prove it, and most cases ended up with a warning from the stock exchange to the company concerned.

The only provision of the Securities and Exchange Law which was recently invoked to deal with insider trading is Art 189 on short-swing trading. Article 189 provides for the recovery of unfair profits obtained by directors or major shareholders of a company by their using information available to them by reason of their positions. If such persons make a profit by purchasing shares within six months after the sale, or selling shares within the same period after the purchase, the company may require this person to surrender such profits to the company (Art. 189, para. 1).

The need for strengthening control over insider trading has been accepted in Japan for some time. This was accelerated by two external factors. First, due to the internationalisation of stock markets, especially with the close links which have developed between stock markets of the United States, Europe, and Japan, it is now possible to take advantage of inside information by dealing in a stock market of another country. Therefore, a concerted international approach to prevent transnational insider trading became indispensable. Since the early 1980s, the United States has concluded agreements on the exchange of information concerning insider trading with Switzerland, Canada, U.K. and Japan.[4]

An incident occurred in 1987 which accelerated this move. A medium-sized chemical company, which was heavily involved in 'financial strategy' – i.e. the practice of an industrial company of investing surplus funds in order to bolster profits, fell into financial difficulties. This company lost 20 billion yen in the sharp

4 *Japan Economic Journal* (Nikkei), 15 March, 1988.

fall of the Japanese bond market. One of the banks which held shares in this company sold its holdings one day before this company announced its losses. A large number of shares were sold on the day before the announcement. The Ministry of Finance and the Osaka Stock Exchange investigated the case. Both failed to prove the existence of insider trading, but the former found that the bank acted against the informal guidance of the Ministry issued to listed companies, and was 'morally responsible'.[5]

Amendments were made to the Securities and Exchange Law in 1988 in order to strengtehn controls over insider trading. Firstly, Art. 190–2, which was newly added, covers insider trading carried out by people 'connected with the company'. Those who have come to know significant facts concerning the business of listed companies are not allowed to sell or purchase securities (including options) of such a company or trade in them for profit, except after these facts have been made public (Art 190–2, para. 1). Securities in this context include listed shares, convertible bonds, bonds with warrants and straight bonds.

The scope of information which is considered to be insider is listed in the Law (Art. 190–2, para. 2). This includes new issue of equities, decrease in capital, distribution of profits, marketing of new products and commercialisation of new technology, and changes in major share holders. In addition, there is a general clause which covers 'significant facts concerning the business, or the assets of the company, which significantly affects the decision-making of investors'. Persons who are prohibited from using insider information include insiders, such as board members or employees of the issuing company, major shareholders with more than 10% of the issued shares of the company, who are entitled to inspect the books of account. If the insider is a juridical person, its board members and employees are considered to be insiders. Those who ceased to be related to a company, for example, because of resignation, are nevertheless regarded as insiders for one year.

There are also quasi-insiders, which include a person who has a power granted by law over the company and a person who is a party to a contract with the company (Art 190–2, para. 1). The first category is understood to cover, *inter alia*, ministerial officials responsible for supervising the industry. The second category includes trading partners of the issuing company as well as underwriters, attorneys, and accountants. In addition, those persons who have learned of significant facts concerning business

5 *Japan Economic Journal* (Nikkei), 7 October, 1987.

from the above-mentioned persons are not allowed to trade in listed shares of the company until these facts are made public (Art 190–3, para 3). Thus, friends or families of these persons, and even a news reporter may be held liable for insider trading.

Another significant provision in the 1988 amendment concerns short-swing trading. The amendment strengthened control over securities transaction by board members or major shareholders of a company. Board members and major shareholders are required to file a report with the Minister of Finance, if they purchase or sell the company's listed shares, convertible bonds, warranted bonds, or straight bonds or options on these securities before the 15th day of the forthcoming month (Art 188). Thus, if the Minister of Finance considers that a board member or a major shareholder has made a profit by short-swing trading within six months, he informs this person of this finding. The latter may file an objection with the Minister. If there is no such objection, the Minister sends a copy of the relevant documents to the company and informs it of the transaction in expectation that the company will demand the surrender of the profits (Art. 189).

Violations of Arts 190–2 and 190–3 entail criminal sanctions of a maximum of six months' imprisonment or a fine not more than 500 thousand yen (Art 200, para. 4).

The insufficiency of the regulatory framework was again felt in 1991, when it was revealed that a majority of securities companies were involved in a series of scandals. Among other matters such as alleged insider trading and market manipulations, a number of securities companies had compensated the loss which their favoured customers incurred in the securities market. About three-quarters of compensation involved losses incurred by fund management accounts which were under the control of the broking department.[6] Some securities companies were suspected of guaranteeing a certain level of return from investment to major customers.

Previously, only guarantee of compensation was explicitly banned by the Securities and Exchange Law (Art. 50). Compensation *per se* was not prohibited, although there was a circular of the securities bureau director which prohibited such acts. The amendment of 1991 made compensation illegal.

There is no provision concerning damages in the Securities and Exchange Law. It is generally accepted that a means of claiming damages for the loss arising from the violation of the Securities and Exchange Law is needed. In fact, most specialists of Securities and Exchange Law are of the view that those who have

---

6 *Financial Times*, 5 August, 1991.

15 Labour law

1. Development of Japanese labour law

Relations between the employer and individual employees are contractual, i.e. based upon the agreement of the parties. Before the end of the War, such contracts were regulated solely by the Civil Code – by the provisions on 'employment' (Arts. 623–631). Employment contracts are categorised as one of the 'typical' contracts provided in the Code, together with contracts of sale, lease, gift etc. However, the Code presupposes that the parties in employment contracts have equal status. This naturally does not reflect the true state of affairs in labour relations where employees normally do not have sufficient power vis à vis the employer. Therefore, laws which supplement the Code and provide protection to employees were needed.

The necessity of protecting the interests of workers became acute in the course of the rapid modernisation which began in the late 19th century. However, the government was slow in reacting to such needs. It was only in 1911 that the government finally enacted the Factory Law, which had met strong resistance from industry. This Law set forth restrictions on the employment of women and children – the main restriction being a 12-hour day. The standards provided in this Law were far below the international standard of the time.

An embryonic form of trade union was formed at the end of the 19th century. In 1897, an association aimed at establishing trade unions (*Rōdo-kumiai kisei-kai*) was established. Under the auspices of this association, several trade unions, such as the steel workers' union, the railway workers' union, and the printers' union were set up. The government reacted by promulgating the Public Security and Police Law (*chian-keisatsu-hō*) in 1900. This law punished the promotion and instigation of strikes as well as 'acts of assault and intimidation' carried out to induce workers to join a trade union. It was actively enforced and served as an instrument to suppress labour movements, which were aimed primarily at improving working conditions.

Although the relevant provision in the Public Security and Police Law was repealed in 1926, other acts such as the Maintenance of Public Security Law of 1925 were available to suppress labour movements. Thus, until the end of the Second World War, the Japanese labour movement was subject to strict restrictions imposed by the government.

A watershed in the development of Japanese labour law came with the occupation by the Allied Powers.[1] In October 1945, as one of the five major reforms, the organising of trade unions was encouraged by the Allied Powers. In the 20 months following the end of the War, around 17,000 trade unions were formed. The first Trade Union Law was enacted in December 1945. This law, however, was considered by American advisers to be 'unduly restrictive' and provided an insufficient guarantee of the autonomy of trade unions.[2] The Law was totally amended in 1949.[3] In the meantime, in 1946, the Law on the Adjustment of Labour Relations, which set out institutions and procedures for settling labour disputes, was enacted.[4] Then in the next year, following the adoption of the Constitution which provided for the protection of workers' rights, the Labour Standards Law was adopted. This Law sets standards for wages, hours of work, annual paid holidays, safety of work, minors and female workers, skills training, rules of employment etc.[5] It was aimed at raising the standards of labour protection to the level of ILO standards.

The policy of encouraging trade union movements by the Allied Powers underwent a change in late 1947. The change involved the status of public sector workers. The post-War labour movement had been primarily led by trade unions in the public sector. The Allied Powers became concerned at the growing power of trade unions in the public sector and opted for the curbing of their power. In 1948, a ban was introduced and government employees were prohibited from conducting collective bargaining and organising strikes. In the same year, the Law on Labour Relations in Public Corporations was adopted.[6] This Law prohibited employees of these organisations from taking industrial action. This difference in the treatment of public and

---

1 As for the history of Post-War reforms in labour law, see W.G. Gould IV, *Japan's Reshaping of American Labour Law*, Cambridge (Mass.), 1984, p. 23ff.
2 *Ibid.*, pp. 27–28.
3 Law No. 174, 1949.
4 Law No. 25, 1946.
5 Law No. 49, 1947.
6 Law No. 257, 1948.

private sector employees remains basically unchanged to the present day.

Thus, basic laws concerning labour relations were all adopted in the years shortly after the end of the Second World War and basically remain unchanged. There are, however, some new laws which were enacted in recent years. These include the Law on Measures for Employment, the Law on Equal Opportunity for Men and Women, and the Law on the Dispatch of Workers.[7]

The Constitution has two provisions directly concerning the rights of workers. Article 27 provides that all people have the right and duty to work. This provision also mandates the government to take adequate legislative and administrative measures to provide opportunities to work. The government has responsibility to provide assistance to those who do not have a job. At present, there are laws such as the Law on Job Opportunities and the Law on Employment Insurance which are designed to assist the unemployed.[8] The former provides for job arrangement and recruitment, training, and employment agencies. Public employment offices run by the Ministry of Labour are responsible for the implementation of this Law. The latter mainly deals with unemployment benefit. An unemployed person may receive benefits amounting to between 60 and 80% of his salary before losing the job for a maximum of one year. Incidentally, the unemployment rate was 2.1% in 1991. It is the lowest of Western indistrialised countries.[9]

Another relevant article in the Constitution is Article 28 which guarantees the right of workers to organise, bargain and act collectively. It prohibits unjust interference with the activities of trade unions by government agencies. This provision has its origin in the Constitution of the Weimar Republic of 1919. The Weimar Constitution, which was in force until the Republic was superseded by the Third Reich, had provided that all agreements and measures intended to restrict or obstruct the freedom of organisation were void. Article 28 of the Japanese Constitution is constructed in a similar manner.

Agreements between employers and employees which violate the rights guaranteed by the Constitution are null and void. Technically, such acts are invalidated on the basis of Article 90 of the Civil Code, which provides for public order and good morals, since employment agreements are basically Civil Law contracts.[10]

---

7 Law No. 132, 1966; Law No. 68,1985; Law No. 88, 1985.
8 Law No. 141, 1947; Law No. 132, 1966; Law No. 116, 1974.
9 *JETRO NIPPON Business Facts and Figures: 1992*, Tokyo 1992, p. 116.
10 K. Sugeno, *Rōdōhō (Labour Law)*, Second edition, Tokyo 1988, p. 18.

Article 28 of the Constitution guarantees three fundamental workers' rights. First, the right to organise and to join an organisation for negotiating with the employer on an equal footing is guaranteed. Organisation in this context includes not only trade unions, but also other temporary organisations of workers. The government as well as employers are prohibited from interfering with the internal matters of trade unions. Discriminatory treatment due to the membership of a trade union is regarded as unfair labour practice and is null and void (Art. 7, para. 1, Trade Union Law).

The second right guaranteed by Article 28 is the right to collective bargaining. Workers are entitled to collectively negotiate labour conditions with their employers. Employers may not refuse to negotiate with the representatives of the employees without justifiable reasons. Unjustified refusal constitutes an unfair labour practice (Art. 7, subpara. 2, Trade Union Law). Agreements made through collective bargaining invalidate employment contracts which are against the agreement.

Finally, Article 28 guarantees the right of workers to act collectively. This includes the right to strike and to take other actions in the course of a dispute. Such actions are exempted from civil and criminal liabilities (Art. 1, para. 2, Art. 8, Trade Union Law).

One problem is the scope of 'industrial actions' guaranteed by the Constitution.[11] In practice, it is sometimes difficult to delineate the boundary between a political and economic strike. Sometimes the demands of the employees are political but at the same time have bearing on the economic welfare of the employees. The courts deny the legitimacy of strikes with purely political demands which are beyond the power of the employer.[12] This is supported by a majority of labour law specialists who contend that the scope of industrial action has to be limited to issues which can be solved through collective bargaining. In cases where a political demand is combined with economic demands, the primary purpose of the action has to be ascertained. If political demands were merely of secondary significance as compared with economic demands, then the action is eligible for protection under the Constitution.

Although the Constitution does not explicitly exclude government employees and workers in the public sector from the protection extended by Article 28, there are laws which impose

---

11 M. Itoh, *Kenpō* (*Constitutional Law*), Tokyo 1982, p. 373.
12 Judgment of the Supreme Court, 26 October, 1966 (*Keishū* 20–8–901). Judgment of Nagoya Appellate Court, 10 April, 1971 (*Rōmin* 22–2–453).

restrictions on their rights. First, certain categories of government employees, such as policemen, firemen, and members of the Self Defence Force are denied all three fundamental rights. Government employees engaged in non-manual works are not allowed to bargain or act collectively. Other government employees, such as post office employees and workers of public corporations are not allowed to act collectively, i.e. they are given the rights to get organised and bargain, but not the right to take industrial action.

The constitutionality of these restrictions has been contested in courts on various occasions. At one stage, the Supreme Court acknowledged the unconstitutionality of the restrictions imposed on the government employees by using the less restrictive alternative test, which had been developed in the United States. However, in 1973, the Supreme Court changed track and gave a broad discretion to the legislature in limiting the rights of government employees and workers of public corporations.[13] The Supreme Court based its judgment on the argument that although Article 28 covers government employees, they are subject to certain restrictions imposed on the ground of the common interests of the people, provided that the restrictions are reasonable. Academic opinion is mostly against the position of the Supreme Court, which virtually gives the government carte blanche to restrict the rights of these employees and workers.

Japan has ratified some of the treaties prepared by the ILO, including the Treaty No. 87 on the Freedom of Association and the Right to Organise as well as Treaty 98 on the Application of Principles of the Rights to Organise and Collective Bargaining. Some lawyers argue that restrictions imposed on the right to organize and to act collectively on government employees and employees in public corporations fail to meet international standards.[14]

2. Relations between the employer and employee

Since the post-War reforms, the contract of employment has not been left to the autonomy of the parties as is the case with other Civil Law contracts, but has come to be subject to various laws which extend protection to employees and set forth rules concerning collective agreements and work conditions. Provisions

13 Judgment of the Supreme Court, 25 April, 1973 (*Keishū*, 23–5–305).
14 See K. Nakayama, *ILO Jyōyaku to Nihon* (*ILO Treaties and Japan*), Tokyo 1983.

of the Civil Code concerning employment contracts are still applicable, but they are only supplementary to the provisions of labour legislation.

The basic law which regulates the relationship between the employer and the employee is the Labour Standards Law. This law sets the standards for working conditions of all workers, except seamen and certain groups of government employees. According to this law, working conditions are to be decided by the employer and the workers on an equal footing (Art. 2, para. 1). The law provides for employment contracts, wages, work hours, work safety, rules of employment, compensation etc. Employment contracts which are against the Labour Standard Law are null and void and are replaced by the conditions provided in the Law (Art. 13, Labour Standard Law). Foreign companies are subject to this Law in so far as they are operating in Japan. On the other hand, Japanese companies operating overseas are not subject to the provisions of this Law.

Labour legislation is supplemented by case law. Significant doctrines concerning equal treatment of sexes, abuse of the right of dismissal and the right to discipline employees have developed out of court rulings. Overall, case law has contributed to broadening the protection of employees provided by the law.

Together with the laws, collective agreements and work rules play a significant role. Collective agreement is concluded between a workers' organisation or a trade union on the one hand, and the employer on the other hand. When a contract of employment conflicts with the standards set by the collective agreement, the offending provision is void, and standards set by the agreement are read into the contract (Art. 16, Trade Union Law).

Work rules are prepared by the employer after consulting the employees. The rules cover shop rules and working conditions. Typical work rules include work time, wages, methods of payment, retirement, etc. If the contract of employment conflicts with the standards set by the rules of employment, the relevant provision is void (Art. 93, Labour Standards Law). Work rules may not contradict collective agreements (Art. 92, Labour Standards Law).

Employers who employ more than ten workers are required to submit their work rules to the Director of the Labour Standards Supervisory Office. When drafting the rules, the employer has to consult the trade union which is composed of more than half of the employees of the workplace. If no such trade union exists, the employer is required to consult the representative of a majority of the workers (Art. 90, para. 1, Labour Standards

Law). The Law merely provides for prior consultation with the trade union and not a joint decision. Therefore, theoretically, the employer may enact work rules against the will of a majority of employees, once he has consulted them. This differs from the joint decision-making system in Germany.

Whether or not the work rules can be unilaterally altered to the disadvantage of the employees was at issue in a case where a bus company introduced, via such rules, a retirement system at the age of 55. A manager who was dismissed after reaching the age of 55 sued the company on the ground that the changes to the regulation did not affect him, since it was a disadvantageous change unilaterally introduced by the company. The Supreme Court ruled that 1) work rules acquire legal force by Article 92 of the Civil Code, which provides for the effect of *de facto* convention, in so far as their content is reasonable, and therefore, is binding upon all employees regardless of whether they have agreed to the rules or not, or whether the rules were known to them individually; 2) in principle, a unilateral change in the rules against the interests of employees which deprives them of their vested interests, or imposes unfavourable working conditions is not permissible; 3) however, individual employees are not eligible to claim that the rules do not apply to them insofar as the rules are reasonable, and instead, should settle the matter through the collective bargaining procedure. In this particular case, the retirement age of 55 was not considered to be unreasonable, when taking into account that the retirement age for ordinary employees in the company was set at 50, and there was the possibility of employing this person on a part-time basis afterwards.[15]

The Labour Standards Law provides that 'workers' under this Law means those who are employed in the offices and work places listed in the Law and receive a salary (Art. 9). Part-time employees and temporary employees also fall within the definition of 'workers'. Even when there was no formal employment contract between the parties, the courts have acknowledged that the Labour Standards Law applies. Thus, people such as an electricity meter reader and a band member working in a cabaret on an annual contract were found to be covered by this Law. Thus the court takes into account the actual relationship – the existence of subordinate employment relations – between the company and the employee, rather than legal

15 Judgment of the Supreme Court, 25 December, 1968 (*Minshū* 22–13–3459: *Shūhoku* Bus case).

formalities.[16] On the other hand, it is sometimes difficult to delineate the boundary between employment relations and relations on a commission basis. In one case, the Supreme Court denied the application of the Labour Standard Law to a sales representative who had worked on a commission basis with a securities company.[17] In another case, a truck driver who worked for a company with his own truck was found to be a worker in the context of the Law.[18]

The equal treatment of employees as regards wages, hours of work, etc. regardless of their nationality, religion, or social status is required by the Labour Standards Law (Art. 3). Dismissal on the ground that an employee was a communist was ruled by the court to be against this provision insofar as he did not participate in activities such as sabotage.[19]

On the other hand, when deciding whether to employ a particular person, the Supreme Court ruled that employers were basically free to set standards and conditions of employment.

According to the Supreme Court, refusal to employ a person with certain political or religious belief is not necessarily against the law. In this particular case, a company was sued for rejecting a person who had taken part in a students' political movement and failed to disclose this fact during the interview.[20] Generally, when an applicant fails to disclose significant information or provides false information at the interview, he bears the risk of dismissal when the fact comes to be known to the company. On the other hand, when the information in question is irrelevant, the dismissal may be regarded as an abuse of rights on the part of the company.

Another problem is sex discrimination. The Labour Standards Law did not specifically refer to sex discrimination in its equal treatment provision. Instead, it prohibited sex discrimination only as regards wages (Art. 4). Since this provision is understood to require equal pay for equal work, it is not against the Labour Standards Law if female workers are not given positions as high as those of male employees and therefore receive lower salary. It

16　Judgment of the Supreme Court, 18 May, 1962 (*Minshū* 16–5–1108: Ōhira Silk Reeling Case).

17　Judgment of the Supreme Court, 25 May, 1961 (*Minshū* 15–5–1322, Yamazaki Shoken case).

18　Judgment of Kanazawa District Court, 27 November, 1987 (*Hanji* 1268–143, *Kitahama Dobokusaiseki* case).

19　Judgment of the Kobe District Court, 20 July, 1956 (*Rōmin* 7–4–838 : Bōki Seizō case); see also the Judgment of the Supreme Court, 22 November, 1955 (*Minshū* 9–12–1793 : Dai-Nippon Bōseki case).

20　Judgment of the Supreme Court, 12 December, 1973 (*Minshū* 27–11–1536: Mitsubishi Jyushi Case).

is usually difficult for female employees to become executives within a company. Only 12.2% of companies with 5,000 or more employees have women at the level of general manager (department head).[1]

In the absence of an explicit provision in the Labour Standards Law, the courts have endeavoured to eliminate sexual discrimination in various ways. For instance, in a case where a company provided in the rules of employment for retirement age of 60 for male employees and 55 for female employees, the Supreme Court upheld the judgment of the appellate court, which had found the regulations to be unreasonable and against public order and good morals as provided in the Civil Code.[2] The equal treatment clause in the Constitution was also cited in this judgment.

In Japan there is a practice that female employees leave the company once they get married. This practice which was written into rules of employment was found to be unjust discrimination. The compulsory retirement of female workers for reason of marriage and childbirth was found to be illegal by the courts.[3] There was another case where a company set the retirement age of female workers at 30. This was found to be an unreasonable discrimination on the part of the company.[4]

After the International Women's Year in 1975, the Law for Equal Opportunities in Employment of Women was drafted as an amendment to the Law on the Welfare of Working Women of 1972. The amendment was adopted and the Law was renamed in 1985.[5] The amended Law is aimed at, *inter alia*, ensuring equal opportunities and treatment of men and women. Discrimination by sex in training, welfare, retirement and dismissal is explicitly prohibited (Arts. 9–11). In the same year, Japan ratified the Treaty on Abolition of Sex Discrimination. However, the new Law does not necessarily meet the requirements of the Treaty. Thus, elimination of discrimination in employment, positioning, and promotion was provided as a target, rather than a legally binding requirement. Effective means of ensuring the implementation of this legislation are also lacking.

1 JETRO, *supra* note 9, 1991 edition, p. 126.
2 Judgment of the Supreme Court, 24 March, 1981 (*Minshū* 35–2–300 : Nissan Motors case).
3 Judgment of Tokyo District Court, 20 December, 1966 (*Rōmin* 17–6–1408 : Sumitomo Cement case); Judgment of Osaka District Court, 10 December, 1971 (*Rōmin* 22–6–1163: Mistui Zōsen case).
4 Judgment of Tokyo District Court, 1 July, 1969 (*Rōmin* 20–4–715: Tōkyū Kikan Kōgyō case).
5 Law No. 113, 1972 as amended in 1985.

Minimum wages are regulated by the Minimum Wage Law.[6] Wages agreed by the employer and the employee which are less than the minimum wage are void, and are replaced by the minimum wage (Art. 5, para. 2, Minimum Wage Law). The Law does not in itself provide minimum wages; instead, it provides for the procedure to determine minimum wages. At present, minimum wages are primarily determined in each prefecture by the Director of the Labour Standards Bureau upon the recommendation of the Minimum Wages Advisory Board. The director, following this area minimum wages, determines minimum wages for the individual industry.[7]

Employers must pay wages in 'currency', i.e. not in kind, directly to the employees, and in one lot (Art. 24, para. 1).

The Labour Standards Law provides for a 40 hour week (Art. 32, para. 1). Working hours were reduced from 48 hours per week in 1987. Employers may not require employees to work more than eight hours a day, or more than 40 hours a week. Employers must give employees at least one day off a week (Art. 35, para. 1). Employers may ask employees to work longer than eight hours a day or 40 hours a week on a particular day or week, provided that the rules of employment provides for the average work hours which do not exceed the limit set forth by the Law (Art. 32–2).

There are various exceptions to the general rule on work hours. A 48 hour week is permissible in service sectors and retail and distribution sectors (Art. 40 and Labour Standards Law Enforcement Rules, Art. 25–2). Furthermore, if the employer concludes a written agreement with the trade union which is composed of a majority of workers and submits the agreement to the Director of the Labour Standards Supervisory Bureau, he may extend the work hours and also make the employees work on Sundays and holidays (Art. 36). If a trade union composed of a majority of workers does not exist, the agreement should be concluded with a person representing a majority of the workers. There is no formal limit on the extension of working hours under this provision, except for work especially harmful to health, such as mining.

The law also guarantees annual holidays. It provides that those who have been employed for one year without interruption and have worked on more than 80% of the working days in that year should be given 10 days' annual paid holidays. This used to be 6 days' before the amendment in 1987. Those who have been

---

6 Law No. 137, 1959.
7 K. Sugeno, *supra* note 9, p. 176.

employed for more than two years are given one extra day's holiday per year in addition to the 6 days holiday (Art. 39). Thus, annual holidays are regarded more as a reward for uninterrupted work. In 1989, employees were eligible for 15.4 paid holidays; actual holidays taken were 7.9 days.[8]

In fact, the working hours of the Japanese are the highest among the industrialised countries. In 1989, the total actual working hours of Japanese workers were 2,159 hours, in contrast to 1,957 hours in the United States and 1,638 hours in the then West Germany. In 1991, the figure fell to 2,006 hours, but still, it is longer than other industrialised countries. Such long working hours result from the Japanese practice of long overtime. In 1989, the average overtime hours was 254 per annum, which fell to 169 hours in 1991.[9] In response to criticisms by foreign countries, the Japanese government has recently undertaken to reduce annual working hours to 1,800.[10]

On the other hand, partly due to the slowdown in economic growth, the five-day working week is gradually spreading in Japan. In 1985, 49.1% of the companies had adopted this system in one way or another. The percentage increased to 58.3% in 1989. However, in small and middle sized companies, a five-day working week is given only once a month or every two weeks.[11]

There are special provisions in the Labour Standards Law concerning minors and women. As regards minors, i.e. those below 15 years of age, there is a prohibition against employment. There are restrictions on working hours for those under the age of 18. For instance, they may not be made to work between 10 o'clock at night and five o'clock in the morning (Art. 61). Employers are prohibited from employing minors to do hazardous work (Art. 62, paras. 1 and 2). As regards the protection of female workers, there are restrictions on working hours. The 10 o'clock to five o'clock rule also applies to women. Furthermore, employers should not let a female employee, who is more than three months' pregnant, work, if she asked for a leave. Employers must also give a woman who had given birth, eight weeks' postnatal leave. However, if a woman who had given birth more than six weeks ago requested to return to work, the employer may let her do so provided that a doctor has

8 JETRO, *supra* note 9, p. 125.
9 *Asahi Daily*, 2 May, 1992.
10 JETRO, *supra*, p. 125.
11 Ministry of Labour ed., *Labour Situation in Charts, 1987*, Tokyo 1987, pp. 269–276.

acknowledged the work to be harmless to her health (Art. 65, paras. 1 and 2).

The Labour Standard Law was, *inter alia*, aimed at giving special protection to women. However, in the recent years, it has been gradually realised that some special protection for women, especially restrictions on working hours, actually narrowed their opportunity to work. Therefore, it was argued that, except for restrictions related to pregnancy and birth, women should be protected in the same way as men, but not more. Thus the amendment of the Labour Standards Law in 1985 relaxed some restrictions on the working hours of women. On the other hand, it should be noted that the protection of female workers in Japan is not sufficient to meet the standards set by ILO Treaty No. 103 on the Protection of Maternity.[12]

Most companies have their own disciplinary rules. Employees are subject to such rules by entering into an employment contract with the employer. Employers may dismiss, ask for the resignation of, suspend, reduce the remuneration of, or give severe or ordinary reprimands to those employees who have violated the rules. Normally, the grounds for taking disciplinary action and the sanctions available are specified in the rules of employment.

When disciplinary measures are taken without reasonable grounds, or administered in an unjust manner by reference to the principles of proportionality and due process, the courts regard it as an abuse of disciplinary power and void.[13] It should be added that even when there are grounds for taking disciplinary actions, if the misconduct is not likely to affect internal order within the company, then disciplinary action cannot be justified.[14]

The grounds for taking disciplinary actions vary from neglect of duty, breach of duty, private misconduct to political activities. As regards political activities, there was a case where an employee of the then public corporation (later privatised) wore a badge with the slogan 'Oppose the invasion of Vietnam, stop the expansion of U.S. military bases' in office hours. When he was ordered by his supervisor to take off this badge, he distributed leaflets of protest. He was reprimanded for violations of the disciplinary

---

12 H. Nakakubo, '*Jyosei-rōdō to Kokusai Rōdō-kijyun* (Female Labour and International Labour Standards)', J. Akita ed., *Kokusai Rōdō-kijyun to waga-Kuni no Shakai-hō* (*International Labour Standards and Social Legislation of Japan*), Tokyo 1987, p. 171.

13 Judgment of the Supreme Court, 16 September, 1983 (*Rōhan* 415 –16 : Daihatsu-Kōgyō case).

14 Judgment of the Supreme Court, 1 November, 1983 (*Hanji* 1100 –151: Meiji Nyūgyō case).

code. The district court and the appellate court found the employee's case to be substantiated and ruled the reprimand to be void. However, the Supreme Court overruled the judgment of the appellate court. According to the majority opinion of the Supreme Court, political activity within a private company may generate political conflict among employees and furthermore, obstruct the managing of the company. It is probable that such activity could affect the stability of the workplace. Therefore, the Court found that it was reasonable for the employer to prohibit political activity by office regulations. A dissenting opinion indicated that political activity only covers those specifically related to a particular political party or group, and thus suggests that the activity of the employee in this case was merely an expression of his beliefs and had no political content.[15]

As regards private misconduct of employees, there was a case where dismissal of a factory worker on the ground of his arrest for a minor crime was contested. The Supreme Court ruled that as the misconduct was committed in his private time and the crime was not significant, and that his position was not of a supervisory nature, his act could not be regarded as having seriously discredited the company.[16] However, in general, the Supreme Court tend to acknowledge that misconduct in the private life of an employee justifies disciplinary action by the employer in cases where the company was seriously discredited even though it had no actual effect on the business.[17]

3. 'Life-long employment' system

The Civil Code provides that the maximum term of a contract of employment is five years (Art. 626, para. 1). According to the Labour Standard Law, the term may not exceed one year (Art. 14). It was the view of the legislature that contracts of employment which were excessively long might result in forced labour and thus constitute unjust restraints on employees. Therefore, a one year restriction was introduced in the Labour Standards Law. Naturally, if both parties agree, the contract can be renewed. If a contract for a longer period is concluded, employees are entitled to rescind the contract after a year. If the labour relationship continues after the expiration of the contract

15 Judgement of the Supreme Court, 13 December, 1977 (*Minshū* 31-7-974: Meguro Denpō-Denwa-Kyoku case).
16 Judgment of the Supreme Court, 28 July, 1970 (*Minshū* 24-7-1220, Yokohama Rubber case).
17 Judgment of the Supreme Court, 15 March, 1974 (*Minshū* 28-2-265).

and the employer does not object, it is deemed to have been renewed (Art. 629, Civil Code).

In reality, a majority of people work in the same company after finishing school and remain there until retirement. A person will find a job in a particular company, receive training there and stay there. Job mobility is fairly low in Japan. Naturally, the employee is legally free to quit and move to another company, but he seldom does so. On the other hand, companies rarely dismiss employees even in recession. Instead, they take measures such as reduction of working hours, reduction of new employments, transferring employees to other sections and eventually to other companies within the group or to subsidiaries. Dismissal is the last resort. While in the United States, if a company suffers a heavy loss, the first thing the management does is to reduce the work force. In contrast, in Japan, the management prefers to cut the dividend rather than reducing the work force. Also in cases of technological innovation and structural changes in the industry, Japanese companies transfer employees to other sections and companies, but they seldom dismiss those who have become redundant.[18]

Dismissal of employees is regulated by the Civil Code and the Labour Standards Law. The Civil Code provides that if an employment contract is with a fixed term, the employer may dismiss the employee only when he has an unavoidable reason (Art. 628). If the contract is not for a fixed term, the employer may propose termination of the contract any time. This takes effect in two weeks (Art. 627, para. 1). In this way, according to the Civil Code, employers have a fairly free hand in dismissing employees. Since this system may produce unfairness against employees, labour legislation, namely the Labour Standards Law, has introduced some limitation on the right of dismissal on the part of employers.

Firstly, an employer may not dismiss an employee during the statutory pre- and postnatal leave, and within 30 days of the end of the latter (Art. 19, para. 1, Labour Standards Law). Secondly, employees cannot be dismissed during the leave arising out of work-related injury or disease and 30 days thereafter (Art. 19, para. 1). Thirdly, in order to dismiss an employee, the employer has to give the employee at least 30 days' notice. If this requirement is not met, the employer must give 30 days' pay in lieu (Art. 20, para. 1).

---

18 R. Onodera, 'Arbeitsverhältnisse in Japan', in P. Hanau et al. eds., *Die Arbeitswelt in Japan und in der Bundesrepublik Deutschland – ein Vergleich*, Köln, 1984, S. 6–9.

Collective agreements often include provisions limiting the dismissal of employees. For instance, an obligation is placed on the employer to consult the trade union. Rules of employment often include some additional requirements.

Further restrictions on the dismissal of employees have developed out of judicial precedents. The courts have found dismissals to be an abuse of rights (Art. 1, para. 3, Civil Code) under various circumstances. The doctrine of abuse of the right of dismissal has thus emerged in court practice.

The Supreme Court ruled that the employer's right to dismiss an employee constitutes an abuse of rights and is therefore null and void, if an objective and reasonable ground does not exist, and cannot be justified by socially accepted standards.[19] In a leading case, a broadcaster was dismissed for failing to broadcast the news twice as a result of oversleeping. However, he did not act intentionally or out of malice, his work record had not been bad, he expressed remorse, and there had been no precedent of dismissal in such cases. Besides, another employee, who should have woken up the announcer had also overslept, but he was merely reprimanded. The Supreme Court ruled that even when there is a formal ground for dismissal, an employer is not always free to dismiss an employee. In this particular case, the Supreme Court found the dismissal unreasonable and void.[20]

Another problem is dismissal for redundancy. Since the oil crisis in 1973, some industries have undergone contraction. As the life-long employment system had already become established at that time, Japanese companies endeavoured to avoid dismissal. However, dismissal was not always avoidable, and in some cases, was contested before the courts. The courts have been fairly strict in judging the necessity of redundancy dismissal. One judgment stated that in order to make such dismissal valid, there has to be a serious crisis in business and efforts should be made to transfer and absorb redundant personnel within the company.[1]

A leading case is the Toyo Oxygen case, where a chemical company dismissed 47 workers of a section producing acetylene gas because of market deterioration. Thirteen workers applied to the court for redress. The district court found the dismissal to be void, but the appellate court overruled this judgment. The latter

---

19 Judgment of the Supreme Court, 25 April, 1975 (*Minshū* 29–1–456: Nihon Shokuen Seizō case).
20 Judgment of the Supreme Court, 31 January, 1977 (*Saikōsai-saibanshū* 120–23: Kōchi Hōsō case).
1 Judgment of the Okayama District Court, 31 July, 1979 (*Rōhan* 326–44: Sumitomo Jyūki Tamashima Seizōsho case).

set three standards for judging whether the dismissal was really unavoidable or not. First, the closure of the section had to be unavoidable and necessary for reasonable business management. Second, there should have been no possibility of transferring employees to similar sections or work places and the dismissal was not arbitrary. Third, employees who are to be dismissed have been selected according to objective and reasonable criteria. The appellate court ruled that the company in this case met these standards. This judgment was upheld by the Supreme Court.[2] Academics add that the employer should consult the trade union and explain the situation on such occasions.

It is generally acknowledged that when dismissing employees by reason of redundancy, the employer must, based upon the doctrine of good faith and fair dealing, make efforts to avoid dismissal. Usually, when a company dismisses workers without trying alternative measures such as transfer within the company, encouraging voluntary retirement etc., such dismissal is found void by the court.

Moreover, procedural fairness is required in redundancy dismissals, as well as in dismissals on other grounds. The employer must explain the situation to the trade union or the workers and conscientiously discuss the matter with them.

In order to cope with recession in the 1970s, instead of making redundancy dismissals, many companies resorted to measures such as transferring employees to another section or work place, secondment to another company within the group, or to subsidiaries.

Initially, companies were thought to have a free hand in transferring personnel within the company. However, in recent years, it has been acknowledged that the company's right to order transfer is not unlimited. If there was an explicit or tacit agreement between the employer and the employee to the effect that the latter must accept transfer, transfer is valid without a specific consent by the employee. If not, he is entitled to refuse the transfer. Whether there was such kind of agreement between the employer and employee is to be judged from the employment contract, collective agreement, rules of employment, and practice within the company. Transfers which involve a change of address, especially, have to be handled prudently.

The courts have adopted a two-tier approach. Firstly, the courts make efforts to ascertain whether any limitation on transfer can be found in the contract, collective agreement, or

2 Judgment of Tokyo Appellate Court, 29 October, 1979 (*Rōmin* 30–5–1002: Tōyō Sanso case).

rules of employment. If there is no explicit or tacit agreement to accept the transfer, the court will quash the transfer order.

Secondly, even when the transfer was explicitly or tacitly agreed by the parties, the courts often find such orders constitute abuse of rights on the part of the employer. The Supreme Court decided on a case concerning transfer of an employee from Osaka to Nagoya. In this case, the court acknowledged that if the collective agreement and the rules of employment provide for a transfer order, and the work place had not been specified at the beginning of employment, the employer has discretion to decide on the work place. This does not constitute an abuse of power unless the transfer is unnecessary for the business, is made out of inappropriate motives or purposes, or excessively onerous to the employee. The Supreme Court went further and indicated that even if the transfer results in the employee's living separately from the family, it is not in itself an abuse of rights.[3]

There was a case where the Supreme Court ruled that a transfer of a school teacher to another secondary school in the same city was appropriate, since it did not entail any disadvantage as regards remuneration, work place, and contents of work.[4]

On the other hand, the courts have acknowledged that the consent of the employee is necessary in cases where the transfer entailed substantial reduction in wages, or significantly hindered the career development of the employee.[5] There was a case where the transferring of a broadcaster with 20 years' experiece, who had been employed specifically as a broadcaster, to another section, was found unreasonable.[6]

Secondments of employees to another company within the group, a subsidiary or a subcontracting company are not rare in Japan. The courts began to treat such secondments in a way similar to transfers within a company as such practices became common.

In some cases, employees who are seconded to another company retain their status in the original company, while in other cases, they entirely leave the company. These two kinds of secondments need a different consideration, since the latter

---

3 Judgment of the Supreme Court, 14 July, 1986 (*Rōhan* 477 – 6: Tōa Paint case).

4 Judgment of the Supreme Court, 23 October, 1986 (*Rōhan* 484–7: Osaka Fukyōi case).

5 Judgment of Wakayama District Court, 14 March, 1959 (*Rōmin* 10–2–127: Wakayama Pile Orimino case).

6 Decision of Tokyo District Court, 23 July, 1976 (*Hanji* No. 820, p. 54 : Nihon Television case).

involves a change of identity in the parties to the contract of employment, whereas the original contract between the employer contract between the employer and the employee remains intact in the former. It is generally considered that in the latter cases, the employee's general or tacit consent basis will suffice, while in the former cases, a more specific consent is necessary.

In the aftermath of the privatisation of Japan National Railway, secondments to a related company were fairly common. In one case, the court acknowledged the existence of a tacit agreement to accept secondment to another company, but suspended the order on the ground that the work after secondment was quite different and that the selection of employees to be seconded was not reasonable.[7]

In most companies, a compulsory retirement age is provided in the rules of employment. The retirement age of workers was previously 55 in most companies. In recent years, the government has been making efforts to raise the retirement age to 60. In 1981, a retirement age of 60 was introduced for government employees; there had been no fixed retirement age before. A new Law which was enacted in 1986 provided retirement at 60 as a target in private industries.[8] It should be noted that a retirement age of 60 is realised in 50 % of the companies.

4.   Collective industrial relations

The basic Law concerning trade unions is the Trade Union Law. It provides for criminal and civil law immunity for the legitimate actions of a trade union. It also deals with the effect of collective agreements and remedies for unjust labour practices. This Law, however, does not apply to non-manual central and local government employees. The Law on Labour Relations in State Enterprises and the Law on Labour Relations in Local Public Corporations apply in such cases.[9]

One of the main characteristics of Japanese trade unions is that they are organised in each company, instead of an industry as a whole or in accordance with particular skills. Employees of a company usually belong to the same trade union, regardless of the kind of work they do. Trade unions of a company form a regional federation and also industrial or occupational federation. These federations in turn form national organisations.

---

7 Judgment of Osaka District Court, 30 November, 1987 (*Hanji* 1269–147).
8 The Law on Stabilization of Employment of Aged Persons, Law No. 68, 1971.
9 Law No. 257, 1948 as amended and Law No. 289, 1952.

The percentage of workers who are trade union members has been decreasing in recent years. In 1975, it was 34.4%, while in 1989, it fell to 26.1%. This is much lower than in the then West Germany (41.1% in 1984) and England (52.0% in 1984), but higher than in the United States (18.0% in 1985).[10]

Trade unions under this Law are organizations and their federations voluntarily organised by employees primarily in order to improve the working conditions and economic situations. Those organisations which allow the participation of supervisors or others representing the interest of the employer, which are subsidised by the employer, or which are primarily with charitable, political or social aims are not regarded as trade unions under this Law (Art. 2).

Trade unions are required to prove that they meet these conditions, and must submit their rules to the labour commission in order to take part in the dispute settlement procedures and have recourse to remedies as provided in the Trade Union Law (Art. 5, para. 1). Labour commissions, which are administrative commissions established at central and prefectural level, have the power to determine the eligibility of each trade union. Trade unions which do not meet the above-mentioned conditions are still protected by the Constitution, and enjoy the same civil and criminal immunities as registered trade unions.

A majority of trade unions have union shop agreements with the employer. However, these agreements merely provide that those who are not members of the trade union should, 'in principle' be dismissed, or have a provision which stipulates that 'when this employee is needed by the company, the company may employ him (or her)'. In this way, a union shop agreement is made flexible in Japan.

Collective bargaining is guaranteed by the Constitution. Trade unions are immune from criminal or civil liability when engaging in collective bargaining. Employers are not allowed to refuse to enter into collective bargaining without justifiable reasons (Art. 7, para. 2, Trade Union Law).

In practice, collective bargaining between the company and its trade union is the commonest form of negotiation. Since this type of collective bargaining can be disadvantageous to employees who are generally in a weaker bargaining position than the company, other methods of collective bargaining have emerged. In some cases, a trade union federation of an industry bargains with a particular company on behalf of the trade union of that company. In other cases, the federation jointly negotiates with

10 Ministry of Labour, *supra* note 21, pp. 341–342.

the company's trade union, or sends a representative to take part in the negotiations between the trade union and the company.

The scope of issues which can be handled via the collective bargaining process is fairly broad. Employers are not free to decide working conditions unilaterally. Terms and conditions of employment are to be discussed in the collective bargaining process. The transfer and dismissal of trade union members as well as the imposition of disciplinary measures are matters which are regarded as being subject to collective bargaining. Issues concerning management and production, such as the introduction of new machinery, changes in production methods, and the reorganisation of a company may also have to be discussed in collective bargaining, insofar as they affect work conditions and employment. In addition, there are issues which are not mandatory to be considered in collective bargaining, but can be discussed via such a process if both parties agree.[11]

If the employer refuses to bargain without justifiable grounds, the trade union may apply to the labour commission for remedies (Art. 27, Trade Union Law). The commission reviews the application and if it is substantiated, will order the employer to take part in collective bargaining. Employees may also apply for mediation by the labour commission (Art. 12).

Employers are not allowed to deal directly with individual employees when there is a trade union within the company. Unlike the United States, where a system of exclusive representation is adopted, in Japan, if there are several trade unions within a company, each trade union is entitled to represent its members. In some cases, there is an agreement between the employer and the trade union that the company recognises a particular trade union as the only one with whom it will negotiate. This kind of agreement infringes the rights of other trade unions within the company and is considered to be void.[12]

Collective bargaining is primarily aimed at concluding or revising collective agreements, which set forth rules concerning the relationship between employer and employees. Collective agreements also set standards of welfare and working conditions of employees and furthermore, provide for the extent of participation or involvement of the trade union in the management of a company.

In some countries, collective agreements are treated as gentlemen's agreements, while in other countries, they are regarded as binding contracts. In the former case, collective

---

11 Sugeno, *supra* note 9, pp. 422–425.
12 *Ibid.*, p. 417.

agreements do not necessarily affect individual contracts of employment. In Germany, collective agreements have a stronger effect. According to the Law of 1918, collective agreements have effects on individual contracts, and moreover, are even binding on those who are not members of the trade union. Japanese law has adopted this German system.

Collective agreements exist in almost all companies with more than 1,000 employees in Japan. Most are concluded on a company basis – i.e. these are agreements between the company and the trade union. General agreements applicable to an industry as a whole or a profession are exceptional.

The content of collective agreements varies. Generally, they begin with general provisions concerning trade union membership, union shop agreement etc. This is followed by provisions regarding trade union activities, personnel management, work conditions, employee's rights and duties and safety arrangements. Furthermore, they can deal with the following – procedures for collective bargaining, the scope of issues and the procedure by which the trade union is consulted by the company, the complaints procedure, and the dispute settlement clause (*sōgi jyōkō*).

Provisions of the contract of employment which conflict with the collective agreement concerning work conditions and other matters affecting the employees' rights and duties are void (Art. 14, Trade Union Law). This is termed the 'normative effect' of the collective agreement. The invalidated part is replaced by the standards set out in the collective agreement. This applies both to cases where the standard set by a contract of employment falls short of the collective agreement as well as cases where the former exceeds the latter. This is similar to American Law, but different from German and French Law.[13] When there is no provision in the contract of employment, the provision of the collective agreement directly regulates the relationship between employer and employee.

The Law provides that the maximum term of agreement is three years (Art. 15, para. 1, Trade Union Law). A provision often found in collective agreements requires that both parties refrain from industrial action in order to revise or delete the provisions of the agreement while the agreement is in force. This obligation is referred to as an 'obligation of peace'. Sometimes, the parties agree to refrain from industrial action altogether. Breaches of such obligation may result in civil liability.

Other provisions often found are those that define the rules

13 *Ibid.*, pp. 446–448.

and procedures in cases of dispute, such as those requiring the party to make efforts for settling the dispute through negotiation, requiring advance notice for industrial action, and those providing for procedures for conciliation and mediation.

The effect of a collective agreement extends to those who are not party to the agreement nor members of the trade union which is a signatory to the agreement. The Trade Union Law provides that when more than three quarters of employees of a factory or an office are subject to a collective agreement, this agreement binds other employees who are engaged in similar kinds of works (Art. 17). However, this does not apply when the remaining minority is organised into another trade union, especially when it has concluded another collective agreement with the employer.[14] Furthermore, the Law provides that the effect of a collective agreement concluded by a great majority of employees in the locality extends to other similar employees and employers within the locality (Art. 18, para. 1). Since collective agreements are usually concluded in each company, and not on an industry or area basis, this latter provision is seldom applied.

5. Industrial action

The Constitution guarantees the right of workers to act collectively. This includes the rights to take industrial action as well as other actions which do not amount to industrial action, such as distributing leaflets, organising meetings, and posting up bills and posters.

Legitimate industrial action is immune from criminal or civil liability. Although the current Criminal Code does not punish industrial action *per se*, it is still possible that statutory provisions relating to the obstruction of business by force, extortion, trespass etc. are applicable to industrial action. The Trade Union Law provides explicitly that legitimate activities of the trade union are regarded as 'socially justifiable acts' in the sense of Article 35 of the Criminal Code, and are immune from criminal liability. By the same token, employers may not claim damages from the trade union or its members for taking part in a legitimate strike or other industrial action. Both criminal and civil immunity emanate from the Constitution, and the provision of the Trade Union Law is understood merely to have confirmed this constitutional guarantee. In addition, employers are not

14 Judgment of Tokyo District Court, 19 July, 1969 (*Rōminshū* 20–4–813: Katsuragawa Seishi Seisakusho case).

allowed to discriminate against employees who have taken part in, or organised legitimate industrial action.

Industrial action has to be legitimate as regards its subject, purpose, procedure and methods. Firstly, an industrial action has to be pursued by a trade union, although it does not have to meet the standards set by the Trade Union Law. For instance, a group of workers temporarily organised for a specific demand is also entitled to criminal and civil immunity, although it is not a trade union in a strict legal sense. On the other hand, wild-cat strikes, i.e. strikes initiated by a small number of workers within the trade union, are not legitimate.

Secondly, the purpose of the industrial action has to be justifiable. In this regard, the legitimacy of a political strike has been a focus of debate. The courts maintain that purely political strikes which have no direct bearing on the improvement of the economic position of the employees are not justified. Since the right to industrial action is guaranteed by the Constitution as a means to facilitate collective bargaining, issues which can not be disposed of in the collective bargaining process cannot be legitimate aims of an industrial action.[15] Some lawyers are of the opinion that industrial action against laws or policies directly related to economic interests of workers are justified.

Thirdly, industrial action has to be procedurally fair. For instance, it is generally not justifiable to resort to industrial action without first making efforts to settle the dispute through collective bargaining. Industrial action taken in breach of peace provisions in the collective agreement is neither justifiable.

Fourthly, forms of industrial action have to be appropriate. Use of force is not justified. As for picketing, there is a disagreement of views. In Japan, picketing plays a significant role in industrial disputes. The difference of opinion focusses on the limits on picketing, i.e. whether picketing is limited to peaceful persuasion or not. In a leading case, a trade union of a mining company started a strike, demanding changes to the collective agreement. In the course of the dispute, some members of the trade union withdrew from the trade union. The company also employed some new personnel, and, together with those who had withdrawn from the union, attempted to break the picketing line and resume business. Trade union members organised a sit-in at the entrance of the mine, formed a scrum, and prevented a mining car from entering the mine. Organisers of the picketing were prosecuted for obstruction of business by force.

15 Judgment of the Supreme Court, 2 April, 1969 (*Keishū* 23–5–685 : Zenshihō Sendai case).

The Supreme Court ruled that the method of strike should be limited to a refusal to work. Preventing the employer from operating his business by force, threat or obstructing the management of his property is not permissible.[16] The Court added that 'various factors and circumstances' should be taken into account when judging the legitimacy of picketing. However, since this judgment, the Supreme Court has been strict in dealing with the breadth of criminal immunity when issues of picketing have arisen.

Employers adopt various measures against industrial action. Employers are free to continue their business by using executive employees and other employees who do not belong to the trade union. They are also free to employ replacements. As for lock-outs, the Supreme Court did not accept that lock-outs were a legitimate practice, but ruled that under certain circumstances when the employer is in an extremely disadvantageous position, a lock-out can be justified as a counter-measure to recover the balance of power between the employer and the employee.[17]

6.   Procedures for the settlement of disputes

Labour commissions are designed to settle industrial disputes and provide remedies against unfair labour practices. The Trade Union Law provides for the Central Labour Commission, Central Seamen's Labour Commission, local labour commissions, and local seamen's labour commission (Art. 19, para. 2). They are independent of the Minister of Labour or governors of prefectures.

Labour commissions are composed of representatives of employers, employees and those who represent the public interest – neutral members. The Central Labour Commission consists of equal numbers (nine each) of members representing employers, employees and the public interest. Members of the Central Labour Commission are appointed by the Minister of Labour. Representatives of employees are recommended by the trade unions. Appointment of those representing the public interest requires the consent of employer and employee representatives (Art. 19).

Labour commissions are responsible for reviewing the

16 Judgment of the Supreme Court, 28 May, 1958 (*Keishu* 12–8–1694: Uhoro Tankō case).
17 Judgment of the Supreme Court, 25 April, 1975 (*Minshū* 29–4–481: Marushima Suimon case).

eligibility of trade unions for the protection extended by the Trade Union Law (Art. 5, para. 1), reviewing complaints concerning unfair labour practices and providing remedies (Art. 7), and 'adjusting (settling)' industrial disputes (Art. 20).

Employers and trade unions are free to establish their own dispute-settlement mechanisms, such as complaint procedures or independent arbitration procedures. If such mechanisms do not exist, or if the parties fail to resolve their differences through these mechanisms, the dispute is brought to the labour commission. Procedures for the settlement of industrial disputes are regulated by the Labour Relations Adjustment Law.[18]

When industrial action has been taken or is likely to be taken, the dispute can be brought to the labour commission (Art. 6). In such cases, the parties are expected to make sincere efforts to solve the dispute by themselves (Art. 2).

The first stage of the procedure once the case comes to the commission is mediation. A councillor appointed by the chairman of the labour commission makes efforts to clarify the issue and solve the difference. This procedure can be initiated by either party in the dispute or by the chairman of the commission *ex officio* (Arts. 10,12, and 13). Parties are free to accept or not accept the advice of the councillor.

The second device as provided by the Labour Relations Adjustment Law is conciliation. A conciliation panel set up within a labour commission hears the views of both parties, drafts a settlement, and recommends it to both parties (Art. 17). The conciliation procedure is initiated on joint application by both parties, or application by either party if there is a conciliation clause in the collective agreement. In disputes involving public utilities, disputes on a major scale, or disputes which seriously affect the public interest, either party to the dispute, the labour commission, or the governor of a prefecture may initiate this procedure (Art. 18).

The third device is arbitration conducted by an arbitration board established within the labour commission (Art. 29). Arbitration procedure is initiated on the joint application of parties or application of either party in cases where there is an arbitration clause in the collective agreement. Arbitrators are chosen by the parties from among those members of the labour commission that represent the public interest (Art. 31–2). The decision has the same effect as a collective agreement and is binding on both parties (Art. 34).

18 Law 25, 1946.

As is the case with the U.S. law, there is a system designed to cope with a state of emergency. The Prime Minister is empowered to start an emergency adjustment (dispute settlement) procedure, when 1) the case concerns public utilities, 2) the dispute is of a large scale, or 3), the dispute involves an industry with a special nature, and therefore, is likely seriously to affect the normal operation of the economy, or is likely seriously to affect the normal life of people. The likelihood of such results has to be present (Art. 35–2). When an emergency adjustment procedure has been triggered, the parties are not allowed to resort to industrial action for 50 days (Art. 38). The Central Labour Commission is expected to do its utmost to solve the dispute.

The Trade Union Law provides for remedies for unfair labour practices. Although the present system has been primarily inspired by the Wagner Law of the United States of America, the definition of such practices differs from that found in U.S. law. Unfair trade practices enumerated in the Trade Union Law include, *inter alia*, 1) disadvantageous or discriminatory treatment of workers who organise or join a trade union, 2) 'yellow dog agreements', 3) unjust refusal to enter into negotiations on the part of the company, 4) interference with the administration of the trade union, or the exercise of control upon the trade union by the employer (Art. 7). Unlike the U.S. Law, unfair labour practices are limited to the acts of the employers; the definition does not cover the acts of trade unions.

Trade unions and employees may claim damages for unfair labour practices by bringing a case to court. In addition, they may pursue a remedy before the labour commissions. Hearings are conducted by those members of the local labour commission that represent the public interest. If a given act is found to be an unfair labour practice, the commission issues a remedial order to recover the *status quo ante* (Art. 27). A majority of cases end in compromise before any formal decision is reached. If either party is not satisfied with the outcome of the first instance, the decision can be appealed to the Central Labour Commission. The decision can be further appealed to the court. The Law on Administrative Litigation applies to these cases.

16 Anti-monopoly law

1. An outline of the system

The industrialization of Japan, which started in the late 19th century, was initiated and promoted by the government from above, rather than by the spontaneous growth of the entrepreneurs from below. At the initial stage, the government promoted and managed key industries and then handed them over to private companies at an extremely low price. This resulted in a domination of the economy by a handful of giant business conglomerates which were called *zaibatsu*.[1]

Furthermore, new laws were enacted in the 1930's in order to facilitate the military build-up, leading to a further growth of business conglomerates. Therefore, the concentration of economic power was not necessarily regarded as a negative phenomenon.

One of the goals which the Allied Forces endeavored to achieve after the Second World War was the democratisation of the economy. This included the dissolution of *zaibatsu* and elimination of the excessive concentration of economic power. It was against this background that the Law on Prohibition of Private Monopoly and Ensuring of Fair Trade (hereafter Anti-Monopoly Law) was enacted.[2] In the same year, the Fair Trade Commission was established in order to implement this law. The Commission is organisationally attached to the Prime Minister's Office, but is guaranteed independence and has quasi-judicial and legislative powers.

The Anti-Monopoly Law, introduced in 1947, was heavily influenced by the antitrust legislation of the United States. It was even stricter than the American law in some respects, since American advisers to Japan were inclined to support the precepts of the New Deal policy, and they intended to introduce a system which they had failed to implement fully in the United States.

1 R. Storry, *A History of Modern Japan*, Harmondsworth 1960, pp. 123–124.
2 Law No. 54, 1947.

However, this law was considered to be too stringent to be applied to Japan, which was a country which had previously rejected any idea of regulating the concentration of economic power and promoting fair competition. Therefore, the restrictions introduced by the Anti-Monopoly Law were relaxed to a certain extent by an amendment in 1953, soon after the end of the Allied occupation.

Another major reform of the Anti-Monopoly Law took place in 1977. At this time there was considerable public criticism of the behavior of major corporations during the oil crisis, and for the first time in the history of the Anti-Monopoly Law, restrictions were strengthened. This amendment introduced, *inter alia*, surcharges for operating illegal cartels, the new concept of 'monopolistic situation' which enables the Fair Trade Commission to order the partition of giant enterprises, and the mandatory submission of reports to the Fair Trade Commission in cases of increase in prices by several leading entrepreneurs of the same product or service if it had taken place within three months.

The Structural Impediments Initiatives Talk between the United States and Japan which started in 1989 resulted in the overall review of the Anti-Monopoly Law and its implementation. The Americans argued that unfair and restrictive trade practices in Japan were impeding the entry of foreign companies into the Japanese market. Practices such as mutual shareholding and the *keiretsu* (business affiliation) system have made it difficult for foreign companies to penetrate into Japan. In order to make the Japanese market more transparent and fair, the strengthening of the Anti-Monopoly Law was proposed.

This was partly realised by increasing the amount of surcharge for illegal cartels by four times and increasing the maximum amount of fines from one million yen to 100 million yen in 1992. A new guidline concerning the distribution system and business practices was published in 1991. While the Fair Trade Commission used to rely on informal measures rather than formal proceedings, in the last couple of years the Commission has come to rely more on the latter. In 1991, for the first time since the oil crisis in the 1970s, a criminal proceeding was initiated against an illegal cartel. Further changes concerning remedies are now being discussed.

The primary goal of the Anti-Monopoly Law is to promote and maintain free and fair competition in the market and to ensure fair trade. Article 1 of the Law provides that the Law is to 'promote free and fair competition, enhance free enterprise, encourage business activity, and increase employment and wage levels'. This provision is interpreted broadly to include fairness of competition and fairness of trade, which are expected to contribute to the protection of the interests of consumers and ultimately, to the democratic development of the nation's economy. In order to achieve these purposes, the Law prohibits private monopolisation, unreasonable restraints on trade, and unfair trade practices.

The agency in charge of implementing the Anti-Monopoly Law is the Fair Trade Commission. The Fair Trade Commission is attached to the Prime Minister's Office (Art. 27). The chairman and four councillors of the Fair Trade Commission are appointed by the Prime Minister with the consent of both Houses and the chairman is attested by the Emperor. The chairman and the councillors are required to be over 35 and have sufficient knowledge of either economics or law. Once they are appointed they may not be removed against their will, except in cases specified by the Law (Art. 31).

The Anti-Monopoly Law regulates the activities of entrepreneurs and trade associations. The Law defines an entrepreneur as a person who carries on commercial, industrial, or financial business (Art. 2, para. 1). They can be either natural or juridical persons. Local authorities, as well as government agencies, may also qualify. The Law also provides for trade associations, which are defined as a union of entrepreneurs or a federation of such unions, which has the promotion of their common entrepreneurial interests as its primary goal.

Measures provided for by the Anti-Monopoly Law can be applied to those entrepreneurs or trade associations which, in one way or another, restrict fair competition in a 'particular field of trade'. Whether foreign markets are included in this definition is not certain. Generally, it is understood that restrictions on fair competition in a foreign market cannot be controlled by the Japanese Anti-Monopoly Law, unless it directly affects the domestic market. The Law has not been applied in an extraterritorial way so far, although there have been some cases where a foreign company was involved in a cartel.[3] In this regard, a study group set up by the Fair Trade Commission reported in 1990 that the Anti-Monopoly Law should be applicable to foreign companies residing outside Japan, if they act against the Law. However, the report added that there may be cases where Japan should refrain from applying its law out of various considerations.[4]

---

3 M. Matsushita, *Keizaihō Gairon* (*An Outline of Economic Law*), Tokyo 1986, p. 49.

4 See A. Negishi, '*Gaikoku-kigyō to Dokusen-kinshi-hō* (Foreign Companies and Anti-Monopoly Law)', *Jurist*, No. 1000, 1992, p. 304.

The Anti-Monopoly Law covers three major areas: private monopolies, undue restrictions on trade, and unfair methods of trading.

2.   Private monopolisation

Article 3 of the Law prohibits entrepreneurs from operating private monopolies. The term 'private monopolisation' means the exclusion or control of business activities of other entrepreneurs by a single entrepreneur, or in conjunction with, or in collusion with, other entrepreneurs, thus substantially restraining competition against public interest (Art. 2, para. 5). This includes prohibition of private monopolisation *per se*, as well as control of excessive concentration of economic power and control of a 'monopolistic situation'.

As regards private monopolisation *per se*, typical acts of excluding other entrepreneurs are unreasonable reductions in price, predatory pricing, and the acquisition of competing entrepreneurs. Control of other entrepreneurs' activity means depriving another entrepreneur of his freedom of decision-making. Typical methods include holding the shares of a competitor, sending in directors, and abusing the bargaining power.

In one case, a tin-manufacturing company exercised control over four smaller companies by holding their shares through intermediaries and sending in directors to these companies. The market share of this company reached 73%. In order to maintain its dominant position, the company restricted the business of these smaller companies by limiting the size of the market to which they sold the goods. The company also prohibited the manufacturing of certain goods and limited the construction of a new plant. When a food company planned to open its own plant for manufacturing tin, the company stopped supplying its products to this company and forced it to abandon the project. The Fair Trade Commission found this to be a private monopoly.[5]

Private monopolisation can also be realised through a concerted action of entrepreneurs. In one case, two dairy companies (at one time a single company which had been split up after the Second World War), collected more than 70% of milk supplies in a region. They colluded with the Agricultural Bank and the

5 Recommendatory Decision of the Fair Trade Commission, 18 September, 1972 (FTC *Shinketsushū* 19–87: Tōyō Seikan case).

regional Federation of Agricultural Cooperatives, exercising influence over them because shareholders and directors of the companies were also on the boards of the Bank and the Federation. The Bank made it a condition of loans to dairy suppliers (farmers) that they did not supply milk to competitors of the two dairy companies. The Federation imposed a similar condition for guaranteeing such loans. For over three years, the Bank extended 300 million yen in loans and was able to affect severely the business of its competitors. Thus, the dairy companies maintained their dominant position and sought to strengthen it further by restricting or eliminating the business of competitors. The Fair Trade Commission found this to be private monopolisation.[6]

In another case, a leading producer of soy sauce which had a market share of 9.3% decided to raise the price of its products, and stopped supplying those retail traders who did not increase their prices. In this business, the price was considered to reflect the quality of the product, and as a result of this company's behaviour, other major companies were forced to raise their prices as well. The Fair Trade Commission found that by controlling the retail price of the product, this company had restrained fair competition.[7]

The Fair Trade Commission is empowered to order an entrepreneur to file reports with the Commission, to cease and desist from acts which are against the Anti-Monopoly Law, to transfer part of the business and take other necessary measures to eliminate any violations. In the above-cited dairy companies case, the Fair Trade Commission ordered that the company cease interference with other companies' activities and sell those shares which the company owned through intermediaries.

Restrictions on private monopolisation also covers prevention of excess concentration of economic power. The Anti-Monopoly Law restricts the holding of shares, the concurrent holding of directorships, the merger of companies and the transfer of business. These restrictions are aimed at preventing the concentration of economic power in the hands of a small number of entrepreneurs.

There is a general prohibition on creating a holding company (Art. 9). A holding company is a company, the primary business of which is to control the business activities of another company

---

6 Decision of the Fair Trade Commission, 28 July, 1956 (FTC *Shinketsushū* 8–12: Yukijirushi Dairy case).
7 Judgment of the Tokyo Appellate Court, 25 December, 1957 (*Kōsai-minshū* 10–12–743: Noda Shōyu case).

by holding its shares. Before the Second World War, *zaibatsu* had controlled groups of companies through such holding companies. This provision was introduced to prevent the re-emergence of such *zaibatsu*. It does not, however, prohibit companies from holding shares if they are at the same time engaged in business. Therefore, it is possible to establish a subsidiary and hold its shares as long as the parent company itself is engaged in some kind of business.

The acquisition and holding of other companies' shares is subject to restrictions. Financial companies such as banks and security companies are prohibited from acquiring or holding more than 5% of the issued shares of another Japanese company. For insurance companies, the ceiling is 10% (Art. 11).

Another restriction on the owning of shares by companies was introduced by the 1977 amendment. Large joint stock companies whose net assets exceed 30 billion yen or which have capital of more than 10 billion yen, are prohibited from acquiring or holding shares of other companies beyond a certain limit. The ceiling is set at the amount of net assets or capital, whichever is the higher. The total price of acquisition should not exceed this ceiling (Article 9–2, para. 1). Some exceptions, such as companies which develop natural resources, are made to this provision.

Even when the shares acquired by a company do not exceeed the ceiling, companies are forbidden to acquire or hold shares of a company if this results in substantially restraining competition in a particular field. They are also banned from acquiring or holding shares by unfair means of trade (Art. 10, para. 1). The Fair Trade Commission issued guidelines in 1981 for the application of this provision.[8] Another guideline which was issued in 1991 also addresses this matter. If a company which is holding shares of another company uses this as a lever to force the latter not to trade with the former's competitors, this constitutes a violation of Anti-Monopoly Law. Similarly, if a company refuses to deal with companies whose shares are not held by this company, this is also against the Law. This arrangement is intended to curb exclusive trade by group companies linked by mutual shareholding.[9]

Interlocking directorship is also covered by the Anti-Monopoly Law. Directors or employees of a company may not combine directorship of another company, if it results in substantial restraint on competition in a specific area of trade. A company is

---

8 M. Nakagawa, *Anti-Monopoly Legislation in Japan*, Tokyo 1984, pp. 89–94.
9 The Fair Trade Commission, *The Anti-Monopoly Act Guidelines concerning Distribution Systems and Business Practices*, 1991.

not allowed to force its competitor to accept its director or an employee to become a director of the latter by resorting to unfair trade practices. In certain cases, when a director or an employee of a company is to combine directorship of a competitor, he has to notify the Fair Trade Commission (Art. 13).

In cases of infringement, the Fair Trade Commission may issue a cease and desist order and take all necessary measures to eliminate the violation, including ordering the sale of the shares.

The Law also has restrictions on mergers. A merger is not allowed, if, as a result of the merger, competition in a particular field is likely to be substantially restrained, or unfair trade practices have been employed in the course of the merger (Art. 15, para. 1). A company which intends to merge with another company must file a report with the Fair Trade Commission (Art.15, para. 2). The merger cannot be carried out until 30 days after the report has been received by the Commission (Art. 15, para. 3). The Commission decides whether the merger is likely to restrain competition substantially within this period. If the conclusion is in the affirmative, the Commission will initiate formal proceedings or recommend that the parties refrain from merging. If the Commission eventually finds that the merger is against the Law, it may prohibit the merger or impose conditions on merger. When the merger is carried out in breach of the Law, the Commission is empowered to bring the case to court and nullify the merger (Art. 18).

As regards merger, the Fair Trade Commission receives almost 1,500 notifications. However, these mainly involve small and medium size companies which are handled by a simplified procedure. In 1992, there were 53 cases of merger of listed companies.[10] The only case of merger which the Fair Trade Commission has handled in a formal proceeding is the merger of the Fuji Steel Corporation and the Yawata Steel Corporation. In the mid 1960s, the Japanese steel industry was dominated by six major companies. The first and the second largest companies decided to merge and filed a report with the Fair Trade Commission in accordance with the Law. The Commission found the merger to be impermissible, because it was likely substantially to restrain competition, and recommended that the merger not go ahead. This was not accepted by the two companies. Therefore, the Commission applied to the Tokyo Appellate Court for an injunction which was granted. The Commission then initiated formal proceedings. Both companies, seeing that it was

10 Commercial Law Centre ed., *Zōshi Hakusho (White Paper on Corporate Finance) 1992*, Tokyo 1992, pp. 151–156.

difficult to obtain approval for the merger, chose to accept the decision of the Commission. Accordingly, the Commission rendered a consentient decision.[11]

The Commission ruled in this case that if, as a result of a merger, the structure of the market changes, becomes less competitive, and an entrepreneur obtains a dominant position within the market, it is a substantial restraint on competition within Article 15, para. 1 of the Law. An entrepreneur is considered to hold a dominant position if he dominates the market, or is capable of controlling the price, quality or quantity of the merchandise above a certain level. In this particular case, the Commission acknowledged, in principle, that the proposed merger would result in a substantial restriction of competition in the market of rails, tin plate and other items. However, the Commission ruled that if necessary measures to prevent unreasonable restraints were adopted, the merger could go ahead. Thus, various measures, such as the transfer of steel mills to other smaller companies as well as sharing expertise with them, and the assignment of shares owned by the parties, were recommended and accepted by the two companies. The idea underlying this decision was that if an effective competitor is created, the proposed merger will not result in a substantial restraint on competition.

The Fair Trade Commission issued guidelines concerning mergers in 1980. There is a simplified procedure for a merger of companies whose total assets are less than five billion yen. In such mergers, the Fair Trade Commission examines the proposed merger on the basis of the application submitted by the parties. When the market share of any party to the merger, or the combined market share of the parties either 1) exceeds 25%, 2) is the largest and exceeds 15%, or 3) is the largest and there is a substantial gap between the share of the second or third largest company, close scrutiny is to be given to the proposed merger. The guidelines set out various factors in detail which should be taken into account in examining the proposed merger.[12]

As part of the measures to prevent or eliminate private monopolization, a new provision concerning a 'monopolistic situation' was introduced by the 1977 amendment. If there is a 'monopolistic situation', the Fair Trade Commission may order the entrepreneur to take certain steps, including transfer of

---

11 Consentient Decision of the Fair Trade Commission, 30 October, 1969 (FTC *Shinketsushū* 16–46: Yawata Seitestu case).
12 Nakagawa, *supra* note 7, pp. 79–83.

business and the restoration of a competitive market in goods or services (Art. 8–4). This provision is expected to deal with a situation where one or a small number of entrepreneurs dominate a particular market and inhibit free competition.

A situation is regarded as monopolistic, if 1) the market share of one company exceeds 50% or the total share of two companies exceed 75%, 2) entry into the market is extremely difficult, and 3) there has been a considerable increase in prices, or a decrease in prices has been limited for a certain period and the entrepreneur has either made considerable profits exceeding the norm set by administrative ordinances or has incurred extremely high sales or administration costs, provided that the total turnover exceeds fifty billion yen (Art. 2, para. 7).

The Commission is empowered to order the partial transfer of business operations or assets, the sale of shares, a change in business methods, and the opening up of the distribution system. The Fair Trade Commission is required to notify the Minister in charge if it intends to take such measures. The Minister may present his views to the Fair Trade Commission (Art. 45–2). In order to initiate formal proceedings in such cases, a public inquiry must be held. A decision of the Commission shall be reached only with the consent of the chairman and not less than three councillors (Art. 55, para. 3). The Commission is not allowed to take any action if it would reduce the scope of a business beyond an appropriate size, undermine the financial position of the entrepreneur, make it difficult to maintain competitiveness in the international market, or when other measures to restore competition have been taken (Art. 8–4, para. 1).

It is fairly unlikely that measures to remedy a monopolistic situation will actually be applied, especially the order to transfer part of the operations of a business.[13] The provision is expected to function as a deterrent, especially in relation to a concerted increase in prices led by a dominant entrepreneur. Its actual implementation is considered to be a last resort.

3. Unreasonable restraints of trade

Unreasonable restraints of trade in the sense used by this Law refers primarily to cartels. The Law defines unreasonable restraint of trade as a concerted action of entrepreneurs in mutually restraining or terminating competition in a particular

---

13 Matsushita, *supra*, note 3, pp. 95–96.

field of trade, resulting in substantial restraints on competition against the public interest (Art. 2, para. 6). The Law prohibits various forms of unreasonable restraints, such as fixing, increasing or maintaining of prices, limiting production outputs or the use of technology, controlling products, facilities, customers, or suppliers (Art. 3). Bid-rigging, which is said to be common in some industries, also falls within this category.

One case involved nine companies which supplied coal to breweries. Three sales companies agreed to raise their retail prices. These companies' share of the market reached virtually 100% of the domestic market for this type of coal. The Fair Trade Commission found this agreement to be a substantial restriction on competition and ordered its revocation.[14]

Mutual restraint does not have to be legally binding. Even a gentlemen's agreement will suffice in certain cases. There is some debate as to whether the parties should be only competitive entrepreneurs, or include entrepreneurs without competitive relations too. In this regard, whether the Law prohibits 'vertical' agreements as well as 'horizontal' agreements became an issue when newspaper companies and newsagents made a tacit agreement regarding the territory of each agent. The appellate court ruled that restraint in the sense of Article 2, paragraph 6 should be mutual, not unilateral, and its content should be the same for all parties. Thus, the court rejected the application of the Anti-Monopoly Law to an agreement of mutual restraint between newspaper companies and newsagents.[15]

It is understood that the agreement does not have to be explicit. In practice, it is often difficult to prove the existence of a mutual agreement among entrepreneurs. A coincidence of action is insufficient; a certain correspondence of will is needed.[16] There have been cases of bid-rigging where the existence of a collusion was at issue. In one case, members of a plywood manufacturers' association were invited for tenders by a government agency. Representatives of the companies discussed the bidding price in advance, and the bids coincided. The Fair Trade Commission ruled that the coincidence of the bidding price was not sufficient to prove concerted action, but in this particular case, it acknowledged the existence of such an action, since each

---

14 Recommendatory Decision of the Fair Trade Commission, 28 July, 1982 (*Shinketsushū* 29–51).
15 Judgment of Tokyo Appellate Court, 9 March, 1953 (*Kōsai-minshū* 6–9–435: Asahi Shinbun case).
16 Decision of the Fair Trade Commission, 30 August, 1949 (FTC *Shinketsushū* 1–62: Yuasa Mokuzai Kōgyō case).

company had predicted actions of the other companies and acted with an intention to match their actions.

In a similar case, oil companies made bids for a government purchase. The companies held several meetings of representatives, and 'had a chat' concerning the bidding price. As a result, the prices quoted by the companies showed uniformity. The Fair Trade Commission found this to be a mutual agreement in restraint of trade, and the appellate court upheld this decision.[17]

Some academics assert that if there is concerted action, and if such action is inconceivable without prearrangement, the existence of such an action itself serves as proof of mutual agreement. However, such a view remains a minority one.[18]

Another problem is related to the widely utilised instrument of administrative guidance. If a cartel has been formed in response to an administrative agency's guidance, does this legitimise the cartel which restrains trade? The Fair Trade Commission has long held the view that although entrepreneurs followed administrative guidance, this does not in itself make an illegal cartel legal.[19] This problem was at issue in the celebrated *oil cartel* cases.

In this case, oil companies which formed the Association of Oil Companies, had mutually restricted the refinement of crude oil. The Ministry of International Trade and Industry was responsible for formulating and implementing policies concerning the supply of oil products. Control was to be effected by restrictions on the supply of oil products and the Ministry implemented this policy by administrative guidance. The Association of Oil Companies decided on the total amount of crude oil to be refined and made corresponding allocations to member companies. The Fair Trade Commission found this cartel to be illegal, and prosecuted the company directors.

The appellate court ruled that the restriction on production was against the Anti-Monopoly Law, but acquitted the defendants on the ground that they had not realised that the act was illegal and had a reasonable ground in believing so. The court, however, referred (obiter) to the relationship between administrative guidance and a cartel, and suggested that if the restraints on production had been consequent on the guidance of the Ministry,

17 Judgment of Tokyo Appellate Court, 9 November, 1956 (*Gyōsaireishū* 7–11–2849: Nihon Sekiyu case).

18 For details of the discussion, see Matsushita, *supra* note 3, pp. 110–116.

19 Interpretations on the Relations between the Anti-Monopoly Law and Administrative Guidances, Fair Trade Commission, 16 March, 1981. Nakagawa, *supra* note 8, pp. 171–173.

the Association should not be held solely responsible. The court accepted that this kind of administrative guidance will almost invariably result in concerted actions by entrepreneurs, and therefore, impermissible.[20]

In this case, the Ministry of International Trade and Industry had set the maximum price for oil products by way of administrative guidance. Oil companies intended to exercise influence over the price and decided to notify the Ministry of the desirable maximum price. In addition, they mutually agreed that once the maximum price was set, they should raise the price to the maximum.

On appeal, the Supreme Court denied that this cartel was based on administrative guidance and found it to be against the Law. However, the court stated in *obiter dicta* that administrative guidance which does not have an explicit legal basis can be justified, if it is made in a reasonable and socially acceptable way and does not contradict the fundamental purpose of the Anti-Monopoly Law. A cartel on price which, seemingly contravenes Anti-Monopoly Law, should not be considered illegal, if it is formed as a consequence of administrative guidance.[1]

Academic opinion varies on this issue. The majority finds such cartels illegal, even though they were formed as a consequence of administrative guidance. After all, administrative guidance is an act of an administrative agency which does not have the power to give an authoritative interpretation of the Law. If such cartels were to be legitimised only because they had been based upon administrative guidance, it means that administrative agencies are free to create exceptions to the Anti-Monopoly Law.

On the other hand, some lawyers support the position of the Supreme Court. One leading specialist in this field is of the opinion that while the existence of administrative guidance does not in itself justify a cartel, there are cases where restraints on competition by such a cartel do not contradict the ultimate goal of the Anti-Monopoly Law. In such cases, a cartel is not against the public interest as provided by Article 2, paragraph 6, and thus is not illegal. The existence and content of administrative guidance should be taken into account when judging whether or not the cartel is against the public interest.[2]

The Law also regulates the activities of trade associations.

---

20 Judgment of Tokyo Appellate Court, 26 September, 1980 (*Kōsaikeishū* 33–5–511: Oil Cartel case).

1 Judgment of the Supreme Court, 24 February, 1984 (*Keishū* 38–4–1287: Oil Cartel case).

2 M. Matsushita *supra* note 3, pp. 122–124.

Trade associations are prohibited from: 1) substantially restraining competition in a specific area of trade; 2) entering into international agreements or contracts which involve unreasonable restraint on trade or unfair trade practices; 3) limiting the present or future number of entrepreneurs in a particular field of business; 4) unreasonably restricting the functions or activities of member entrepreneurs; and 5) forcing entrepreneurs to employ unfair trade practices (Art. 8, para. 1). Whether or not the association is a juridical person does not matter.

When a manufacturers' cooperative for school uniforms decided to raise its prices by 20%, it encouraged its members to follow. The Fair Trade Commission found the resulting increase in price to be against this provision.[3] In another case, a grocers' cooperative made it a rule that members should not sell goods to retail traders who were not members and it instructed its members who violated this rule to cease such activity. The Fair Trade Commission ordered the cooperative to repeal the rule.[4]

Controlling a concerted increase of price by entrepreneurs is not easy, since it is difficult to prove the existence of an agreement. The Fair Trade Commission had planned to introduce a requirement to disclose production costs when raising prices, but this proposal met with objections from companies, and instead, the amendment of 1977 introduced the compulsory reporting of simultaneous price increases in goods or services by those entrepreneurs who have a large share in a particular market. If more than two entrepreneurs, including the one with the largest share in the market, increase prices by the same or similar amount within three months, the Fair Trade Commission may ask these entrepreneurs to file a report explaining the reasons for such price increases (Art. 18–2, para. 1).[5]

Another novelty concerning the prohibition of cartels is the system of surcharge, which was introduced in the same year. This is designed to deprive the entrepreneur of any excess profit he may have obtained from operating a cartel. When an entrepreneur exercises unreasonable restraint on trade in relation to prices, the Fair Trade Commission may impose surcharges (Art. 7–2).

Initially, the maximum amount of surcharge was calculated on the basis on one half of 4% of the sale during the period of the

---

3 Recommendatory Decision of the Fair Trade Commission, 29 June, 1973 (FTC *Shinketsushū* 20–41: Hifuku Kumiai case).
4 Recommendatory Decision of the Fair Trade Commission, 13 January, 1966 (FTC *Shinketsushū* 13–99: Seikashō Kyōdōkumiai case).
5 S. Imamura, *Dokusen-Kinshi-hō*, revised edition, Tokyo, pp. 357–366.

operation of the cartel for manufacturers, 2% for retailers and 1% for wholesalers (Art. 7–2, para. 1). This amount was raised to a full 6%, 2% and 1% respectively in 1991.

4.   Unfair trade practices

The Anti-Monopoly Law prohibits unfair trade practices (Art. 19, Art. 2, para. 9). The 1982 Guideline designates 16 types of acts which are likely to inhibit fair competition as unfair trade practices.

The prohibition on unfair trade practice is intended to prevent the emergence of private monopolies by regulating acts which may lead to such monopolies. This covers not only unfair methods of competition, but also deceptive practices. It should be added that these provisions concerning unfair trade practices are closely related to consumer protection legislation. In this regard, the Law against Unjust Premiums Advertisement and Labelling, the Law against Unjust Competition and some other laws also play a significant role.[6] Furthermore, restrictions on unfair trade practice contribute to the protection of entrepreneurs in economically weak positions. This especially applies to the prohibition of abuse of a dominant bargaining position. The Law on the Prevention of Delay in Payment for Subcontracted Works is also intended to serve a similar purpose.[7]

The constitutionality of the delegation of legislative power to the Fair Trade Commission was once challenged in the Commission's proceedings. It was argued that such a blanket delegation of legislative power undermined the supremacy of the Diet, but the Commission rejected this argument by pointing out that the Law sufficiently specifies the scope of delegation, and besides, restriction of unfair trade practice must be flexible enough to cope with complicated and changing economic phenomena which are impossible to regulate by means of primary legislation only.[8]

The first category of acts which constitute unfair trade practices covers, among other things, the joint refusal of companies to deal with a third company, discriminatory pricing, and discrimination in terms of trade. A common example of a joint refusal is a boycott. In one case, a refusal by wholesale traders which caused

6 Law No. 134, 1982, Law No. 14, 1934
7 Law No. 120, 1956.
8 Decision of the Fair Trade Commission, 11 October, 1968 (FTC *Shinketsushū* 15–84: Morinaga Shōji case).

difficulties to a retail trader (grocer) in finding alternative supplies was ruled to be an unjust refusal.[9]

Discriminatory pricing means unjustly supplying or purchasing commodities or services at prices that discriminate between regions or parties. In one case, a manufacturer of floorboards encouraged some builders to join a cooperative in order to maintain the retail price of floorboards. The builders who did not join the cooperative were forced to buy the boards at a higher price. This was found to be discriminatory by the Fair Trade Commission.[10]

The second category of unfair trade practices is unjust pricing. Naturally, selling at a reduced price is not in itself against fair competition, but if the price is unreasonably reduced in order to eliminate competitors, it is against the Law. In practice, however, it is often difficult to demarcate the boundary between reasonable and unreasonable reductions in price. The Fair Trade Commission's defines sales at an unreasonably low retail prices as a continuous supply of goods or services at a price which is excessively below the cost incurred, or other kinds of supply of goods and services at an unreasonably low price, which are likely to cause difficulties to a competitor's business (para. 6).

In one case, a newspaper company sold papers at 500 yen (2 pounds) for a month's subscription in certain areas in order to attract new readers. Although the price was nominally the same as cost, the Fair Trade Commission ruled that this cost was inconceivable without a subsidy from the parent company. The Tokyo Appellate Court ruled that the price should not only be below market price, but should also be lower than cost, if it is to be considered an unreasonably low price. The court acknowledged that 500 yen was unfair, and ordered the newspaper company not to sell the paper at a price lower than 812 yen.[11]

The third category of unfair trade practice is deceptive soliciting and soliciting by unreasonable benefits. In one case, the Fair Trade Commission recommended that a company retract an offer for a color television set to those who purchased air conditioners from a certain retailer.[12] The Law prohibits sales by

---

9 Decision of the Fair Trade Commission, 24 December, 1965 (FIC *Shinketsushū*, 13–87).

10 Recommandatory Decision of the Fair Trade Commission, 7 February, 1980 (FTC *Shinketsushū* 26–85: Tōyō Linoleum case).

11 Decision of Tokyo Appellate Court, 30 April, 1975 (*Kōsai-minshū* 28–2–174: Chūbū Yomiuri Shinbun case); Consentient Decision of the Fair Trade Commission, 24 November, 1977 (FTC *Shinketsushū* 24–50).

12 Recommandatory Decision of the Fair Trade Commission, 6 February, 1968 (FTC *Shinketsushū* 14–99: Tsunashima Shōten case).

deceptive advertisement or labelling, as well as sales by excessive benefits. The above-mentioned Law against Unjust Premiums, Advertisement, and Labelling is also applicable here. The Fair Trade Commission is empowered by this Law to set the maximum of benefits which can be offered, and also to designate an acceptable form of advertising (Art. 2).

In addition to the above-mentioned unfair trade practices, the Anti-Monopoly Law prohibits 'tie in' sales, dealing on exclusive terms, and the imposition of conditions regarding the retail price. In 'tie in' sales, the seller makes it a condition of sale that the buyer purchase other goods sold by the seller. Dealing on exclusive terms means making it a condition not to deal with competitors. Thus, acts of imposing conditions on dealing with others which unjustly restrict any of their transactions with a third party are regarded as unfair trade practices.

Suppliers of goods often make it a condition of sale that the buyer (retail traders) observe the sales price when reselling the goods. In principle, prices should be determined by the market and such control of resale prices is considered to be unfair trade practice. The Law provides for some exceptions, but they do not apply when such control of retail prices results in unreasonable infringement of the interests of consumers (Art. 24–2). Furthermore, impediment of a competitor's business and interference with the internal affairs of a competing company is considered to be an unfair trade practice.

One of the features of Japanese Anti-Monopoly law lies in the emphasis placed on the abuse of a dominant bargaining position (Art. 2, para. 9, item 5). It is unlawful, *inter alia*, to force the other party, who is in a continuous trade relationship, to purchase related goods or services, or to offer money, services, or other economic benefits, to impose on the other party disadvantageous terms of trade or to change those terms to the disadvantage of the other party. These acts have to be unjust in the light of the normal trade practice and have to be committed by abusing a dominant bargaining power. In one case, a major department store was found to have abused its dominant position against its suppliers. Suppliers had been competing for a place in this prestigious store. The department store virtually forced the suppliers to purchase goods and services from the store and made them pay the cost of refurbishment.[13]

Several cases involve banks because they tend to hold a

13 Consentient Decision of the Fair Trade Commission, 17 June, 1982 (FTC *Shinketsushū* 29–31: Mitsukoshi case).

position superior to other companies. In one case, a bank made it a condition of a loan that the managing director and executive directors be selected on its instruction. This was found to be an unjust use of its dominant position.[14] Another example involved a bank's request for a company, which sought a loan, to borrow more money than it needed. The excess amount was to be deposited at the bank, enabling the bank to gain an unfair interest on the loan. This was also found to be an unfair trade practice.[15]

The strengthening of control over unfair trade practices has gained momentum recently in the U.S.–Japan Structural Impediments Initiatives Talk, since this was thought to be vital to make the entry of foreign companies into the Japanese market easier. Among other issues, the practice of company *keiretsu* was blamed as exclusive and unfair. *Keiretsu* designates companies which are linked together by continuous business relations. The term is still not preceisely defined, but it is generally acknowledged that there are three types of *keiretsu*; suppliers *keiretsu*, distribution *keiretsu*, and company groups.[16]

A typical example of suppliers' *keiretsu* can be found in the car and home appliances industry, in which major manufacturers have a network of suppliers of parts and components. In order to maintain the quality and the timing of the supply, a majority of these suppliers exclusively service a single manufacturer. These suppliers are mostly medium and small sized companies, and are usually not subsidiaries of the manufacturers. The manufacturer often holds a minority share of these suppliers and sends in directors.

This arrangement has an advantage, since in this way, manufacturers can maintain a constant supply of parts and components of a high quality tailor-made to their needs. In addition, Japanese companies have adopted the 'just in time' delivery system in order to minimise the stock of parts and components. *Keiretsu* is the most suitable way to meet the requirements for this system. On the other hand, it was argued that this whole network of suppliers has worked against the entry of foreign suppliers. Also the relationship between these

---

14 Recommendatory Decision of the Fair Trade Commission, 6 November, 1953 (FTC *Shinketsushū* 5–61:Nihon Kōgyō Ginkō case).
15 The Judgment of the Supreme Court, 20 June, 1977 (*Minshu* 31-4-449: Gifu Shinyōkumiai case). See also K. Sanekata, *Dokusen Kinshi Hō* (*Anti-Monopoly Law*), revised edition, Tokyo 1992, pp. 345–347.
16 T. Taikgawa, '*Keiretsu heno Dokkinn-hō niyoru Kisei* (Regulation of *Keiretsu* by the Anti-Monopoly Law)', *New Business Law*, No. 487, 1991, pp. 6–9.

powerful manufacturers and suppliers can be a problem under the Anti-Monopoly Law, since there might be abuses of dominant bargaining position by manufacturers.

As regards distribution *keiretsu*, again, the car industry and home appliances industry serve as examples. Manufacturers have developed a network of sales companies and dealers in order to maximise the sale of their products. These sales companies and dealers used to sign an exclusive agreement with the manufacturer not to deal with other manufacturers' products. Therefore, if foreign manufacturers come into the Japanese market, they were unable to use the exisiting sales network, and had to develop his own from the scratch. This was considered to be unfair. Since their early 1980s, such exclusive arrangements are treated as against the Anti-Monopoly Law by the Fair Trade Commission. However, there still is a practice of prior consultation if a sales company or a dealer intends to deal in another manufacturer's product. On the other hand, it is reported that some car dealers have started to deal with other manufacturers' cars.

As is the case with suppliers' *keiretsu*, this system, despite some criticisms, has some advantages. It contributes to keep the sales price at a certain level and to ensure proper service to the consumers. However, it is problematic not only from the view point of foreign companies, but from the view point of Japanese consumers. For example, in the home appliances market, large discount shops have mushroomed. Some manufacturers reacted by putting pressure on the wholesale traders not to supply products to these discount shops. Employees of the manufacturer constantly monitor sales prices and when they find a large discount in prices, they may trace the supply route and block it.

The third type of *keiretsu* is company groups. There are six major company groups, some of which originated from the pre-War *zaibatsu*. Group companies usually include banks and a trading house in addition to various companies involved in different areas of industry. They are, to a certain extent, linked by mutual shareholding and cross directorship. These company groups have been criticised at the Structural Impediments Initiatives Talks for being involved in exclusive practices. In fact, a recent survey demonstrates that these company groups is not as exclusive as they seem. The percentage of shares of a group company held within the group is around 20%. These companies mutually hold shares, but most of the stable shareholders are from outside the group. A majority of trade is conducted with companies outside the group.

The Fair Trade Commission addressed this problem of *keiretsu* in the 1991 Guideline on Distribution Systems and Business

Practices. The Guideline takes the position that *keiretsu* per se is not against competition. It has some economic rationale, for instance, in pursuit of efficiency and quality. If a continuous trade relationship has been formed on the free choice of the company based upon commercial consideration such as price, quality, service etc., such relationship is not against the Anti-Monopoly Law. However, there are some *keiretsu* practices which impede fair competition. The Guideline is intended to strengthen the enforcement of the Law in such areas.

There are some acts which are, in principle, against the Law. These are cutomer allocation, boycotts and retail price maintenance. The permissibility of other acts is decided on a case-by-case basis, taking into account their effect on competition. The Guideline deals with three main areas; suppliers' *keiretsu*, distribution *keiretsu* and sole distributorship. Various issues including restrictions on trading partners in dealing with competitors, unjust reciprocal dealings, exclusionary conduct by means of holding shares of trading partners, restrictions on distributors' handling of competing products, interference in distributors' management, and unreasonable obstruction of parallel imports are covered.

5.   Regulations on international agreements

The Law prohibits entrepreneurs from entering into an international agreement or contract which constitutes an unreasonable restraint on trade or unfair trade practice (Art. 6, para. 1). The Fair Trade Commission is empowered to order entrepreneurs to rescind such agreements or contracts. Entrepreneurs who have entered into an international agreement or contract are required to file a report with the Fair Trade Commission and submit a copy of such an agreement or contract within 30 days of its conclusion (Art. 6, para. 2). Since this requirement was considered to be a burden by foreign companies, the Fair Trade Commission has narrowed the scope of agreements which are to be notified. The latest change of the rule took place in 1992.

In 1972, an agreement between Japanese and German companies producing rayon was found to be against the Law. In this case, three major Japanese producers of rayon (who controlled the majority share of the domestic market) reached an agreement with German (West) companies not to export goods to the others' 'traditional markets,' and mutually limited the amount of exports to their 'common markets' such as the United

States. They also agreed to set the minimum sales prices for each country within their 'common market.' The Fair Trade Commission found that this agreement substantially restricted competition in export of rayon. However, it refrained from deciding upon the legality of this international cartel itself and instead found that the three Japanese companies mutually restricted competition in a substantial way and ordered rescission of the agreement.[17] Incidentally, in this case, the Japanese Fair Trade Commission acted in coordination with the German Federal Cartel Office. West German companies involved in this agreement were fined by the Cartel Office.

This provision of the Anti-Monopoly Law does not mean that the law can be applied in an extra-territorial way. Japanese law acknowledges extra-territorial application only when there is an explicit provision. However, if an international agreement or contract involving unfair restraint on trade or unjust trade practices which was concluded abroad has an effect in Japan, the Japanese Anti-Monopoly Law can be applied to such acts.[18]

The number of formal decisions taken by the Fair Trade Commission concerning international agreements and contracts is small, but the Commission relies more on administrative guidance without resorting to formal procedures. In this way, the Commission has been fairly active in controlling international agreements and contracts.[19]

6.   Exemptions

The Anti-Monopoly Law provides for exemptions concerning certain acts. In addition, there are 15 individual laws which provide for exemptions of cartels for various reasons. At present, six of them are operational.

The Anti-Monopoly Law provides for seven categories of exemptions: 1) railway companies, electricity and gas companies and other companies, which by virtue of the nature of their business, constitute monopolies; 2) legitimate acts based on specific laws and orders, such as the Law on Local Railways and the Law on Hygiene of Foods; 3) exercise of rights as provided by laws concerning intellectual property; 4) acts of certain kinds

---

17 Recommendatory Decision of the Fair Trade Commission, 27 December, 1972 (FTC *Shinketsushū* 19–124: The case of Asahi Kasei Kōgyō and others).
18 Matsushita, *supra* note 3, pp. 179–180.
19 *Ibid.*, p. 188.

of cooperatives, such as consumers' cooperatives; 5) maintenance of retail prices for certain categories of goods; 6) depression cartels; and 7) rationalisation cartels (Arts. 21, 22, 23, 24, 24–2, 24–3, 24–4).

A depression cartel is formed with the authorisation of the Fair Trade Commission, when the prices of goods fall below the average costs of production and a majority of producers are likely to discontinue business. This kind of cartel may be formed in order to limit production output, the volume of sale, and production facilities. A rationalisation cartel is designed to enhance rationalisation of enterprises by taking concerted action, for example, to reduce costs and increase efficiency.

Some of these exemptions do not contradict the fundamental aims of the Anti-Monopoly Law, while others are regarded as a 'retreat' from the Anti-Monopoly Law in the interest of different policy goals.[20]

The narrowing down of these exemptions has been at issue in the Structural Impediments Initiatives Talks. The Fair Trade Commission is reviewing these exemptions. Some of these exemptions are considered to have outlived their significance. Exemptions in retail price maintenance may also be narrowed.

7. Procedures

The Anti-Monopoly Law provides for administrative measures, such as cease and desist orders, orders to eliminate violations and take corrective measures and orders to pay surcharges. Criminal sanctions are also available. Those who incurred loss from the violation of the Anti-Monopoly Law by entrepreneurs may sue for damages.

The Fair Trade Commission is empowered to order entrepreneurs to cease violations of the Law and to take necessary measures to eliminate such violations (Art. 7). Such measures range from partial transfers of business operations, transfers of shares, termination of merger plans, deletion of certain clauses from contracts, rescission of agreements, to dissolution of cartels. The Commission must follow a formal quasi-judicial procedure in issuing such orders. In cases of urgency, the Commission may apply to the Tokyo Appellate Court for an interlocutory injunction (Art. 67).

Any person who considers that there has been a violation of the Law is entitled to report it to the Fair Trade Commission and

20 Imamura, *supra* note 11, pp. 194–209.

request that appropriate actions be taken. The Commission is required to conduct an investigation on receipt of such a report. It is also empowered to start investigation *ex officio*. In the course of investigation, the Commission may require witnesses or persons involved to appear for questioning, experts to appear and give evidence, and the submission of accounts and other documents. The Commission may enter any place of business or other premises in order to investigate business activities and the financial status of those involved, and inspect the accounting records (Art. 46, paras. 1 and 2).

If a violation is found as a result of an investigation, the Commission either recommends entrepreneur(s) to take appropriate measures, or initiates formal proceedings. Of the two procedures, the Commission seems to prefer the former. If the person accepts the recommendation, the Commission may render a recommendatory decision without taking formal proceedings (Art. 48). Even when the illegal act has ceased, the Commission may still recommend that certain action be taken.

If there is a violation of the Law and the Commission considers that it is in the public interest to have the case dealt with via formal proceedings, it renders a decision to start formal hearings (Art. 49, para. 1).

Hearings can be conducted either by the Fair Trade Commission or by a Hearings Commissioner (administrative law judge). Most cases are handled by Hearings Commissioners. The hearing is conducted on an adversarial system. An official of the Commission is entrusted with the task of pursuing the charge brought against the respondent. The respondent has a right to be represented by an attorney (Art. 52).

The Hearings Commissioner *does not* have the power to render a final decision. When the hearing is completed, he drafts a decision, and sends it to the Commission and the respondent. The respondent may file an objection to the draft. The Commission will take this into consideration in rendering a formal decision (Art. 54).

After the Commission has decided to initiate formal proceedings, if the respondent accepts the validity of the facts and the application of law as indicated in the decision to open the hearing and offers to accept it without a formal hearing, the Commission may render a consentient decision. The respondent in such cases is required to submit a plan of action which describes the steps he will take in order to remedy the breach of the Law (Art. 53–3).

Decisions of the Fair Trade Commission are subject to judicial review. The Tokyo Appellate Court has exclusive jurisdiction over such cases. Those who have had their legal interests infringed by a decision have standing to bring the case to Court.

In one case, a Japanese company concluded an international agreement which was against Article 6, paragraph 1 of the Law. The Fair Trade Commission recommended that the company rescind the agreement, and the company accepted it. The foreign party to the agreement brought the case to court. The Tokyo Appellate Court denied standing to the foreign party, and the Supreme Court upheld this decision, basing its judgment on the ground that the decision of the Commission was not binding on the foreign party, which was a third party to the proceedings, and thus its legal interests had not been damaged.[1]

When the Court reviews a decision of the Fair Trade Commission, if it finds that the facts as determined by the Commission are based on substantial evidence, then it is bound by these facts (Art. 80, para. 1). The Court merely reviews the case on points of law.

The Law also provides that an entrepreneur who has created a private monopoly, unreasonably restrained trade, or resorted to unfair trade practices is liable for damages. For instance, where consumers have purchased goods or services at a high price maintained by a cartel, they are entitled to claim damages.[2] The entrepreneur cannot be exempted from liability by claiming the absence of intention or negligence (Art. 25). This is considered to be a special arrangement to tort law, which is based on fault. Claims on the basis of Article 25 can only be made after a decision has been rendered by the Fair Trade Commission as to the legality of the entrepreneurs' actions and has taken effect. The Tokyo Appellate Court has an exclusive jurisdiction over such claims for damages too.

Unlike in the United States, where a body of case law developed out of litigations brought by citizens, in Japan, suit for damages has been rare. There are various reasons for this. First, such claims require a formal decision of the Commission confirming the violation of the Anti-Monopoly Law. However, since the Commission relies more on informal measures, a formal decision is not necessarily available. Second, there is always a difficulty in proving the causation between the violation of the Anti-Monopoly Law and the loss. The scope of loss is often

---

1 The Judgment of the Supreme Court, 28 November, 1975 (*Minshū* 29–10–1592: Amano Seiyaku and Novo Industry case).
2 Judgment of the Tokyo Appellate Court, 19 September, 1977 (*Kōsai-minshū* 30–3–247: Matsushita Denki Sangyō case).

difficult to prove too. Third, material and information concerning the violation are usually not in the hands of the plaintiff.

There was a case where a group of consumers filed suit for damages for the loss incurred by a cartel of oil companies during the oil crisis. The plaintiffs based the litigation on general tort law, instead of Article 25 of the Anti-Monopoly Law. While the lower courts upheld the claim, the Supreme Court reversed the judgement on the ground that there was insufficient proof of the causal links between the cartel and the increase in prices.[3] There was a public outcry against this judgment, and the Fair Trade Commission started reviewing the system in order to make litigation eaasier. This issue was also raised in the Structural Impediments Initiatives Talks.

The Anti-Monopoly Law also provides for criminal sanctions. A maximum of three years' imprisonment or a fine of five million yen (approximately twenty thousand pounds sterling) can be imposed by the court for various violations of the Law. If representatives or employees of a company violates the Anti-Monopoly Law, the company itself may be fined (Art. 95). If a representative of a company failed to take preventive measures while knowing that a violation of Anti-Monopoly Law was being planned, or to take corrective measures after he has found that such a violation had taken place, this representative may also be fined (Art. 95–2). Only the Fair Trade Commission has the power to initiate criminal proceedings at the Tokyo Appellate Court via the High Prosecutors Office of Tokyo (Art. 96). In 1992, the maximum amount of fines was raised to 100 million yen (approximately forty thousand pounds sterling).

There was a proposal by the United States to introduce punitive damages, but this was turned down as being alien to the Japanese criminal and civil law system.

---

3 Judgment of the Supreme Court, 8 December, 1989 (*Minshū* 43–11–1259, Tsuruoka Tōyu case).

17 Civil procedure

1. Civil cases in Japan

The first Code of Civil Procedure was promulgated in 1890 during the first codification period of Japanese Law. Initially, the government intended to model the Code on French Law. A draft was prepared on the basis of the French Code of 1806. Another draft was worked out by the French adviser Boissonade. The government, however, changed its policy in the early 1880s when it learned of the new German Code which had been enacted in 1877. As this was the most recent code of civil procedure, it was considered to be a better model for the Japanese Code. A Prussian adviser was invited from Germany to produce a draft.[1] The Code was adopted in 1890, and remains in force today, although it has undergone major reforms on two occasions.

Soon after its promulgation, the Code was criticised for its rigid and cumbersome procedure. After all, the Code was a close imitation of the German Code and so had developed in a different environment. Thus, it was not necessarily suited to Japanese conditions in its original form. Therefore, the Code was amended substantially in 1926. The Code of Civil Procedure of Austria, adopted in 1895, served as the model. This latter Code stressed the interests of Society as opposed to the interests of the parties, and strengthened the role of the judge at the expense of the parties.

Thus, until 1945, the influence of the Continental legal system was dominant in the development of the Japanese Civil Procedure system.

Another major reform of the civil procedure took place after the Second World War. Some elements of American procedure were introduced during the period of occupation by the Allied Forces. Whereas the previous system relied heavily on the initiative of the judge rather than that of the parties, this second

1 S. Takayanagi, *Nihon-Hōsei-shi* (History of Japanese Law), vol.2, Tokyo 1965, pp. 190–192.

reform introduced the adversarial system. For instance, cross-examination of witnesses, in principle, replaced the interrogation of witnesses by the presiding judge. However, the predominantly German approach to civil procedure still remains.

The Constitution provides that no person shall be deprived of the right to have access to the courts (Art. 32). The Law on Courts further provides that the courts adjudicate all legal disputes except those matters specifically provided in the Constitution (Art. 3).

Civil cases in Japan can be roughly classified into four categories. The first comprises ordinary civil cases involving disputes between citizens. 114,402 such cases were newly accepted by the district courts, while 97,355 cases were accepted by the summary courts.[2] These include, *inter alia*, claims for repayment of debts, claims for eviction from buildings or land, claims for damages, claims concerning family matters, and claims for transfer of movables. The Code of Civil Procedure as well as the Rules of Civil Procedure are applied in these cases. The Rules are enacted by the Supreme Court, which is vested with rule-making powers by the Constitution.

The second category comprises special proceedings for claims for payment of bills and cheques. Such proceedings were introduced by the 1965 amendment of the Code of Civil Procedure (Art. 444 ff.). As a rule, documentary evidence only is permitted in order to ensure the speedy resolution of the dispute. The plaintiff may demand during the hearing that the formal proceedings be initiated, without the consent of the other defendant. Although an appeal is not allowed against the judgment, the losing party may lodge an objection within two weeks. Then the case will be dealt with by formal proceedings. There were approximately 9,000 such cases in 1991.

The third category involves family affairs. Typical cases include divorce proceedings and claims for recognition of paternity. The family court mainly deals with such cases. In divorce cases, if the parties fail to reach agreement in conciliation proceedings before the family court, then the case is transferred to the district court.

The fourth category is administrative cases. These cases include claims for revocation of administrative decisions. Before the end of the Second World War, there was a special administrative court to deal with these kinds of cases. However, the jurisdiction of the court was limited, and furthermore, the administrative court was part of the Executive branch. After the

---

2 The Supreme Court, *Shihō-tōkei-nenpō (Annual Report of Judicial Statistics) 1990*, Tokyo 1991, p. 3.

War, administrative courts were abolished, and now their jurisdiction is given to the ordinary courts. The current legislation which forms the basis of the procedure is the Law on Administrative Litigation, which was enacted in 1962. The Code of Civil Procedure supplements this legislation. There are approximately 800–900 administrative cases annually.

In recent years, the emergence of a new, 'modern type of litigation' has become noticeable. Typical examples include medical malpractice cases, product liability, environmental protection and pollution cases. These cases primarily involve claims for damages and injunction, and therefore, fall within the category of oridinary civil cases or administrative cases, if the other party is the state. However, they have some characteristics which are not found in the 'traditional types of litigation'. Firstly, these cases are a response to new phenomena which the legislature had not expected. There is no precedent and therefore, the courts are expected to create law or influence the policy-makers by their judgments. Secondly, there can be a number of litigants involved in such cases. In some cases, there may be only a few litigants, but the judgment may affect a number of people, for example, in claims of citizens for damages inflicted by cartels. Thirdly, unlike a majority of traditional litigation, there is an inequality in the bargaining power of the parties. For instance, in product liability cases, there is an obvious inequality in the knowledge and expertise as well as information which the manufacturer and the plaintiff have.

It is acknowledged that the present system of civil procedure is not necessarily capable of coping with these new types of litigation. The reform of the Civil Procedural Code is now being discussed by the Legislative Advisory Commission. Issues relevant to these new types of litigation are addressed in the discussions.[3]

2. Basic rules of Civil Procedure

The jurisdiction of the court is detailed by the Code of Civil Procedure. All people within the territory of Japan fall within the jurisdiction of Japanese courts. As a rule, territorial jurisdiction of the court is defined by the place of the defendant's *general forum*. In the case of natural persons, the general forum is his or her domicile. If the domicile is not in Japan, or is unknown, his

3 '*Minjisosho Tetsuzuki ni kansuru Kento Jiko* (Issues to be Considered in Civil Procedure)', *Jurist*, No. 996, 1992, pp. 61–79.

place of residence is the forum. If the place of residence is not in Japan, or is unknown, his last place of residence in Japan is the forum (Art. 2). As for juridical persons, the forum is where its principal office or place of business is located. If there is no such office or place of business, the domicile of the principal person who runs the business serves as the forum.

In addition to the general forum, there are *special fora*, which are listed in Articles 5 to 21 of the Code. These include, *inter alia*, the place where an obligation is to be performed, the place where a tortious act has taken place, the place where the real property at issue is located and the place where a ship is registered. Furthermore, the parties may agree to a specific choice of forum (Art. 25). If the defendant responded to a suit without objection, he is regarded to have accepted the jurisdiction (Art. 26).

Both natural and juridical persons can be parties to litigation (have capacity to sue and be sued). In addition, associations and foundations without juridical personality are given capacity, provided that there is a representative or an administrator (Art. 46). The Law does not specify the scope of organisations without juridical personality which can be parties to litigation. The Supreme Court has acknowledged the capacity to become parties of an organisation which was established to enhance the welfare of repatriated citizens, and also of an organisation of inhabitants of a specific area.[4] These associations or foundations are required to have an organisational body, decide issues by a majority vote, to be independent of each member, have a representative and have established rules concerning the administration of any property.

Foreign citizens and juridical persons have capacity to be a party to litigation.

Those who have capacity to sue and be sued do not necessarily have procedural capacity, i.e. capacity to act as a party in the proceedings. For instance, minors and people without civil law capacity are not entitled to act on their own in the proceedings; they have to be represented either by a legal representative or by an attorney whom they have appointed.

Standing in a particular case is granted on a case by case basis. Consideration is made from the viewpoint of who are the appropriate parties to solve the given dispute most effectively and properly. Standing to sue is generally acknowledged for those who have a right under the substantive law and are suing in order

4 Judgments of the Supreme Court, 15 October, 1964 (*Minshū* 18–8–1671), 19 October, 1967 (*Minshū* 21–8–2078).

to settle a dispute concerning this right. In some cases, standing to sue is accorded to persons other than the holder of the disputed right. Thus, an executor of a will can sue and be sued. This is also the case with shareholders' litigation (derivative action), in which a shareholder is entitled to sue on behalf of the company.

With the increasing activities of consumers' organisations and other citizens' groups in other fields such as the protection of the environment, the problem concerning the status of such organisations or groups as regards civil procedure has become a current issue. Since these organisations or groups often lack even the requirements to be accorded capacity under Article 46 as associations without juridical personality, it is likely that the court will not acknowledge them as parties to litigation. In such cases, if the group or organisation is to proceed, all members may have to become plaintiffs of a joint litigation.

There was a case where several persons sought an injunction against an electricity company in respect of a power plant. They also sought to reinstate the seaside area affected by the plant to its condition prior to the building of the plant. They claimed that they represented the area in order to preserve the environment. The Supreme Court ruled that such an action is not possible without specific commission from the inhabitants of the area.[5]

The present law enables members of a group or organisation to avoid the inconvenience of jointly having to be parties to the action. This is the system of representative action, which came from England. In representative litigation, a person or persons selected by the parties acts as the party in litigation on behalf of all parties. The Code provides for three requirements; there should be multiple parties involved, they should share a common interest, and the parties entrusted to initiate and proceed with the litigation should be selected from among the parties (Art. 47). Common interest is understood to mean that the parties share the rights or obligations which are the subject of the litigation (cf. Art. 59). All parties have to be specified in the pleading: this is in contrast to class action.

The system of Class Action as provided by the U.S. Federal Rules of Civil Procedure, Section 23 (b) (3) does not have its counterpart in Japan. In the U.S. – Japan Structural Impediments Initiatives Talk which started in 1989, it was pointed out that arrangements for litigations initiated by a group of people were insufficient in Japan. For instance, in cases where citizens

5 Judgment of the Supreme Court, 20 December, 1985 (*Hanji*, 1181–71: Buzen Power Plant case).

incurred loss from violations of the Anti-Monopoly Law or Securities and Exchange Law by companies, it proved to be difficult for them to claim damages. In the view of the Americans, such flaws in the system have inhibited the proper implementation of these laws. Therefore, it was suggested that class action should be introduced.

In fact, a proposal had been made by some lawyers and academics to improve the system, and a draft law was published.[6] At present, introduction of class action, which is a uniquely American institution, seems to be unlikely. On the other hand, it is generally accepted that the current system for group litigation is inadequate. A new system in line with the German *Verbandsklage* is now being discussed.

In order to sue, the plaintiff must have a *legitimate interest* in having his rights protected by the court. This concept is explained in two ways; one school of thought asserts that in order to utilise the judicial system provided by the State, a legitimate interest on the part of the plaintiff is needed. Another school of thought approaches the problem from the viewpoint of whether there is a legitimate interest on the part of the plaintiff to settle the problem with the defendant by means of litigation.

Interest to sue becomes an issue in a variety of cases. For instance, when a plaintiff initiates, after May Day, litigation against the local government to rescind a decision not to permit public demonstrations on May Day, he does not have a legitimate interest to require rescission of the decision, although he may have an interest in claiming damages.

One of the most discussed issues in this respect is the confirmation by the court of a legal relationship that no longer subsists. A typical case is that of a parental relationship with a deceased person. In one case, a mother initiated court proceedings to have the parental relationship with her son, who had died in the War, established in law. The Supreme Court acknowledged that such a claim was possible, as it was a prerequisite of the plaintiff qualifying for a State benefit.[7] In such cases, the deceased is represented by the public prosecutor.

There are two kinds of representatives in proceedings: legal representatives and representatives commissioned by a party to the proceedings. The former mainly represents those who are without procedural capacity, such as minors and persons without civil law capacity. The latter can be further divided into two

---

6 A. Takeuchi et al, *Jurist*, No. 672, 1985, pp. 16–21.
7 Judgment of the Supreme Court, 15 July, 1970 (*Minshū* 24-7-861).

types: those who, by virtue of their appointed position, are entitled to be a party, and those who are commissioned by a party to represent that party in a specific case. The former includes business managers and a ship's Master. The latter are attorneys commissioned by the party. The latter category of representatives have to be qualified and registered as attorneys except in cases handled by the summary courts (Art. 79, para. 1).

In contrast to German law, Japanese law does not require parties to appoint attorneys. Parties are allowed to take part in the proceedings without an attorney. Actually, at the summary court level, and even at the district court level, litigation without an attorney is not uncommon. At the district court level, both parties were represented by an attorney in 50% of the cases in 1990.[8]

The concept of the object of litigation (*Prozessgegenstand*) was introduced from Germany before the Second World War and has played a significant role in the theory of Japanese civil procedure, although the term itself does not appear in the Code. Previously, the object of litigation was understood to be the the a claim of a right provided by substantive law. This theory was influenced by the German theory which was prevalent up to the 1930s.

In recent years, another school of thought concerning the object of litigation appeared. This school asserts that the object of litigation is not the right *per se*, which is provided by substantive law, but instead, is the contested legal interest supported by assertions concerning substantive rights. Thus, for instance, claims for compensation arising from medical malpractice can be based either on tort or contract law. If the classical theory is strictly applied, a claim based on tort and a claim based on contract are two different objects of litigation. In contrast, the new school asserts that the object of litigation is one in such cases.

The concept of the object of litigation is important when deciding the possibility of joinder of claims, the scope of *res judicata*, the limits on the alteration of the claim, and prohibition of double litigation. The new theory is primarily based on practical considerations as to how the scope of litigation should be demarcated in order to ensure the optimum settlement of dispute. If, for example, after losing a claim based on tort, the plaintiff is able to bring another claim in contract law in the same dispute, it will be burdensome not only to the court, but also to the defendant. Therefore, by acknowledging that the object of litigation is the same in both claims, the plaintiff is expected to

---

8 The Supreme Court, *supra* note 2, pp. 128.

pursue both tortious and contractual claims, and thus settle the dispute in one case.

Among academics, this new theory commands majority support. So far, the attitude of the court is not so clear-cut.

3.   Pre-trial procedure

The plaintiff is required to present a claim to the court with jurisdiction. In the complaint, in addition to the name of the plaintiff, the substance of the claim as well as its factual grounds should be specified.

Interlocutory measures which are designed to secure the enforceability of the prospective judgment are provided by the Law on Civil Interlocutory Measures.[9] There are two kinds of measures: provisional attachment and provisional disposition. Provisional attachment is used in order to preserve the property at issue which belongs to the debtor. Without such protection, the defendant could dispose of the property before the judgment is rendered and becomes enforceable. The plaintiff's claim has to be in monetary terms or convertible to money. Provisional attachment is possible when, without attachment, the enforcement of judgment is likely to be impossible, or extremely difficult.

There are two types of provisional disposition: provisional measures to preserve the object in dispute, and provisional measures to establish an interim legal relationship between the parties. The former is a remedy for creditors who have a claim against property other than money. When provisional attachment is possible, this remedy is not available. For instance, when a dispute concerns real property and there is a chance that the defendant will sell it to a third party before the case is settled, the plaintiff may apply for provisional disposition.

The latter type of provisional disposition is used in order to terminate imminent harm to the plaintiff. In this type of provisional disposition, the court temporarily acknowledges the plaintiff all or part of relief sought by the plaintiff, before final judgment is rendered. Thus, in libel cases, the plaintiff may seek provisional disposition to prevent the publication of a libellous statement. This disposition is also available when it is needed to prevent serious damages to a continuing legal relationship.

These provisional measures are frequently used by the parties. At the district court level, such measures are used in almost half

9 Law No. 91, 1989.

of the cases. It is pointed out that although the consequence of these provisional measures can be serious to the defendants, these measures are sometimes available too easily. There was a case where the constitutionality of a provisional measure to prevent the publication of a libellous article in a journal was disputed from the viewpoint of freedom of expression. The Supreme Court ruled that in principle, provisional measures to prevent publication should not be allowed in matters concerning public interest. However, in this particular case, considering the fact that the contents of the article were not true, that the article was not intended to promote the public interest, and that the victim was likely to suffer irreparable damage, the Court acknowledged the constitutionality of the measure.[10]

Even prior to the action, the parties may ask the court to examine evidence, i.e. take evidence from witnesses, experts or prospective parties. It may also order a party to produce documents or conduct on-the-spot inspection (Art. 343). This is designed to preserve evidence, which may otherwise be difficult or impossible to examine at trial. The party who applies for such orders has to justify their ground. A typical textbook example of such a measure is a case where a witness is seriously ill and is unlikely to be able to give evidence at trial.

In Japan, full discovery of evidence is not available, unlike the United States.[11] In recent years, existing provisions on the preservation of evidence have been utilized in order to achieve the same goal as discovery. In medical malpractice cases, the plaintiff often applies for the preservation of evidence in order to copy or photograph clinical records in the hands of the defendant. In one case, the plaintiff applied for the preservation of a clinical record on the grounds that since the patient was dead, the records might be lost and that the doctor might alter the records. These grounds were accepted by the court.[12] The opinion of lawyers is divided as to whether or not this system should be broadly used as a substitute for discovery or not.[13]

Parties are required to submit briefs in advance of the hearing. These should include the matters which the party intends to assert at the hearing. These matters are listed in the Code (Art. 244).

---

10 Judgment of the Supreme Court, 11 June, 1986 (*Minshu* 40–4–872 : Hoppō Journal case).
11 T. Hattori and D. Henderson, *Civil Procedure in Japan*, Looseleaf, New York 1985, pp. 6–4 – 6–6.
12 Decision of Tokyo District Court, 18 March, 1972 (*Kaminshū* 23–1/4–130).
13 H. Inoue, M. Itoh, and I. Sagami, *Korekarano Minjisoshōhō* (*Perspectives of the Law of Civil Procedure*), Tokyo 1984, pp. 153–162.

In complicated cases, a formal pre-trial hearing is sometimes conducted by the Court. Whether or not this hearing is conducted is left to the discretion of the Court. The purpose of this procedure is to sort out the contested issues and evidence in order to speed up the subsequent formal hearing. The hearing is conducted by one of the judges who will be on the bench of the formal hearing. Pre-trial hearings are usually held in camera.

At the pre-trial hearing, the parties submit their cases and present lists of evidence which they intend to produce at the hearing. Thus, at this stage, the issues which are contested and the evidence which is to be produced become clear. Since the judge is empowered to encourage the parties to reach a compromise at any stage, the parties may sometimes reach agreement at this stage.

As a rule, issues which were not raised in the pre-trial proceedings or evidence which was not produced there cannot be raised or produced in the formal hearing.

Pre-trial hearing is not widely utilised. This is due primarily to the difficulty in preparing materials and collecting sufficient evidence at such an early stage of the procedure. In less than 1% of cases, is this procedure utilised.

4.   Hearing procedure

The hearing is conducted in an open court, either by a single judge or by three judges. In the district courts, a case can be dealt with by a single judge, unless otherwise provided by law. In almost 95% of cases, the case is handled by a single judge.

Japanese judges often handle more than 100 cases simultaneously. They have to conduct hearings of several cases a day, and therefore, the time alloted to each case is limited. Thus, the hearings are not held consecutively. Because of this time delay, the memories of witnesses and even the judge can fade. As a result, the judge is forced to rely on written evidence instead of oral testimony and presentation of the parties.

Inspired by the American system, the holding of 'consecutive trials' was recommended some time ago. The Rules on Civil Procedure has a provision which states that the hearings should be held consecutively insofar as it is possible, and when this is not feasible, the interval between sittings should be kept to the minimum (Art. 27). However, in practice, there is still an average of one month's interval between each sitting of the court.

The shortage of personnel, including judges, and of court rooms is said to be the primary cause.

The judge (or a presiding judge) who is assigned to a particular case, examines the complaint. At this initial stage, the judge (or the presiding judge) examines the complaint from a technical point of view and checks whether it is properly formulated. Then a copy of the complaint is served on the defendant. At the same time, the defendant is informed of the date of the first hearing and asked to submit a written reply to the claim.

The hearing is conducted in open court under the direction of the judge. The Constitution provides that where the judges agree unanimously, they may decide not to open the trial to the public. However, in cases of political crimes, offences concerning press and publication and cases involving the fundamental rights of citizens, the Constitution requires that the trial be conducted in open court.

In some categories of civil and commercial cases, for example, in cases involving the liquidation of juridical persons, adjudication is conducted in a non-adversarial manner. In such cases, the hearing is held in camera, and the court must examine evidence *ex officio*. If a case which should be adjudicated by ordinary civil procedure is handled in such a manner, it is regarded as an infringement of the right to have access to the court and have a public hearing.

Parties are required to appear in person, or be represented by a counsel. They present their claims and counter-claims, and produce evidence.

The object of litigation is set by the party: thus, the scope of judicial inquiry is demarcated by the parties. It is the parties which produce the issues (*Streitstoff*) at dispute and contest them before the court. The court may not take into account a claim which has not been submitted by the parties (Art. 186). Furthermore, it may not decide on matters which are not disputed by the parties (Art. 257). The plaintiff is free to alter the claim until the termination of the hearing, insofar as the grounds for the claim remain unchanged. However, alterations which may result in excessive delays are not allowed (Art. 232, para. 1).

This adversary principle (*Verhandlungsmaxime*) is not un-limited. One such limitation is the power of the court to clarify issues. The court is entitled to ask questions of the parties concerning legal and factual matters (Art. 127, para. 1). The court may encourage the parties to produce evidence. The non-exercise of this power may serve as a ground for appeal. Thus, the court must exercise this power under certain circumstances.[14]

14 Judgment of the Supreme Court, 12 April, 1966 (*Minshū* 20-4-560).

There was a case where the claim of the plaintiff could not be fulfilled unless he changed the legal grounds for the claim. The Supreme Court ruled that in cases where, if the plaintiff had based the complaint on different grounds, his claim can be upheld and the dispute can be settled, and if there was some misunderstanding or carelessness on the part of the plaintiff in not doing so, the court may exercise its power to clarify the matter and encourage the plaintiff to reconsider the legal basis for his claim.[15]

The parties are free to dispose of the claim (*Dispositions-maxime*). Thus, the plaintiff may withdraw his claim. The parties may reach settlement or acknowledge the claim of the opposite party, either partly or completely. In such cases, the court is not allowed to make further inquiries. The court may encourage the parties to reach settlement at any stage of litigation (Art. 136, para. 1). In fact, more than one third of civil cases end within the court settlement.

At the hearing, the principle of oral hearing and the principle of directness are applied. As for the former, it should be noted that there is much reliance on written pleading and replies. Thus, at the hearing, the parties often refer to the written pleading and replies. When one party raises an issue not included in the pleading, the opposite party will usually ask the court to allow him time to prepare a written reply. The judge (or judges) will study the pleading and other documents in chambers rather than in the court room.

Concerning the latter principle, the judge who has handled the hearing and examined the evidence must render the judgment. A change in the composition of the Bench often occurs before the case is resolved. In such cases, the hearing has to start afresh, but usually, the parties agree to use the protocols made by the court without objection.

The presiding judge is more active in Japan than in the Courts of Anglo-American countries. Although their powers have been reduced after the Second World War, presiding judges still play a dominant role in the hearing. In addition to the above-mentioned power of inquiry, a judge may ask questions if he finds some contradiction or lack of clarity in the arguments advanced. In exercising this right, he may order the parties to submit documents and other items in their possession, conduct inspection and commission expert opinions. This is considered to be necessary so as to avoid any unfairness which may result from the failure of parties to argue their cases properly.

---

15 Judgment of the Supreme Court, 11 June, 1970 (*Minshū* 24–6–516).

The burden of proof has been a focus of discussion in recent years. The traditional view held is that the burden of proof becomes an issue when the judge fails to be convinced of the essential facts of the dispute. The degree of confidence which the judge should reach in order to render judgment is not always clear-cut. It is generally agreed that the judge should establish facts to the extent acceptable to ordinary people, but there were cases where 'epidemiological proof' was found to be sufficient (see Chapter 10).

In cases where the judge fails to be convinced, one of the parties has to bear unfavourable judgment. The onus of proof rests with this losing party.

The allocation of the burden of proof is based on the principle that the party bears the burden to prove essential facts which serve as grounds for the application of a legal norm favourable to him. Thus, the plaintiff has to prove essential facts for the application of the legal norms which are the basis of his asserted right, while the defendant has to prove essential facts which enable the application of norms which work against such norms. For instance, in a claim for repayment of money, the plaintiff has to prove the existence of the debt, while the defendant has to prove that for some reason, the debt does not exist, is void or has been extinguished.

As can be seen from these formulae, the allocation of the burden of proof was based primarily on the wording and construction of substantive law. However, this principle is not necessarily valid in some cases. For example, the Civil Code provides that a person obtains ownership of an immovable if he has possessed it openly and peacefully for ten years; however, a person who was aware that he did not have ownership cannot obtain ownership. In such cases, the above-mentioned theory does not give an answer to the question of who should prove that the possessor knew that the property was not his. In other words, does the possessor have to prove that he was unaware that he did not have ownership, or does the genuine owner have to prove that the possessor was aware of this fact?

The traditional view is still maintained by the court with some modifications. Some academics have voiced their scepticism about the validity of the traditional view. Although both views do not have much difference in the actual allocation of the burden of proof, the recent view takes into account some practical considerations such as the difficulty of proof and the doctrine of good faith and fair dealing, or collateral estoppel. Others assert that the probability of the given fact should be considered. Thus, while the traditional view allocated the burden of proof primarily on the provisions of the substantive law, the recent views pay more attention to procedural problems in allocating the burden of proof.

There are instances where the burden of proof is reversed out of practical considerations. This happens in some kinds of tort cases, as well as in contract law. Provisions concerning the liability of the employer and supervisor obligates them to prove that they were not at fault (Civil Code Arts. 714 and 715). These are exceptions to the general provision on tort (Civil Code Art. 709). Furthermore, Article 415 of the Civil Code provides that the obligor is liable for the impossibility of performance when the obligor is at fault. The court has long maintained that unless the obligor proves that he was not at fault, he is liable.

An issue of recent years is whether or not the party which does not bear the burden of proof should still bear some kind of a burden to explain the facts and even to submit relevant documents under certain circumstances. This is discussed in relation to pollution cases, cases of medical malpractice, and consumer protection cases. In such cases, the plaintiffs do not have access to the relevant materials and usually lack specialist scientific knowledge, while the defendants have such materials and expertise. For the sake of fairness, it is necessary to require the defendant in such cases to 'clarify the matter' by producing documents and giving explanations. This is achieved by ordering the defendant to submit relevant documents, offer explanation, and even to produce evidence to refute the claim.

The Code has a provision which requires the possessor of a document to submit it to the court (Art. 312). This provision covers documents 'which have been made for the interest of the party who bears the burden of proof, or which have been made for the legal relations between the possessor and such a party'. Under this provision, some lower courts have acknowledged the duty of a hospital to submit medical records for the interest of the plaintiff in medical malpractice cases. At the same time, courts tend to refuse to order submission of such records when the defendant in pollution cases moved for submission of such documents.[16]

In recent years, some courts have ordered the submission of documents in the possession of the government in cases concerning government tort liability. In a case concerning the liability of the State for a military plane crash, the appellate court ordered the government to submit the official report on the

---

16 For instance, Decision of Tokyo Appellate Court, 17 September, 1984 (*Kōminshū* 37–3–164).

accident filed by the Self Defence Force.[17] A similar decision was adopted in a case where inhabitants of an area sued the government, demanding rescission of a decision to build an atomic power plant.[18]

It is because the provisions of the Code are too narrow, that some academics propose the introduction of a general duty on the party which does not bear the burden of proof to assist the opposite party in the clarification of disputed facts.[19]

Formerly, the examination of witnesses was conducted by the judge, and the parties could only ask supplementary questions. However, under the influence of American Law, the system of cross-examination was introduced after the War. Now the witnesses are first questioned by the parties. The judge may then ask supplementary questions. The order of hearing as well as the prohibition on asking leading questions and some evidential rules are provided by the Rules of Civil Procedure. In practice, cross examination is not necessarily effective in Japan. This is partly due to the fact that the parties are not always successful in questioning the opposite party's witnesses because of the lack of materials.

The court is empowered to subpoena witnesses. In practice, the court seldom resorts to compulsory measures. The Code provides for some instances where a person may refuse to testify. First, if the testimony is likely to result in criminal prosecution or punishment of the witness, his family or his employer, he may legitimately refuse to testify. This applies also when the matter concerns issues which may humiliate these people (Art. 280).

Furthermore, people of certain professions, such as doctors, midwives, attorneys, etc. may refuse to testify when questioned about information which has been obtained via professional contact with clients. Since the Code does not provide specifically for journalists and other reporters in this category, the issue of whether they can be compelled to testify at the trial has been raised. The Supreme Court denied this privilege to a news reporter in 1952,[20] but there was an appellate court decision in 1979 which allowed a reporter not to testify on certain issues.[1]

---

17 Decision of Tokyo Appellate Court, 7 August, 1975 (*Kaminshū* 26–5/8–686).
18 Decision of Takamatsu Appellate Court, 17 July, 1975 (*Gyōsaireishū* 26–7/8–893: Ikatagahara Atomic Power Plant case).
19 P. Arens, 'Die Grundprinzipien des Zivilprozessrechts', *Humane Justiz*, 1977, S. 1–5. See also *Minjisoshō-zasshi* vol. 29, 1983, p. 29ff.
20 Judgment of the Supreme Court, 6 August, 1952 (*Keishū* 6–8–974: Ishii reporter case).
1 Decision of Sapporo Appellate Court, 31 August, 1979 (*Kaminshū* 30–5/8–403).

Evidential rules in the Japanese civil procedure are not as complex as those in Common Law countries. The Code and the Rules have various rules regarding evidence, but there is virtually no restriction on the evidence which can be produced in the court. The admissibility of evidence, including hearsay evidence, is almost entirely left to the discretion of the court. This is explained by the fact that since Japan does not have a jury system and professional judges who are sufficiently trained in assessing evidence handle the cases, detailed rules are not necessarily needed.

When assessing evidence and forming their views, judges are not bound by any particular rules except for reason and rules of experience (the principle of free assessment of evidence).

In civil procedure, the admissibility of illegally obtained evidence has not been a significant topic. On the other hand, the recent development of technological aids has led to discussion of problems such as the admissibility of recorded conversation. The court generally allows recorded conversation to be produced, unless it has been obtained in an anti-social way.[2]

There are three kinds of court judgments. The first is a judgment in a narrow sense which is rendered when the court has decided on the procedural legality of the claim or on the substantive matter of the case. Thus, the court may dismiss the case on procedural grounds, or uphold the claim of either party by a judgment. A hearing must precede the rendering of a judgment.

The second form is a decision by the court, and the third form is an order by a single judge. In rendering decisions, it is up to the court to decide whether a hearing is needed. Decisions and orders are used when the Court or a judge rules on relatively minor technical issues.

The judgment becomes formally binding when the period for appeal expires. If an appeal is made against the judgment, the judgment does not become binding until the appeal is formally rejected and this decision takes effect. When a judgment is binding, it also becomes enforceable.

The scope of *res judicata* is determined by the object of litigation. The confrontation between the classical school and its critics is especially intense here, but the difference in outcome is not so great, although the scope of *res judicata* tend to be narrower in the classical theory.

The Code provides that only the formal adjudication contained

2 Decision of Tokyo Appellate Court, 15 July, 1977 (*Tōkōhanji* 28–7–162).

in the judgment is binding. The reasoning of the judgment is not binding (Art. 199, para. 1). However, influenced by German theory and the doctrine of collateral estoppel, a theory which gives binding force to the ratio is gaining support. For instance, seller X sued buyer Y for the price of merchandise. Y claimed that the sale was void, and this was acknowledged by a judgment of the court. X then sued Y to return the merchandise. This second case is not barred by *res judicata*, since the first litigation merely confirmed that X did not have the right to payment from Y. The problem is whether in the second litigation Y is entitled to assert that in fact the sale was valid and that he is not obliged to return X the merchandise. In the first litigation, the validity of the contract for sale was not in itself the object of litigation and did not form part of the formal adjudication. It was merely part of the reasoning. Therefore, the judgment on the validity of the contract is not binding on Y, and technically, he is entitled to assert the validity of the contract in the second litigation.

However, since Y had actually contested the validity of the contract once in the first litigation, it is unfair to allow him to make such a claim. Therefore, the new theory asserts that, for the sake of fairness, once the party has contested a major issue, the result should serve as a basis for the judgment of related claims. The proponent of this theory based this effect on the doctrine of good faith and fair dealing or estoppel, which is different from *res judicata*.[3] A recent reappraisal of the concept of *res judicata* has led some academics to consider this to be an effect of *res judicata* itself.[4]

Generally, two appeals are allowed in civil procedure. The first appeal, which is called a *kōso* appeal, must be filed with the superior court within two weeks. The second appeal against the decision of the superior court is called a *jōkoku* appeal. When the appellate court is the court of first instance, only one appeal is allowed.

A *koso* appeal may be lodged whenever the party is dissatisfied with the original judgment. The appellate court examines the fact in the same way as the court of first instance did. The hearing is not a review of the original judgment, but is a continuation of the hearing of the first instance. Thus, the result of the hearing at the first instance forms the basis of the appeal court's judgment, together with the additional facts found by the appeal court.

The second appeal is strictly on legal points. The grounds for appeal are limited to errors in the interpretation of the

---

3 K. Shindo, *Minji-soshōhō* (*Civil Procedural Law*), Second edition, Tokyo 1989, pp. 425–436.
4 Inoue et al., *supra* note 13, pp. 222–225.

Constitution, contravention of the Constitution and violation of the laws and ordinances which apparently affects the judgment (Art. 394). The court of the second appeal is bound by the facts established by the original judgment. It inquires only into the appropriateness of the application of laws and ordinances.

The basic law for costs is the Law on Costs for Civil Litigation which was enacted in 1971.[5] Generally, costs are born by the party which lost the case, but there are some exceptions. If the winning party has caused excessive extra costs because of making unnecessary claims or defences, or has delayed in making claims or defences, he may also have to bear such costs.

The costs cover expenses of the court as well as those of the parties (Art. 2). Unlike in the United States and Germany, the attorney's fees are not included in the costs, and therefore, and are generally irrecoverable. The reason for this is partly due to the inequality in access to attorneys in rural and urban areas. Also requiring the losing party to pay attorney's fee of the winning party may discourage people from bringing cases to court. There are proposals to make the attorney's fee recoverable, but this has yet to be accepted. The Supreme Court ruled in a tort case that when a person had no choice but to sue a tortfeasor because this person did not voluntarily pay damages, the plaintiff's attorney's fee should be regarded as part of the damages and thus recoverable.[6] In practice, in tort cases, the Court takes into account the attorney's fees when deciding on damages. According to the Tokyo District Court's practice in traffic accident cases, 10% of the damages awarded reflect the fees of the attorney.

5.   Enforcement of judgments

The basic law which regulates the enforcement of judgments is the Law on Civil Execution.[7] This Law covers the execution of judgments provided in the Code of Civil Procedure and the realisation of real security rights. Previously, the execution of judgments and interlocutory measures as well as the realisation of security rights were part of the Code of Civil Procedure. In addition, the Law on Auction provided for the realisation of security rights. These laws were enacted in the 19th century and

5 Law No. 40, 1971.
6 Judgment of the Supreme Court, 27 February, 1969 (*Minshū* 23-2-441).
7 Law No. 4, 1979.

have long become out of date. However, their reform was held up for various reasons. In 1966, the Law on Bailiffs was enacted and finally in 1979, the Law on Civil Execution was enacted. The Law on Civil Execution combined the previously separated procedures of civil execution and the realisation of security rights, streamlined the hitherto complicated procedures, and substantially modernised the procedure.

Civil execution procedure is divided into execution for monetary claims and non-monetary claims. There are separate procedures for the execution of monetary claims over immovables and movables as well as other property rights such as a credit the obligor has against a third party. Ships are regarded as movables in the Civil Code, but in relation to execution, they are treated as quasi-immovables.

Monetary claims are realised in the civil execution procedure by way of direct enforcement. In contrast, the realisation of non-monetary claims can take various forms. In some cases, the judgment obligation is realised by a third person at the cost of the obligor (substitute enforcement). There are also cases where the execution is secured by ordering the obligor to pay a certain amount of money to the obligee until he complies with the judgment (indirect enforcement).

The agencies in charge of executing judgments are the courts and the bailiffs (Art. 2). The court is in charge of execution over immovables, ships, credits and other property rights. It also has jurisdiction over the execution of judgments ordering someone to do or not to do something. Generally, the court which deals with execution of judgments is the district court. The bailiff is an independent judicial agency who works in the district court. The bailiff primarily handles execution of monetary claims over movables and claims for transfer of movables and immovables. Although they are separated, there are instances where the bailiff acts on behalf of the court, or where the bailiff is required to obtain the court's permission.

In order to initiate the execution procedure, the judgment obligee must have a title (*saimu-meigi*) to execute. A title is an official document which certifies the existence of a right to claim and its scope which the law has granted the power to be executed. Agencies of civil execution must judge the enforceability of the judgment solely by the title. A title for execution is usually a court judgment which has taken effect, but in addition, court judgments with a declaration for provisional execution and other documents provided by the Law can form a title for execution (Art. 22). It should be noted that a judgment of a foreign court which can be executed, as well as a foreign arbitration award can serve as a title for execution (Art. 22, para 6, also Code of Civil Procedure, Art. 200).

Furthermore, an execution clause (*shikkōbun*) is needed for execution. This certifies the validity and enforceability of the title. The execution clause is granted by a court clerk, or in some cases, a public notary (Art. 26, para. 1).

The first step in the execution of monetary claims is attachment of the property. In execution over movables, the bailiff takes possession of the property at issue. In execution of titles over immovables, ships and credits, the court declares that the property is attached, i.e. the judgment debtor is prohibited from disposing of the property. There is a risk that property which belongs to a third party could also be seized if it is in a judgment obligor's possession. In such cases, those who have appropriate rights over the property may file an objection to the execution (Art. 38, para. 1).

The second stage of execution of monetary claims is the procedure to convert the property into money. The primary means of selling the property in the execution proceedings are bidding and auction (Arts. 43, para. 1, 134). For immovables, the court decides the minimum sale price, and if this price is not achieved by auction or bidding, the court may adopt other measures to sell the property.

There is another way to execute a title over immovables. This is the system of compulsory administration. The court appoints an administrator who manages the property and the owner is deprived of his right to use and profit from it. The profits made from the property are paid to the creditors (Art. 93).

The methods for the execution of non-monetary claims vary. As for the transfer of immovables, the bailiff discharges the possession of the judgment debtor and transfers it to the creditor. An obligation to do something or not to do something can be enforced not by direct enforcement, but by way of substitute enforcement or indirect enforcement. As a principle, indirect enforcement is allowed only when direct enforcement and substitute enforcement are not available. For example, a judgment to remove a building is executed by a third party commissioned by the court at the expense of the owner. It should be noted that unlike German law, indirect enforcement in Japan does not include detention of debtors. In cases where a declaration of will on the part of the judgment debtor is at issue, a court judgment may be substituted for his will (Art. 173, para. 1).

The Law on Civil Execution also provides for the realisation of security rights. Unlike the execution of unsecured credits and claims, title for execution is not needed in order to realise security rights. However, submission of a document which certifies the existence of a security right, such as a copy of the land register, is required.

18   Criminal law and procedure

1.   The proposed reform of criminal law

The legislation regarding criminal law in Japan consists of the Criminal Code and other laws which provide for individual crimes. The latter are generally designated as 'special criminal laws'. Various specific laws such as the Law on Misdemeanours, the Law for the Prevention of Disruptive Activities, the Regulations for the Control of Explosives, the Law on the Punishment of Violent Activities and the Law on the Prevention of Prostitution are examples of such special criminal laws.[1] In addition, there are a considerable number of administrative law provisions which lay down penalties for their breach. These include the Law on the Prevention of Air Pollution, the Law on Government Employees and the Anti-Monopoly Law.[2]

The Criminal Code is divided into the General Part and Special Part. The former lays down the general principles and basic concepts of criminal law such as intention, negligence, attempt, accomplice, etc. The latter lists individual types of crimes. General rules put forward in the General Part of the Criminal Code apply to special criminal laws as well.

The present Criminal Code dates back to 1907. The first comprehensive criminal code to be enacted after the fall of the Tokugawa Shogunate in 1867 was the *Shinritsu-kōryō* of 1869. This was primarily influenced by the Chinese Ming and Ching codes as well as the laws of the Tokugawa Shogunate. This was supplemented by further legislation – the *Kari-keiritsu* in 1873. These statutes, however, proved to be unsatisfactory for a country which aspired to achieve equality with Western European countries. Therefore, attempts to draft another code based upon a Western European model were made in the 1870s. This finally resulted in the enactment of the Criminal Code of 1880. A French adviser, Gustave Boissonade, was in charge of the

---

1 Laws No. 39, 1948, No. 240, 1952, No. 60, 1926, and No. 118, 1956.
2 Laws No. 97, 1968, No. 54, 1947 and No. 120, 1947.

drafting process, but the content of his draft was watered down at the last stage. Consequently, although the Code was heavily influenced by the French code, some influences of German Law can also be detected. It should be noted that the principle of *nulla crimen sine lege* was first introduced by this Code.

The Criminal Code of 1870 was replaced by the Criminal Code of 1907. In contrast to the 1870 Code, the new Code was primarily based upon German Law. A new school of thought in criminal law and criminology promoted by Italian and German scholars had emerged at this time in Europe and influenced those who were involved in preparing the draft. This new theory laid emphasis on the sociological factors which caused crimes and substituted the concept of rehabilitation for that of retribution. Ever since the enactment of this Code, the influence of German law and legal theory on the interpretation and study of criminal law has been overwhelming.

This Criminal Code was amended soon after the Second World War in order to bring it into line with the new Constitution. Thus, crimes against the imperial family were repealed as a result of the change in the status of the Emperor. Espionage and other crimes which presuppose a state of war were also removed from the Code. The newly-endorsed principle of equality of sexes necessitated the abolition of crimes such as adultery. Furthermore, with the increased guarantee of the freedom of expression, the provision which punished disruption of public peace and order was removed and the provision regarding libel was amended. Under the present Code, if the libellous statement concerns a matter of public interest and was made for the benefit of the public, the person who made this statement is not punishable, provided that he proves that the statement is true (Art. 230–2).

Since the amendment of 1947, the Criminal Code has undergone successive amendments involving specific crimes. The latest major amendment of 1986 concerned computer-related crimes.

Calls for a total amendment of the present Code started in the 1920s when a programme for the reform of the Criminal Code was prepared. In 1931, a 'provisional draft' (*Karian*) of the general part was completed, followed by the special part in 1941. This attempt to reform the Code failed mainly due to the outbreak of war.

In the mid–1950s, the Ministry of Justice started to work on a new criminal code. A subcommittee on criminal law of the Legislative Advisory Committee was commissioned to review the existing Code. It concluded that the Code should be totally amended, and prepared a draft to this effect. This was approved by the Committee in 1974. However, this attempt by the government to amend totally the Criminal Code met with fierce opposition from a majority of legal academics and practising attorneys.

The underlying tenor of the draft itself was the principal target for criticism.[3] The draft was based upon the 'provisional draft' prepared under the previous Constitution in the 1920s and 1930s and thus did not take into account the democratic developments which had taken place after the Second World War. It was not surprising that the draft gave priority to the maintenance of public security rather than to the safeguarding of individual rights. There was excessive emphasis on the ethical nature of criminal law. Criminal law was considered primarily to be an instrument to maintain the ethical standards of the people and preserve traditional virtues. In contrast, opponents of the draft regarded criminal law primarily as a device to protect citizens from violations and infringements of their rights and interests. In their view, criminal law should refrain from interfering with ethics; after all, in this age of pluralism, it was considered to be impossible to agree on ethical absolutes.

The draft's overwhelming concern for public security was demonstrated by the introduction of special 'security measures' for those who were found by the court not guilty or only partly responsible on the ground of insanity. At present, these people are sent to psychiatric hospitals in accordance with the Law on Mental Health.[4] Jurisdiction in such cases is given to the Ministry of Public Health. This corresponds with the idea that since these people are not convicted criminals, they should come under procedures that are not those of criminal law. In contrast, the draft provided for security measures to be applied to these people as an alternative to, or in addition to punishment. The principal purpose of these measures is the maintenance of public security and not therapeutic treatment. The draft provides explicitly that these measures are to be applied when needed for the maintenance of public security. They are to be applied not in psychiatric hospitals but in institutions under the jurisdiction of the Ministry of Justice. The term for such measures is three years, but this is renewable twice. For those who are highly likely to commit a crime in respect of which imprisonment for more than two years is applicable, there is no limit to the number of renewals. These measures are also applicable to psychopaths.

---

3 R. Hirano, 'The Draft of the Revised Penal Code: A General Critique', *Law in Japan*, vol. 6, 1973, pp. 49–64.
4 Law No. 123, 1950.

It is generally agreed that the present system of treating these offenders is not immune from criticism. However, the system proposed by the draft was considered to have gone too far towards the maintenance of public security at the cost of the rights of the mentally ill.

Another point related to the concern of public security in the draft was the treatment of recidivists and habitual offenders. Maximum terms of imprisonment can be doubled for recidivists. Indefinite sentences are made applicable to habitual offenders.

Furthermore, there was a general trend of overcriminalisation in the draft. It incorporated various provisions in the Chapter on crimes against the interest of the State and increased the penalties for them. For instance, preparation for the purpose of causing public unrest was made a crime while the present Code punishes only attempts. Collective insubordination of prisoners was also added to the list of crimes. Divulging of official secrets which is currently found in the Law on Government Employees was 'upgraded' and included in the draft criminal code with increased penalties.

In total, the draft added more than 20 new crimes to the present Code and, moreover, increased the penalties for a number of crimes. The approach of the draft to victimless crimes and moral crimes was particulary criticised. For instance, the draft did not pay due attention to safeguarding freedom of expression and even extended the scope of provisions regarding the circulation of obscene publications and increased the penalties. Abortion, which is seldom punished, still remains in the draft and its scope is even extended.

The draft was subjected to a barrage of opposition. The Japan Federation of Bar Associations, the Japan Association of Psychiatry, the Japan Newspapers Association and various other organisations expressed their opposition to the draft. The Ministry of Justice retreated from its initial position and in 1981, published a paper entitled 'Current Policy on the Reform of the Criminal Code'. In this policy statement the Ministry declared that where provisions had been fiercely criticised, provisions of the present Code were to remain unamended. The penalties for the crimes provided in the special part of the present Code would also remain unchanged. The Ministry of Justice thus abandoned the idea of amending the Code on the basis of the draft of 1974.

On the other hand, the idea of introducing special security measures for the mentally ill has not been renounced. The Ministry has announced that it is considering the introduction of 'therapeutic measures' instead of the proposed 'security measures'. This is also criticised, since it is not clear why the present system of compulsory therapeutic treatment should be entirely replaced by a new system.

In any case, taking into account the lack of consensus, it is unlikely that the total reform of the present Criminal Code will be realised in the near future.

2.   The general part of the criminal code

For an act to be punishable, it has to fulfill three basic requirements. An act is criminal when it coincides with the definition of a specific crime (*Tatbestand*), is against the law (*rechtswidrig*) and is blameworthy (*schuldig*). As is the case in Germany, specialists of criminal law in Japan have endeavoured to work out a systematic theory of crime incorporating these three requirements. Although it is often overlooked by academics, this theoretical framework with its three components is designed to assist judges in deciding whether or not a specific offender is punishable.

In order to be acknowledged as a crime, an act has to fall within the definition of a specific crime, for example, homicide or theft. The principle of *nulla crimen sine lege* is acknowledged in Japanese law. It has its basis on the Constitution which guarantees due process of law in Article 31 and prohibits retrospective application of criminal law in Article 37. Thus, only laws which were enacted by the Diet may provide for punishment. However, there are two exceptions to this rule: delegated legislation and local regulations as mentioned in chapter 3.

As a corollary of this principle, the application of criminal law by way of analogy is not allowed. Nevertheless, there are cases where the courts have interpreted the provisions of the Code rather flexibly. There was a celebrated case in the 1900s where a person who used electricity without permission was found guilty of theft. Before this case, the object of theft had to be corporeal things, but the court in this case ruled that it would suffice if the object was controllable.[5] In a more recent case, the court acknowledged that forgery of a photocopy was punishable in the same way as forgery of the original document. Thus, the court has extended the meaning of 'document' to cover photocopies.[6]

Substantive due process requires that the definition of specific crimes should not be vague. At least theoretically, the Supreme Court has recognised this requirement, but there has been no

5 Judgment of the Supreme Tribunal, 21 May, 1903 (*Keiroku* 9–14–874).
6 Judgment of the Supreme Court, 30 April, 1976 (*Keishū* 30–3–452).

case where it found a provision invalid because of vagueness.[7]

The fact that a given act coincides with the definition of a specific crime does not necessarily justify punishment. Although in most cases, such an act can be presumed to be a crime, there are cases where it is not against the law for some reason. A typical example is self defence – a defensive act against imminent and unlawful attack on the 'rights' of a person (Art. 36). This also applies to extreme necessity (Art. 37). Another exemption is a legitimate act either based on the law or performed as part of a legitimate business (Art. 35). For instance, industrial action may be regarded formally as an obstruction of business by force, but is not punishable, since it is made legitimate by the Law on Trade Unions in so far as it is carried out without violence (Art. 1, para. 2). An operation by a physician is not punishable as an assault, since it is his legitimate business.

An act is punishable only when the person who committed the act had *mens rea*, i.e. he either had an intention to commit the crime or has acted negligently. Negligence is punishable only when there is an explicit provision. As a rule, Japanese criminal law does not acknowledge absolute responsibility. However, there are two exceptions to this rule. Firstly, there are provisions for vicarious responsibility where a juridical person is held liable for the acts of its employees. Secondly, there are cases where the offender intended a certain act but the result of his action was more serious than he had expected. For instance, A assaulted B who died as a result of this attack. Although A had not intended to kill B, he is responsible for B's death. Such cases do not constitute homicide, but are punishable under another provision.

The concept of negligence has become an issue of dispute in recent years. Negligence is understood to be a breach of the duty of care. It is the content of this duty of care which is the focus of controversy. One school of thought maintains that negligence is punishable because of the failure to foresee the outcome of an act. Another school of thought lays emphasis on the failure to avoid the outcome of the act. Even when the outcome of the act could have been foreseen, this does not mean that the actor was negligent. There should have been an opportunity to avoid the outcome of the act and only when the actor proceeded to carry out an act with 'impermissible risk', may he be found negligent.

In addition to these theories, another theory of negligence has emerged. This was partly a result of the serious pollution and

---

7 For instance, see the Judgment of the Supreme Court, 23 October, 1985 (*Keishū* 39–6–413).

other crimes involving major corporations which arose since the mid–1960s. The new theory claimed that foreseeability of the outcome of one's act was not always necessary. In certain cases, a mere feeling of anxiety that a harmful result might occur is sufficient for negligence. This new theory was designed to cope with the situation where major corporations and senior executives managed to avoid criminal responsibility while their low-ranking employees were held responsible. In a case where a dairy company produced and sold dried milk tainted with arsenic and caused death to children, the appellate court found the director of the plant responsible on the basis of this theory. In this case, the court ruled that it was impossible for the employees to foresee that the raw materials were tainted by arsenic, but nevertheless found the defendant guilty, since they must have felt 'anxiety'.[8]

However, this new theory is criticised since it amounts to absolute responsibility and is not compatible with the basic idea underlying the present Code. The judgment of the above-mentioned case is rather an isolated case and recent judgments indicate that foreseeability is still required.[9]

If the person in question is insane, he cannot be held responsible for his act. Criminal insanity is defined as the ability to distinguish right from wrong and act accordingly (Art. 39, para. 1). Schizophrenia and manic depressive psychosis are typical causes of insanity, but sometimes, mentally-retarded persons are also found to be insane under this provision. The Code also provides for those whose ability to distinguish right from wrong and to act accordingly has been considerably diminished. Penalties for such people are reduced (Art. 39, para. 2).

Minors of less than 14 years of age are not held responsible for criminal actions (Art. 41).

There are cases where a crime is committed by more than one offender. The Criminal Code provides that if more than two persons jointly commit a crime, they are joint principals (Art. 60). In addition, the Code provides for instigators and helpers (Arts. 61 and 62). Instigators are treated in the same way as the principal, while penalties for helpers are less severe than for the principal.

Whether it is possible or not to punish a person who did not

---

8 Judgment of Takamatsu Appellate Court, 31 March, 1963 (*Kōkeishū* 19–2–136).

9 M. Maeda, '*Keihō Sōron Kōgi (Lectures on the General Part of Criminal Law)*, Tokyo 1988, pp. 362–368.

actually take part in committing a crime, but has masterminded it and conspired with the others as a principal is a matter of dispute. The legislature seemed to have thought that this kind of a person should be punished as an instigator. However, the court has developed a theory that such a person should be punished as a principal. In a case which was decided in 1958, a person who did not take part in the crime, but had masterminded it and conspired with those who actually carried out the crime was prosecuted. The Supreme Court ruled that this person was a principal on the ground that he had used the act of the others as an instrument to commit a crime.[10]

The main penalties provided by the Code are as follows: capital punishment, imprisonment with compulsory labour, imprisonment without compulsory labour and fines (Art. 9). Imprisonment can be for life, or a maximum of 15 years.

3. Specific crimes in the special part

The definition of each crime is not necessarily as specific as compared with the laws of some other countries. In total, the Special Part has less than 180 provisions. For instance, there is only one provision on homicide, which provides that a person who kills another shall be punished by death, life imprisonment or imprisonment for more than three years (Art. 199). This is even different from the German Criminal Code which had served as a model for the present Japanese Code. It was probably the influence of the new school of thought on criminal law and criminology of the late 19th century which resulted in these simplified arrangements of the Code.

Crimes are classified in accordance with the nature of the legal interest which the law intends to protect: crimes against the interests of the State, crimes against the interests of society and crimes against the interests of individuals. Some people add crimes against morals and ethics to this classification. Originally, the Special Part of the Code began with crimes against the imperial family. These provisions were deleted by amendments made after the War. The present Code starts with crimes against the interests of the State – treason.

In recent years, there have been moves to provide further protection for State secrets. At present, the Code does not penalise the unauthorised release of such secrets. Instead, the Law on Government Employees and the Law on Local

10 Judgment of the Supreme Court, 28 May, 1958 (*Keishū* 12–8–1718).

Government Employees cover the unauthorised release of official secrets. As for military secrets, the Law on the Self Defence Force and a special criminal statute based upon the Mutual Security Agreement with the United States have some penal provisions.[11]

However, the government considered the present system to be inadequate and therefore included some new provisions in the draft criminal code. When it seemed unlikely that the draft would be adopted, the government prepared a separate draft on the law for the protection of State secrets. State secrets in this draft cover military secrets as well as secrets touching on international relations which need protection for the defence of the country. Acts which are punishable are handing over official secrets to a foreign country, the searching for and collecting of such secrets and their release.

This draft met with criticism from various quarters. Firstly, it was not clear why the present system was considered so inadequate as to warrant new legislation. Secondly, the draft did not give due consideration to freedom of information and the right of access to government information. For instance, the collection of information by the media would be hampered by this draft. Thirdly, the definition of State secrets in the draft was vague and was likely to lead to an extension of the criminal law. This is in contrast with the German Criminal Code which has a provision exempting certain information concerning matters against fundamental tenets of the democratic system from protection as a State secret (StGB 193).

The draft was submitted to the Diet as a bill in 1985 but has failed to be endorsed.

One of the salient characteristics of the Code is its leniency towards moral crimes. Homosexuality has never been punishable. Abortion is punishable by the Code, but another law which was enacted after the War made abortion for economic reasons legitimate. Therefore, abortion has been virtually decriminalised. Crimes of facilitating prostitution are covered by a separate law, but prostitution *per se* is not a crime.[12]

Another issue which has been discussed in recent years is the concept of death in criminal law. The Code does not have any provision on this matter. The issue was raised by the first heart transplant operation which took place in Japan in 1968. The donor had been brain dead for a while and then was declared to be clinically dead. Some people questioned whether the donor

11 Laws No. 120, 1947, No. 261, 1950 and No. 138, 1952.
12 The Law on Prevention of Prostitution, Law No. 118, 1956.

was really dead at the time of the heart transplant. The public prosecutor's office conducted a thorough investigation and found that the basis for prosecuting the physician for causing death by negligence was lacking.

A government committee has recently accepted brain death as a sufficient ground for a finding that death has occurred. However, lawyers and the public have yet to reach a consensus on this matter.

Protection of trade secrets was another issue which has attracted attention in recent years. The present Code does not have a provision which directly deals with industrial espionage. If the act involves industrial secrets embodied in a document or a product, their transfer to a third party may be punishable as theft or embezzlement. However, when the act involves disembodied information, the applicability of the Code is very much limited. In 1988 this issue was raised in the U.S.-Japan bilateral negotiations on intellectual property. A new provision was introduced to the Law against Unfair Competition in 1989 in order to make breaches of trade secrets punishable (see Chapter 12).

Since the comprehensive amendment of the Criminal Code came to a standstill, some separate laws were enacted to cope with changes resulting from high economic growth and rapid technological developments. One such case involved pollution. Pollution had always been a serious problem in Japan since its modernisation and rapid industrialisation starting at the end of the last century. In the mid–1960s, as Japan was achieving high economic growth, pollution of the environment became even worse. River pollution caused the deaths of inhabitants in several areas and many people suffered from asthma in areas close to industrial sites. Against this background, the draft criminal code initially included provisions on pollution offences. Later, this part was separated from the draft and submitted to the Diet as a separate law.

The bill was adopted with some amendments as the Law on the Punishment of Pollution Offences against Human Health in 1970.[13] The Law punishes the intentional or negligent discharge of harmful substances which endanger human life or health in the course of entrepreneurial activities (Arts. 2 and 3). The company is punishable together with the actual offender. However, this provision has seldom been invoked; there have been only three cases of prosecution. In a recent judgment, the Supreme Court denied the applicability of this provision to a case where a person mistakenly unloaded sulphamic acid into the wrong tank and as a

13 Law No. 142, 1970.

result, the inhabitants suffered from the effects of chlorine gas. The court ruled that this kind of an accident should not be regarded as a negligent act in the course of entrepreneurial activities in the sense of this Law. The defendant – an employee – was convicted by a provision of the Criminal Code but the company was found not guilty of violating the above-mentioned Law.[14]

4.   An outline of criminal procedure

The history of the law of criminal procedure in Japan, in a way, demonstrates the uniqueness of the reception of foreign law in Japan. The first systematic Code of Criminal Procedure was the Code of Criminal Instruction of 1880. This Code was primarily based upon the French Code of 1808, but had some provisions which came from German Law. Since the system of courts and the procedures provided by this Code proved to be too cumbersome, the Code was soon replaced by a new one which followed the German model. This Code in turn was replaced by another Code in 1922 which again was patterned on German Law.[15] Thus, criminal procedure in the pre-War period was entirely based upon the Civil Law system.

Radical changes to criminal procedure were introduced after the Second World War on the initiative of the Supreme Commander of Allied Powers. The Constitution incorporated a provision requiring the due process of law and guaranteed the right to a defence and other related rights in the Bill of Rights. This necessitated a fundamental reform of criminal procedure. American advisers worked on the draft code of criminal procedure together with Japanese academics, judges, attorneys and officials. This work resulted in the present Code of Criminal Procedure which was enacted in 1948. This time, the Code was basically modelled on American Law.

What is interesting is that, despite the overwhelming influence of American Law on the Code, in practice, the influence of German Law can still be seen in the implementation of the Code. This is particulary evident in the process of investigation as well as the reliance at the trial on written documents – dossiers prepared by the police and the public prosecutors.

14 Judgment of the Supreme Court, 22 September, 1987 (*Keishū* 41–6–255: *Daitō Tessen* case).
15 S. Takayanagi, *Nihon-hōsei-shi* (*Legal History of Japan*), vol. 2, Tokyo 1965, pp. 289–293.

The first stage in the procedure is investigation. Investigation is primarily conducted by the police and public prosecutors. Usually, the police conduct investigations at the initial stage. This is followed by a supplementary investigation conducted by the public prosecutor. The Constitution provides that no one shall be apprehended except on the basis of a warrant issued by a judge (Art. 33). The same rule applies to search and seizure (Art. 35). This requirement of warrants is designed to place the power of investigative officers under judicial control. As for arrest, there are two exceptions to this rule. Firstly, when the suspect is caught red-handed, a warrant is not needed (Art. 212). Secondly, if there is a sufficient ground to believe that the someone has committed a crime which is punishable by death, life imprisonment, or more than three years' imprisonment, he may be arrested without a warrant provided that there was no time to obtain a warrant (Art. 210).

The suspect must be brought to the public prosecutor's office with the documents and evidence within 48 hours of arrest (Art. 203, para. 1). If the public prosecutor finds that the suspect should be detained, he is required to ask the judge to authorise detention within 24 hours (Art. 203, para. 1). Thus, at the maximum, it takes 72 hours for a suspect to be brought before a judge. Suspects have the right to remain silent, which is guaranteed by the Constitution (Art. 38). The suspect should be notified of this right as well as the right to counsel immediately after his arrest (Art. 203, para. 1). If a defendant is unable to afford defence counsel, the state will assign one (Art. 37, para. 3 of the Constitution). However, this right is available only after indictment.

The maximum period of detention prior to being charged is 10 days which is renewable once (Art. 208). There is no limit to the length of detention after being indicted. Bail is available only after being indicted and even then, its applicability is fairly limited. Therefore, some defendants have to spend months awaiting trial. In practice, suspects are often detained in a jail attached to the police station, although they are supposed to be detained in a prison. This practice of putting suspects and defendants under the control of the police is criticised, since it may jeopardise their right to remain silent and to consult their counsel.

Suspects and defendants placed under confinement are guaranteed the right to have access to defence counsel. They are entitled to be interviewed by counsel without any official being present (Art. 39, para. 1). However, public prosecutors and police officials may designate the time, place and the length of interview for suspects, provided that it is necessary for investigation (Art. 39, para. 3). This provision is implemented in practice as if interview with defence counsel depends on the permission of the public prosecutor. In cases where the suspect does not admit guilt, interview with the defence counsel is severely restricted, sometimes only twice in twenty days and ten minutes for each.

During detention, suspects are interrogated by the police and public prosecutors. Records of statements made before police officials and public prosecutors are prepared for possible use at the trial. Thus, detention often turns out to be an institution aimed at obtaining evidence from the suspect rather than an institution designed to ensure that the suspect does not flee.

Arrest and detention of a suspect for a lesser crime in order to interrogate him in relation to a more serious crime is not uncommon. This practice has been criticised by academics and practicing lawyers as a breach of Constitutional safeguards, but has not ceased. The Supreme Court ruled that when there are sufficient grounds to arrest and detain a suspect for a certain crime, it is permissible to interrogate him for another crime which is closely linked to the first one.[16] However, there are lower court decisions which have found such a practice to be illegal in some other circumstances.[17]

Prosecution is the exclusive power of the public prosecutor (Art. 247). Citizens may bring complaints to the police or public prosecutors, but cannot prosecute on their own. Public prosecutors have a broad discretionary power in deciding whether or not to prosecute, even when they are convinced of the suspect's guilt. When making this decision, the public prosecutor takes into account the character of the offender, his age and circumstances in which he was brought up, the gravity of the offence, and the circumstances after the commission of the offence (Art. 248). Thus, if the offender repented and paid compensation to the victim, this may be taken into account in some crimes.

This system which has developed in practice and has since been incorporated in the Code was based upon the idea of 'special deterrence'. It was considered desirable to handle some offenders by a process other than that required by normal criminal procedure for the purpose of their re-education and rehabilitation. On the other hand, there is always the possibility of misuse or abuse of such a wide discretionary power. Furthermore, since

16 Decision of the Supreme Court, 9 August, 1977 (*Keishū* 31–5–821: *Sayama* case).
17 For instance, the Judgment of Osaka Appellate Court, 19 April, 1984 (*Kōkeishū* 37–1–98: *Kobe Matsuri* case).

public prosecutors try to exercise this discretion prudently, the investigation stage tends to become meticulous and thorough. Therefore, once a person is prosecuted, there is a high probability that he will in fact be found guilty. Indeed, the acquittal rate at trial is around 0.1 percent. In 1990, 49,821 defendants were found guilty, while only 61 were acquitted.[18] This might, perhaps, undermine the significance of public trial.

After the decision to prosecute is made, the case is brought to the court of first instance. In most cases, this will be a summary court or a district court. No evidence or documents may accompany the indictment, since this could prejudice the impartiality of the judge (Art. 256, para. 6). More than 90% of cases are handled by a single judge. At this stage, the public prosecutor may transfer cases involving minor offences to a summary procedure conducted on the basis of documentary evidence only. The summary courts which handle these cases may impose a maximum 200,000 yen (approximately 800 pounds) fine. Around 90% of cases are handled via this procedure.

Although the Law on Jury Trial was enacted in 1923, the jury system did not function properly in Japan for various reasons. The Law was suspended in 1943. At present, criminal procedure is conducted without a jury or lay assessors.

Trials are held in public. Although some exceptions are allowed by the Constitution and the Code, trials are seldom closed. At the beginning of the trial, after the public prosecutor has read out the indictment, the presiding judge asks the defendant whether he admits his guilt or not. Since Japan has not adopted the arraignment procedure, even if the defendant admits his guilt, the evidence has to be examined.

Trials are not held consecutively; there is, on average, a one month interval between hearings. It takes on average three to four sittings until judgment is rendered. In approximately 90% of cases tried at the district court, defendants admit their guilt. In such cases, they are handled in a fairly short period, while in contested and complicated cases especially where more than one defendant is involved, it is not rare for the court to take years in reaching a conclusion. In 1990, there were more than 1,000 cases pending for more than a year at the district court level.[19]

The defendant has a constitutional right to be assisted by counsel. This right can be waived, but in cases where the death penalty, life imprisonment or imprisonment exceeding three

18 Supreme Court of Japan, *Shihō-tōkei-nenpō* (*Annual Report of Judicial Statistics*), Criminal Cases, Tokyo 1991, p. 204.
19 *Ibid.*

years can be imposed, the presence of a defence counsel is mandatory (Art. 289, para. 1). In fact, at the district court, around 97% of defendants are assisted by counsel, a majority of which are assigned by the court.[20]

The trial is adversarial in character in contrast to the 'inquisitorial' mode under the previous code. The parties, instead of the judge, take the initiative in producing and examining evidence. Under the previous code, it was the judge who interrogated witnesses; interrogation of defendants by the judge was also allowed. The present Constitution guarantees the right of the defendant to examine all witnesses and as a corollary, hearsay evidence is not allowed (Art. 37, para. 2). Accordingly, the Code has introduced the system of cross examination (Art. 320, para. 1). The defendant cannot be forced to testify under oath unless he so wishes.

However, this new system introduced by the present code did not function exactly in the way expected. The Code provides for various exceptions to the hearsay rule, for instance if the statement was made under special circumstances which give it high credibility and if it is essential to prove material facts (Art. 321, para. 1 subpara. 3). Furthermore, statements by the defendant made before trial can also be admitted, insofar as it includes admissions that are damaging to the defendant or it was made under circumstances which give special credibility to the statement (Art. 322, para. 1). The defendant may also agree to the use of hearsay evidence.

Because of the relaxed admissibility of hearsay evidence, statements of the defendant and witnesses made in the course of the investigation play a crucial role at trial. The trial is conducted mainly on documentary evidence rather than the fresh testimony of the witnesses. It is a common practice that these statements are not even read out aloud in court. Only summaries are given, and even this is often dispensed with. This heavy reliance on documentary evidence is in a way inevitable, since trials are not held consecutively and can last more than a year. It is likely that the memories of witnesses will fade. However, this makes the investigation stage the most crucial part of the criminal procedure and preempts the significance of trial.[21]

The court has a free hand in evaluating evidence (Art. 318). As an exception, a person shall not be convicted if the only evidence against him is his confession. Corroborative evidence is required in such cases (Art. 319, paras. 2 and 3).

---

20 Supreme Court of Japan ed., *Outline of Criminal Justice in Japan*, Tokyo 1990, pp. 36–37.
21 R. Hirano, *supra*, note 3, pp. 138–142.

There is no separate procedure for sentencing. Evidence produced in order to prove guilt is also taken into account by the judge in determining the sentence. The range of discretion given to the judge in sentencing is rather broad. For instance, in homicide, the judge can impose the death penalty, life imprisonment, or imprisonment of between three years and fifteen years.

An appeal to higher courts is allowed both for the defendant and the prosecution. The first appeal – *kōso* – is made to the Appellate Court in most cases. The primary grounds for a *kōso* appeal are: non-compliance with procedural law, errors in the application of law and errors in fact-finding which apparently affected the judgment, as well as inappropriate sentencing (Arts. 379–382). The *kōso* appeal is not a procedure *de novo*. It is designed to review the judgment of first instance, but in exceptional cases, it may involve the examination of witnesses and other evidence.

The second appeal – *jōkoku* – is made to the Supreme Court. *Jōkoku* is allowed on the ground of violation of the Constitution or erroneous interpretation of the Constitution and conflict with the precedents of the Supreme Court (Art. 405). In addition, the Supreme Court may accept appeal on its discretion if the case involves significant matters on the interpretation of law (Art. 406).

19 Foreign relations law

1. The law on nationality

The basic law concerning nationality is the Law on Nationality of 1950. This Law was substantially amended in 1984 in order to meet the requirements of the Convention on the Elimination of All Forms of Discrimination against Women which Japan ratified in 1980.[1]

A person is a Japanese national if, 1) at the time of birth, either of the parents is a Japanese national, 2) the father who died prior to the birth of the child was a Japanese national, 3) in cases where a child was born in Japan, and both of his or her parents are unknown, or are without any nationality (Art. 2). Japanese nationality can also be obtained by legitimation or naturalisation (Arts. 3 and 4).

Before the 1984 amendment, the Law provided that if the father was a Japanese national at the time of the child's birth, the child shall be a Japanese national. However, this did not apply to cases where the mother was a Japanese national but the father was not. Therefore, if a Japanese man married a foreign woman, his child was entitled to Japanese nationality, while if a Japanese woman married a foreign man, her child was not entitled to Japanese nationality. This was considered to be unfair and also inconvenient, since if the father's home country adopted the principle of *jus soli*, the child would be without nationality. There was a case where the issue came to court. In this case, a child of a Japanese woman who married an American was refused registration because of the lack of nationality. The district court rejected the argument of the plaintiff that the provision of the then applicable Nationality Law was unconstitutional.[2] The Law was amended in 1984 in this respect and this differential treatment between sexes was abolished. The present Law

---

1 Law No. 147, 1950 as amended.
2 Judgment of the Tokyo District Court, 30 March, 1981 (*Hanji* 996–23).

provides for *jus sanguinis* for both paternal and maternal lines (Art. 2).[3]

Japanese nationality can be obtained by legitimation. An illegitimate child does not acquire the status of a legitimate child by marriage of his or her father and mother. A separate act of recognition by the father is required. When legitimated, a child under 20 years of age acquires Japanese nationality, provided that the father or mother was a Japanese national at the time of birth and is still a Japanese national, or was a Japanese national at the time of death (Art. 3, para. 1). Before the 1984 amendment, the Law had also discriminated between cases where the father was a Japanese national and the mother was a Japanese national. This has now been changed as is the case with the acquisition of nationality by birth.

The Law also provides for naturalisation as a ground for acquisition of nationality. Naturalisation is subject to the permission of the Minister of Justice. The Law sets out minimum requirements for naturalisation. The applicant must have been domiciled in Japan for more than five years without interruption, must be of twenty years or more of age and have capacity by the law of the home country. He must demonstrate 'good behavior and character', that he is able to provide for himself (including the possibility to be supported by his spouse's or relative's income who lives with him), and is of no nationality or with the acquisition of Japanese nationality, loses foreign nationality, and has never plotted or advocated the overthrow of the Constitution and the government, or formed or taken part in such an organisation (Art. 5 para. 1).

For those who have special links with Japan, such as those who are married to a Japanese, the requirements are relaxed. Thus, a spouse of a Japanese national who has been domiciled or resident in Japan for not less than three years without interruption and is at present domiciled in Japan may acquire nationality. The same applies to a person who has been married for not less than three years and has been domiciled in Japan for not less than a year (Art. 7). Furthermore, a child of a Japanese national who is domiciled in Japan may also be naturalized in a similar way (Art. 8).

Persons with dual nationality are required to choose either one of the nationalities within two years. If this person is under the age of 20, he or she is obliged to choose nationality before he or

3 R. Yamada and F. Tsuchiya, *An Easy Guide to the New Nationality Law*, Tokyo 1985, pp. 2–15.

she becomes 22 (Art. 14, para. 1). The choice is made either by renouncing either of the nationalities, or by declaring his or her choice of Japanese nationality and renunciation of the foreign nationality (Art. 14 para. 2). This declaration is made by filling in a form provided by the civil registration section of the relevant local authority.

A Japanese national who was born in a foreign country and has acquired foreign nationality by birth needs to reserve Japanese nationality within three months of birth. Otherwise, the child will lose Japanese nationality. However, this person may recover Japanese nationality if he or she is under 20 years of age and is domiciled in Japan by filing a notice with the Minister of Justice (Arts. 12 and 17).

2.   The status of aliens

It is generally accepted that aliens in a foreign country are subject to the laws of that country in the same way as its nationals. Thus, as a rule, fundamental rights provided in the Constitution are afforded both to Japanese nationals and to aliens.[4] The Supreme Court acknowledges this in principle.[5] However, some exceptions are allowed in this respect. Firstly, the right to vote and to assume office in the government are denied to aliens. Secondly, social rights, such as the right to work, the right to receive free education and the right to a minimum civilised and healthy life are not automatically guaranteed to aliens. Thirdly, some economic rights are restricted. For instance, aliens are not allowed to enter certain professions such as notaries and pilots. Furthermore, they are excluded from the mining, fishing and telecommunication business. Thus, only Japanese nationals can be shareholders in the Japan Telecommunication and Telegrams (NTT). Licences to undertake telecommunication business are often denied by law to a person who does not have Japanese nationality.

Aliens who are permitted to stay in Japan are required by the Law on Aliens Registration to register with their local authority within 90 days of their entry into Japan (Art. 3).[6] Taiwanese and Koreans who came to Japan before the end of the Second World War as well as their children born before the San Francisco Peace Treaty came into force in 1952 are treated as *de facto* residents

---

4 M. Ito, *Kenpō* (*Constitutional Law*), Tokyo 1982, p. 194.
5 Judgment of the Supreme Court, 4 October, 1978 (*Minshū* 32–7–1223).
6 Law No. 125, 1952.

under the Law on Immigration Control and Recognition of Refugees.[7]

Aliens of more than sixteen years of age must be fingerprinted at the time of registration (Law on Aliens Registration, Art. 14, para. 1). Fingerprinting has become a focus of controversy in recent years. It was considered to be a 'degrading' practice which is not found in other countries. Some cases have been brought to the court on the basis that this requirement constitutes 'unequal treatment' and is thus contrary to the Constitution and the International Covenant on Civil and Political Rights.[8]

In one case, the plaintiff, who was an American married to a Japanese, refused to have her fingerprints taken at the time of the renewal of registration since it was unpleasant and the reasons for such a practice was unclear. The plaintiff applied for re-entry permission to the Minister of Justice before leaving the country for the Christmas holidays. The Minister did not grant permission on the ground that the plaintiff had refused to have her fingerprints taken. The plaintiff filed suit for revocation of the decision of the Minister and claimed damages. The district court rejected the argument of the plaintiff pointing out that the re-entry of aliens into Japan is not guaranteed by either the Constitution or the International Covenant on Civil and Political Rights.[9]

In another case, a person of Korean origin who came to Japan in 1937 with his parents refused to have his fingerprints taken and was prosecuted. The defendant argued that this practice infringed his right of privacy as guaranteed by the Constitution. The appellate court accepted that the taking of fingerprints may constitute a breach of the Constitution if it is forced arbitrarily. However, the court found this practice to be constitutional in so far as it is reasonable and necessary in order to achieve appropriate administrative purposes.[10] There are still some similar cases pending.

Since there has been strong opposition to this practice from foreigners living in Japan, the government made some concessions in 1987 and has reduced the number of occasions when fingerprints are taken, normally only once when a person registers anew.

As for immigration control, the Law on Immigration Control was amended in 1981 in order to facilitate the cross-border

---

7 Cabinet Ordinance No. 319, 1951 (later upgraded to Law No. 126, 1952).
8 K. Itoh, *Law in Japan*, vol. 20, 1987, pp. 48–54.
9 Judgment of Tokyo District Court, 26 March, 1986 (*Gyōsaireishū* 37–3–459).
10 Judgment of Tokyo Appellate Court, 25 August, 1986 (*Hanji* 1208–66).

movement of people. In addition, Japan ratified the Treaty on the Status of Refugees and its Protocol in the same year and the amendment incorporated the necessary changes.

The Civil Code provides that aliens enjoy private rights except in cases where it is prohibited by international treaties, laws, or ordinances (Art. 2).

Whether an alien has capacity to perform juristic acts – i.e. to conclude a contract, to establish a company, etc. – are primarily issues determined by the law of his home country (Law on the Application of Laws, Art. 3 para. 1). This also includes the capacity to act as a party to civil procedure, but does not cover acts concerning Family Law and the Law of Succession. If an alien who does not have capacity in his home country performs a juristic act in Japan, he is deemed to possess capacity provided that he is a person with full capacity by Japanese law (Art. 3, para. 2).

As for juridical persons, the governing law is the law of the country of incorporation. Companies incorporated under Japanese law are 'domestic' companies while those incorporated under foreign law are 'foreign' companies. Foreign commercial companies are also recognised as companies by the Civil Code (Art. 36, para. 1). Entities which are not juridical persons in the home country, for example, partnerships in the United Kingdom, are also granted the status of juridical person by this provision. In principle, foreign companies enjoy the same rights as Japanese companies.

There are some businesses in which foreign companies are not permitted to engage. These include mining, broadcasting, telecommunications, aviation and fishing. In the area of securities and finance, the barriers are gradually being removed as a result of the internationalisation of the market. For example, in the securities business, the Law on Foreign Securities Companies was amended in 1980.[11] This permits foreign securities companies to engage in business in Japan subject to a licence by the Minister of Finance. As late as 1990, more than 50 foreign securities firms were operating through branches in Japan. Foreign banks are also granted licences to conduct business in Japan provided that Japanese banks are treated in the same way in the home country of the foreign bank (Law on Banks, Article 4, para. 3).[12] If a foreign bank intends to open a branch in Japan, each branch has to be licensed by the Minister of Finance (Art. 47, para. 1).

11 Law No. 85, 1980.
12 Law No. 59, 1981.

The Commercial Code provides that foreign companies which intend to engage in business continuously in Japan must select a representative in Japan, open an office and register with the local legal bureau (Art. 479). For a transaction without registration, the individual who performed the transaction is liable jointly and severally with the company (Art. 481, para. 2). Foreign companies which are duly registered have the same rights and duties which corresponding Japanese companies enjoy, except in cases provided by law (Art. 485-2). Under extreme circumstances, the court, upon the request of the Minister of Justice, shareholders, creditors and other interested parties, may order the closure of the office of a foreign company. These include instances where the office was established for illegal purposes, where the office did not start business within a year after registration or ceased business within the same period, or became insolvent without justifiable grounds (Art. 484, para. 1).

Organisational matters are regulated by the law of the country where the company was incorporated. However, a certain category of companies incorporated abroad is subject to the same regulations as companies incorporated under Japanese law. Companies which have their main office in Japan and aim to conduct business primarily in Japan are treated as 'domestic' companies even when incorporated in a foreign country (Art. 482). In one case, a company which was incorporated under Delaware Law had its main office in Delaware and opened an office in Tokyo. However, the company in fact had no place of business nor employees in the United States and operated mainly in Japan. The court ruled that Article 482 was applicable to this case.[13]

Whether a foreign company has the right to be a party in civil proceedings depends upon the law of the home country.[14] There have been cases where a partnership's capacity to sue was at issue. In one case, a Kenyan partnership, which is not a juridical person but has capacity to sue in Kenyan Law, was held to have such capacity in Japan as well.[15]

The Law on Bankruptcy provides that in bankruptcy proceedings, foreign individuals and juridical persons have the same status as Japanese persons on the basis of reciprocity (Art. 2). Where bankruptcy is declared in Japan, it has effect only on property located in Japan. A declaration of bankruptcy in a

---

13 Judgment of the Supreme Court, 4 June, 1954 (*Hanta* 40–73).
14 Judgment of the Supreme Court, 22 November, 1959 (*Hanji* 211–13).
15 Judgment of Tokyo District Court, 9 August, 1960 (*Kaminshū* 11–8–1647).

foreign country does not have effect on property located in Japan (Art. 3, para. 2).[16]

Taxes are levied by central government as well as prefectural and municipal governments. Basic laws regarding national income taxes are the Law on Corporate Tax, the Law on Individuals' Income Tax and the Law on Special Measures of Taxation.[17] Local taxes are regulated by the Law on Local Taxes.[18] The system of tax payments includes the power to withhold tax on salaries, dividends and interest on corporate bonds and bank deposits.

Foreign companies are taxed only on income arising in Japan. The primary Law which provides for taxation on companies is the Law on Corporate Income Tax. Major source incomes which are taxable are as follows: 1) incomes from business or assets in Japan, 2) incomes from providing personal services in Japan, 3) incomes generated from lease of immovables, 4) interests and dividends received in Japan, 5) interests for loans to entities doing business in Japan, 6) royalties on industrial property rights. Foreign companies with a permanent business establishment – i.e. a branch, factory, office etc. – in Japan are liable for corporate income tax basically in the same way as Japanese companies.

Those without such establishments must pay withholding tax for their income derived from the business activities. If a foreign company has construction or installation projects or supervises such activities in Japan for more than one year, or if it conducts business through certain types of agents, it should file a tax return and pay corporate income tax on its net income for these activities.[19]

In addition to corporate income tax, there are two kinds of local tax imposed on companies: enterprise tax and inhabitant tax. The former is levied on net income while the latter is levied at a flat rate in proportion to corporate capital and the amount of the corporate income tax.

The most relevant law for the taxation of individuals' income is the Law on Individual Income Tax. There are two types of tax payers: residents and non-residents. Residents are further divided into permanent residents and non-permanent residents. Non-permanent residents are those who do not intend to live in Japan

---

16 Law No. 71, 1922.
17 Law No. 33 and No. 34, 1965.
18 Law No. 226, 1960.
19 T. Kuboi, *Business Practices and Taxation in Japan*, Revised Edition, Tokyo 1989, pp. 69–75.

permanently and have continuously maintained a domicile or residence for not more than five years in Japan. A foreign individual who accepts employment in Japan is generally classified as a non-permanent resident upon his arrival if his conditions of employment require continuous residence in Japan for one year or more.

Permanent residents are liable to pay tax on all their income regardless of source. Non-residents and non-permanent residents are subject to national income tax only on income arising in Japan, unless, in the case of the latter category, the foreign source income is paid in Japan or remitted to Japan. Japanese source income of those who fall within the former category is subject to a withholding tax while those in the latter category have to follow the same procedure as permanent residents.

The above-mentioned system of taxation is modified by bilateral tax treaties. Japan has concluded such treaties with more than 35 countries including most European countries, Canada, United States, Australia, Korea, India, Malaysia and Singapore.[20]

3. Regulations over foreign investment and trade

The basic Law on foreign exchange and investment is the Foreign Exchange and Foreign Trade Control Law of 1949. A fundamental reform of the foreign exchange system and the liberalisation of controls over foreign investment had been discussed in multilateral fora such as IMF and OECD as well as in bilateral negotiations for some time since the 1960s. Accordingly, measures for capital liberalisation were adopted from 1967 onwards and culminated in the total amendment of the Law in 1979.[1] The Foreign Investment Law of 1950 was abolished at the same time. Capital transactions are now covered by the Foreign Exchange and Foreign Trade Control Law.[2]

The new Law marked a shift from the system of selective permission of incoming capital flow to a generally permissive system. Thus, the present Law declares that foreign exchange, foreign trade and capital transactions are basically free from

20 *Ibid.*, p. 133.
1 J. Horne, *Japan's Financial Markets*, Sydney 1984, pp. 142–172. A. Kawamura, 'History of Japanese Foreign Exchange and Foreign Investment Control', in Kawamura ed., *Law and Business in Japan*, Tokyo 1982, pp. 73–87.
2 Law No. 228, 1949 as amended in 1979 by Law No. 65.

restrictions. In contrast to the previous system, a transaction is permitted unless there is an explicit prohibition. Only minimum necessary controls and adjustments are to be exercised by the government (Art. 1).

Whether this amendment represents a total restructuring of the previous system is often questioned by foreign lawyers. One attorney pointed out that the amendment fell short of a total restructuring, since broad discretion is given to the ministries in creating specific exceptions to the permissive principle.[3] Much of the implementation of the Law is left to cabinet ordinances, ministerial ordinances as well as various circulars and notices. This may make the system confusing and sometimes incomprehensible to foreign businessmen.[4]

The present Foreign Exchange and Foreign Trade Law covers the following transactions: 1) foreign exchange business, 2) payment transactions, 3) capital transaction and service transactions including 'technology induction agreements', 4) direct 'inward' investments, 5) foreign trade.[5]

In order to conduct foreign exchange business, banks must be licensed by the Minister of Finance. The conclusion of correspondent agreements with overseas banks is also subject to licence requirements. In addition to the Bank of Tokyo which is authorised by the Law on Foreign Exchange Banks, major Japanese banks and more than 70 foreign banks are authorised as foreign exchange banks.[6] Authorised foreign exchange banks must report their business to the Minister of Finance (Art. 15). Furthermore, they have a duty to ensure that the payments and transactions concerned are in compliance with licensing and other requirements as provided by the Law (Art. 12).

Japan is a signatory to the IMF Articles of Agreement and accepted Article 8 in 1964. Payments generated from foreign trade are not controlled unless they fall within the category of 'special methods of payment' as specified in the ministerial ordinance. These include credit and debit entries between the accounts of residents and non-residents, prepayments or deferred

---

3 A. D. Smith, 'The Japanese Foreign Exchange and Foreign Trade Control Law and Administrative Guidance: the Labyrinth and the Castle', *Law and Policy in International Business*, 1984, p. 418.

4 As for cabinet and ministerial ordinances concerning foreign trade and investment, see *Japan: laws, Ordinances, and other Regulations concerning Foreign Exchange and Foreign Trade*, Tokyo 1987.

5 M. Matsushita and T. Schoenbaum, *Japanese International and Trade Law*, Tokyo 1989, pp. 116–122.

6 The list is given in *supra* note 5, pp. 90–93.

payments in excess of a year and set-offs. Furthermore, the Minister in charge is empowered to require licenses in cases other than these where it is specially needed in order to maintain Japan's balance of payments, to ensure implementation of the present Law and ordinances, or when it is needed for the faithful implementation of international treaties or agreements (Art. 16).

Capital transactions as provided in the Law cover, *inter alia*, the following transactions: 1) transactions involving the creation, alteration, or extinction of claimable rights which arise from a deposit agreement or a trust agreement between residents and non-residents, 2) transactions concerning the creation of claimable rights on the basis of a loan agreement or a guarantee agreement between residents and non-residents, 3) acquisition of securities denominated in foreign currency by a resident from a non-resident, or acquisition of securities by a non-resident from a resident, 4) issuing or offering of securities overseas or issuing or offering of securities in foreign currency in Japan by residents, 5) issuing or offering of securities overseas denominated or payable by yen by non-residents, 6) inter-office transfer of funds, 7) acquisition of immovables and related rights overseas by residents, or in Japan by non-residents (Art. 20).

The scope of transactions which are subject to license of the Minister of Finance or the Minister of International Trade and Industry came to be fairly limited although there are reporting requirements. There are only a few types of capital transaction which are subject to license including the issue of Euro-yen bonds by non-residents (Art. 21, para. 1, Art. 24). However, the Minister retains the power to tighten controls and make the transactions subject to licence in cases where otherwise, Japan's balance of payment would become difficult to maintain, results in drastic fluctuation in the yen exchange rate, or results in a massive flow of funds which adversely affects the financial or capital market in Japan (Art. 21, para. 2). The ministers are empowered to recommend or order the alteration or suspension of capital transaction in cases where the transaction adversely affects international financial markets or discredits the country, has adverse effects on the financial or capital markets of Japan, adversely affects the business of a specific industry or the smooth functioning of the economy, or is against international peace and security or public order (Art. 23, para. 2).

The Law provides for direct inward investments by foreign investors separately from capital transactions. Direct inward investments include: 1) acquisition of shares or other equity interests of a company except for listed shares, 2) any acquisition by assignment, from a non-resident individual, of shares or equity interests of a non-listed company which the non-resident individual had possessed before becoming a non-resident, 3) any acquisition of listed shares and shares traded over the counter by a foreign investor which results in the holding of 10% or more of the outstanding shares when combined with the holdings of juridical persons and other bodies which have special connections with the investor, 4) creation of branches, factories and other places of business in Japan or any substantial changes in their type or business objectives, 5) lending of money over a year exceeding a certain amount to a juridical person which has its principal office in Japan (Art. 26, para. 2).[7]

Foreign investors in this context includes non-resident individuals, juridical persons or other organisations established under foreign law or those with principal offices abroad and also companies which are controlled by those who fall within these two categories. Japanese companies with 50% or more of their shares or capital held directly or indirectly by a non-resident individual or a foreign company and those companies with non-resident individuals occupying more than half of the seats on the board are regarded as foreign investors (Art. 26, para. 1).

Foreign investors must report to the Minister of Finance and the Minister in charge of the relevant business, the purpose, amount of investment and the time of investment (Art. 27, para. 1). Formerly, a prior notice was needed, but now, only in exceptional cases is advance notice required.[8] In such cases, those who give notice to the relevant ministers have to wait for thirty days before carrying out transactions. During this waiting period, the ministries review the intended transaction to see that *inter alia* it does not affect national security or public order, and that it does not have serious adverse effect on the smooth administration of the economy (Art. 27, para. 2). The Minister of Finance and the minister in charge are empowered to recommend changes or suspension of the transaction upon advice of the Foreign Exchange Council (para. 5). If the investor refuses to accept the recommendation, the ministers may order alteration or suspension of investment (para. 10).

In practice, routine transactions are treated as a matter of course and notices are accepted without any difficulty in so far as they do not fall within the categories of investments reserved under the Code of Liberalisation of Capital Movements of the OECD. So far, there has been no reported case of a recommendation or order to alter or suspend direct investments

---

7 For details, see The Bank of Tokyo, *supra* note 5, pp. 99–104.
8 Matsushita and Schoenbaum, *supra* note 5, pp. 186–188.

in such transactions. However, in areas such as oil industry and agriculture, the Ministry of International Trade and Industry exercises controls over foreign investors by way of administrative guidance. Furthermore, transactions involving designated technology and designated companies are carefully reviewed by relevant ministries.[9]

The Foreign Exchange and Foreign Trade Control Law provides for 'technology induction contracts' along with direct foreign investments, separately from other trades in services. Presumably, the legislature had considered the introduction of technology as one of the means of potential foreign control of Japanese companies. The phrase 'technology induction agreement' covers agreements on the assignment of industrial property rights and other rights concerning technology, licensing contracts to use these rights, and the providing of technical or managerial guidance by a non-resident (Art. 29). Until 1991, in order to conclude or alter such agreements, the parties had to give prior notice to the Minister of Finance and the Minister of International Trade and Industry. There was a waiting period of 30 days as is the case with direct inward investments.

With the amendment of 1991, as a rule, a post de facto report is sufficient, and only in exceptional cases, an advance notice is required (Art. 30, para. 1). In such cases, the ministers have powers to make recommendations or orders of alteration or suspension similar to those in inward foreign investments (Art. 30, paras. 1 and 2).

This waiting period is actually waived in all cases except twelve designated technologies permitted under the OECD Code. Designated technologies include aircraft, weapons, nuclear power, space technology and computers.[10] For some of these technologies, prior negotiation with the Ministry of International Trade and Industry is required.

Unlike capital transactions, the export and import of goods has been relatively free from restrictions. The Law provides that the export of goods is to be allowed with minimum restrictions (Art. 47). The Law on Export and Import Transactions provides for some restrictions in order to prevent unfair exportation and ensure orderly importation.[11] Unfair exportation includes the export of goods which may infringe industrial property rights or copyrights protected in the country of destination, export of goods with false representation of country of origin, as well as

---

9 Smith, *supra* note 21, pp. 461–468.
10 The Bank of Tokyo, *supra* note 5, pp. 158–160.
11 Law No. 299, 1952.

goods which greatly differ from the specifications given in the contract (Art. 2).

The Foreign Exchange and Foreign Trade Control Law provides for export licenses for certain kinds of goods and services for certain destinations, and transactions with certain specified methods of transaction or payment. A person who intends to export goods to a destination which is designated in a cabinet order as an area where international peace and security are obstructed is required to obtain a licence from the Minister of International Trade and Industry (Art. 48). The same applies to technology (Art. 25, para. 1). Initially, these arrangements primarily involved CoCom controlled goods and technology. Japan joined CoCom in 1950 and enforces CoCom controls through a national list of strategic goods and technology. The list is published together with other controlled items in a cabinet order and is administered by the Ministry of International Trade and Industry.

The significance of CoCom control was considerably reduced with the collapse of the socialist regime in the former Soviet Union and Eastern Europe. On the other hand, since the Gulf War, the necessity of multilateral control over mass destructive weapons was felt. Japan is a member of various international fora including the Australian Group countries which control chemical and biological weapons, the Zander Committee which deals with nuclear technology and the Missile Technology Control Regime.

In addition to strategic items, certain goods require export licences in order to ensure domestic supply. There are also goods which cannot be exported such as cultural properties of significance.

4.   Rules of conflict of laws

Rules regarding conflict of laws are provided by the Law on the Application of Laws (*Horei*).[12] This Law, which was enacted in 1898, underwent a major change in 1989. The amendments were basically aimed at ensuring equal treatment of men and women. In addition, some provisions concerning points of contact were streamlined.

The Law provides that the validity and the effects of a juristic act are to be determined by the law of the parties' choice. The form of a juristic act is governed by the law governing the validity of such an act. These provisions are applicable to contracts. If the

12 Law No. 10, 1898 as amended.

choice of law by the parties is unknown, *lex loci actus* is to be the governing law (Art. 7). Before resorting to the law of the place where the juristic act has taken place, implicit intention of the parties has to be sought from various circumstances including the type and contents of the agreement, nationality of the parties, place where the act has taken place, place of performance, arrangements for dispute settlement, language of the agreement etc.

If, however, the application of a foreign law is against public policy and good morals, such law is not applicable (Art. 33). This provision is often applied in cases where a party to the marriage comes from countries where divorce is not allowed. Japanese courts have granted divorce by denying the application of Philippine law as being against public policy.[13]

Properties (movables and immovables) are governed by the law of the place where they are located (Art. 10, para. 1). Ships and aircrafts are ruled by the law of the country where they are registered. Goods in transition are governed by the law of the country of destination.

The validity and the effect of the obligation arising from tort are governed by the law of the place where the tortious act took place (Art. 11, para. 1). Whether this means the place where the act was committed, or where the results have emerged has been discussed for some time. There is a third view which points out that it is impossible to apply a single rule to various types of tort, and therefore, a proper law should be found on a case-by-case basis, taking into account specific circumstances of the given case.

There are cases where jurisdiction of the Japanese court is at issue. Formerly, the majority view was that jurisdiction of the court should be surmised from the provision of the Code of Civil Procedure. However, at present, the view that jurisdiction should be determined not by the provisions of the Code which deal with domestic litigations, but from the viewpoint of which jurisdiction is the most suitable in terms of a speedy, fair and appropriate settlement of the case.

In one case, A was travelling in South East Asia when his plane crashed. Heirs of A sued a Malaysian airline company in Tokyo. The Supreme Court ruled that the jurisdiction should be decided on considerations such as fairness between the parties and whether the litigation can proceed appropriately in a speedy manner. Provisions of the Code of Civil Procedure, such as those concerning the address of the defendant, location of the assets of the defendant, the place where the tortious act has been committed, etc. should be taken into account. The court found

13 Judgment of Tokyo District Court, 27 February, 1981 (*Hanji* 1010–85).

that a Japanese court had jurisdiction over this case, taking into consideration that the airline company had an office in Tokyo.[14]

There are instances where the same case is considered by courts in different jurisdictions. For instance, Company A was sued by a sales company in the United States for the loss resulting from alleged fault in the machinery which it had exported to the United States. Company A then initiated a case in Japan against the U.S. company in order to have the absence of obligation confirmed. Thus, the same case came to be pending both in the United States and Japan. This was presumably aimed at blocking the enforcement of the U.S. judgment in Japan in case the Japanese party lost. The U.S. company claimed that the litigation in Japan was unlawful, since the case was already pending in the United States.

Under the Japanese Code of Civil Procedure, no person may initiate litigation on the same case which is already pending at court (Art. 231). In such cases, the second litigation is unlawful and the court has to reject the case. If there is a judgment which has come into force, a new litigation involving the same case cannot be brought to the court. The court is of the view that these provisions apply only to litigations within Japan. In the above-mentioned case, and in other similar cases, the court found that the existence of a case pending in a foreign court did not hinder litigation in Japan.[15] In this particular case, the judgment in the United States came into effect and the plaintiff applied for its enforcement in Japan. The court rejected the application on the ground that since there was a judgment which was in force in Japan on the same case, it was against public policy to enforce the U.S. judgment in Japan.[16]

Recently, there are views which cast doubt on such an approach. Some experts suggest that if there is a likelihood or possibility of the given foreign judgment being enforced in Japan, then the first litigation should be respected and the second litigation initiated in Japan should either be suspended or rejected.[17]

Foreign judgments and arbitral awards are enforceable under certain conditions in Japan.

The Code of Civil Procedure has a provision on the enforcement of foreign judgments. A foreign judgment which has

---

14 Judgment of the Supreme Court, 16 October, 1981 (*Minshū* 35–7–1224).
15 Judgment of Tokyo District Court, 30 May, 1989 (*Hanta* 703–240).
16 Judgment of Osaka District Court, 22 December, 1977 (*Hanta* 361–127).
17 M.Dogauchi in *Shōgai Hanrei Hyakusen (100 Selected Cases on Conflict of Laws)*, Tokyo 1986, pp. 220–221.

taken effect is enforceable in Japan provided that 1) jurisdiction of the foreign court has not been denied by law or treaty, 2) if the losing party is Japanese, he has been properly notified of the litigation and served documents or has accepted the jurisdiction, 3) the judgment is not against public order or good morals in Japan, 4) there is a reciprocal arrangement (Art. 200). As for the second requirement, Japan is a signatory to the Treaty on Civil Procedure and the Treaty on the Delivery of Documents and Notification concerning Civil and Commercial Cases.

The requirement of reciprocity has been a focus of controversy. The recent majority view interprets reciprocity rather flexibly and unless the foreign country imposes excessively strict conditions on the enforcement of a Japanese judgment, the requirement of reciprocity is met. This becomes an issue when a foreign country makes it a rule for the court to review the judgment of a Japanese court on merit before allowing enforcement. Since a Japanese court does not consider a foreign judgment on merit when deciding its enforceability, in such cases, there is no reciprocity. Thus, the enforcement of a judgment of a Belgian court was denied on this ground.[18]

As regards arbitration awards, Japan is a signatory to the Convention on the Recognition and Enforcement of Foreign Arbitration Awards. Even before the ratification of this treaty, Japanese courts have acknowledged that the existence of an arbitration agreement would block the litigation. It is up to the party (and not the obligation of the court) to refer to the arbitration agreement.

---

18 Y. Kikuchi, 'Gaikoku Hanketsu no Shonin Shikko (Recognition and Enforcement of a Foreign Judgment)', in N.Motoki and K.Hosokawa eds., *Shogai-Soshō-Hō (Transnational Litigation Law)*, Tokyo 1989, pp. 130–136.

Appendices

Appendix 1 Legal profession and related professions

	1956	1966	1976	1986
Attorneys	6,040	7,687	10,792	13,159
Chartered Accountants	1,185	3,127	5,222	7,895
Tax Attorneys	7,644	15,827	32,436	47,342
Judicial Scriveners	—	11,758	13,958	15,260
Patent Attorneys	966	1,425	2,293	2,947
Judges	1,597	1,787	1,912	2,009
Public Prosecutors	1,000	1,082	1,173	1,173

(Source: *Jurist*, Special Issue on State Judicial Examination, 1987, p. 98).

Appendix 2   Population per Attorney

Japan	9,199
U.S.A.	358
U.K.	879
Germany (West)	1,291
France	3,468

(Source: *Jurist*, *ibid.*, p. 86).

Appendix 3   Civil cases at the District Court level

	Total	Judgment	Decision	Order	In-the-Court Settlement	Abandonment	Acceptance	Withdrawal	Others
Total	112,140	48,986	521	961	39,305	131	1,093	18,906	2,237
1 month or less	4,602	122	91	115	380	–	53	3,225	616
2 months –	14,659	6,089	136	396	3,780	6	514	3,514	224
3 months –	16,343	10,017	80	129	3,857	14	210	1,902	134
6 months –	21,701	10,363	125	180	7,573	22	181	3,014	243
1 year –	18,831	6,184	50	85	9,147	36	96	2,972	261
2 years –	18,907	7,601	32	33	8,459	33	27	2,402	320
3 years –	8,355	4,012	3	11	3,249	6	5	897	172
4 years –	3,985	2,064	3	5	1,404	6	4	393	106
5 years –	1,996	1,072	1	3	628	3	–	220	69
More than 5 years	2,761	1,462	–	4	828	5	3	367	92

(Source: *Shihō-tōkei Nenpō* (*Annual Judicial Statistics*), Civil Cases, 1991, Tokyo 1992, p. 122).

Appendix 4   Average time needed in criminal cases

Time needed in each instance

Summary Courts   2.6 (months)

District Courts   3.5

  tried by a collegiate body 8.5
  single judge   3.1

First Appeal   5.0

Second Appeal   5.4

Time needed from indictment to the final judgment

First Appeal   13.2

Second Appeal   23.3

(Source: *Shihō-tōkei Nenpō* (*Annual Judicial Statistics*), Criminal Cases, 1991, Tokyo 1992, p. 21).

Appendix 5 Types of companies

(1 million yen ≠ 4 thousand pounds)

Amount of Capital / Types of Companies	less than 5 million yen	5 million to less than 10 million	10 million to less than 1 billion	100 million to less than 1 billion	1 billion or more	Total	Percentage
Joint Stock Companies	416,610	216,123	320,190	19,488	3,450	975,861	52.7%
Limited Liability Companies	615,159	160,387	53,168	416	21	829,151	44.8%
General Partnership	4,509	1,162	523	13	—	6,207	0.3%
Limited Partnershp	24,076	4,077	2,259	17	—	30,429	1.6%
Others	4,331	1,393	4,073	308	20	10,025	0.5%
Total (percentage)	1,064,505 (57.2%)	383,142 (20.7%)	380,213 (20.5%)	20,242 (1.1%)	3,491 (0.2%)	1,851,673 (100%)	100%

Cited in T. Okushima, *Prep Kalsha-ho (Introduction to Company Law)*, Second Edition, Tokyo 1991, p. 39.

Appendix 6 Financing by listed companies (all stock exchanges)

(yen mil.)

Year or Month	Offering to Shareholder			Public Offering			Private Placement			Total of Stocks			Straight Bonds		Convertible Bonds		Total of Bonds	
	No. of Cases	Amount Raised	Excess over Par	No. of Cases	Amount Raised	Excess over Par	No. of Cases	Amount Raised	Excess over Par	No. of Cases	Amount Raised	Excess over Par	No. of Cases	Amount Raised	No. of Cases	Amount Raised	No. of Cases	Amount Raised
1 (1989)	32	726,212	675,641	227	5,830,283	5,635,078	22	102,272	97,343	716	8,848,609	8,,473,351	18	580,000	431	8,496,189	719	18,751,524
2 (1990)	39	824,870	776,979	121	1,975,399	1,909,971	21	314,620	301,585	578	3,792,440	3,636,563	43	1,828,000	190	3,498,150	391	9,175,841
3 (1991)	40	218,028	196,757	27	125,847	123,854	19	103,532	94,394	395	807,735	757,447	57	2,314,700	103	1,306,099	443	7,925,347
3 (1991) 6	5	20,050	18,267	2	8,219	8,094	1	8,900	8,400	120	60,903	57,652	2	120,000	9	164,133	53	955,320
7	1	6,216	5,772	–	–	–	2	5,163	4,895	107	33,826	32,195	6	290,000	13	119,128	68	1,169,334
8	1	3,168	2,904	–	–	–	2	26,138	23,260	90	41,927	38,222	4	20,000	22	282,384	74	1,025,378
9	–	–	–	1	21,616	21,536	1	6,469	6,367	95	59,779	58,017	1	129,700	5	109,818	19	344,479
10	6	41,779	38,574	–	–	–	–	–	–	103	81,331	75,800	1	10,000	9	132,432	25	330,440
11	2	7,728	6,822	–	–	–	–	–	–	92	30,370	28,094	8	320,000	15	226,053	34	633,843
12	4	30,780	28,421	1	2,030	1,973	1	493	450	62	57,253	53,778	8	320,000	14	101,208	44	667,717
4 (1992) 1	1	911	–	–	–	–	2	5,549	5,051	56	15,256	13,370	3	90,000	6	95,860	16	285,664
2	2	3,113	2,691	–	–	–	2	2,804	2,328	48	10,047	8,948	4	200,000	8	70,287	25	432,566
3	11	87,310	78,277	2	1,255	1,206	4	33,499	29,778	63	133,319	119,876	7	245,000	19	363,020	48	809,259
4	3	9,722	8,520	–	–	–	2	28,375	26,460	39	56,826	52,891	4	240,000	3	31,000	19	408,841
5	–	–	–	–	–	–	1	4,495	3,903	45	23,169	21,563	9	460,0000	–	–	15	512,032
6	2	8,063	7,375	–	–	–	2	6,139	4,866	40	35,803	33,092	7	310,000	–	–	10	332,275

Source: Tosho-tokei-geppo (Monthly Statistical Review of the Tokyo Stock Exchange), 1992 No. 7, pp. 71.–72

Appendix 7 Mergers and acquisitions involving Japanese companies

(Number of cases)

	1990	1991	1991 (Jan to June)	1992 (Jan to June)
IN–IN	304	258	135	122
IN–OUT	463	260	143	120
OUT–IN	17	13	7	16
Total	784	531	285	258

(Amount involved)   (million yen)

	1990	1991	1991 (Jan to June)	1992 (Jan to June)
IN–IN	342,333 (143)	453,260 (127)	232,750 (67)	221,692 (56)
IN–OUT	3,257,084 (360)	678,026 (182)	282,390 (99)	224,769 (71)
OUT–IN	21,410 (6)	58,103 (8)	13,367 (7)	
Total	3,620,827 (509)	1,189,389 (327)	538,561 (170)	459,828 (134)

Sources: Daiwa Securities

In–In: M & A between Japanese companies
In–Out: M & A abroad by Japanese companies
Out–in: M & A in Japan by foreign companies

Appendix 8   Reported crime per 100,000 inhabitants

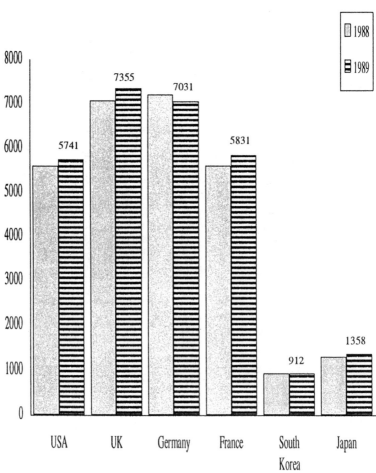

(Source: Ministry of Justice ed., *White Paper on Crime 1991*, Tokyo 1992).

Index